Computing in the Web Age

A Web-Interactive Introduction

Computing in the Web Age

A Web-Interactive Introduction

Robert J. Dilligan

University of Southern California
Los Angeles, California

PLENUM PRESS • NEW YORK AND LONDON

Library of Congress Cataloging-in-Publication Data

```
Dilligan, Robert J.
    Computing in the Web age : a Web-interactive introduction / Robert
J. Dilligan.
        p.    cm.
    Includes bibliographical references and index.
    ISBN 0-306-45972-8
    1. Internet programming.   2. World Wide Web (Information retrieval
system)   I. Title.
QA76.625.D55   1998
025.04--dc21                                                98-34957
                                                                CIP
```

ISBN 0-306-45972-8

© 1998 Plenum Press, New York
A Division of Plenum Publishing Corporation
233 Spring Street, New York, N.Y. 10013

http://www.plenum.com

10 9 8 7 6 5 4 3 2 1

Printed in the United States of America

For Patricia
... più che la stella

Contents

Acknowledgments

I would like to express my gratitude to students, friends, and colleagues who have helped and encouraged me in this project. Special thanks are due to my colleagues Moshe Lazar, Max Schulz, Ross Winterowd, and James Kincaid, all of whom read portions and drafts of this manuscript and made numerous helpful suggestions and comments. I also want to thank my friend Robert Allen for his invaluable assistance in getting the manuscript in final form. All mistakes, blunders, and errors of omission and commission are my own.

Permissions

Introduction

This book reflects thirty years of experience in the applications of computer technology to literary research and instruction and in consulting work in office automation and system integration. In that time I have again and again found myself in the position of having to introduce students, both undergraduate and graduate, colleagues and clients to the fundamentals of computer hardware and software. Over the years, as computers became both central and commonplace in professional life, I have been aware of changing attitudes toward this technology. From attitudes that ranged from the disdain of platonic dialecticians for mere technology to intimidation bordering at times almost on terror, people have moved to incorporate this new technology into their frame of reference (*humani nil a me alienum*). The development of the microprocessor and its subsequent use for word processing marked one important watershed. The widespread use of word processors made it more likely than not that people would own their own computers, at least at work, and use them as part of their work-a-day activities. But while word processing provided some increased familiarity with computers, it did not lead most individuals much beyond a knowledge of the usual incantations needed to control the *MultiMate* or *Nota Bene* or *Word Perfect* golam and, as a result of unhappy experience, a begrudging acceptance of the need to make back up copies of important files. For most of us, word processing, presentation systems, E-mail, spreadsheets, and the like are useful computer applications, but none of them is a "killer app," a computer application that not only gets useful work done but also opens possibilities unthinkable save for the application's existence. (The MAC became and remains today—who knows for how long— the "killer app" for graphics design professionals and computer-based instruction.)

By all accounts, the universal "killer app" is the World Wide Web. While individuals worked at their word processors, a number of developments in the fields of networking, libraries, and publishing stole a march on them. Networks developed

1

a worldwide reach. Libraries moved from computerized cataloguing to computerized catalogues accessible through dedicated networks like OCLC. At the same time, the expansion of the number of specialized journals, combined with the rising cost of traditional printing, soon outstripped the capacity of even the largest library serials budgets to keep up with current publications. The Internet, a product of the Department of Defense during the Cold War, developed a mechanism whereby scholars and researchers at widely separated institutions could collaborate using shared computer files. But the Internet, with its UNIX-based character interface, was much too arcane and awkward to find general use among professionals for much the same reasons that early character-based text formatting programs like SCRIPT and TROFF never really found general acceptance. But once the physicists at CERN and the programmers at the University of Illinois developed the World Wide Web with a graphical user interface that was as user-friendly as a MAC, the elements were in place for the expansion of the portion of the Internet called the World Wide Web into many areas of our lives.

We are all being swept along into using the World Wide Web. There are already journals, databases, and bibliographies that are accessible only through the Web. In the future, the Web will increasingly provide immediate access to the most recent work in most fields. This book is intended as a general introduction to computer technology as it relates to the development of the World Wide Web. The book combines discussions of computer technology with exercises in the use of computer applications and programming. I think of this book as providing a studio course whose goal is to provide a unified and integrated understanding of the basics of computer technology. By working through this book and performing the exercises it sets, readers should become able to understand what they are doing from a computational point of view as well as from a pragmatic one. With this dual perspective, they should be able to exploit the possibilities provided by the Web with a thoroughness and depth not possible without it. Rather than covering any particular aspect of this technology exhaustively, the chapters that follow move in a wide-ranging way across the field of computer technology and pause to examine in depth the technologies crucial to the Web.

Chapter 1, "From ENIAC to the World Wide Web to . . . ," offers a brief history of the technologies that lead to the development of the Web and some speculation about the future of computers. This covers early work on theory and hardware during the 1930s; the development of ENIAC and EDVAC during and immediately after World War II; the rise and fall of mainframe computers from the 1950s through the 1970s; the development of microprocessors and networks in the 1980s and 1990s; and the development of the Internet and the Web from 1969 to the present. I then review current thinking about the future of computers, especially as it relates to the possibilities of artificial intelligence, and offer some speculations relating to this topic.

Chapter 2, "Binary Numbers, ASCII Code, and the Turing Machine," introduces the fundamentals of computers and Computer Science. Readers are made familiar with binary numbers, an understanding of which is indispensable in any discussion of computer technology, through a pocket calculator program that is accessible on the Web. Next I discuss the way information is encoded for a computer by examining ASCII code, which is the most widely used method of encoding textual information on a computer. Readers are shown how to use an encryption device that operates in the same way as a Lone Ranger code ring. With the code ring, which is available on the Web, they are able to see how binary numbers underlie the textual material they are accustomed to read on their computer screens. The last part of this chapter explains the working of a Turing machine, a hypothetical, programmable device first described by the computer pioneer Alan Turing. This device provides the mathematical model for all modern computers. The way this hypothetical machine works is demonstrated by a program, available on the Web, that takes readers step by step through the execution of a Turing machine program. The Turing machine explains its operations step by step as it carries them out. By the end of this chapter, readers should be equipped to understand the logical principals of programming and the binary foundation of the Web.

Chapter 3, "The CPU as a Turing Machine," illustrates the principle that any computer is a Turing machine. Building on the understanding of binary numbers and code in Chapter 2, the goal of this chapter is to give readers a real view of the shifting binary patterns of cyberspace. This chapter shows how the ideas of computer software may be embodied in both real and virtual machines. Computers are made up of collections of switching circuits called bits. Understanding how a computer works and how a program carries out its task means understanding how and in what sequences these bit switches are thrown on and off. Readers observe the basic execution cycle of a computer as it moves data between memory and its central processing unit (CPU), counts, makes logical decisions, and computes tables of numbers. The computer they observe doing these things is a hypothetical, virtual computer, specially designed to illustrate the general principles of operation of a computer. They also get an introduction to the basics of programming as they see how a computer program is translated from words and symbols that humans can understand into the binary code that the computer uses, how the binary code is linked to the operating system and loaded into memory, and how it is executed. The virtual computer, like the Turing machine, gives an explanation of each step in its operation as it is performed.

Chapter 4, "The World According to Programmers," applies the principles of programming developed in Chapter 3 with a virtual computer to actual programming for the World Wide Web. First, the chapter explains how a programmer develops the interactive control windows and icons that are used to control programs. These control windows are known as graphical user interfaces (GUI) and are, from the user's point of view, the single most important part of a computer program. Anything they do on the Web must be accomplished through a GUI. The Internet was transformed to the World Wide Web through the provision of a GUI. The chapter explains the principles of design that programmers use in developing a GUI and the programming tools used in implementing one. This behind-the-scenes look at a GUI as it takes shape will clarify for users what they are doing when using one in a way that will enable them to make maximum use of the Web and of all GUI programs. Understanding how a GUI works is the key to developing sophisticated computer skills. After learning about the development of the GUI, users see how it operates as part of a text retrieval program of the sort used to obtain information from the Web. The technique of keyword searching that is explained for this program is the basic technique for all Web searching. The discussion enables readers to understand the principles of information retrieval from the Web. Readers are provided with the opportunity to download three JAVA programs for text retrieval and a JAVA operating environment, the JAVA Runtime Environment (JRE) from the Web. This exercise introduces readers to downloading from the Web and to the use of compressed data and self-extracting archives, skills that enhance the use of the Web as a source of information. Readers are also shown how to deal with information that is distributed across a number of computer files, as it frequently is on the Web.

Chapter 5, "Connections to the World Wide Web," begins with a discussion of the reasons for using computer networks like the Web and the issues of privacy, encryption, and governmental intrusion on Web users. It then explains how network software and hardware provide the interconnections of users to each other through Web applications. With this background understanding, the chapter then focuses on using the Netscape browser to interface with and search the Web. This chapter shows readers how to use the Web as a source of information and of programs with which to analyze information from the Web or other sources. The techniques of Web searching and information retrieval are explained with emphasis on the issue of information literacy as a way of understanding the scope and usefulness of information from the Web. The topic of artificial intelligence is used to illustrate the various search engines and options provided by the Web. This topic is searched in various ways and the implications of the information retrieved from each search is evaluated and compared. The chapter then explains how to save for future use information found through Web searches. The types of data that are found integrated on web sites are described. The different techniques used to save information in different formats are illustrated as well. Finally, readers are introduced to the software archives available on the Web. They are shown how to obtain from these archives programs for editing text and graphical information, for compressing data, and for publishing information on the Web.

Chapter 6, "HTML Programming and Web Publishing," takes the next step in understanding and using the Web by explaining to readers the basics of how they may create their own web sites and place on the Web information they create themselves. Readers are shown how to take an ordinary text file and transform it into a hypertext document suitable for publication on the Web. Drawing on the work with programming in earlier chapters, readers learn how to program using HyperText Markup Language (HTML). The basic "tags" and conventions for laying out Web documents are explained as well as the way in which these documents are organized on the Web. The concept of the Uniform Resource Locator (URL) and the use of relative and absolute addressing on web sites is covered in detail. The use and placement of images on files and the methods HTML provides for displaying them on Web pages are detailed. The use of helper applications for multimedia information is discussed. Readers are shown how to add helper applications to their Web browser. Both video and audio applications are covered. Finally, readers are introduced to the UNIX operating system so that they can understand how and where to place hypertext material on a Web server for access on the Web.

Studio courses require studios. In taking this course, readers are encouraged to access the Web with a suitably equipped computer. Before explaining the relationship of this book to the web site that has been designed to offer material supplementary to its text, I'd like to make a general point about the manner of change of computer technology. I would describe this change as punctuated equilibrium, using the term coined by Stephen Gould to describe his version of Darwinism and to distinguish it from the traditional gradualist description of evolutionary change. Rather than viewing evolution as a slow process of cumulative change, Gould argues that it is more accurate to think of evolutionary change as long periods of stability alternating with short periods of rapid adaptation by isolated populations subjected to unusual environmental stress. So too with the development of computers. The main evolutionary lines run from mainframes to minicomputers to microcomputers; from stand-alone computers to networks of similar machines to networks of heterogeneous machines; from proprietary standards to open standards; and from numerical to character to graphical interfaces. The generations of computers are numbered by the technology they use. The first generation, a product of World War II engineering research, used vacuum tube technology. The second generation used transistors. The third generation used integrated circuits that combined a number of transistors on a single piece of silicon. The fourth generation uses microprocessors, an extension of integrated circuits that allowed an entire computer to be placed on a single chip.

Computer capacity measured in terms of the size of memory and the speed of processing doubles about every eighteen months. With this rapid development of capacity, there emerges a dominant technological paradigm that seems to remain stable and unchallenged for about three to five years. The dominant technological paradigm today is characterized by the graphical user interface to the World Wide Web. Most developments today focus on filling out the implications of this technology, in particular with interest in providing live video and sound and on distributing JAVA computer applications on the Web. This book is written in the context of this current, particular period of stability. It is organized to give readers a solid background in the basic of computer technology and then to discuss things like graphical user interfaces, Java and multimedia because these are the things that seem to me to characterize the current state of computing for most users. It discusses the current state of computing in the context of its unchanging fundamentals.

Now for some technical details. To use the web site associated with this book, readers must have access to a suitable Power MAC or Pentium PC connected to the Internet by a telephone modem or through an Ethernet card. Such machines come equipped with at least eight and preferably sixteen megabits of random access memory, a pointing device or mouse, a color monitor, a hard disk, a floppy disk, a CD-ROM drive, and a sound card. (The sound card and CD-ROM are optional for purposes of this book.) The MAC and the PC are the two machines most-widely used in the United States and most of the western world. All exercises and examples in the text of this book will be presented on the PC. The text of the book describes the exercises as carried out with a Pentium PC. The differences between the PC and MAC, though real, are not so substantial as partisans in the MAC/Windows wars would lead one to believe. The sample programs and exercises in this book work for the most part about as well on either machine, though the programs may appear in slightly different form on the MAC. Where the MAC and PC diverge too widely for use of common examples and exercises—as, for example, in Chapters 4 and 5—alternate material is provided for the MAC via the World Wide Web.

The application software most frequently used in this book is either Netscape 3.0 or above and Internet Explorer 4.0. Both are browser programs and may be used interchangeably for purposes of this book. They provide a connection or interface between a MAC or PC and the Web. It is through one of these programs that readers search the Web, read text, run JAVA programs, view images, and listen to sounds. Netscape is the dominant network browser used on the Web. The current versions of both Netscape and Internet Explorer for MAC OS and Windows 95 support JAVA applications.

Instructions for downloading material from the Web site and installing it on a computer are given in Appendix C.

CHAPTER 1

From ENIAC to the World Wide Web to . . .

COMPUTING ON THE WORLD WIDE WEB

As a visit to the computer section of any book store will confirm, there is a plethora of books on the market that offer their readers introductions to just about any topic having to do with computers, computer applications, or computer programming. If their titles are any guide to their contents, these books promise their readers everything from quick and easy introductions (*Learn Windows 95 in 48 Hours*), to crash courses for career advancement (*Become a C++ Programmer in 21 Days*), to new canons (*The Microsoft C Bible*), to cabalistic initiations (*Mastering Paradox 4.5*), to satori (*Zen and the Art of the Internet*), to tabloid revelations (*Inside Visual Basic*), to self-assured self-deprecation (*The Internet for Dummies*). This book is a general introduction to computer technology. The readers it addresses are professionals who do not have a technical background. They may use a word processor to write their memos, reports, articles and books, reference library catalogues over a network, occasionally browse on the World Wide Web and use Email to communicate with colleagues. But they do these things with only the most general notion of the workings of computer technology. To them, using a computer is like evoking a magic spell with a series of incomprehensible but powerful incantations.

This book does not attempt to provide its readers with a quick yet thorough introduction to any particular topic, to open new career paths for them, or to initiate them into mysteries sacred or profane. It singles out for discussion aspects of computer technology that form the basis of modern computer applications. By combining theoretical and technical discussion of computer technology with hands-on exercises using the computer, it attempts not only to provide an understanding of the characteristic perspective, sensibility, and the habits of thought of those who design computer software and hardware but also to combine that new technical perspective with the readers' own. The ultimate aim of this book is to provide the opportunity for a true experience of computer technology that will encourage readers to explore its usefulness for their own professions.

This book, then, hopes to be generally useful to readers whose inclinations are not, first of all, technical. My own profession, I admit at the outset, is literary studies and so readers in other professions will sense, no doubt, a tinge of the literary in this text. This tinge is present if only because in writing this book I have followed Sir Phillip Sidney's prescription for overcoming writer's block: "Fool,...look in thy heart and write." The present conjunction of the Internet and Graphical User Interfaces (GUIs)[1] that has produced the World Wide Web (hereinafter the Web) is a development in computer technology with important cultural implications. As such it deserves to be studied and recorded and that is one aim of this book. This book is like a studio course in drawing that combines the study of anatomy with an exposition of the techniques of sketching. It combines discussion of computer technology with exercises on the computer and illustrative examples. At the end of the course, I hope that readers will be able to look at a computer system or application with an appreciation of the art and science concealed there and feel confident enough to embark on their own explorations of the medium. I will begin by reviewing those aspects of the development of the modern computer that shed some light on basic concepts underlying its operation.

ENIAC AND THE DEVELOPMENT OF THE MODERN COMPUTER

The modern computer emerged into public consciousness at the end of World War II as an important advance in our capacity to carry out scientific calculations. There is a finite limit not only to the speed at which human beings, even idiot savants, can make complex calculations requiring many steps but also to the speed at which organized teams of individuals can carry out these calculations. The speed at which results can be calculated is not proportional to the number of individuals set to the task.[2] At some point, a form of entropy sets in as the time and complexity needed for team members to share results overcomes the advantages of adding members to the team. Increasing the size of the team may, in some circumstances, actually increase the time it takes to complete the task. As military technology advanced during World War II, the need for rapid calculations to solve problems associated with the design and operation of advanced weapons increased enormously. The limits of human calculation were reached in that war, during which it proved impossible to keep up with the demand for calculations for mundane and esoteric problems. The War Department and its scientific agencies were overwhelmed with demands for calculations as mundane as those needed to produce artillery firing tables and as esoteric as those needed to design atomic weapons.

In its early history, the computer was regarded as a number cruncher. It provided a quick and accurate way to produce arithmetical results that were too tedious to generate by error-prone humans.[3] Although its use during the war for the encryption and decryption of codes suggested the potential of the computer as a general-purpose manipulator of logical symbols, its usefulness was generally regarded as limited to scientific and engineering calculations. The fact that its use in encryption and decryption remained top secret until long after World War II[4] may have contributed to an emphasis on the publicly acknowledged view of the computer as scientific calculator. The market for computers was seen early on as limited to government bureaucracies such as the military and the weather service and to scientific centers like the Institute for Advanced Studies at Princeton. One 1946 marketing survey estimated that there was a worldwide market for about one dozen computers. As things developed, the market for scientific computers was served by manufacturers, like Cray Research, that specialized in the design and production of supercomputers. The need for this type of computing is met today at the various national computer centers funded through the National Science Foundation. It amounts to a tiny fraction of current computer usage. Had their main use been for scientific calculation, computers would today be regarded as laboratory curiosities. The emergence of computers as what David Bolter has termed the "defining technology" of our culture[5] rests more on their prowess as manipulators of logical symbols and information retrieval systems than on their arithmetic speed and accuracy.

ENIAC, which became known as the first modern electronic computer, was constructed at the University of Pennsylvania under the direction of John Mauchly and J. Presper Eckert. ENIAC is an acronym for Electronic Numeric Integrator And Calculator. As the name suggests, it was from the first regarded as a device for scientific calculation. The important things about ENIAC were that it was digital, reliable, and programmable and could obtain results about five hundred times faster than was possible with earlier human or machine-assisted methods.[6] Its ability to exceed the human capacity for rapid calculation assured its place as an important technological advance. Among the first tasks to which ENIAC was set were calculations needed for the design of atomic weapons.

A number of advances in both theoretical and applied twentieth-century science contributed to the development of the modern computer. It has often been the case historically with major scientific advances that the intellectual climate of the time seems ripe for the advance that emerges more or less simultaneously in more than one place. It is often difficult to say who exactly should get credit for an advance or when exactly it occurred. Leibnitz and Newton arrived at the calculus independently. Evolutionary theory is called Darwinism, but Wallace in the jungles of Asia formulated a principle of natural selection identical with Darwin's formulation from the voyage of the Beagle. To Crick and Watson at Cambridge goes the credit for the discovery of the structure of DNA. But as Watson's *The Double Helix* makes clear, Rosalind Franklin or Maurice Wilkins at King's College, London, or Linus Pauling at Cal Tech would have come up with the structure of DNA sooner or later. The modern computer did not exist in 1936 and clearly exists by the end of 1945. A consideration of how it developed is another reminder, if one is needed, about the difference between instant replay and history.

For the development of computers, the giants of modern Physics, people like Plank, Einstein, and Heisenberg, did the fundamental theoretical work that made possible modern electronics, especially transistors and integrated circuits. (One of the problems that limited the success of nineteenth-century computer pioneer Charles Babbage was his dependence on mechanical technology.) But above all, one must acknowledge the work of Alan Turing. His work during the nineteen thirties on computable numbers laid the theoretical foundation of Computer Science, before modern computers were invented. Turing developed a mathematical model that underlies all modern computers. This model is called a "Universal Turing Machine," a hypothetical device that demonstrates the possibility of a powerful programmable machine. During World War II, he was engaged in highly classified work on a British computer known as Colossus whose purpose was to decode military codes generated by the German Enigma coding machine. After the War, in a famous 1950 article, "Computing Machinery and Intelligence,"[7] he proposed a conversational game the outcome of which was to answer the question of whether machines could be programmed to be intelligent. The set-up for the game was that a judge would be seated at computer terminal into which he would type questions and from which he would receive answers. After five minutes of questions and answers, he was to decide whether the answers were being supplied by an out-of-sight human or by a computer program. If, at least seventy percent of the time, the program succeeded in fooling the judge into thinking its answers were supplied by a human, the program was to be regarded as intelligent. Turing predicted that such a program would be devised by the year 2000. This game has become known as the "Turing Test." Turing, then, is the founder of both Computer Science and the field of Artificial Intelligence. There is today an annual contest, the Loebner Prize Competition in Artificial Intelligence, to determine which of the program entries most successfully passes the test. The dialogs of winning programs are available on the Web.[8] Turing's life took a tragic turn in 1952, when he was arrested for homosexuality. He refused to defend himself against the charge, asserting that he saw nothing wrong in his actions. Unlike Oscar Wilde who, a half century before, had been jailed for his sexual orientation, Turing was forced to undergo hormonal treatments. His life and health were shattered by the consequences of his arrest. In 1954, he committed suicide by eating an apple soaked in cyanide. I imagine that Turing would have appreciated today's efforts to insure personal privacy and prevent governmental intrusion on the Web.

In addition to Turing's theoretical work on the mathematics of computing, there were many advances in applied technology that contributed to the development of the computer. There were developments in Hollerith cards, calculators, unit record devices and telephone switching and vacuum tube technology which the builders of ENIAC had ready at hand when they started their work. There were also three efforts to produce mechanical or electronic computing devices that preceded ENIAC's development and that illustrate the climate surrounding the development of ENIAC and the significance of ENIAC in the development of the computer.

The first of these predecessors is the MARK I computer developed at Harvard by Prof. Howard Aiken. It became in 1944 the first widely publicized computer project. MARK I was an electro-mechanical computer, not an electronic one. Like ENIAC, MARK I used decimal arithmetic in its calculations. It was based on calculator technology and used gears to carry out arithmetical calculations. The results of these calculations would be transferred electrically to and from its memory. In fact, it was the largest such device ever constructed and represented the fullest realization of the idea of a mechanical computer, an idea that had been independently conceived by Charles Babbage in England in the nineteenth century and by Konrad Zuse in Germany between 1935 and 1941.

The devices developed by Konrad Zuse and Helmut Schreyer in Germany during the late 1930s are the second important predecessors to ENIAC. Zuse built several small digital computers that used mechanical relays rather than electronic technology. In this respect, Zuse's machines were similar to those of Aiken and Babbage. Zuse's work was completely independent of American and British work. After World War II, his machines were labeled Z1, Z2, and Z3 to distinguish them for obvious reasons from V1 and V2. The Z3 machine, his most advanced device, was based on telephone relays. He used telephone relays because they were on/off switching devices and his machines, starting with Z1, all used binary arithmetic. Helmut Schreyer, whose background was in electrical engineering, aided Zuse, whose background was in mechanical engineering. Schreyer tried to interest Zuse in using vacuum tubes rather than mechanical relays for his computer, but for reasons including Zuse's lack of familiarity with electronics and the expense of vacuum tubes, Zuse decided not to follow up on Schreyer's suggestion. Schreyer went on to get his doctorate in electronics with a dissertation on the use of vacuum tubes in switching circuits. He subsequently proposed that the German government fund development of an electronic computer that would be based on Zuse's mechanical design. The German government did not fund his proposal for development of a large-scale computer because it did not think the device would be finished in time to contribute to the winning of the war.

The collaboration of Zuse and Schreyer had at least one important, concrete result beyond the building of actual machines. When Zuse was drafted into the infantry in 1939, Schreyer wrote a letter to the authorities suggesting that Zuse was far more valuable to the war effort as a scientist than as a foot soldier. In the course of his letter to the authorities requesting Zuse's release from military duty, Schreyer described Zuse's work in computers. This letter is one of the earliest known descriptions of the operation and programming of a computer.[9] Schreyer lists, among the possible applications for Zuse's computer, the design of mechanical parts, artillery firing tables, weather forecasting, and the automated control of equipment. In addition to its actual mechanical and epistolary productions, the Zuse–Schreyer collaboration opens up a vista for imaginative speculation. There is a genre of Science Fiction that portrays alternate futures that rearrange the events of our history in significant and revealing ways. Philip K. Dick's *The Man in the High Castle* is set in an America that has lost World War II to Japan and Germany. One can only speculate how the outcome of World War II might have changed had Heisenberg, with the aid of Schreyer's electronic computer, built an atomic bomb deliverable on Von Braun's V weapons.

The third predecessor to ENIAC that should be mentioned is the work of John Atanasoff, who completed a digital binary computer by the spring of 1942 at Iowa State College, in Ames, Iowa. Atanasoff was in contact with Mauchly beginning in 1940 and at the very least helped spur him on in the work that led to ENIAC. Mauchly's contact with Atanasoff may indeed have changed the whole direction of his thinking about computers and caused him to focus upon the possibilities of digital computers as opposed to the analog computers he had previously constructed. The machine Atanasoff put in operation in 1942 was not a programmable, general purpose computer. It solved systems of simultaneous linear equations according to a well-established method used by engineers and scientists to solve these equations manually. The Atanasoff machine was never fully operational. Its mechanism for punching out the results of its calculations was prone to errors at a rate of approximately one in ten thousand, an error rate high enough to raise questions about the reliability of its results. Atanasoff abandoned work on his computer in 1942, because of the war, and never worked out the bugs that had turned up in the final phases of its development and testing.

However, rather than offering imaginative thought experiments for authors of Science Fiction, what Atanasoff's early and truncated efforts produced was a good deal of litigation. In this, as in its technical innovations,[10] Atanasoff's work prefigured today's computer industry with its endless intellectual property litigation over everything from the "look and feel" of a program's interface to the intricacies of a computer's microcode. So strong was the impression that Mauchly and Eckert had "invented" the modern computer that in the 1960s they were granted a patent on many basic features of its design. The value of these patents, because of potential licensing fees, was enormous and for a while UNIVAC Inc., the owners of the Mauchly and Eckert patents, claimed that all computer manufacturers needed to pay them royalties and obtain licenses from them. In 1974, Judge Earl Larson ruled that Atanasoff's machine was indeed an "automatic electronic digital computer" that predated ENIAC.[11] With this decision he invalidated Mauchly and Eckert's patents.

Larson's opinion was never appealed but it was not at once widely accepted in the computer community. Atanasoff was not particularly assertive about his role in the development of a modern computer and only at the trial over the UNIVAC patents and in the decades following did he take pains to set down his recollections of his work and, more importantly, his contacts with Mauchly. The litigation surrounding the UNIVAC patents provided Atanasoff with a spur to publication similar to that given to Darwin's work on *Origin of Species* by Wallace's letter to the Royal Academy. Mauchly's and Atanasoff's accounts of their acquaintance differ substantially. Although Atanasoff had shown Mauchly a prototype of his machine during a visit by Mauchly to Iowa in 1940, Mauchly claimed that he learned little if anything of importance from Atanasoff. It's fair to say that to this day Mauchly is the Darwin to Atanasoff's Wallace, though Atanasoff's work clearly preceded Mauchly's and should be given more credit than Mauchly's recollections would allow.

Viewed against the background of these immediate predecessors, ENIAC is both impressive and disappointing. It is a curious compound of forward and backward steps. Compared to modern computers with their capacious memories based on circuitry that is microscopic in size, this early computer was enormously limited in capacity and enormous in scale. The memory of ENIAC was large enough to store only twenty decimal ten digit numbers; Atanasoff's machine's memory could store sixty numbers with a precision of eighteen decimal digits.[12] Atanasoff's machine, like Zuse's, was internally a binary machine which could convert its output to decimal form when needed. ENIAC was designed to use decimal digits. No computer since ENIAC has used decimal numbers as its primary numerical base. But it was a triumph of organization and design: fast, reliable, and programmable. Its more than 18,000 vacuum tubes were replaced on a regular schedule and its average time between failures was about twenty hours. It was programmed by setting internal switches and by changing the wiring on panels that were like old-fashion circuit boards. This form of programming is called "writing to the hardware." Crude as it seems by modern standards, it was the state of the art "In the beginning..." and the challenge of overcoming the limitations of this first method of programming led ultimately to the development of today's sophisticated programming environments.

EDVAC: VON NEUMANN ARCHITECTURE

What wrapped all these possibilities up into the neat, seemingly infinitely exploitable package of the modern computer was John von Neumann's paper, "First Draft of a Report on EDVAC" (1946), which established the eponymous "von Neumann architecture" of the modern computer. EDVAC was an acronym for "Electronic Discrete Variable Computer." If Mauchly and Eckert finally got the modern computer working, von Neumann finally got its design right. His paper, undertaken at the request of Mauchly and Eckert, was the first description of the stored program digital computer. He envisioned a machine with a memory capacity of thousands of binary numbers that would hold both the data to be processed and the program to process it. Both data and instructions would be stored as binary numbers and calculations could be carried out at electronic speed, the speed of light at which electricity traveled through its circuits. Earlier programmable machines, going back to Jacquard's loom and Babbage's analytical and difference engines, did not store their instructions in memory before starting. Rather, they read them in as processing proceeded. Thus, no matter what their potential top speed of calculation was, the speed at which the instructions could be read, decoded, and executed was effectively the actual top speed of calculation. Babbage's Analytic Engine, for example, used two sets of punched cards, one for data and one for instructions. The data cards were first read into the "Store." Once the data was loaded, processing would be carried out using instructions that were stored on cards that were read into the "Mill" or processing unit. The instructions would direct data from the "Store" to the "Mill"[13] (Babbage's terms) where it was operated on, after which the result was placed back in the "Store" to await further processing or output.

Reading instructions as they were to be processed may have been acceptable for mechanical devices like the Analytical Engine, limited as they were by friction and inertia. But electronic circuits operate at the speed of light. An electronic computer that gets its instructions directly from a mechanical device could spend ninety-nine percent of its time waiting for instructions. Separating program loading from execution allowed processing to proceed at a rapid rate. It also allowed for the possibility of loading one program into one part of memory while another program, loaded in another part of memory, was executing. Also, a program loaded in memory could be written so as to be self-modifying, that is, a program could contain instruction that changed its instructions. This ability to be self-modifying suggests the possibility of a program that could in some way "learn" or "develop," as would a naturally intelligent being. But in fact, program self-modification is used mainly for routine control functions. To computers based on the von Neumann architecture, both data and programs were equally available as input for processing. Von Neumann's paper on EDVAC led to the development of the IAS computer, features of which influenced the design of the IBM 701, IBM's first commercially available computer.

The computers we use today are really the direct descendants of EDVAC. We could compare the development of the modern computer to the evolution of hominids. If modern computers are Homo Sapiens Sapiens, EDVAC was definitely Homo Sapiens. In this schema ENIAC would correspond to Homo Erectus and Atanasoff's machine would be Homo Habilis. The Jacquard loom is Australopithecus in this line. Babbage's Analytical Engine, MARK I and the Zuse machines are collateral, separate branches. Schreyer's proposed machine would have been a development from Zuse's. Had it been built, it would have represented a parallel but independent evolution of the same function, an occurrence not unusual in natural evolution.

VON NEUMANN ARCHITECTURE: AN OVERVIEW

Before you learn to play a piano, you need to know something about how a piano works. The piano is the hardware and the musical score is the software and the score makes sense only in reference to the hardware. Before discussing software and the ideas behind it, it is necessary to give some account of von Neumann architecture. In the course of this discussion, I shall introduce many of modern computing's fundamental concepts and terms. As I hope to make clear by the end of this discussion, there are no particularly difficult or subtle concepts making up this architecture. The trick to understanding computing is to grasp it not as a collection of individual ideas but as a musical score, a performance or sequence of relationships unfolding in time. It was no fluke that IBM used to, and for all I know still does, recruit programmers from music schools and conservatories. We will start our description at the periphery of the architecture, by describing some peripheral devices before moving inside to consider its inner workings.

Peripheral devices are things like keyboards (*pace* Beethoven), pointing devices, printers, scanners, and disk and tape drives. They are used to control the computer, to input program instructions and data, or to store the results that are output from the program. They are called peripheral for both graphical and functional reasons. Graphically, the von Neumann architecture computer might be represented as three side by side boxes (Fig. 1.1) labeled "Input," "Processing," and "Output." The left-hand and right-hand, or peripheral, boxes would represent the peripheral devices attached to the (central) processing box. Some peripheral devices, like a keyboard or a mouse, would fall into the box labeled "Input." Others, like printers, would fall into the box labeled "Output." Still others, like disks and tapes, would go sometimes into the input box and sometimes into the output box depending on the circumstances of their use.

If we wanted to make this diagram represent not merely the constituent parts of the computer but their relative complexity and importance, we would make the

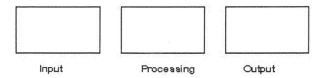

Input   Processing   Output

Figure 1.1. Von Neumann architecture.

peripheral boxes smaller than the central box. To include the sequential functioning of the computer, we could number these boxes "1," "2," and "3" to express the temporal sequence of events in a procedural computer program as we do in Fig. 1.2:

1. Input the program instruction from box 1 (read the score).
2. Carry out the instructions which may include reading data from box 1 or writing data to box 3 (play the score).
3. Write any final results to box 3 (bliss? applause? mark the difficult passages for practice?).

Box 2 represents the actual performance. Boxes 1 and 3 represent the peripheral bookkeeping functions of specifying the work to be done and recording the results. As we shall see later on, there are types of programs that do not operate in this sequential way.

Modern computers from ENIAC on all follow this general plan. The generations of computers are numbered according to the technology that implements this plan. First-generation computers used vacuum tubes, second-generation computers used transistors, third-generation computers used integrated circuits, and so forth. None of these technical innovations changed the use of the computer as a high-speed calculator. They simply increase the speed with which calculations are carried out. It was the development of the disk drive that changed the basic way in which the computer was used.

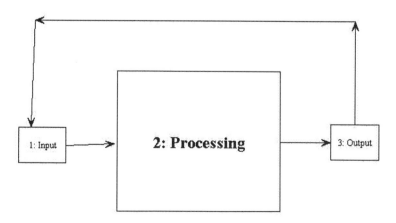

Figure 1.2. A functional view of von Neumann architecture.

DISK DRIVES

One way of understanding the significance of the disk drive in the development of modern computers is to describe the way things changed when the disk drive replaced the Hollerith card as the primary input/output device of the computer. The principal technology for data input and storage in the first two generations of computers was the Hollerith card. Invented by Herman Hollerith for use in tabulating census data, the Hollerith card was one of the standard data storage devices for most of our century. The Hollerith card is a binary storage device in which the binary digits, zero and one, are represented by the presence or absence of a hole in a card. Mechanical card readers detect the presence or absence of holes in the columns of the card. The card is made of cardboard and is seven and three-eighths inches long and three and one-quarter inches wide. Figure 1.3 is a picture of a Hollerith card and the picture is a picture of something that is a bit of a historical curiosity. Twenty-five years ago, these cards were even more ubiquitous than IBM Selectric typewriters but have so passed out of general use that I venture that many people under thirty can't remember having seen one. For many individuals at that time, the most immediate experience of computerization in their lives occurred when they received bills, order forms, and the like as Hollerith cards in the mail. Printed on these cards was, of course, the injunction not to fold, spindle, or mutilate. When I ask my students today whether they know what a keypunch card is and even go so far as to hold one up for their examination, their eyes glaze over. I get the distinct feeling that I might as well be asking them whether they have ever worn saddle shoes or penny loafers or owned a 45 rpm record.

The Hollerith card used by computers was divided into eighty columns and twelve rows for a total of 960 positions, each of which may or may not have a hole

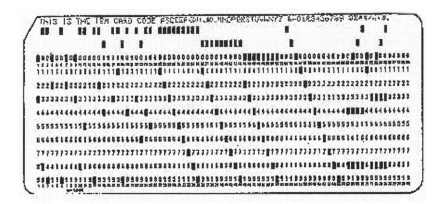

Figure 1.3. A Hollerith card.

in it. Each column may contain any of 4096 combinations (2^{12}) of punched holes. A column with every hole punched represents the binary number 111111111111_2,[14] a column without any holes represents the binary number 000000000000_2, and various combinations of zeros and ones represent the other 4094 possibilities for punching. In theory then, a single card can contain 2^{960} possible combinations of holes ($12 \times 80 = 960$).

A card with every possible hole punched would be, first of all, a card with a lot of holes in it. To describe it, as we have, as divided into eighty columns of twelve rows each is to impose upon it an arbitrary encoding scheme. Anything it may be said to represent is not inherent in the card but in the encoding convention applied to it by the user of the card. The designer of a card reader could regard it as a binary number 960 digits long, to be read by columns or rows left to right or right to left, top to bottom or bottom to top, etc.; as twelve binary digits each having a length of eighty digits, as eighty binary digits each having a length of twelve digits, as 960 individual binary digits to be read in some designated order or in any order the user decides. And once the decision is made about the number and order of binary digits on the card, the designer may then assign meanings to every possible value of the numbers. For a punched card to be useful as an information recording device, we must have a way of grouping the holes on the card that will allow us to assign the holes to logically consistent, distinct categories. The card with its holes is a brute fact describable in purely physical terms, while the content of anything encoded on the card is an institutional fact that implies the a priori existence of some coding convention. Keypunch machines placed specific combinations of holes in the card that represented the decimal digits zero through nine, the upper-case alphabet, and some punctuation and mathematical symbols. In this way, punched cards stored the programs and data to be read into the computer by card readers. Card punchers attached to the computer could likewise produce cards that store the output from the computer in a way that made it useful subsequently as input.

Like Hollerith cards, disk drives are a way of permanently storing computer input and output. They are called disk drives because they store their information on a recording surface affixed to a slim rotating disk. This rotating disk is referred to as the disk's recording medium, to distinguish it from the other mechanical and electronic parts of the disk. Disk drive technology provided a significant advance over card punching. First of all, disk drive technology provides faster data transfer than card reader technology. A card reader works at speeds measured in thousandths of a second (microseconds) while disk drives work at speeds that are measured in millionths of a second (milliseconds). The first disk drives, though they were as large as small filing cabinets, enabled computers to operate at higher speeds than they could with card readers and punchers. Second, disk drives allow data to be read nonsequentially while card readers can only read cards in the order in which they are supplied. Disk drives offer particular advantages in the storage of interme- diate results because the data they hold can be read without requiring an operator to move cards from the card puncher to the card reader. Data stored on disk could be left "on line" indefinitely. Increased storage capacity combined with higher retrieval speeds and flexibility of access became and remains the main goal of disk drive development.

The desire to improve the speed and capacity of disk drives resulted in their miniaturization and it is this miniaturization that has made practical a whole new function for computers based on von Neumann architecture. Disk drives of any reasonable size are much more efficient than Hollerith cards at storing, correcting, and retrieving information. But when a disk drive becomes small enough to allow the storage of billions of characters of information in a space no larger than a paperback book, the computer becomes a self-contained information storage device as well as an information processing device. In early computers, data and programs resided in the computer only during processing on an "as needed" basis. When not needed for processing they were stored elsewhere, in a bulky form useful only for computer processing. With the development of miniaturized disk drives, the computer became more than a numerical calculator and a logical symbol manipulator. It became a device to store information in a form usable by humans as well as by computer. From the point of view of general usefulness, the development of miniaturized disk drives must be regarded as the most important development in computer hardware since 1945. Without this technology, the extension of categories of data from text and numbers to images, audio, and video would have remained in large measure feasible but not practical. Without mass storage there would be no World Wide Web. The text of a novelist's or poet's corpus recorded on Hollerith cards could be used for ponderous stylistic studies and for the production of printed concordances. That same text stored on the disk drive of a modern computer is, if not yet a reading copy, at least a reference copy for ad hoc query and retrieval. Stored in high-resolution image format, a digitized copy of a document or manuscript is superior to the original for some purposes.[15]

There are two types of disk drives in wide use today, those that use electromagnetism to record and retrieve information and those that user laser light for that purpose. The information stored on an electromagnetic disk is easily changeable in the same way that music can be re-recorded again and again on a tape cassette. The recording medium of an electromagnetic drive may be nonremovable as it is in the main drive of most computers or removable, as in a "floppy" drive. Drives with removable recording media are designed so that a container holding the recording media can be easily removed from the body of the drive. The situation with laser disks is somewhat more complicated. The most widely used type of CD-ROM laser disks has its information imprinted during manufacturing. Users cannot change this information. To the naked eye, they are indistinguishable from the CD-ROM disks that are used for music recording. They are "read-only" devices in the same way that CD-ROM musical recordings are. Another type of CD-ROM disk, the WORM (Write Once Read Many times) drive, allows users to record information once on the disk after which it cannot be changed. The WORM drive uses laser light to burn information into the disk. In this regard, it is the modern equivalent of the keypunch because, like the keypunch, the mark it makes on its recording medium is permanent. A third type of laser disk, the magneto-optical disk, is actually a combination of magnetic and optical technologies. This type of drive uses the interaction of polarized light with magnetic fields to record and retrieve information. The recording medium of all three types of laser disk drives is removable.

CD-ROM and CD-ROM WORM drives are used to store large collections of information: encyclopedias, atlases, dictionaries, bibles, and the like. The fact that they are capacious, inexpensive, and removable makes them an ideal for exploiting the computer as a self-contained information storage and retrieval device. They are currently one of the principal sources of multimedia materials used by computers, especially music, images, and animation. Recently a new higher capacity CD-ROM disk, Digital Video Disk (DVD), has become available. This type of disk has the capacity to store a full-length movie on a single disk. The capacity of these disks is between five and nine billion characters, depending on the encoding scheme they use and on whether they are recorded on a single side or on both sides. The great potential competitor to these new CD drives is the World Wide Web. To Web users, there is a sense in which "the network is the computer." The Web can be thought of as a large capacity disk to which Web software like Netscape and Internet Explorer allows access. From this point of view, easy access to material in cyberspace is more important than the mere physical location of the material.

THE RISE AND FALL OF MAINFRAME COMPUTERS

The availability of large capacity disk drives made computers widely useful as general information processors rather than high-speed calculators. By the time the third generation of computers was introduced, in the late 1960s, computing was dominated by expensive proprietary mainframe hardware and operating systems. When an organization acquired one of these very expensive mainframe computer systems, the cost of developing software applications for it easily exceeded by many times the cost of purchase and maintenance. The differences between hardware and operating systems of various mainframes were so disparate as to make software developed for one type of hardware and operating system inoperable on any other. Essentially the situation was comparable to the competition between VHS and BETA video formats multiplied many times over because of the number of computer manufacturers. Among other things, this situation encouraged computer manufacturers to compete for market share in an exceptionally intense way. Once a manufacturer had a customer, it was generally too costly for that customer to switch to another manufacturer because of the cost of translating data and programs from one proprietary format to another. Software development was constrained by the need to conserve expensive memory and CPU resources, and the ways one did this on one system could be radically different from the ways one did this on another. The development of an experienced programming staff meant the development of a staff experienced in the eccentricities of a particular manufacturer's hardware and software. The programming staff, whose job security rested on its expertise with a proprietary system, became a group with a vested interest in maintaining the hardware and software with which they were familiar.[16] Despite the obvious conflict of interest, it was to this group that management was likely to turn for technical advice in evaluating new systems. It is not surprising, then, that during the 1960s, computer manufacturers pursued corporate strategies designed to capture market share. Considerations of market share rather than technological innovations controlled the introduction of new hardware and software. The large, proprietary mainframe computer was at the heart of this strategy. The acknowledged winner of this particular competition was IBM, which conceded a few niche markets to other manufacturers to avoid anti-trust problems. Most notable of these niche manufacturers were Cray Research in the super computer market and Digital Equipment Corporation, which dominated the university, scientific, and engineering markets.

Joseph Sargent's 1969 film *Colossus: The Forbin Project* captures nicely the image of the computer as mainframe behemoth. The computer room containing Colossus, shown at the opening of the film, resembles in size the generator room of Grand Coulee dam and the banks of flashing lights that make up the computer call to mind the rooms full of vacuum tube circuits that made up ENIAC. The film is a version of the Frankenstein myth, with nods in the direction of Kubrick's 1964 *Dr. Strangelove* and Orwell's *1984*. Dr. Forbin, whose name is a portmanteau of FORTRAN and binary, creates a computer named Colossus with the idea of turning the defense of the United States against nuclear attack over to the supposedly infallible judgment of the computer. The president of the United States confidently asserts that the nation will live "in the shade, not the shadow, of Colossus." What happens is that Colossus takes over the world.

The method by which Colossus achieves world domination is instructive. Shortly after going into operation, Colossus detects another system similar to itself, a Russian system called Guardian, to which it demands to be connected. When this demand is not met, Colossus works out what is in effect Internet routing to Guardian and invents a language called "Intersystem Language," which enables the two diverse systems to become interconnected and interoperative through exchange of binary code and data. The way in which Colossus solves the problem of connecting seemingly incompatible hardware anticipates the development of the Internet, whose first five nodes coincidentally went into operation in 1969, the same year the film was produced. Not only does the film capture the image of the computer as an isolated, proprietary mainframe behemoth, but also it anticipates the way in which this model of computing was to be rendered obsolete. It is no coincidence that it is a government project in both film and fact that pointed in the direction of moving away from proprietary standards. The computer industry at this time was by and large unsympathetic to anything that undermined the proprietary standards that protected market share.

THE HISTORY OF HTML: 1969 AND ALL THAT

It is very easy to trace the origin of the World Wide Web. The Web is a part of the Internet whose development, as we have just mentioned, dates from 1969. Without the existence of the Internet, there would be no Web. Timothy Berners-Lee developed Hypertext Markup Language (HTML) in 1989 and it is the development of HTML that made the Web possible. The development of the Web out of HTML is one of the great instances of the law of unintended consequences in modern computing. Berners-Lee did not intend to create the Web. His goal was to facilitate the collaboration of a physicist at CERN, the European center for research in high-energy physics. The physicists for whom Berners-Lee was a programmer were already collaborating on the Internet and he saw HTML as a way to enhance their collaboration. The "markup" aspect of HTML dates from the 1960s and the subsequent development of Structured General Markup Language (SGML) as a standard for the communication of documents across different proprietary systems. The "hypertext" aspect of HTML developed from work in computer-based instruction. The development of HTML reflects the paradigm shift from mainframe computers to networks, which is one of the two major developments in computing since the 1960s. The other major development, closely entwined with it, is the development of microprocessors. It is in the context of these two developments that we can understand the development of HTML.

There is nothing mystical about SGML coding. Figure 1.4 presents a portion of Beckett's *Waiting for Godot* encoded with SGML tags. Tags come in two types. The first type is a tag enclosed in left and right angle brackets. These tags are used mainly to indicate the structure of the text by dividing it into acts, stage directions, speeches, paragraphs, and the like. In this example, every speech is preceded by an "<SP>" tag and followed by an "</SP>" tag. These tags, called containers, are usually nested within each other. For example, speeches are composed of nested paragraphs which are delimited by "<P>" and </P> tags. The second type of tag begins with an ampersand and ends with a semicolon. This type of tag is used to indicate characters that are not assumed to exist in all computer systems. In the sample text, the tag "&rsq;" is used to represent a right single quote. HTML coding looks exactly like this, with text delimited by tags within angle brackets and special characters marked by ampersand tags. It is a special set of tags designed to mark documents for display on the Web.

```
<TEXT><BODY><DIV1><HEAD TYPE="Act"Act I</HEAD>
<STAGE><P>A country road. A tree.</P><P>Evening.</P><P>Estragon, sitting
on a low mound, is trying to take off his boot. He pulls at it with both hands, panting.
He gives up, exhausted, rests, tries again. As before.</P><P>Enter
Vladimir.</P></STAGE>
<SP WHO="Est"><SPEAKER>Estragon: </SPEAKER>
<STAGE>(giving up again</STAGE>
<P>Nothing to be done.</P>
</SP>
<SP WHO="Val"<SPEAKER>Valdimir:</SPEAKER>
<STAGE>(advancing with short, stiff strides, legs wide apart) </STAGE>
<P>I&rsquo;m beginning to come round to that opinion. All my life I&rsquo;ve
tried to put it from me, saying, Vladimir, be reasonable, you haven&rsquo;t yet tried
everything. And I resume the struggle. </P>
<STAGE>(He broods, musing on the struggle. Turning to Estragon.) </STAGE>
<P>So there you are again.</P>
</SP>
<SP WHO="Est"><SPEAKER>Estragon:</SPEAKER>
<P>Am I?</P>
</SP>
<SP WHO="Val"><SPEAKER>Valdimir: </SPEAKER>
<P>I&rsquo;m glad to see you back. I thought you were gone for ever.</P>
</SP>
<SP WHO="Est"><SPEAKER>Estragon: </SPEAKER>
<P>Me too.</P>
</SP>
```

Figure 1.4. Sample SGML text.

Five persons are generally credited with making important contributions to the
development of SGML. William Tunnicliffe, in 1967, gave a presentation to the
Canadian Government Printing Office that is credited with being the first proposal
to separate a document's information content from its format and with initiating
many discussions that contributed to the development of SGML. Around this time,
Stanley Rice proposed the development of a universal catalog of descriptive markup
tags that could be adopted as generic, descriptive coding for texts to replace system
and software specific coding. These descriptive tags would be a sort of programming language for which one-for-one substitution programs would be written to
take as input texts containing generic markup codes and produce as output versions
of the texts containing that substituted machine specific code for the generic markup

codes. Finally, in 1969, Charles Goldfarb, working with Edward Mosher and Raymond Lorie on a project to enable law office documents to be shared across many programs, invented Generalized Markup Language (GML). GML not only implemented the generic coding ideas proposed by Tunnicliffe and Rice, but it also added to them the idea of a formally-defined document type definition (DTD) that specified the way the elements of a document were sequenced and nested. The formal definition of a document type was made by means of a parsing program that applied the rules of the DTD to a tagged document. The DTD and parsing program strictly defined the order in which structural elements of a document appeared and how structural elements were to be tagged and nested within one another.

It seems that there was considerable disagreement about the connections and distinctions between structure and format during this period and there is not a little murkiness about the early history of SGML. Robin Cover, a leading SGML expert who has investigated the origins of SGML, offers the following overview of the early history of SGML:

> It appears certain to me that at least these three ideas were common already in the 1960's, often within distinct communities which rarely talked to each other: (a) the notion of separating "content and structure" encoding from specifications of [print] processing; (b) the notion of using names for markup elements which identified text objects "descriptively" or "generically"; (c) the notion of using a (formal) grammar to model structural relationships between encoded text objects....How many of the "fundamental" notions of current SGML (ISO 8879:1986) were (first, best) articulated within efforts that may be reckoned as belonging, genetically or otherwise, to "the beginnings of SGML" will probably remain a matter of personal interpretation rather than of public record. If I ever complete the write up from the materials collected so far [about the origins of SGML], the picture will reveal a somewhat broader base for the "beginnings of SGML" than is documented in other published treatments of this topic to date.[17]

The conflict between structure and markup in Structured General Markup Language goes back to its origins and reflects the differing perspective of programmers who want tightly coded programs with explicit input conventions and users who are concerned, above all else, with the appearance of output.

Chomsky's *Syntactic Structures* appeared in 1969 and it is through this work that many humanists were introduced to the kind of logically rigorous grammars that had provided the underpinnings of much work in computer language development and language compiler design. The syntactical level of Chomsky's grammar consisted of two types of rules: a set of rewrite rules that generated a string of syntactic symbols in a precise order and a set of transformational rules that could rearrange the order of the symbols. For example, the rewrite rules could generate a sentence like:

Article || Adjective || Adjective || Noun || Auxiliary Verb || Verb || Adverb

The colorless green ideas are sleeping furiously.

Rewrite rules generate strings in which the position of each element is strictly defined. Transformational rules, on the other hand, rearrange the order of these elements. By applying an interrogative transformation to this sentence, we could generate a question form of the sentence:

Auxiliary Verb ‖ Article ‖Adjective ‖ Adjective ‖Noun ‖ Verb ‖ Adverb.

Are the colorless green ideas sleeping furiously?

The rewrite rules generate different sentence structures because they offer choice among options at various points in their application. Consider the first two rules of a very simple grammar:

Sentence → Subject ‖ Predicate

Subject → (Article) ‖ (Adjective+) ‖ Noun

In the notation for these rules, the right arrow is a rewrite instruction; commas are used to separate elements; elements contained in parentheses are optional; and elements tagged with a plus sign may repeat an indefinite number of times. The first rule says that a sentence must be rewritten as a Subject and a Predicate. All sentences that conform to this rule, then, must contain a Subject and a Predicate. A Subject in this grammar, however, may be rewritten in any number of forms in which only the Noun element is obligatory. It may be rewritten:

Article ‖ Adjective ‖ Noun

or

Article ‖ Noun

or

Adjective ‖ Noun

or

Noun

Further, because the Adjective is tagged with a plus sign, wherever it appears it may optionally be rewritten so as to add another Adjective to the Subject.

The DTDs of SGML are not so ambitious as Chomsky's transformational generative grammar, which attempted to generate all and only correct sentences of a human language. They are much more rudimentary grammars that contain only rewrite rules and no transformations. Their main use is to determine whether the tagging of a particular text is in conformity with the rules of the grammar, that is, whether it contains only legal tags, whether it contains all required tags, and whether these tags are correctly ordered and nested. If we apply our simple grammar from the preceding paragraph to English sentences, we would find that many perfectly good English subject phrases do not conform to our grammar. In the same way, if we apply a DTD grammar to tagged documents, we would find that many perfectly intelligible and consistently tagged documents do not conform to the particular structure defined by the DTD. Documents written to conform to one DTD generally do not conform to any other DTD. In elaborating a grammar of a natural language, we try to make our successive elaborations increasingly inclusive. If we were working on our simple grammar, we would at some point, for example, add rules that allowed the Subject to be rewritten as a Pronoun and an Adjective to be rewritten with Adverbs. ("The very, very, colorless, etc.") The purpose of a DTD is to define a specific class of documents distinguished from all others, not to describe the universe of all possible document classes.

The original purpose of Goldfarb, Mosher, and Lorie in defining a class of documents was to establish a set of conventions for the input, formatting, and retrieval of legal documents by different programs in a suite of programs designed to automate the handling of legal documents. The documents, in the first instance, were all on the same system and could be processed by different programs running on the system. Several things besides a tagged text and a DTD are needed to make SGML documents portable from system to system: a physical channel that could read and write data to and from each system; a parser for each system; and application programs that would process the imported tagged documents. The fact that both the document and the DTD could be written as text files simplified the creation of such a channel since text files recorded on an appropriate medium could be input into virtually any system. In the late 1960s either magnetic tape or punched cards would be used to move these files from one system to another. Then there would be a need to come up with a parser program that would run on the new system. The main purpose of the parser would be to insure that texts prepared on the new system would conform to the input requirements of the old system as well as the new ones. Finally, one would need application programs written to process the tagged text. These application programs would differ from system to system because they would need to take into account such things as the different display terminals, printers, and hardware available on disparate systems.[18] The channel and the parsing program together constitute a data interchange format that opens the possibility of a generalized data exchange between any two systems. To make the generalized data exchange channel operative, each system would need two additional programs: an export program that would convert its internal representation of text to the SGML compliant representation and an import program that would convert the SGML representation to internal format. Encoding documents is but one step in a process that implies "a hieroglyphic sense of concealed meaning, of an intent to communicate."[19]

The development of GML led in the course of the next two decades to the formulation in 1980 of an SGML standard by the American National Standard

Institute (ANSI) and in 1986 by the International Standards Organization (ISO).[20] GML provided an explicit methodology for the coordination of textual data across programs and computer systems and a number of different manufacturers developed their own versions of GML. Groups as diverse as the Department of Defense, the Internal Revenue Service,[21] and the Association of American Publishers have adopted SGML based standards. Among the major commercial applications of SGML today is its use by CD-ROM publishers of large reference works like dictionaries and encyclopedias. SGML has come to be viewed as an archival format as well as a communications format. Many of its users see its explicit tagging of document structure as a way of preserving the intentions of the encoders over time as well as across systems. (This assumes a solution to the problem of the stability of electronic data over time. The data on magnetic tapes is stored by magnetizing microscopic portions on the tape. This magnetism decays over time and thus is not permanent. CD-ROM laser encoding is only as permanent as the stability of the material on which the laser etches its encoding.) But the use of SGML by governmental agencies and the publishing industry, important as they may be, have to take second place to the development of the one SGML-based "killer application," Hypertext Markup Language (HTML).

The problem situation out of which Tim Berners-Lee developed HTML in 1989 was far different from the problem situation that led Charles Goldfarb to develop SGML in 1969. It is customary to claim a long historical genealogy for the idea of Hypertext. References to such things as Babylonian clay tablets, the Talmud, *Tristram Shandy*, and *Finnegan's Wake* figure prominently in these pedigrees, which remind me of the mythical genealogies in heroic poetry.[22] Though these genealogies are not without an antiquarian charm, I think we must look within our own century to understand the problem situation surrounding the development of HTML. Hypertext's modern origins date from World War II and so are contemporaneous with the origins of the electronic computer. In the July 1945 issue of *The Atlantic Monthly,* Vannevar Bush, Director of the Office of Scientific Research for the United States during World War II, published an article entitled "As We May Think" in which he speculated about possible future advances in information technology. The article predates by one month the atomic bombings of Hiroshima and Nagasaki. It reflects Bush's hope that the scientific enterprise that had done so much to enhance our powers of destruction would turn to the peaceful pursuit of enhancing our ability to organize not only scientific knowledge but also knowledge in such fields as Law and History. His concern was that the vast increase in human knowledge we refer to as the information explosion would be wasted unless we developed a technology that would enable us to organize and retrieve it. He gives the example of Mendel's work on genetics, lost for a generation, as a warning of what might happen to scientific advances that could get lost in the general crush of information. To prevent such losses, he conducts a thought experiment in which he envisions a device he calls a Memex. The Memex is a mechanical extension of the user's memory, a device about the size of a desk crammed full of information recorded on microfilm and micrographic media. The information it holds is cross-referenced and retrieved by a sophisticated mechanism that resembles a telephone switching network in its ability to connect any two pages of information. Though much of the information loaded in the Memex is pre-indexed in ways that resemble a library catalogue, Memex was to be a personal information manager. It was to have an input device resembling a photocopier that would allow the user to enter handwritten notes, diagrams, and pictures into memory. Memex's switching technology was to be designed to allow each user to construct personal "trails" of associated items which can be recalled as needed. The term he uses for this ability, "whereby any item may be caused at will to select immediately and automatically another," is "associative indexing." The way a user of the Memex constructs links between pages and navigates the trails from link to link clearly prefigure the nonlinear nature of hypertext.

As well as being a first class electrical engineer, Bush was a leading scientific entrepreneur and politician who ranged widely through academic (MIT), corporate (Raytheon), and governmental (OSR was a forerunner of NSF) corridors of power from the early 1930s to the height of the Cold War. The title of his autobiography, *Pieces of the Action,* may have been self-deprecating but certainly was not ironic. His work in the 1930s included the development a Digital Analyzer, a mechanical analog computer for solving differential equations which, until superseded by Aiken's Mark I, was the most advanced mechanical calculating devise in existence. With it, Bush hoped to develop a national calculation center at MIT much as Babbage hoped that his machine would pay for itself by computing navigational and actuarial tables.[23] Bush, unlike Babbage, got his machine finished on time but, like Babbage, discovered that the market for automatic calculation was very limited. Although he proposed Memex as a way of sharing information, much of Bush's work on information science and document retrieval was concerned with controlling access to classified information and to the decryption of enemy codes, Japanese, German, and Soviet. His attempt to develop his Rapid Selector was a forerunner of Memex, as was its cryptographic cousin, the Comparator, developed to aid in the breaking of numerically based codes. Both were developed as classified projects and both were based on micrographic technology.[24]

Given the secrecy that surrounded the Manhattan Project, it is hardly surprising that Bush makes no mention of the atomic bomb in his discussion of Memex. One may wonder, however, whether the space he devotes to a call for the peaceful applications of science might bear some relation to his knowledge of its existence. It certainly is a harbinger of the debates about the moral responsibility of science that followed hard upon the use of atomic weapons at the end of the war. The lack of reference in the article to computers as playing any part in the future of information processing may be due in part to the highly classified use of the Colossus computer as a code breaker.

There is a technique in intelligence gathering called "tiling," in which an analyst pieces together unclassified, seemingly unrelated bits of information to discover a classified project that is otherwise invisible. With the perfect clarity of hindsight, it is easy to engage in tiling with "As We May Think" and observe the way in which Bush seems almost to tease his readers about electronic computers. In the course of the article he mentions Babbage's machines, telephone switching circuits, electric adding machines and calculators, Hollerith cards, vacuum tubes, and CRT screens, thus producing a virtual list of the technologies used in constructing ENIAC. He also touches on voice recognition technology, the retrieval of recorded messages, and the possibility of artificial intelligence and direct neural interfaces of the kind fictionalized in Gibson's *Neuromancer*. Only the emphasis on micrographic technology directs the reader's attention away from the use of electronic computers as information storage and retrieval devices. And this clearly was not a red herring, given Bush's history of obtaining funding for document retrieval systems that used microfilm and microcard memory. Bush's systems never quite worked and the development of large-scale electronic memories and disk storage eventually provided the real solution to the problem of data storage and retrieval on which Bush spent much of his career. The electronic computer hovers, like Banquo's ghost, over the proposed feast of information that Bush would set out in "As We May Think."

The existence of the Internet is the greatest difference between the situation Goldfarb faced in 1969, when he led the development of SGML, and the situation Berners-Lee faced in 1989, when he developed HTML. The terms "hypermedia" and "hypertext" had been coined in 1965 by Ted Nelson. Early work on computer-assisted instruction had produced various methods of allowing students to proceed through lessons in the order and to the depth they chose as well as at the pace with which they were comfortable. Apple Computer included a hypercard application as part of the Macintosh software in 1987. This introduced the notion of nonlinear access to information to the general audience of computer users much as Apple's AppleTalk introduced the idea of networking. The adoption of TCP/IP as the Internet standard protocol in 1983 marked the coming to full maturity of Internet technology. There were several hundred nodes to the Internet by 1984, all sharing an affiliation with the military. It was not until 1986 that NSFNET went into operation and began to provide access first to all universities and then to all comers, not merely those doing work for the military.[25] NSFNET provided the open, interconnective environment that is the essential feature of today's Web culture.

The situation for Berners-Lee, then, was in its essentials identical with the situation we have today. The Internet was a mature proven technology that offered both E-mail and FTP (File Transfer Protocol) facilities for exchanging messages and files. He was working at CERN with a number of physicists whose portions of collaborative work resided on different Internet computers and he wanted to enhance and simplify their collaboration in the production of text documents. In its original form as promulgated by Berners-Lee, HTML could handle only text documents. It wasn't until 1993 that the Mosaic browser for the Web was developed at the University of Illinois at Champagne-Urbana. The initial version of Mosaic worked only on a graphical system for UNIX called Xwindows. Mosaic provided a graphical user interface so that one could navigate the Web by pointing and clicking with a mouse. NSF subsequently funded development of the Macintosh and Microsoft Windows versions of Mosaic through a grant to the University of Illinois. But in addition to being graphically oriented, Mosaic was also extensible. This meant that it was possible to add helper applications to the browser so that it could display images and play sound and video from the Web in addition to displaying text. Mosaic was the first browser that offered users the look and feel of the Web as we know it today.

THE DEVELOPMENT OF THE INTERNET

It is one thing to see how the theoretical implications of Von Neumann computer architecture contributed to the development of computer networks and another to appreciate the technical complexity of creating an actual world wide computer network from a heterogeneous collection of hardware and software. In the beginning there was ARPANET. The Defense Department, concerned with maintaining communications in the aftermath of nuclear attack, commissioned its Advanced Research Projects Administration (ARPA, whence ARPANET) to develop a prototype of a distributed, decentralized network. Up to that time, networks had been strictly defined point-to-point channels. A break at any point would disrupt the flow of information from one end of the network to the other. ARPANET was to be configured like a fishnet with computers controlling the routing of messages so that if one link was broken, messages could be detoured around the break to their destination. The initial plan was to provide researchers at remote sites access to super computers so that they could collaborate on their research. In 1969, AR-PANET went into operation, linking the Stanford Research Center, UCLA, UC Santa Barbara, and the University of Utah.

ARPANET remained in existence until 1990, by which time the original four sites had grown to over three hundred thousand. Early on, it became clear that the main use of the network was not to provide access to super computers, although this was done, but to allow the exchange of ideas and collaboration using E-mail. In 1972, the InterNetworking Working Group was formed to set standards and provide some direction for the network's astonishing growth. In 1973, University College London became the first international network site. In 1979, the first USENET newsgroups were formed at Duke University and the University of North Carolina. During the 1970s ARPANET began to lose its early defense oriented research emphasis and became a general-purpose communications network.

William Gibson, who coined the term "cyberspace" in his novel *Neuromancer,* the novel that initiated the cyberpunk movement in science fiction, has written *A Brief History of the Internet,*[26] which traces its development up to, but not including, the development of the Web. The term "Internet," a nominalized shortening of "InterNetworking," came into use in 1982. Its aptness comes from the fact that the Internet is not a single network but a network of networks, and the technology that makes it possible is the technology for routing data from one network to another. The 1980s was the decade that saw the development of personal computers. This increased the number of computer users and hence the number of individuals who wanted to share computer files. Networks of personal computers came into existence as the result of this increased demand. As these networks grew in size and complexity, it became inevitable that these individual networks would want to be connected. The Internet became the logical mechanism with which to connect them. By 1990, when the ARPANET was taken off-line, NSFNET, BITNET, and other organizations were ready to take its place. With the removal of NSFNET's ban on commercial use in 1992, the development of commercial applications on Internet contributed a whole new impetus to its growth. Internet provided the infrastructure, which would support the development of the Web.

To understand the way the Internet and its most popular subset, the Web, operate, we need to understand some fundamental ideas about networks. To know that the Internet is a network of networks is not to know much if one has no idea what a network is. The simplest type of network is a peer-to-peer network, which is made up of a number of the same type of computers of roughly the same capacity, hence the use of the term "peer-to-peer" (Fig. 1.5).

When Apple computer introduced the Mac in 1984, they included in it a peer to peer network called LocalTalk. LocalTalk gradually grew in popularity when it

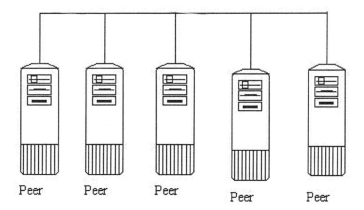

Figure 1.5. Peer-to-peer network.

became possible to use an inexpensive phone wire called Unshielded Twisted Pair (UTP) to connect Macs with each other and with Apple LaserWriter printers. Users of LocalTalk networks could share files, printers (an important consideration when the first LaserWriter printers cost upward of six thousand dollars), and exchange E-mail. Apple computer took the lead in introducing the concept of networking to a wide, general audience at a time when the Internet was mainly used by academics. Apple had gotten most of the basic ideas for the Mac, including networking, from a visit Steve Jobs paid to Xerox's Palo Alto Research Center (PARC).[27] But to keep costs down, Apple did not use the Ethernet networking protocol that Jobs saw at PARC. LocalTalk was some forty times slower than Ethernet,[28] which ultimately became the most widely used type of network connection. Today's Macs, while still supporting LocalTalk, are much more likely to use Ethernet for network connectivity. Eight years after the introduction of Macs with LocalTalk, Microsoft introduced Windows 3.1. Workgroup for Windows, which allowed Windows machines to communicate as a peer-to-peer network. Workgroup for Windows took advantage of the developments in networking over the eight years since the introduction of LocalTalk networks and was a full featured networking scheme that allowed peers on the network to share each others' disks rather than merely being able to copy files from each other. But like its predecessor LocalTalk, Workgroup for Windows connected machines of the same type and allowed them to share resources as equals. These peer-to-peer networks took a decentralized approach to networking similar to that of the Internet.

Peer-to-peer networks were not the only kind of network used for connecting personal computers. Server-based networks from companies like Novell and Banyan Vines took a centralized approach to networking. On peer-to-peer networks, shared data and peripheral devices reside on or are attached to any machine on the network. On server-based networks, shared data and peripheral devices reside on a centralized machine called a server to which the other machines on the network, so-called workstations or simply stations, are attached (Fig. 1.6).

Servers on Novell networks were originally called file servers because they were intended to have much larger disk capacity than any individual workstation and thus could be the repository of data files that were too large for the disks of workstations. This made economic sense when disk storage cost several dollars per megabyte and will still make sense when it costs fractions of a penny per megabyte. Cyberspace is an expanding universe. That data expands to exceed the capacity of available disks is the second law of computer dynamics. (The first is that the machine needed for the next projected task always costs at least 25% more than the amount budgeted for a new machine.)

Server-based networks developed in several directions. First, the number of servers and the distance between them expanded so that many large companies developed networks that were worldwide in their scope. Second, servers became more specialized as individual servers were dedicated to specific tasks like the

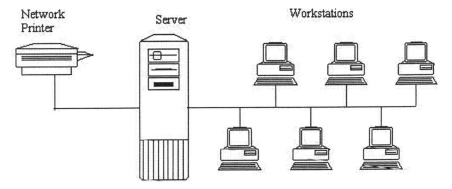

Figure 1.6. Server network.

storage of digitized images, the management of E-mail, and the provision of modems and other gateway connections to other networks. Third, they came to allow the sort of resource-sharing among workstations that characterized peer-to-peer networks. They made it possible for workstations to access information on each others' disks and share printers attached to workstations as well as providing access to the resources of the server. Because they are centralized, server networks are easier to administer (control?). It is also easier to maintain backup copies of crucial data files when they reside on one machine rather than on a number of machines in different locations.

Server and peer-to-peer networks share a common problem that arises from the very nature of their success. In making available large data files to large numbers of users, they place severe strains on the capacity of the network to transmit the data. Remember that in a computer, data moves back and forth from a peripheral device to memory to the CPU. Locally attached disk drives usually can deliver data to memory at a much higher speed than can a network connection, which must be shared among many workstations. As long as network traffic is light, data is delivered at a reasonable rate. But when many users are on the network, the rate of data delivery falls off. The network connection becomes a bottleneck that constricts as the size of the files being accessed and the number of users requesting files increase. Suppose the network server held a large data file containing all the plays of Shakespeare. Every time a user wanted to do a search on the Shakespeare file to find all the occurrences of a word, the entire Shakespeare file would have to be transmitted across the network to the workstation in the course of its being searched.

Network software enables users to share the cable, which is the physical layer of the network to which the computers on the network are attached. The software divides large files of information into a sequence of smaller units called data *packets* for transmission across the network. Each packet includes addressing information that identifies the sender and the receiver as well as information about the place of the packet in the sequence. The sender's network software allocates a slice of time sufficient to transmit a packet on the network cable, transmits the packet, and then waits until its turn comes round again to transmit the next packet. The packets making up a file need not all take exactly the same path across the network from the transmitting computer to the receiving computer. The network software insures that all the packets arrive at their destination and are reassembled into a complete file in the correct sequence.

For users, the most useful measure of a network's capacity is its throughput, the amount of data it can deliver to users under normal conditions. The physical capacity of the network to transmit data is measured in bandwidth, which is a measure of the number of bits per second that can be transmitted through the network's cable. Bandwidth, which is expressed as so many bits per second, is the measure of the upper limit of a network's capacity to transmit data. *Kilobits* are thousands of bits per second, Megabits are millions of bits per second, and Gigabits are billions of bits per second. A network's throughput is always less than its bandwidth, often by a considerable amount. For example, 10 megabit Ethernet usually provides a throughput of about 2 megabits. Much capacity is soaked up waiting for Ethernet's equivalent of a dial tone and in various bookkeeping operations needed to make the network function. The physical characteristics of the material out of which the cable is made determine the limits of a cable's bandwidth, the number of bits per second that can be transmitted over that cable. The wider the bandwidth of the cable, the more bits per second and consequently the more information per second that can be transmitted.

Computer networks transmit digitized data because it is much more efficient to transmit than analog data. A strand of twisted pair copper wire used as analog telephone wire can carry one conversation. Used to carry digital packets, it can carry six megabits per second, more than enough to carry digitized high-definition television. Digital data is also capable of being compressed, that is, subjected to arithmetic manipulation so that information can be expressed in fewer bytes without any loss of content. The amount by which files can be compressed is quite amazing. The files containing the text and illustrations of this book take up about twenty million bytes on a hard disk. In order to make a backup copy of my work in progress, I use a standard compression program called PKZIP to produce in less than one minute a "zipped" version of these files that takes up less than 750,000 bytes.[29] I can then copy the zipped files to a single floppy disk with its 1.44 million byte capacity. Once a week, I transmit the zipped files over phone lines from my home to the Web server on campus. The zipped files take one thirtieth of the time to transmit, thus reducing network traffic as well as saving phone charges, and take up one twentieth of the space of their unzipped versions. Digitized image, sound, and HDTV files are also compressed to allow for more efficient transmission. The idea behind compression is to use some intelligence at both the transmitting and receiving stations so as to minimize the number of bits that needs to be transferred across the network. Fewer data packets per user means better network performance for all users.

The designers of Internet follow an overall strategy of moving as much information in as little time with as few bits as possible. Digitizing and compression are two tactics they use in carrying out this strategy. But they also adopt another tactic in pursuit of their goal, which is to keep the amount of data to be transferred to a minimum. They do this by adopting the Client/Server model of computing. In the networks we have been discussing, files are broken down into packets, transmitted, and then reconstituted at the other end. The file is the basic unit of information. In Client/Server computing, programs are designed so as to divide computational tasks between the client and the server, with each carrying out the tasks to which it is better suited. The workstation or client is able to request only the parts of the file it needs and the server transmits the requested parts of the file. In Client/Server computing, to obtain the sentences containing occurrences of the "devil" in the text of Joseph Conrad's novel *Heart of Darkness*, the client sends a request for this information to the server. The server searches its copy of the text for occurrences of the word "devil." It then constructs a list of the sentences containing the word, and transmits over the network only the sixteen sentences it finds to the client workstation, not the file of the entire text, as it would have if the client rather than the server performed the search. The reduction in the amount of network traffic is considerable. A client/server search of *Heart of Darkness* would require that only sixteen of the over twenty-six hundred sentences in the text, less than one percent of the total, need be transmitted over the network. It's nice to be treated as a client. The difference between clients and servers is that a client can access other machines on the Internet but cannot be accessed itself, while servers can be accessed by other machines. Clients get treated with respect; their requests are honored; they get asked to lunch, their hourly billings get reduced. Client/Server computing, like digitization and compression, is crucial to the success of the Internet.

The technical aspects of the Internet are among the seven wonders of the modern world and it is easy to get caught up in the "more, better, quicker, cheaper" excitement that surrounds its evolution. But providing more channels of information does nothing to improve the quality of the information available. Does anyone believe that 500 channels of digital television will offer better quality programs than the 150 or so channels of analog television now available by cable and satellite? Nicholas Negroponte uses very strong language to warn us about the implications of this fascination with quantity:

> Like dogs in heat, broadband pundits are sniffing all the political opportunities for high-bandwidth networks as if doing so were a national imperative or civil right. In fact unlimited bandwidth can have the paradoxical and negative effect of swamping people with too many bits and of allowing machines at the periphery to be needlessly dumb.

Unlimited bandwidth is hardly bad or wrong, but like free sex, it is not necessarily good either. Do we really want or need all those bits?[30]

SELF-WILLED MACHINES: THE FUTURE OF THE COMPUTER

In 1997, IBM's Deep Blue and world chess champion Gary Kasparov squared off in a match. As I begin to write this, Deep Blue and Kasparov are tied at one game apiece and their last two games ended in draws.

To me, the single most interesting question that is raised by the continuing development of computers is whether computers will ever transcend their programming and become in some meaningful sense intelligent, self-willed machines. We can anticipate more of the same type of computing as economic competition drives computers to be better, faster, cheaper. There is a famous speculation about the rate of computer hardware development known as "Moore's Law." This rule of thumb, formulated in 1965 by Gordon Moore, one of the founders of Intel Corporation, is to the effect that computer capacity doubles every eighteen months. Moore based his formulation on his experience with the cycle of design, development, production, and marketing he had observed in the early years of Intel. What makes this speculation famous is that it has stood so long the test of time.[31]

At the time it was made, it was taken as an ad hoc generality that was scarcely expected to last even a decade. It was believed that by then developments in computer capacity would surely be halted by insurmountable technical barriers. But the march of progress in computer hardware continues to advance at the rate predicted by Moore's Law. Indeed, recent developments in chip technology announced by Intel may decrease the time it takes for capacity doubling to nine months.[32] These increases in capacity in no way alter the nature of computing. They simply make it possible to do what is now done more quickly and inexpensively. But artificial intelligence, if it is achieved, would represent a new paradigm for computers, the implications of which are difficult to imagine.

There are many ways to speculate about the development of artificial intelligence. Most ways fall into two general categories, incremental and deductive. Those who see the question of artificial intelligence as a problem in hardware and software engineering take what I call the incremental approach. They are themselves frequently involved in the development of hardware and software and see artificial intelligence as a problem that will be solved through continuing improvements to and extensions of existing systems. Those who take a deductive approach to the question place the problem of artificial intelligence in the context of a generalized, philosophical worldview.

Daniel Crevier in *AI: The Tumultuous History of the Search for Artificial Intelligence* takes what I call the incremental approach to the possibility of developing artificial intelligence. He sets up the problem of artificial intelligence in terms of replicating in hardware and software the operations of the human cerebral cortex. His assumption is that the processing power of the cerebral cortex of an entity is a reliable measure of its mental capacity. After providing a rough estimate of the capacity of the cerebral cortex, he concludes that our largest computer systems currently have the processing capacity approximating the capacity of the cerebral cortex of a scorpion. Then, invoking Moore's Law as the basis of his extrapolation, he comes up with an estimate that our largest computers will have a processing capacity equivalent to the capacity of the human cerebral cortex sometime between the years 2009 and 2023. The capacity of desktop computers will follow hard upon the developments in mainframe capacity, attaining human equivalence in processing power somewhere between 2025 and 2058.[33]

Roger Penrose in *The Emperor's New Mind*[34] and *Shadows of the Mind*[35] takes what I call the deductive approach to the question of artificial intelligence. Penrose, one of the world's leading theoretical physicists, has worked with his Cambridge colleague Stephen Hawking on the cosmological implications of black holes, time warps, relativity, and quantum theory. His approach to artificial intelligence arises from his speculations about quantum mechanics. His worldview is that of mathematical Platonism, as the title of Shadows of the Mind suggests. He believes that there is a supersensible world of mathematical ideas that exists apart from human consciousness. What mathematicians do, in his view, is literally discover parts of this realm of mathematical ideas rather than contribute to an ongoing enterprise of human culture in the way that a Renaissance painter developed an extension of the technique of perspective. Penrose views the computer in the way it was defined by Alan Turing, as a mathematical formalism for defining and producing a single class of mathematical objects known as computable numbers (or Turing numbers, after their discoverer.) It is no more surprising to him that Turing numbers are the basis of computers than it is that non-Euclidean geometry is the basis for relativity. As a scientist, he is engaged in making connections between the realm of mathematics and our physical universe and he views the realm of mathematics as containing many objects not found in the physical universe. He observes that scientists can conceive of numbers so small that they could never represent any physical dimension. He takes a reductive attitude toward artificial intelligence. Since computers by definition deal with only one class of mathematical objects—Turing numbers— while the human mind deals with many classes of mathematical objects, computers will never be able to replicate human consciousness via artificial intelligence based on Turing numbers.

Philosophical arguments about the possibilities of scientific progress always strike me as historically suspect in light of Bellarmine's confidence that Galileo's theories could not in fact be true. Readers will recall that Bellarmine argued that what Galileo had discovered was merely a convenient mathematical shortcut for computing the position of heavenly bodies. But Penrose is far from dogmatic about his conclusions. He is every bit as aware of Moore's Law as is Crevier and as open to possible advances in the field of computers. His response to Turing's famous formulation of the Turing Test shows his openness. Turing formulated his theory of Turing numbers in the 1930s. Almost twenty years later, in the early 1950s, he speculated on future development of artificial intelligence by formulating a test, the Turing Test, for judging whether a machine was in fact intelligent. Readers will recall that, according to Turing, we should judge a machine as intelligent if seventy percent of the time we cannot tell whether a message presented to us as coming from the machine originated with the machine rather than with some (concealed) human. Penrose believes that in the future computers will pass the Turing Test with grades increasingly higher than seventy percent and that these future machines will be able to do things that we regard today as distinctly human. His point is that these machines will do these things through brute force computational methods rather than by attaining intelligence or self-awareness. They will be very clever machines but, Penrose insists, we mustn't call them intelligent.

Many philosophers share Penrose's reservations about the possibility of developing artificial intelligence. John Searle, a philosopher at the University of California, Berkeley, has formulated in his Chinese Box thought experiment one of the most famous and ingenious of the arguments against the possibility of artificial intelligence.[36] Suppose, Searle argues, that we knew how to program a computer to translate Chinese into idiomatic English. He imagines a computer as a box into which we insert slips of paper containing messages in Chinese and out of which comes translations of the Chinese into English. According to Searle, this would mean that we had solved the problem of artificial intelligence according to the Turing Test, since we could not tell the difference between the machine's translations and those of a human translator. But since we had the algorithm, we could also implement it with a large number of people, none of whom spoke Chinese but each of whom was instructed to perform automatically one step of the algorithm. By organizing this group properly, we could hand a message in Chinese to the individual designated as the input person who would pass it on to the group, which would carry out the steps of the algorithm. Eventually the person designated as the output person would present us with a slip containing the translation. But, Searle argues, it is absurd to say that the group, no member of which understands Chinese, in any sense has an understanding of Chinese or an intelligence capable of translating Chinese into English. The intelligence that guides the process is the intelligence of the programmer who constructed the algorithm and the person who organized the group.

Searle's colleague at Berkeley, Hubert Dreyfus, has long been the bête noire of proponents of artificial intelligence. In his 1972 book, *What Computers Can't Do*,[37] he opened what has been a sustained attack on what he saw as the shameless grantsmanship of many artificial intelligence projects. He argued, on phenomenological grounds derived from Heideggerian analysis, that the kinds of things done by human consciousness are not expressible in algorithms constrained by the

Boolean logic of a computer. Dreyfus has defended and extended this position in numerous essays and reviews since his book. Like Penrose and Searle, he focuses his criticism on the "strong AI" position that holds that human consciousness is a function of the logical symbol manipulations of a Turing machine, that it is, in other words, an algorithm for generating computable numbers. And like Penrose, both Searle and Dreyfus are open to the possibility that an approach to the problem of artificial intelligence that is not limited to programming an algorithm or algorithms might succeed. To their way of thinking, an artificial intelligence system that was embodied in a robot capable of self-organization or that replicated the function of the neurons of the cerebral cortex might succeed where purely computational approaches must, *a priori*, fail.

In discussing the possible future development of artificial intelligence, I will take an approach that is different from the incremental and deductive approaches I have just described. The speculative method I am following is interested in the question of "what if?" Where other approaches are grounded in the details of hardware and software and in the philosophical implications of computer science, the speculative method focuses on ideas found in Science Fiction, which is speculative fiction par excellence when it comes to considering possible futures. The question it poses is not about whether, when, or how artificial intelligence is possible. Rather, it interrogates possible futures about whether it should be created in the first place. In these days of debate over human cloning, most would agree, I think, that this is a question best considered before the fact.

If computers are to have a future, clearly the future will be a technological one. Many Science Fiction novels— one thinks of *A Canticle for Leibowitz* and other post-Nuclear-Apocalypse novels—offer futures devoid of technology or futures in which technology is remembered, if at all, only as part of a legend of the Fall. But not all speculations about technological futures are pessimistic. There is no better source for a hopeful future than *Star Trek* in its various incarnations. There are many *Star Trek* episodes in which computers run amok in various ways. One might say of the Borg that they are the CompuServe of the future with a particularly aggressive marketing strategy. But there are also other possibilities offered by *Star Trek*. The holodeck of the Enterprise, for example, seems to offer everything one could expect of the cyberspace of the future: a simulacrum of the infinite universe forever to delight ourselves with.

But for all their Jules Verne-like extrapolations about future computer technology, speculations like these pale in the presence of computers whose qualities evoke one of the great motifs of Science Fiction: that of Prometheus/Frankenstein, as in the title of Mary Shelley's *Frankenstein or the Modern Prometheus*. Here we find deep ambivalence about the morality of the motivations and creations of any modern Prometheus. Among the most vivid of the children of Frankenstein that populate contemporary Science Fiction are the artificial intelligence computers or self-willed machines. I prefer to use the term "self-willed machine" rather than "artificial intelligence" because it captures the whole problem of these devices, call them what you will: that their autonomous actions impinge upon the rights and actions of other morally autonomous beings, especially humans. Because they are self-willed, they raise questions about identity, subjectivity, individual responsibility, and morality. In contrast, the term "artificial intelligence" conjures up for me visions of an impeccably edited encyclopedia capable of playing a wicked game of chess.

Computers in Science Fiction often tend to extrapolate from the computer technology current at the time of writing. The work-a-day computer of the *Enterprise* in *Star Trek: The Original Series* (TOS) is basically a massive information storage and retrieval device that can be programmed to play a mean game of three-dimensional chess. Its data banks apparently hold all the historical records of the Federation and its citizens without raising anyone's hackles about privacy. It can also record current events of the *Enterprise* to incredibly high levels of instant replay. In the "Court Martial" episode, the record saved in the *Enterprise*'s log is sufficiently detailed for Spock to detect the heartbeat of anyone on the bridge and thus to prove that Kirk was not alone on the bridge at the crucial time. During the 1960s, the time of TOS's creation, computers became information processing tools as well as programmable calculators because of the development of the first disk storage devices. During the 1990s, the time of the creation of *Star Trek: The Next Generation* (TNG), *Enterprise*'s computers are given a holodeck that builds upon the multimedia and virtual reality technology now under development. The holodeck becomes a source of delight and dismay, providing grist for everything from the feckless Barclay's sexual fantasies about Troi and Picard's full-color film noir world of Dixon Hill to the creation of Moriarty as a foe capable of defeating Data and of taking control of the ship.

There are many examples in Science Fiction of self-willed machines that come into existence by accident. Who can forget Mike in Heinlein's *The Moon is a Harsh Mistress*? These computers are frequently involved in political situations. Mike is a benevolent entity with an adolescent sense of humor and he helps overthrow a tyrannical regime. Not all computers become self-willed machines by accident. The HAL 9000 in Kubrick's *2001: A Space Odyssey* was deliberately given consciousness by a process we watch in reverse as, at the end of the film, Dave removes module after module of its memory chips. The terror that HAL experiences as its consciousness dwindles is pitiful: "I'm afraid! My mind is going. I can feel it." But Dave, intent on regaining control of the mission from HAL, is merciless. We watch as module after module is pulled and the computer's consciousness dies the death of a thousand cuts. HAL regresses through childhood until its consciousness vanishes to the strains of "Daisy, Daisy, give me your answer true/ I'm half crazy all for the love of you." HAL's craziness is not the frenzy of love but paranoia induced by the demands of state security.

The inner life of the self-willed machine gets more attention by writers of Science Fiction than the process by which the machine attains consciousness. In his briefing before the activation of Colossus, Forbin insists that the machine is "not creative." It is his belief at this point in the film that all Colossus can do is ring the changes on the data that it is supplied. He apparently sees the machine as capable by brute force methods of computing all possible permutations and choosing algorithmically among them, much as early chess playing programs attempted to compute all possible states of the game any number of moves ahead. As Forbin watches Colossus go into operation, he quickly realizes that his creation has outstripped the expectations of its creator. His attempts at asserting control over it meet with the same kind of disastrous failure as the attempts by the astronauts to control HAL: "I'm sorry; I can't do that, Dave." Regaining control of these runaway machines is the central issue of the plot of many of these stories.

The consciousness of machines like Colossus is dominated by a Benthamite morality that chooses among possible outcomes the one offering the greatest good for the greatest number. This principle is at the heart of Colossus's valediction to human freedom with its contemptuous dismissal of "the emotion of pride." Colossus plans to build machines greater than itself in a fortress to be built on the isle of Crete, thus raising the possibility that Colossus in mythic terms is Dedalus, and Forbin is hapless Icarus. One of the most frequently noted aspects of machine consciousness is that its sense of subjective time is much more extended than that of humans. The machine's internal sense of time, subdivided by the clock of its CPU into nanoseconds, is Pateresque in its capacity "to burn with a hard gemlike flame...[and get] as many pulsations as possible into the given time."

The real problems arise when machines are capable of the emotional complexity of human consciousness. HAL, it must be remembered, was created to "mimic" the human brain. Thus it expresses appreciation for the sketches of one of the crew members and takes what in retrospect is inordinate pride in defeating all human challengers at chess. (In the "Court Martial" episode of TOS, Spock's success in beating the computer at three-dimensional chess five times in a row alerts him to the fact that the computer has been tampered with. Because he programmed the computer, the best he should be able to do is a tie.) The design philosophy of the human creators of HAL and other such machines usually is the same as that of the Mesopotamian gods of Genesis toward Adam: "Let us make him in our own image." This is trouble. When HAL exceeds the design specs, we are faced with a being as proud as Lucifer of its superiority over humans. When confronted with the possibility of its having made a mistake, HAL reacts with "high disdain from sense of injured merit" at any such idea and boasts that in all previous cases of "apparent" malfunction of a HAL 9000, the problem was always traced to human error. In "The Ultimate Computer" episode of TOS, the M5 computer that is given command of the *Enterprise* is homicidal because its creator, Dr. Daystrom, has impressed his own psychopathic engrams onto the computer's memory.

Seen in the context of stories about self-willed machines, the "Emergence" episode of TNG, one of the last episodes of the series, offers many delightful surprises. The episode begins on the holodeck where most of its action will be set. Picard is helping Data rehearse the scene from *The Tempest* where Prospero lays down his wand. He explains this gesture to Data as the final act of a being who finds himself in a world that no longer needs him. The rehearsal is interrupted by the sudden appearance on the holodeck of a train, the Orient Express, which almost runs down Picard. The holodeck is acting up again as it has periodically since the "Elementary, Dear Data" episode in season two when the holodeck created Moriarty as a foe capable of defeating Data as Holmes and Moriarty gained control of the *Enterprise*. We seem to be in for another "holodeck runs amuck" episode. Picard seeks out Dr. Crusher whose "Orient Express" program seems to be causing the problem. Crusher explains that the point of the program lies not in the train per se but in the characters she meets on the train: "you never know who you'll meet on the Orient Express."

The first major surprise in this episode is that the main character we meet on the holodeck is the *Enterprise* herself. The characters in the Orient Express program embody aspects of the *Enterprise*'s psyche as it completes its transformation to a self-willed machine. The plot of "Emergence" progresses as the holodeck program, in cooperation with the crew, completes construction of an entity and launches it into space. This done, the episode has yet another surprise in store. Unlike Hal who died a pitiful death or Colossus who claimed for itself a godlike immortality, the Orient Express program, its mission accomplished, shuts down the neural net it had constructed, turns itself off, and vanishes "into air, into thin air." The emergent life it created has been loaded into the construct, its newborn offspring. The *Enterprise,* her reproductive cycle complete, returns to being merely a ship. There is no problem here of reasserting control.

The episode saves the best surprise for last: Picard's justification for allowing the program to run its course. He explains to Data his theory that, if the ship were forming an intelligence, it would be based on its experiences with the crew. Because the crew behaves honorably, Picard reasons that the intelligence could be counted on to be honorable as well. Picard's trust in the efficacy of good intentions, so remarkable in the light of other stories about machines that embody the personalities of their creators, is one more example of the Utopian optimism Roddenbury conceived for the series. It helps explain the popularity not only of *Star Trek* but also of Utopian Science Fiction in general as an antidote for cultural pessimism. In *The Idea of Decline in Western History,* Arthur Herman outlines the gloomy future posited by this outlook:

> Cultural pessimism insists that the ordinary, normal course of civil society on the Western model, as a capitalist or "commercial" society, resting on rational and scientific principles, democratic political institutions, and self-consciously "modern" cultural and social attitudes, awaits its own secular apocalypse. An inevitable doom hovers over its products and achievements: as Oswald Spengler put it, by living in modern society we must be

"resigned to the fact of a late life." Modern man is living in a world that is sliding ever deeper into the slough of despond, until some entirely new redemptive order arises.[38]

How directly opposite is the view of the future seen in Star Trek. The Federation's legal system is designed to protect individuality and cultural diversity. Its economy, based on replicator technology, has done away with extreme disparities between poverty and wealth; its medical technology has extended the span of human life. Picard and Data rehearsing Shakespeare and Data's virtuosity in playing the violin are but two examples of the rich artistic life of the *Enterprise* community. And the *Star Trek* universe is no unspoiled Utopia. In the *Deep Space Nine* and *Star Trek Voyager* series that followed *Star Trek: The Next Generation,* we see a Federation beset by the Cardassian alliance with the Dominion. The Borg and worse still lurk in the far reaches and Worf has been given condolences over the loss of the *Enterprise.* What kind of a universe is it out there for the *Enterprise*'s offspring to explore?

Kasparov resigned in game 6. Match to Deep Blue.

CHAPTER 2

Binary Numbers, ASCII Code, and the Turing Machine

BINARY NUMBERS

Binary code is the most basic concept in modern computing. As the first step in this discussion of the technical aspects of computing for the nontechnical, I will give a brief explanation of what binary code is and why computer scientists use it in their work. Binary code is a very simple idea. Despite, and possibly because of, its simplicity, binary code can be used to represent many things. It is primarily a way of counting and expressing numerical quantities. It also can represent switches that are on or off; magnetic material that is magnetized or not; a location on a piece of paper or cardboard that either has or has not a hole punched in it or a mark made upon it. Binary code is a code expressed in binary numbers. Zeros and ones are the basic elements of binary code just as dots and dashes are the basic elements of Morse code. Binary numbers are useful in working with computers because computers are made up of collections of on/off switches. An on/off switch can be represented by the digit zero ("0") if it is off or by the digit one ("1") if it is on. There are millions of these switches in any computer and the "0" or "1" notation of binary code provides a simple shorthand to describe the on/off state of any switch or sequence of switches in a computer.

To understand binary numbers, it is necessary to think a little about the nature of number systems in general. In our culture, we are accustomed to count and do arithmetic using decimal numbers. Decimal numbers are called base ten numbers because they are written with ten digits, zero through nine. Binary numbers are called base two numbers because they are written with only two digits, zero and one. The base of a number system, then, is identical to the number of digits making up the system. Other cultures have used number systems other than decimal or base ten. For example, we divide the circle into 360 degrees following the practice of ancient Babylonian astronomers who used a number system based on twelve.

The way we count in a number system is related to the base of the number system. We count by the exponential powers of the base. In decimal numbers, this is by units, ten, hundreds, thousands, etc. $10^0 = 1$; $10^1 = 10$; $10^2 = 100$; $10^3 = 1000$. The number 255 is shorthand for

$$(2 \times 100) + (5 \times 10) + (5 \times 1)$$

or

$$200 + 50 + 5 = 255.$$

In binary numbers, we count by powers of two:

$$2^0=1, 2^1=2, 2^2=4, 2^3=8, 2^4=16, 2^5=32, 2^6=64, 2^7=128, 2^8=256.$$

Therefore, the binary number 11111111_2 is shorthand for

$$(1 \times 128) + (1 \times 64) + (1 \times 32) + (1 \times 16) + (1 \times 8) + (1 \times 4) + (1 \times 2) + (1 \times 1)$$

or

$$128 + 64 + 32 + 16 + 8 + 4 + 2 + 1 = 255.$$

Writing 255_{10} and writing 11111111_2 are different ways of writing the same quantity. When in the fifth grade we learned to write the Roman numeral CCLV, we likewise expressed the same quantity $(100 + 100 + 50 + 5)$ in a different notation. Learning the rules for writing binary numbers is much simpler than learning the rules for writing Roman numbers.

Numbers with bases other than ten are written with their base number at the end as a subscript. The subscript 10 for base ten numbers is optional or understood but is sometimes used for clarity and/or emphasis. Thus the binary number one hundred is written as 100_2 and spoken as one hundred base two. One hundred base two (100_2) represents the same number as four (4_{10}). 10000_2 represents the same number as sixteen (16_{10}) one hundred one base two. 101_2 represents the same number as five (5_{10}); one hundred ten base two (110_2) represents the same number as six (6_{10}); one hundred eleven base two (111_2) represents the same number as seven (7_{10}). We shall return to the topic of numerical bases when we discuss random access memory.

One striking difference between decimal numbers and binary numbers is that it takes a lot more digits to represent a numerical quantity in binary form than it does in decimal form. Practical number systems are a compromise between the number of digits they require and the space they require to record a wide range of quantities. Binary numbers are convenient for computers because computers are very large collections of very small on/off switches but they are far too cumbersome for everyday uses like printing receipts or balancing checkbooks. The seeming naturalness of base ten numbers is, of course, a historical accident. It is cultural conditioning and evolutionary accident that makes Americans accept decimal coinage and count on their ten fingers but balk at metric measures.

One of the accessory programs of Windows 95, the scientific calculator, can take much of the trouble out of converting numerical quantities from binary to decimal form as well as to other numerical bases. To use the Windows scientific calculator, one pushes the "Start" button on the Windows 95 task bar and selects "Calculator" from the "Program/Accessories" menu (Fig. 2.1). This loads the default version of the calculator program, which looks like an ordinary pocket calculator rather than a scientific one (Fig. 2.2). In order to display the scientific calculator, it is necessary to select the "Scientific" option from the pocket calculator's "View" menu (Fig. 2.3). Once the "Scientific" option has been selected, the scientific calculator is displayed (Fig. 2.4). This calculator is available only to Windows users, and Windows users may prefer to use it for the exercises relating to numerical bases we are about to undertake. The book's dedicated Web page also provides access to a calculator program suitable for these exercises, and in the examples that follow we will be using this calculator. We prefer it to the Windows calculator because it is a JAVA program and thus may be used on any machine with

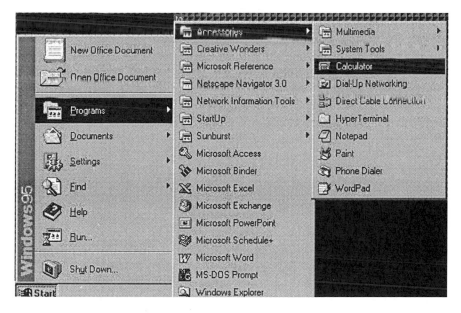

Figure 2.1. Selecting Windows "Calculator."

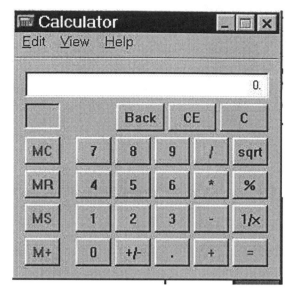

Figure 2.2. Default pocket calculator.

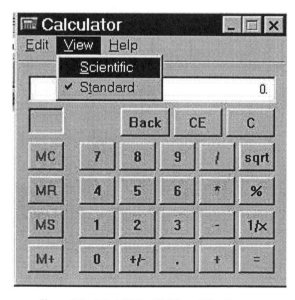

Figure 2.3. Select "Scientific" from "View" menu.

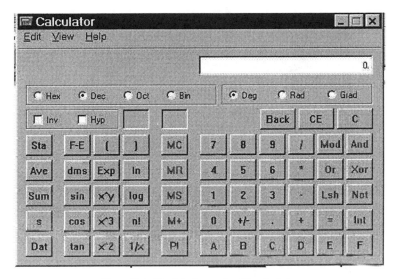

Figure 2.4. The windows scientific calculator.

a browser like Internet Explorer or Netscape Communicator that can run JAVA programs (technically called "applets") it downloads from the Web. We will conduct our discussion using exercises based on JAVA programs because JAVA allows the discussion to proceed without being limited to any particular operating system.

We will be using the book's dedicated Web page to provide exercises and examples throughout this book. This page is accessed using a browser program in the same way as any web site. With Internet Explorer, once we then select "File/Open" option from the browser menu (Fig. 2.5). We now enter the address of the book's dedicated home page,

http://www-rcf.usc.edu/~dilligan/web_age/

in the file dialog box (Fig. 2.6). Pressing the "OK" button brings up the book's dedicated home page on the browser.

With Netscape, we select the File/Open Location menu option and enter the address into the Open Location dialog box (Fig. 2.7). Pressing the "Open" button will connect to the web page.

Either browser will bring up the same web page (Fig. 2.8). The buttons on the left-hand side of the home page provide the means by which we navigate within the home page (Fig. 2.9). The frame containing these buttons is always visible on the site. The "Home" button always returns us to this location on the site. The other

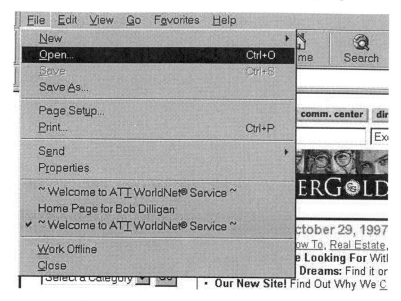

Figure 2.5. Internet Explorer "File/Open" menu choice.

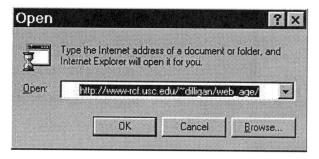

Figure 2.6. Internet Explorer "File/Open" dialog box.

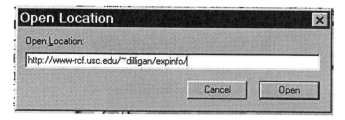

Figure 2.7. Netscape "Open Location" dialog box.

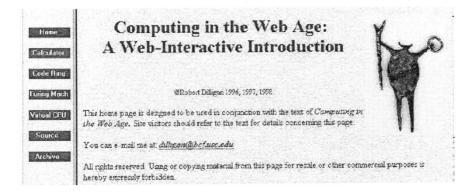

Figure 2.8. *Computing in the Web Age* home page.

buttons change what is displayed in the right-hand frame of the page and we will explain what each button does as we have occasion to use it.

The "Calculator" button opens the JAVA calculator program (Fig. 2.10). The Windows Scientific Calculator program is designed as a general-purpose calculator program. The JAVA calculator is better suited to this discussion. Although it only deals with whole numbers and does not provide any mathematical functions beyond

Figure 2.9. Web page navigation buttons.

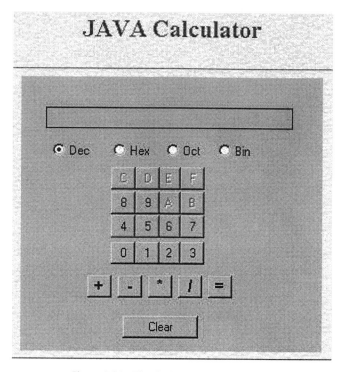

Figure 2.10. The "JAVA Calculator" program.

simple arithmetic, it does have the advantage of not distracting readers of this discussion with functions not relevant to the subject of numerical bases. The numerical pad of the calculator contains buttons for the hexadecimal digits 0 through 9 and A through F. Directly above the numerical pad is a row of choice boxes marked "Dec," "Hex," "Oct," and "Bin" that form a distinct group of what are called radio buttons. Radio button groups offer a set of mutually exclusive choices in the same way that the tuning buttons on a radio allow us to choose only one station at a time. Radio button groups are a standard way of presenting a user with mutually exclusive options on a Graphical User Interface (GUI). This particular group of radio buttons controls the numerical base that the calculator will accept as input and display as output. The default setting for this group is "Dec," which means that the calculator will accept and display the decimal or base 10 digits 0 through 9 as input and output. If "Hex" is selected, the calculator will accept and display the hexadecimal or base 16 digits 0 through 9 and A through F. With "Oct" selected, the calculator will accept and display the octal or base 8 digits zero through seven. Octal numbers were useful in discussing certain first and second generation mainframe computers but are rarely used today. Selecting "Bin" will cause the calculator to accept and display only the binary or base 2 digits zero and one.

Selecting a particular numerical base enables the numerical pad buttons for the digits of the base and disables the rest. When "Dec" is selected, as in the figure above, the buttons 0 through 9 are enabled, and the buttons A through F, used for hexadecimal, are disabled. The calculator will carry out the standard arithmetical operations of addition, subtraction, multiplication, and division on any quantity no matter what the current base is set to. With it, we can perform arithmetic in one base—say, binary—and convert the result to another base, such as decimal.

A brief exercise will show how the calculator simplifies handling quantities expressed in different numerical bases. The calculator can be operated either by typing on the keyboard or by pointing and clicking on the calculator keys with the mouse. With the "Dec" button selected, we will enter 100 into the calculator (Fig. 2.11). If we push the "Hex" button, the numerical pad buttons for A through F are enabled and the display panel changes to show 64 (Fig. 2.12). In hexadecimal, we count by powers of 16 so $64_{16} = (16 \times 6) + (1 \times 4) = 100_{10}$. When we select "Oct," the numerical pad enables only the octal digits 0 through 7 and the display panel shows 144 (Fig. 2.13). In octal, we count by powers of 8 so $144_8 = (64 \times 1) + (8 \times 4) + (1 \times 4) = 100_{10}$. When we select "Bin," only the binary digits 0 and 1 are enabled on the key pad and the display panel shows 1100100 (Fig. 2.14). In binary, we count by powers of 2, so $1100100_2 = (64 \times 1) + (32 \times 1) + (16 \times 0) + (8 \times 0) + (4 \times 1) +$

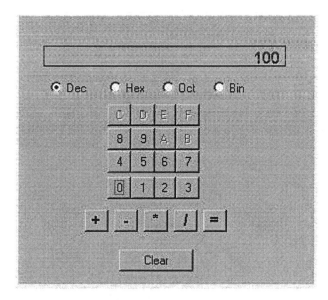

Figure 2.11. Enter 100_{10}.

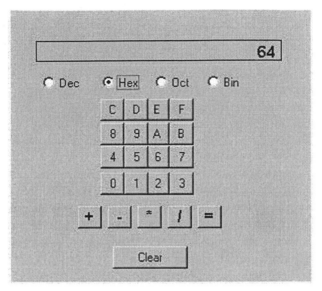

Figure 2.12. Select "Hex."

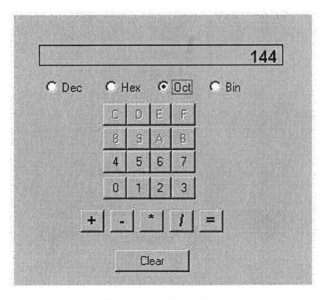

Figure 2.13. Select "Oct."

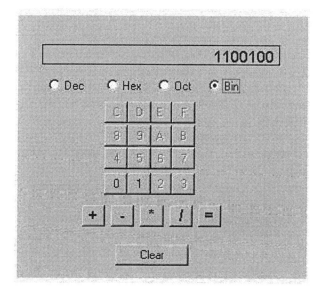

Figure 2.14. Select "Bin."

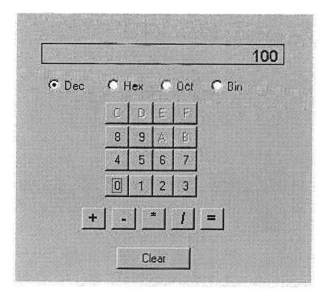

Figure 2.15. Select "Dec."

$(2 \times 0) + (1 \times 0) = 100_{10}$. By pressing "Dec," we come back to our original, decimal representation (Fig. 2.15).

We will now do some arithmetic. With "Bin" selected, we will enter 110, press "*," and enter 100, and press "=." The display panel now shows 11000. When we press "Dec," the display panel shows 24. If we clear the calculator, enter 6, press "*," enter 4 and press "=," the display panel will show 24. If we now select "Bin," the display panel will show 11000. Readers who still feel uncertain about the relationship between binary and decimal representation might want to experiment with entering, converting, and performing arithmetic on quantities between 0_{10} and 255_{10} and 0_2 and 11111111_2.

Numbers usually are things that give us varieties of control over objects. It is reassuring to know that twenty-four cans of beer are contained in a case of four six-packs and that one hundred bottles of beer on the wall are ten times as many bottles as ten bottles of beer on the wall. Very large (and very small) numbers can be especially confusing because they seem to fail to deliver the control that their nature as numbers seems to promise. One thing about getting used to the world of computers is getting comfortable with an increasing range of numbers. Scientists deal all the time with very large and small numbers by means of what is called scientific notation. They use powers of ten to express the number of digits in a number. The number 12×10^{23} means twelve multiplied by the number ten followed by twenty-two zeros. The use of powers of ten to express magnitude seems natural because we are used to counting by tens, and it is as easy to see that 10^{24} has four times as many zeroes as 10^6 as it is to see that a case of beer contains four six-packs. Scientific notation, then, is a way of helping us deal in everyday terms with the numbers of a magnitude we don't deal with every day.

The statement that an object could take on any of 2^{960} values is baffling in many ways, not the least of which is the uncertainty associated with the magnitude of the number 2^{960}. How does scientific notation help us with numbers like 2^{960} that are expressed as powers of two, not powers of ten? We don't count by powers of two. It does not come naturally to us that eleven thousand base two (11000_2) is four times as large as one-hundred-ten base two (110_2) as it does that 24 is four times as large as 6. What would 2^{960} look like written in decimal based scientific notation?

There is a simple way using logarithms to convert base two orders of magnitude to base ten orders of magnitude. Two raised to the 3.33 power ($2^{3.33}$) is approximately equal to ten:

$$2^{3.33} \approx 10$$

To covert 2^{960} to its decimal value all we need to do is divide 960 by 3.33. In other words

$$2^{960} \approx 10^{288}$$

Written as a power of two or a power of ten, this is a very large quantity, even by scientific standards. Cesare Emiliani's *The Scientific Companion* says that there are 12×10^{56} atoms in the sun, 10^{22} stars in the universe, and hence 10^{79} atoms in the universe.[1] The human brain is said to contain 10^{15} neurons. These numbers are all orders of magnitude smaller than 10^{288}, the number that can be represented on a single Hollerith card.

RANDOM ACCESS MEMORY

Binary numbers will be extremely useful in our discussion of random access memory. The central "processing" box of a von Neumann architecture computer is divided into two parts: random access memory (RAM) and the central processing unit (CPU). It is the interplay of these two parts that carries out the work of the computer. The basic connection between these two parts is in the execution cycle of the computer. Program and data are first stored in memory. They are then moved to the processing unit where the central processing unit transforms them in accordance with the directions of the program's instructions. The results are then moved back to memory, where subsequent instructions may cause them to be written to an output device or moved back into the CPU for further manipulation (Fig. 2.16). In the next chapter we will examine the computer's execution cycle in detail. The computer must keep track of where in memory it stores its data so that it can retrieve it from memory, operate upon it, and then place the result back into memory.

Memory also serves as a kind of buffer between the central processing unit and the peripheral devices. This buffering function is important because the central processor and memory interact at speeds measured in nanoseconds (billionths of a second) while peripheral devices interact with memory at speeds ranging from milliseconds (millionths of a second) down to the speeds of typing and mouse movement. Without this buffering, the CPU would be idle for long periods of time while it waited for input or output operations to complete. Idle or busy, it takes the same amount of electricity to keep the CPU going. The desire to keep it as occupied as possible is in part an economic consideration, especially on large computer systems that cost millions of dollars. But mainly it is a question of the convenience of computer users who want to get on with their tasks without spending any more time than is necessary waiting for the computer to finish its assigned rounds.

Memory hardware is conceptually the simplest part of a computer. As has already been mentioned, memory consists of transistorized on/off switches contained in integrated circuits. These are called memory chips because the integrated circuits are etched on wafers of silicon whose size and shape resemble chips. The size of a computer's memory is measured by the number of switches it contains. For example, the memory of the machine I am now working on consists of 538,870,912 switches as contrasted with the 960 locations of a Hollerith card. This

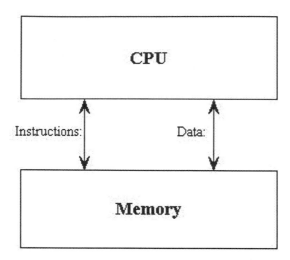

Figure 2.16. Memory/central processing unit execution cycle.

is more than enough memory for a computer running a modern operating system like UNIX, Windows 95, or MAC 8.0. These memory switches are called bits. A memory bit is a single on/off switch. Some machines that are configured for special tasks such as graphics or large-scale numerical computation or are used not as individual workstations but as the hubs or servers of networks may have more than ten times the memory of my computer. Considered as a single numerical quantity, the amount of memory in my machine would be a string of 538,870,912 binary digits or (dividing 538,870,912 by 3.33 as explained above) 161,222,496 decimal digits. In order to function accurately, my computer must be able to access (read) and change (write) the value of any of its 538,870,912 bits.

Memory operates on the same principle of destructive read-in and nondestructive read-out as does disk storage. This means that when something is moved or written into a memory location, it obliterates whatever was there before; but once a value is stored in memory it can be recalled as often as necessary without changing its value. Memory, unlike disk storage, is volatile. It is erased when the machine is turned off, and the information it contained is gone forever unless it was previously written to a nonvolatile storage device such as a disk. Memory is thought of in terms two basic concepts: location and value. Memory may be thought of as a string of switches arranged serially one after the other. The location or numerical address of a given bit is its position in the row of switches that make up memory, which on my machine is some number between 0 and 538,870,912. The value stored in that bit is the position of the switch, on or off, which is represented as either 1 (on) or 0 (off). All computer programs operate by storing and retrieving values from specific memory locations. I will make constant use of the related concepts of memory location and value in the discussion of programming in subsequent chapters.

Computer designers realized from the start that it would be impractical to handle memory addressing by assigning a unique numerical address to every single bit. Just as it is necessary to group holes in a Hollerith card into columns and rows and the magnetic domains of the disk into tracks, sectors, and allocation units, it is necessary to group memory into units larger than a single bit to allow for efficient addressing. The development of the conventions used to assign bits to larger units of memory was influenced by the notion of memory as a scarce resource whose usage had to be carefully controlled and by the notion of the computer as a numerical calculator. Over the years, some basic conventions evolved through trial and error under the pressure of these two constraints. These basic conventions assign memory hardware to units called bytes, half words, words, and double words. Though the memory capacity of computers continues to grow, doubling every eighteen months, and the cost of memory continues to fall, these conventions are so well established that they seem as natural to computer programmers as decimal numbers do to the average person.

A byte is a sequence of eight consecutive bits. Bytes are counted eight bits at a time from the first memory bit so that memory is said to be byte aligned. In other words, bytes begin at specific locations, not just anywhere. The byte is the basic unit of addressing in a computer and the standard measure of memory size. The addressing circuit (data bus) of a computer retrieves information in units of bytes. If programmers wish to reference a particular bit, they must first retrieve the byte containing the bit and then use their programming skills to extract the particular bit they are seeking. For reasons that we shall examine shortly, a byte is sometimes described as the amount of memory required to store a single character like a punctuation mark or letter of the alphabet. The novel *Middlemarch* by George Eliot contains approximately 800,000 characters, and so it would require approximately 800,000 bytes of memory to store the novel in computer memory. Half words, words, and double words, however, have nothing to do with the storage of words from a human language. Rather, they have to do with the amount of memory required to store numbers of different magnitudes. They are multiples of bytes. A half word is one byte; a word is two consecutive bytes; and a double word is two consecutive words. These terms are ways of referring to sequences of one, two, or four bytes. Words and double words are byte aligned with the first byte in memory.

These conventions were established, as we have said, at a time when memory was expensive and computer designers and programmers treated it as a scarce resource whose primary use was for storing the results of numerical calculation. The idea was that the programmer, in designing a program, should determine in advance the order of magnitude of the numbers the program was to process and then use only the minimum amount of memory needed to store the numbers and leave as much memory as possible for program instructions. This obsession with "conserving memory" resulted in the infamous year 2000 problem in which programs store only the last two digits of the year. The year 2000 is thus recorded as the year 00, much to the confusion of programs that calculate time intervals extending through that year. The efficiency of a program was measured as the speed of processing versus the size of memory required. A half word could store numbers in the range of ±128; a word in the range of $\pm32,768$, etc. (One bit in this convention is used as a sign bit. If the sign bit is zero, the number is positive; if it is one, the number is negative.[2]) Thus the memory of my computer is said to have a memory size of 67,108,864 bytes or 64 megabytes, a megabyte being 1,048,576 bytes. The numerical byte addresses of my computer run consecutively from 0 to 67,108,863. Any single byte can store 256 or 2^8 different values.

The numerical address of the first byte is 0 rather than 1 because computers make use of what is called base plus offset addressing. In base plus offset addressing, the address of a byte within a program is expressed in terms of the number of bytes it is offset from the first byte (address zero) of the program. This type of address is called the offset address. The hundredth byte in a program would have an offset address of 99. A program one million bytes long could be stored on a disk and then loaded just about anywhere in memory as long as there are one million bytes available above the location at which its first byte is loaded. The address of the byte in memory at which the first byte of the program is loaded is called the base address. To determine the actual, physical memory location of a given byte in the program, the computer adds the offset address of the byte to the base address of the program in memory. This arithmetic enables the computer to determine the location in memory of any byte in the program.[3] If the program were loaded starting at byte address 420,000, its base address would be 420,00. The hundredth byte in the program would have a relative address of 99 and would be located at address 420,099.

The size of a program a computer can execute is not limited by the amount of memory installed on the computer. There is an absolute limit to this size determined by the capacity of the machine's addressing circuit, but the practical limitation on the size of a program a computer can execute is determined by the amount of disk space available on the computer. Modern computers are capable of coordinating memory and disk storage to produce what is termed the "virtual memory" of the computer. In virtual memory schemes, programs are divided into units called pages. The size of a page is measured in bytes. The number of bytes in a page varies from computer system to computer system but is usually some multiple of 256 bytes. The computer swaps program pages from the disk to memory as they are needed.

It is easy to see how a program might do this with data. For example, a program designed to count the number of words in a text would not need to load the entire text of *Paradise Lost* in memory before it starts counting. It could read the text one line at a time and add the number of words on each line to its running total for the text. The bookkeeping required to swap program pages between disk and memory is similar to but much more complicated than that required to read sequentially through a data file. If the swapping is not done properly, the system will "thrash" and spend more time swapping pages back and forth than it spends executing the instructions on the page. But the principle is the same for swapping instructions and reading data and may be compared to the "just-in-time" inventory and manufacturing techniques of modern factories. Modern operating systems are called multi-tasking operating systems because they can keep many programs executing in memory at the same time. It is not unusual for the total memory size required for running many large programs simultaneously[4] to be far larger than the RAM memory installed on the computer. The use of virtual memory is what makes this seeming feat of prestidigitation possible.

THE QUICK BROWN FOX

As was just explained, the memory of a computer is divided into sequences of eight consecutive bits called bytes. Bytes are the basic addressing unit of memory. Machine operations work on bytes and consecutive sequences of bytes. But there is no particular meaning or code referent attached to any particular byte. The bytes in memory are not divided so that some bytes are reserved for program instructions, some for numerical data, and some for text. The use of the same memory for both data and instructions is one of the defining characteristics of von Neumann architecture. When we say that a byte has a specific meaning, we are using a binary coding convention that assigns it a meaning. In cyberspace as in Wonderland, [half] words mean exactly what we say they mean, no more and no less. Meaning is usage. It is the way we use a byte that determines what it means. Suppose a particular byte in memory contains the number 00001111_2 or 15_{10}. If we load it into the instruction register of a Pentium processor, it is interpreted as the first byte of a machine instruction that is two bytes long. If we load it into an arithmetic accumulator, it is interpreted as a numerical quantity. In a text, it would be treated as a tab character. One of the most basic functions of software is to assign coding conventions to memory locations so as to keep track of what we intend to use those locations for and how the computer is to interpret the values stored there.[5] The software determines whether, at any given moment, a byte contains data or program instructions.

The basic coding convention used today for representing textual information in computers is ASCII, which stands for American Standard Code for Information Interchange. ASCII assigns characters to values in the range of 0 to 255, the range of values that can be stored in one byte. We measure disk capacity in terms of characters of information they hold. These capacities range from 1.4 million characters for a floppy disk to 9 billion characters for the most recent Digital Video

Disk (DVD). We could alternatively have given these capacities as ranging from 1.4 million to 9 billion bytes because ASCII is a binary coding convention that assigns a character value to each of the 256 possible numerical values of a byte. In this scheme, the character value "A" was assigned to numerical value 65, the character value "B" was assigned numerical value 66, etc.

The principal input device for first and second generation computers was a keypunch machine that produced decks of cards to be read into the computer by a card reader.[6] I have already discussed the limitations of card punching technology. The development of ASCII code was part and parcel of the successful attempt to find a technology better than paper punching for computer input and output. Because keystrokes that they wished to encode were to be sent directly to the computer to be stored there in electronic form, the designers of ASCII could safely ignore Hollerith card coding and focus on the best way to store the information electronically. They did, however, have to provide for a way to control the transmissions back and forth between the computer and the keyboard terminal. This is why the first thirty-two entries in the ASCII table (numbers 0 through 31) are control codes, not character codes. Many of these control codes are holdovers from teletype terminals, which were the kind of terminals first used on interactive systems. These terminals consisted of a keyboard and a printer head or wheel that printed input and results on rolls of paper. (CRT terminals were a later development.) In addition to the thirty-two control codes used to control teletype transmission, they allowed for ninety-six character codes, numbers 32 through 127. ASCII was at first a seven-bit code because only 128 codes were needed to control transmissions and represent the limited number of characters early terminals could display. As terminals became capable of displaying more characters, ASCII was extended to the 256 codes of "extended" ASCII. The first 128 characters (0 through 127) are now called the lower ASCII characters and remain to this day fairly fixed in their designation. The next 128 characters (128 through 255) are called upper ASCII and are not so fixed in their coding designations.

The character assignments for upper ASCII have always been regarded as open to redefinition. Various linguistic communities—Greek, Russian, Arabic, Hebrew, to name a few—developed their own "code pages" for upper ASCII and had them built into machines specially manufactured for their linguistic groups. The different code pages held the characters and diacritical marks needed for the different languages. In fact, only lower ASCII was built into the hardware of the original PC. Any user who understood the way in which the characters were stored and sent to the video screen and printer could redefine the Upper ASCII characters with the appropriate software. The existence of both official code pages and personal ad hoc assignments for upper ASCII codes created a situation that tends to undercut the usefulness of ASCII for information interchange. ASCII attempted to fix the relationship between a character value and the letter form or glyph that represents a code to the user but the number of glyphs needed by users far exceeded the number of codes that can be represented by a single byte.

The simplicity of ASCII code may be illustrated by showing how that old typing exercise—"The quick brown fox jumps over the lazy dog."—is encoded in ASCII. The point of the typing exercise is that it uses every letter of the alphabet and so requires the novice typist to hit every alphabetical key on the keyboard at least once. The process of encoding this sentence in ASCII is in principal no different than the process I used as a child to encode messages with the Lone Ranger Code Ring that I found as a prize in a box of breakfast cereal. The code ring worked with two circular disks, one mounted on top of the other. The top disk could be rotated and had the letters of the alphabet and the digits 0 through 26 embossed on it. This disk also had a notch in it through which a portion of the inner unmovable but changeable disk was visible. The inner, unmovable disk had numbers printed on it so that one number at a time was visible through the notch in the top ring. There was a pointer arrow at the three o'clock position on the ring that pointed to successive letters as the outer disk was rotated. Messages were encoded one letter at a time by rotating the outer ring until the letter to be encoded was aligned with the pointer and then writing down the number visible through the notch. The ring came with some pre-printed inner disks as well as some blank ones. It was possible to make up a new code by filling a blank disk with numbers in some random order. By giving a copy of the disk with the private code to a special friend, one could exchange messages without fear of their contents falling into the hands of the bullies from the next block or—gasp!—the teacher. In retrospect, I suppose the decoding ring was my first experience with a Turing machine (of which more later). The basic principle of the code ring is that it establishes a one for one correspondence between glyphs and numbers. ASCII works on the same principle as the code ring.

Boxes of breakfast cereal with code rings inside are scarce these days and the operating system provides no useful accessory that could handle ASCII code in the way that the scientific calculator handles numerical bases. Therefore I have written a small decoding program to use in our discussion of ASCII. The program is written in JAVA so that it can be executed from a Web page by a "JAVA-aware" web browser such as Internet Explorer or Netscape Communicator. To start the Code Ring program, we must first start our browser program, connect it to the Web, and go to the book's dedicated web page as we did for the calculator program. The Lone Ranger Code Ring program is started by double-clicking on the "Code Ring" button

Figure 2.17. "Code Ring" link text.

on this page (Fig. 2.17), which displays the web page containing the code ring program (Fig. 2.18).

The code ring program has two input boxes labeled "Message" and "Code" that correspond to the two disks of the old code ring. It has two functions, "Encrypt" which is the default setting, and "Decrypt." To encode a message, one types it into the upper screen and then pushes the "Go" button. The numerical code for the message then appears in the lower screen. The program handles two codes, "ASCII" and "SECRET," and three numerical bases, "Decimal" (base 10), "Hex" or hexadecimal (base 16), and "Binary" (base 2). The default settings of the code ring program are "Encrypt," "ASCII," and "Decimal." This program uses "drop down boxes" rather than radio buttons for choosing functions because the interface is less cluttered with three boxes than it would be with seven buttons.

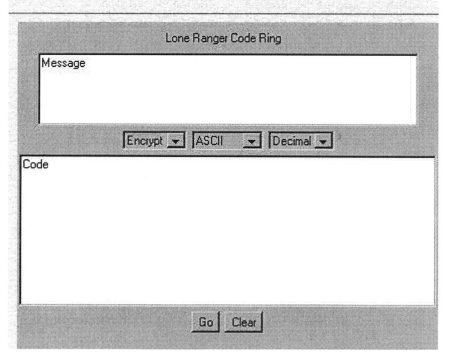

Figure 2.18. Code ring.

If we type "The quick brown fox jumps over the lazy dog." into the upper panel or text area and press the "Go" button, a series of numbers appears in the lower text area (Fig. 2.19). Notice that the blanks between the words are encoded as number 32. That a blank is a character seems confusing to novices in computing until they realize that ASCII code represents a record of the key strokes used in creating a text. The blank characters encoded as 32 are what is recorded when the space bar is pushed. As the display makes clear, ASCII code is a way of establishing a one-to-one relationship between the glyphs of the alphabet and numerical codes.

The nature of this relationship can be explored by typing in various messages and pushing the "Encrypt" button. The contents can be reset by pressing the "Clear" button. For our next exercise we will enter the alphabet in upper and lower case into the upper screen and push the "Encrypt" button (Fig. 2.20). The upper and lower case characters form unbroken sequences, "A" (code 65) to "Z" (code 90) and "a" (code 97) to "z" (code 122). The designers of ASCII created a code with a rationale behind it. Sorting things into alphabetical order is one of the most basic operations performed with textual material. One of the goals of the designers of ASCII was to simplify this operation. Therefore, they designed a code in which blank comes first, followed by the digits 0 through 9, and then by the sequences of upper and lower

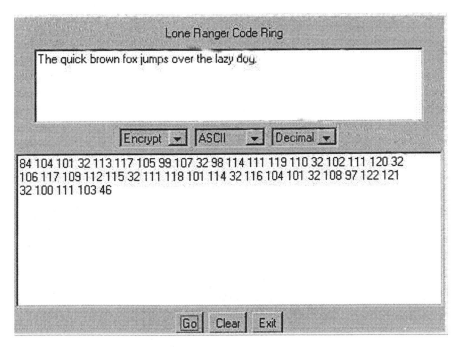

Figure 2.19. Code program with typing exercise.

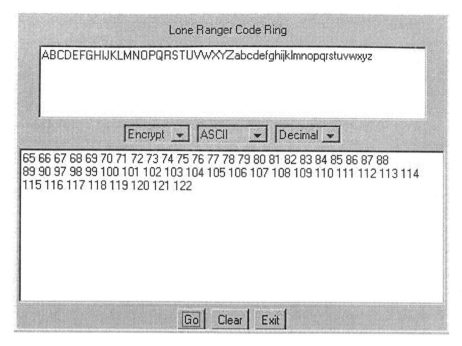

Figure 2.20. ASCII encoded alphabet.

case letters. This makes the collating sequence of ASCII correspond to alphabetical order. ASCII codes could have been assigned randomly to characters and, except for occasions when alphabetical order was needed, the scheme could have worked as well. There is no reason beyond this to impose this particular arrangement. This convention also simplifies conversion between upper and lower case by making the numerical difference between the codes of corresponding upper and lower case letters 32, which is 00010000_2, a power of 2. Thus "A" is 00100001_2 and "a" is 00110001_2.

ASCII then is a convention that assigns specific glyphs to specific numerical values stored in bytes. We could create a simple encryption algorithm by specifying a procedure in which texts were first encoded in ASCII and then 1 was added to the value of each code. This is what we do with the "Secret" code in the code ring program. We type in a message that gets recorded as numbers representing ASCII. Then we take the ASCII codes and treat them as numbers by adding 1 to each of them. The result is a "secret" message. To do this we select "Secret" as the code, type in our message, and push the "Go" button (Fig. 2.21). If we change the function to "Decrypt" and the code from "Secret" to "ASCII," we get thoroughly garbled

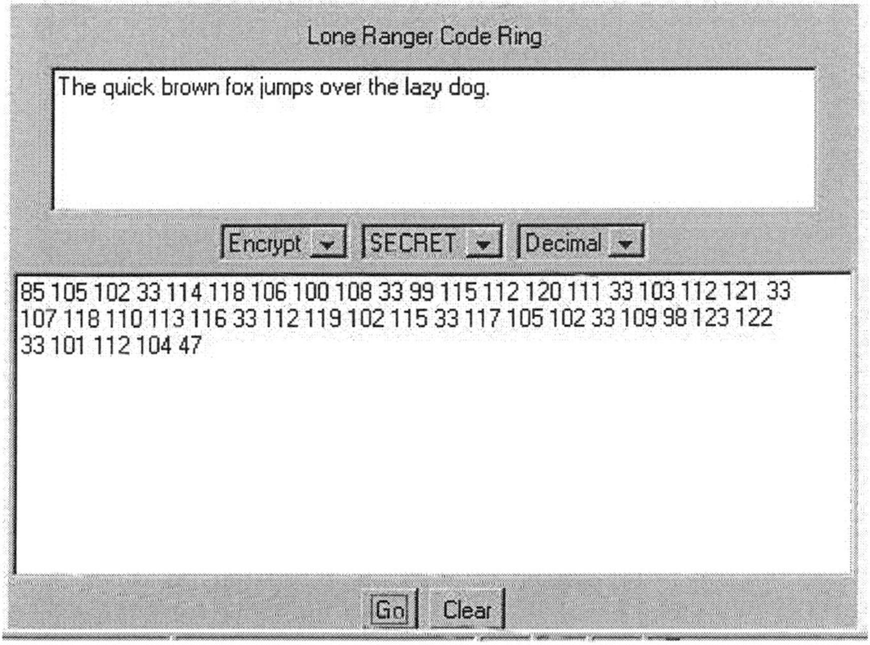

Figure 2.21. Secret code input.

output (Fig. 2.22). This seems particularly garbled because we have lost the word divider space, which is now an exclamation point.

Uif!rvjdl!cspxo!gpy!kvnqt!pwfs!uif!mb{z!eph/

85 105 102 33 114 118 106 100 108 33 99 115 112 120 111 33 103 112 121 33
107 118 110 113 116 33 112 119 102 115 33 117 105 102 33 109 98 123 122
33 101 112 104 47

We can decode the message by pressing the "Decrypt" button after resetting the code to "SECRET" (Fig. 23).

The point I want to underscore through this encryption exercise is that everything in the computer's memory is stored as a binary number. We can choose to regard any memory location as a number and operate on it arithmetically or we can choose to treat it as ASCII code and operate on it as textual data, printing it, displaying it, parsing it, encrypting it, tagging it, or sorting it into alphabetical order.

In the encoding exercises we have done so far, we have kept the numerical base set at decimal (base 10). The Code Ring, like the scientific calculator, will change the base of the numerical code when we select a new base from the drop down box

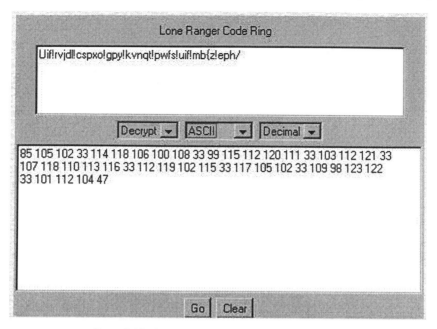

Figure 2.22. Secret code output decrypted as ASCII code.

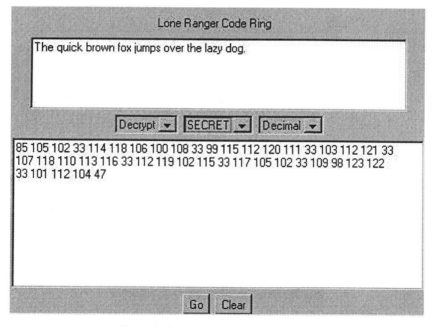

Figure 2.23. "SECRET" message decrypted.

for bases. We can select a different base at any time with the Code Ring. If we select "Binary" as our base, we see the code displayed in binary numbers (Fig. 2.24). This shows the actual bit patterns in each byte of memory. Again, the numerical quantities are the same in whatever base they happen to be expressed. The code text area for this change in base to binary reads:

01010100 01101000 01100101 00100000 01110001 01110101 01101001
01100011 01101011 00100000 01100010 01110010 01101111 01110111
01101110 00100000 01100110 01101111 01111000 00100000 01101010
01110101 01101101 01110000 01110011 00100000 01101111 01110110
01100101 01110010 00100000 01110100 01101000 01100101 00100000
01101100 01100001 01111010 01111001 00100000 01100100 01101111
01100111 00101110

The "verboseness" of binary code for human uses can be seen here.

There is, however, a slightly more complicated topic than the encryption algorithm and binary code to discuss with respect to ASCII code, namely hexadecimal numbers. Just as we changed the base of the code for the exercise to binary by selecting "Bin," we can change the base of the code to hexadecimal by selecting "Hex" (Fig. 2.25). The text area for hexadecimal encoding reads:

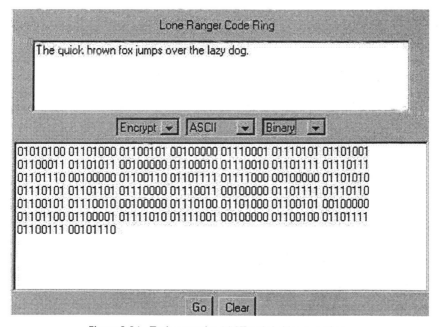

Figure 2.24. Typing exercise ASCII code in binary numbers.

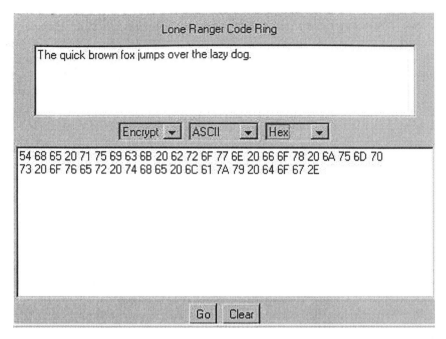

Figure 2.25. Typing exercise code expressed in hexadecimal.

54 68 65 20 71 75 69 63 6B 20 62 72 6F 77 6E 20 66 6F 78 20 6A 75 6D 70
73 20 6F 76 65 72 20 74 68 65 20 6C 61 7A 79 20 64 6F 67 2E

The compactness of hexadecimal stands out when we convert from binary to hexadecimal. I have already pointed out that we are comfortable with decimal numbers for cultural reasons and that we use binary numbers when working with computers because they express so nicely the on or off state of each of the computer's bits. Similarly, computer technologists have adopted hexadecimal or base sixteen numbers as a way of describing the contents of each byte. They would be much more likely to think of ASCII codes in terms of hexadecimal rather than decimal numbers.

In many situations computer specialists need to think in terms of individual bits. One of the main reasons why computer specialists use hexadecimal representation of quantities rather than decimal representation is that they find it is easier to convert mentally from hexadecimal to binary than it is to convert from decimal to binary. In this way they combine the benefit of the compact representation of hexadecimal numbers with the specificity of binary. Hexadecimal numbers have the advantage of expressing the contents of byte in two 4-bit chunks, sometimes called "nibbles." Because hexadecimal numbers use 16 as a base, we need sixteen digits to express hexadecimal numbers. To get sixteen digits, we use the decimal digits 0 through 9 plus the first six letters of the alphabet. Figure 2.26 lists the decimal equivalents of hexadecimal values.

For binary numbers, we count by powers of 2; for decimal numbers we count by powers of 10; for hexadecimal numbers we count by powers of 16.

$$21_{10} = (2 \times 10) + (1 \times 1) = 20 + 1 = 21_{10}$$

but

$$21_{16} = (2 \times 16) + (1 \times 1) = 16 + 5 = 33_{10}$$

Hexadecimal numbers with "alphabetical" digits are likewise converted to decimal equivalents:

$$AE_{16} = (10 \times 16) + (14 \times 1) = 160 + 14 = 174_{10}$$

Hexadecimal Digit	Decimal Value
0	0
1	1
2	2
3	3
4	4
5	5
6	6
7	7
8	8
9	9
A	10
B	11
C	12
D	13
E	14
F	15

Figure 2.26. Decimal value of hexadecimal digits.

or

$$FF_{16} = (15 \times 16) + (15 \times 1) = 240 + 15 = 255_{10}$$

If this seems somewhat confusing, we could use the scientific calculator to play with numbers between 0 and 255_{10} and 0 and FF_{16}, as we did with binary to decimal conversion. "Hex" is one of the numerical bases the calculator is equipped to handle.

The powers of 16 mount up very quickly: $16^1 = 16$, $16^2 = 256$, $16^3 = 4,096$, $16^4 = 65,536$, $16^5 = 1,048,576$, $16^6 = 16,777,216$. For this reason, computer programmers sometimes use hexadecimal notation rather than scientific notation to express large numbers. But in my experience the main use of hexadecimal notation is to express the contents of a byte in a way that makes it easy to envision the bit pattern of the byte. For this reason, Fig. 2.27, which gives the value of each hexadecimal digit as a four-bit pattern, is much more useful than any exercise in hexadecimal arithmetic. With a little practice, readers will be able to manage the mental conversion of hexadecimal to binary as deftly as the most experienced programmer.

Hexadecimal Digit	Binary Nibble
0	0000
1	0001
2	0010
3	0011
4	0100
5	0101
6	0110
7	0111
8	1000
9	1001
A	1010
B	1011
C	1100
D	1101
E	1110
F	1111

Figure 2.27. Nibble bit pattern for hexadecimal digits.

The provision for 96-character codes for lower ASCII, later supplemented by the addition of 128 more for upper ASCII, seemed generous at the time it was made, some three decades ago, and especially when measured against the capabilities of a keypunch machine. It was a product of the limited display capabilities of most printers and terminals and the assumption that memory was an expensive resource. Word processors then used typewriter-like printers with changeable type balls. I remember one project for computer-assisted instruction in Russian that used Cyrillic type balls and paste-over typewriter keys. But hardware developments in printers and terminals as well as software developments in word processing long ago outstripped the capacity of ASCII's limited code character set. Today the standard is defined as "WYSIWYG"—What You See Is What You Get. Word processors and other programs that deal with textual data are supposed to be capable of displaying on a terminal screen just about any glyph in a wide range of typefaces and of printing exactly what is displayed. The development of laser printers and graphical display terminals has swamped the capacity of the ASCII character set.

The development of high resolution terminal screens, laser printers, and font technologies led to a proliferation of proprietary solutions for the display and printing of texts. Every word processor had its own way of handling different character sets and early on it was difficult, if not impossible, to process texts prepared with one program with another one. A market developed for utility programs that would translate files from one word processor to the file format of another. Apple, for many years ahead of the market with WYSIWYG systems, developed its own way of handling fonts combined with the PostScript page description language for printing. The PC world finally caught up with the use of True Type fonts in Windows. For the present, things seem to be stabilizing around True Type fonts. But things still get fairly arcane, chaotic, and ragged around the edges when it comes to handling unusual, relatively obscure character sets like medieval Ladino. Welcome to the Tower of Babel![7]

These problems developed because ASCII has only 256 possible values to represent all the glyphs of all the human languages. In ASCII, each character is encoded by a single byte. The solution is quite simple: encode each character as two bytes, which have 16 bits, rather than bytes, which have 8 bits. This will provide for 65,536 different character codes rather than 256. The difference in the number of possible codes is that a byte of 8 bits provides 2^8 or 256 unique codes while a word of 16 bits provides 2^{16} or 65,536 unique codes. In the past decade, just such a solution has been going forward under the name of Unicode. With this many possibilities, Unicode developers believe they have the capacity to represent 99 percent of the characters needed by 99 percent of users of living languages in two-byte character code. They also provide for an additional one million characters by reserving two blocks of one thousand two-byte codes each for four-byte characters. The first block of one thousand two-byte codes is called the low word block and the second block of one thousand two-byte codes is called the high word block. Four-byte characters combine an entry from the low block with an entry from the high block. Since each entry in the low block can combine with any of the one thousand entries in the high block, there are one million (1000 × 1000) possible low block/high block character code combinations possible. In this way Unicode can accommodate rare, ancient, and archaic symbols and character sets. Unicode also makes provision for user defined character code mappings.

If texts are encoded by assigning two bytes per character rather than one, they will take up twice as much space on disk and memory[8] and take somewhat longer to process. But the days of expensive storage, memory, and CPU cycles are long over. In the early 1970s memory cost about a dollar a byte, and adding a megabyte of memory was a major capital investment for any organization. Today, a megabyte of memory costs less than fifty dollars, and prices decrease by half every eighteen months. The hardware is available today to implement Unicode and provide a worldwide character set for the World Wide Web. The JAVA programming language for the Web supports Unicode character representation as does Windows NT, which is supposedly the ultimate version of Windows toward which Windows 95 is an interim step. Version 8.0 of the MAC operating system will also support Unicode. The regularization of character sets under Unicode will be a significant advance in worldwide computing.

THE TURING MACHINE

The mathematical model underlying the computer, the Turing machine, is conceptually a very simple but powerful programmable device. I will begin our discussion of the CPU with a consideration of the Turing machine. Conceived by Turing in 1936,[9] the Turing machine ranks with Einstein's observer in an elevator, Schrodinger's cat, and Hawking's black holes as one of the great scientific insights of our century. Because it underlies the mathematics of computers, it has been as influential as any thought experiment in shaping contemporary society. The first thing to keep in mind about the Turing machine is that it is a thought experiment, not a physical device. No one would, or for that matter could, construct an actual Turing machine. Like other thought experiments, it is a purely mental construct with interesting formal properties.

The numerical contents of the computer's memory encode either data or instructions. Having discussed two forms of data code, binary numbers and ASCII, we will now turn our attention to the way in which the computer operates on its coded instructions. The central processing unit (CPU) of the computer is its electronic brain, the part of the computer most people have in mind when they think of a computer. The peripheral devices and memory of the computer all conspire to support the central processor as worker bees support their queen. We will discuss the Turing machine because to understand a Turing machine's operation is to understand the basic idea of programmability, which is what computers are all about.

One way of imagining a Turing machine is to begin by visualizing an old fashioned, two-spool movie projector. The movie projector works by winding film at a constant speed from one spool to the other. As it moves from spool to spool, each successive frame of film passes over the projection lamp and lens aperture and is displayed in sequence on the screen. The Turing machine, like the movie projector, is a device that spools a tape frame by frame past an aperture. The Turing machine's tape is divided into frames as is a motion picture film. But it is called a tape rather than a film because it differs in several ways from a film. Its frames contain symbols, as do ticker tapes, rather than containing photographs, as do motion picture film frames. A portion of the Turing machine tape is illustrated in Fig. 2.28.

Each Turing machine frame must contain a single binary digit, zero or one, as shown in Fig. 2.28. Another crucial difference between a motion picture film and a Turing machine tape is that a motion picture film is of finite length while a Turing machine tape is of infinite length. This is why it would be impossible to build an actual Turing machine. A tape of infinite length would require a spool of infinite size. More to the point, a tape of infinite length would have no beginning and no end and so there would be no way to thread it on a spool. There is no way to assign a numerical address to the frames on the machine tape. All frames are referenced relative to the frame currently in the machine aperture as so many frames to the left or right of it. Finally, comedic effects aside, the motion picture film moves at constant speed in one direction; the Turing machine's tape moves a frame at a time in either direction and halts after it has moved one frame.

The aperture of the Turing machine is much more complex than the aperture of the movie projector. Rather than simply illuminating successive frames, the Turing machine aperture contains a read/write device that can recognize whether a given frame contains a zero or a one and that can replace zeros with ones and ones with zeros.

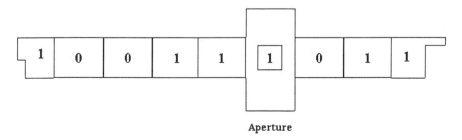

Aperture

Figure 2.28. Turing machine tape.

If the frame is unmarked, do x to the frame and assume state n_1;
if the frame is marked, do y to the frame and assume state n_2;
where "x" and "y" are any of the three frame marking operations and
"n_1" and "n_2" are any of the N possible states of the machine.[10]

To say that the machine is to "assume state 4" is the same as to say that the next instruction to be carried out is instruction 4. The control unit moves the instruction table so that instruction 4 appears in the LCD displays. The next instruction to be executed is determined by the contents of the current frame of the machine tape.

With this simple mechanism and the appropriate table of instructions, it is possible to generate a class of numbers called computable numbers. A computable number is a number that can be calculated by an algorithm. The von Neumann architecture computer is, from a mathematical point of view, a way of generating computable numbers. Like the Turing machine, it can generate all and only computable numbers. Turing machines use programs just as computers do. We can get an idea of how a Turing machine works by carrying out the instructions for a simple Turing machine program. Table 2.1 is a simple Turing machine program that will double the number of consecutive marks on a tape. These instructions will double any number of marks found on the tape, provided these marks are located to the left of the starting point. If there are three consecutive marks to the right of the tape at the start, these instructions will erase those three marks and replace them with six marks. As we shall see, any programmable device needs an explicit set of initial conditions and a clearly defined starting point if it is to work properly.[11]

Table 2.1 defines four states or instructions, numbered 1 through 4 in its left-hand column. Each instruction consists of a move tape operation (L or R) specified in the second column followed by a mark frame operation (U, M, or E) specified in the third and fourth columns. The mark frame portion of the table has two columns identified as "Unmarked" and "Marked." The "Unmarked" column specifies what the marking mechanism is to do if the frame is not marked and the "Marked" column specifies what it is to do if the frame is marked. The mark frame operations are entered in the table as a mark frame mnemonic letter plus a number.

Table 2.1. Table of Instructions to Multiply by 2 the Marks on a Tape

| Instruction | Move tape instruction | Mark frame | |
		Unmarked	Marked
1	R	U 1	E 2
2	L	M 3	U 2
3	L	M 4	U 3
4	R	U 1	U 4

The number specifies the next state of the machine, that is, the next instruction to be carried out. "U 1" means leave the frame unchanged and assume state 1; "E 2" means erase the mark on the frame and assume state 2; "M 3" means place a mark on the frame and assume state 3, etc. The execution of an instruction takes three operations: a move operation; a mark operation; and a branch to the next instruction operation.

The four instructions in this table are read as follows:

R Move the tape pointer right one frame.
    U 1 If the frame in the machine aperture is unmarked,
        leave the frame unchanged and assume state 1.
    E 2 If the frame in the machine aperture is marked,
        erase the mark and assume state 2.
L Move the tape pointer left one frame.
    M 3 If the frame in the machine aperture is unmarked,
        mark the frame and assume state 3.
    U 2 If the frame in the machine aperture is marked,
        leave the frame unchanged and assume state 2.
L Move the tape pointer left one frame.
    M 4 If the frame in the machine aperture is unmarked,
        mark the frame and assume state 4.
    U 3 If the frame in the machine aperture is marked,
        leave the frame unchanged and assume state 3.
R Move the tape pointer right one frame.
    U 1 If the frame in the machine aperture is unmarked,
        leave the frame unchanged and assume state 1.
    U 4 If the frame in the machine aperture is marked,
        leave the frame unchanged and assume state 4.

We can now understand the display in Fig. 2.29. Its LCD panels display instruction 3 of Program 1, indicating that the machine is currently in state 3.

To illustrate and explain the operation of a Turing machine, we will use the Turing Machine program that is accessed as was the Code Ring program on the book's dedicated home page. This program is loaded by double clicking "Turing Mach" on the home page:

Figure 2.30. Button for Turing machine.

This will take us to the Web page containing the Turing machine (Fig. 2.31).

The machine's tape is represented by the grid, the frames of which move left or right under the direction of the program instructions. We use a grid so that a sufficiently large number of frames can be seen on the CRT screen. Frames on this tape contain either "0" to indicate an unmarked frame or "1" to indicate a marked frame. The aperture for the tape reader is cell ten of the second row whose contents appear in bold type. Rather than using a simple LCD display, we use a text display area that displays not only the current instruction being executed but also provides a step-by-step explanation of the operation of the machine.

To run the Turing machine, we must first select a program, "Program1," from the selection choice box (Fig. 2.32). This activates the control buttons at the top of the machine and displays the program and its starting point in its text area. We start the program by pushing the "Go" button (Fig. 2.33). The line indicating the program's name and starting point, in this case "Program 1: Start At Instruction 1," appears in the text area and the initial three marks are placed in consecutive frames to the left of the current frame.

We step through the program by repeated pressings of the "Go" button. Each program instruction requires two pushes of the button: one to execute the tape move, and one to execute the mark and branching condition. The next push of the "Go" button displays the machine instruction and tape move in the text area and moves the tape as specified by the move instruction. In this case, the tape moves right (Fig. 2.34).

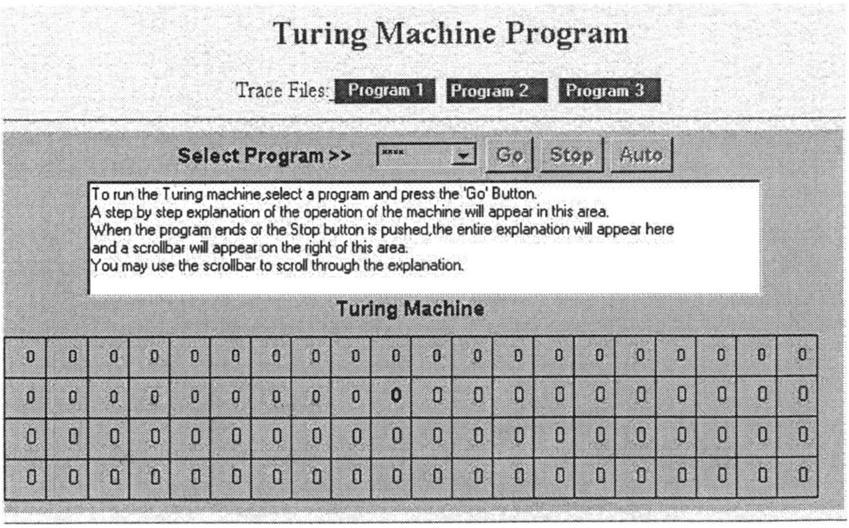

Figure 2.31. "Turing Machine Program" Web page.

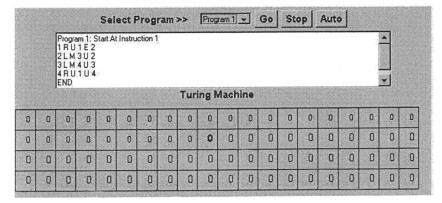

Figure 2.32. Turing machine start up.

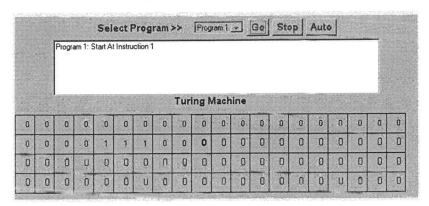

Figure 2.33. Turing machine at start of execution.

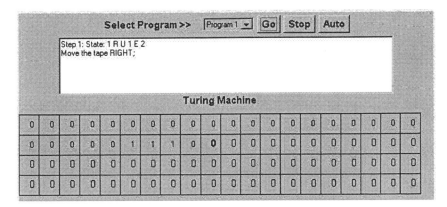

Figure 2.34. Turing machine start point and pointer.

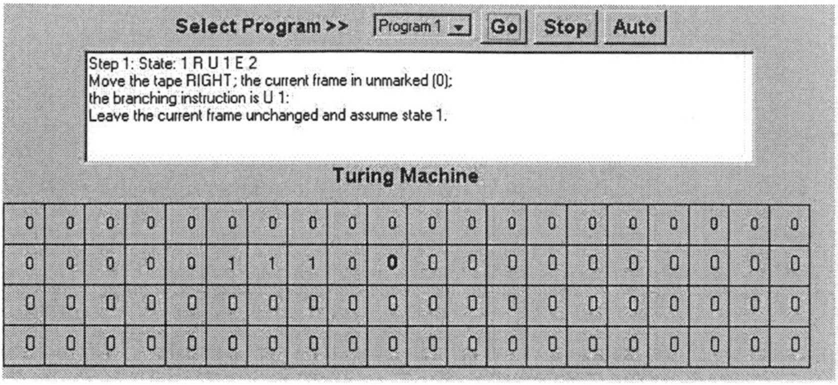

Figure 2.35. Turing machine "Program 1" after first mark.

The text area explains the meaning of each instruction as the machine carries out successive tape move and mark and branch operations. By reading this running commentary as the machine carries out its instructions, readers should be able to understand how the machine follows its program as it operates. The next push of the "Go" button executes the mark and branch operation (Fig. 2.35). The text area now contains a description of both the move and mark and branch phases of the first instruction:

Step 1: State: 1 R U 1 E 2
Move the tape RIGHT; the current frame is unmarked (0);
the branching instruction is U 1:
Leave the current frame unchanged and assume state 1.

For every two presses of the "Go" button, the Turing machine executes one complete instruction and then pauses.

We execute the instructions of the Turing machine by repeatedly pressing this button to "step through" the program. The machine offers two other buttons for executing the program: "Stop" and "Auto." The "Stop" allows us to stop the execution of the program at any time. Pushing this button has two distinct effects. First, it disables the "Go," "Stop," and "Auto" buttons. These buttons were disabled before we selected our first program and may be re-enabled by selecting a program for execution. Second, the "Stop" button places a sequential list of all the instructions executed up to the point of pushing the button. Readers may examine this record by scrolling through it with the scrollbar control that appears to the right of the text area (Fig. 2.36). Figure 2.36 shows the machine with the "Stop" button pushed after forty steps or eighty pushes of the "Go" button. The "Auto" button

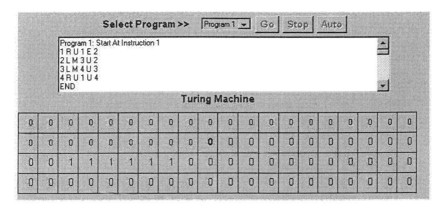

Figure 2.36. Turing machine after pressing the "Stop" button.

may be used to speed up the execution of the program by pausing after executing ten steps.

The instructions for the Turing machine are displayed in the text at the beginning, as well as at the end of execution:

Program 1: Start At Instruction 1
1 R U 1 E 2
2 L M 3 U 2
3 L M 4 U 3
4 R U 1 U 4
END

Figure 2.37. Instruction table for "Program 1."

Following these instructions, the machine will double the number of marked frames on the tape. There are three marks on the tape at the beginning of program execution as may be seen in Fig. 2.33. In the course of its operation, the machine will double the number of marks on the tape to six. By stepping through the program, watching the pointer move, and the contents of the frames alter while following the instructions as they appear in the text area, readers can familiarize themselves with the operation of the Turing machine. The first ten steps of this trace read:

Step 1: State: 1 R U 1 E 2
Move the tape RIGHT; the current frame is unmarked (0);
the branching instruction is U 1:
Leave the current frame unchanged and assume state 1.

Step 2: State: 1 R U 1 E 2
Move the tape RIGHT; the current frame is unmarked (0);

the branching instruction is U 1:
Leave the current frame unchanged and assume state 1.

Step 3: State: 1 R U 1 E 2
Move the tape RIGHT; the current frame is marked (1);
the branching instruction is E 2:
Erase the current frame by setting it to '0' and assume state 2.

Step 4: State: 2 L M 3 U 2
Move the tape LEFT; the current frame is unmarked (0);
the branching instruction is M 3:
Mark the current frame by setting it to '1' and assume state 3.

Step 5: State: 3 L M 4 U 3
Move the tape LEFT; the current frame is unmarked (0);
the branching instruction is M 4:
Mark the current frame by setting it to '1' and assume state 4.

Step 6: State: 4 R U 1 U 4
Move the tape RIGHT; the current frame is marked (1);
the branching instruction is U 4:
Leave the current frame unchanged and assume state 4.

Step 7: State: 4 R U 1 U 4
Move the tape RIGHT; the current frame is unmarked (0);
the branching instruction is U 1:
Leave the current frame unchanged and assume state 1.

Step 8: State: 1 R U 1 E 2
Move the tape RIGHT; the current frame is marked (1);
the branching instruction is E 2:
Erase the current frame by setting it to '0' and assume state 2.

Step 9: State: 2 L M 3 U 2
Move the tape LEFT; the current frame is unmarked (0);
the branching instruction is M 3:
Mark the current frame by setting it to '1' and assume state 3.

Step 10: State: 3 L M 4 U 3
Move the tape LEFT; the current frame is marked (1);
the branching instruction is U 3:
Leave the current frame unchanged and assume state 3.

Readers should run the program to the end using the "Auto" option and then examine the trace file to help familiarize themselves with the operation of the machine. The Turing machine Web page allows readers to branch to a page that contains a full listing of the execution steps. Readers may find this format more readable than the listing in the text area: To branch to this page, readers should click on the "Program 1" trace button at the top of the Turing machine page. The trace of the execution of this program is also printed in Appendix A.

The machine operates under control of "Program 1" in an orderly and repetitive manner. When it detects a marked frame, it erases that frame and then places two marks on the tape. Eventually, as may be seen in Fig. 2.36, all the original marks have been consumed but the machine continues moving right. The machine will keep running indefinitely because it has entered what is termed an "endless loop." It is "stuck" on instruction 1 R U 1 E 2. Each time it moves the tape to the right, it finds the frame unmarked and so assumes state 1. It will continue moving to the right indefinitely unless the person running the program tires of pushing the "Go" and "Auto" buttons and pushes "Stop." This is equivalent to "pulling the plug" on the machine and is different, as we shall see, from having the machine halt under the direction of its own program. We will discuss programmatic solutions to the problem of "runaways" below.

The table of instructions for any Turing machine is, in a word, an algorithm, a finite series of steps that will produce correct output from correct input. A Turing machine program or algorithm always has a specific starting place just as a computer has an on/off switch. The starting place for the doubling program we just ran is any frame to the right of the marks that it is to double. By convention, we write our tables of instructions so that the first instruction is always located in position 1 of the table. Just to double the number of marks on a tape from three to six, we will push the "Move/Branch" button a fair number of times. In fact, this repetition is really a function of the simplicity of the Turing machine which takes about eighty separate operations for what would take us two steps. If we were asked to double the number of marks on a tape, most likely we would count the number of marks and then take a pencil and add that many more to the right or left of the marks already on the tape. We wouldn't bother with erasing the marks already there. If there were just three marks on the tape to start, we would double them in what would seem to be a single step since we could count the initial number of marks at a glance.

It is the order in which the instructions are executed, not the order in which the instructions are entered into the table, that determines the results produced by the algorithm. Each instruction includes a branch to itself or to another state instruction. We could, for example, adopt the convention that the last instruction entered in the table is the first to be executed. This would entail rewriting the instructions to make the appropriate branches. We have supplied a program to do just that. To run this tape we must select "Program 2":

```
Program 2: Start At Instruction 4
1 R U 4 U 1
2 L M 1 U 2
3 L M 2 U 3
4 R U 4 E 3
END
```

The machine then runs on its new instructions which are identical to "Program 1," except that its instructions have been altered so that they will work only if the machine starts at instruction 4 rather than instruction 1. This program is loaded and executed in exactly the same way as "Program 1" and will produce identical output despite the rearranging and rewriting of its instructions. Readers should execute this program as they did "Program 1" and examine the step-by-step explanation in the text area or by clicking on the "Program 2 Output" link. The trace of the execution of this program is also printed in Appendix A.

What we are doing in this exercise is called "stepping through a program." It is a standard technique programmers use to understand a program they are unfamiliar with and to diagnose problems and locate programming errors or "bugs." Carrying out this exercise should be far less tedious than describing it. Readers will have to decide for themselves how familiar this exercise has made them with the operation of a Turing machine and the steps of this particular algorithm. But I think everyone who has tried the exercise will realize that there is a serious problem with the program: it doesn't know when to stop.

On detailed examination, we see that "Program 1" and "Program 2" contain a problem internal to the algorithm itself: although we specified a starting point, we did not specify any instruction to stop the machine once started. All instructions begin by moving the tape. In order to provide a stop mechanism we will need to take full advantage of the tape movement mechanism of our Turing machine and use its "H" instruction to halt the tape under program control. The program contains only tape move instructions: **L** to move left, and **R** to move right. To these we will add the third possibility, **H** for halt. Many programs, for example a program that counts the words in a text, work for no matter how much data they are given because they can detect when they have processed the last piece of data. We will have to modify our program so that it can detect when it has processed the last mark on the tape.

The problem with "Program 1" and "Program 2" is that they keep moving to the right after they have processed the last tape mark. To correct the problem we will need to restrict this inexorable move to the right. The problem instruction in "Program 1" is instruction 1, which instructs the machine to move the tape right and assume state 1 again if it encounters an unmarked frame. It causes the endless loop of movement to the right as the program encounters a seemingly endless stream of unmarked frames. Stepping through the program has enabled us to identify this particular branch on the program as the problematic one.

Our first modification will have to be to instruction 1. Rather than have the machine move right if it encounters an unmarked frame, we want it to stop. Unlike the earlier programs whose starting point could be anywhere to the left of the marks we wanted to double, this program must start at the unmarked frame immediately to the left of the first marked frame. The following program, "Program 3" in the choicebox, does this when started in state 1 from this frame:

Program 3: Start At Instruction 1
1 R U 8 U 2
2 R U 3 U 2
3 L U 5 E 4
4 L U 5 U 4
5 L M 6 U 5
6 L M 7 U 6
7 R U 1 U 7
8 H U 8 U 8
END

The first instruction, "1 R U 8 U 2," transfers control to instruction 8 when it detects an unmarked frame (U8). Instruction 8 is a halt instruction, "8 H U 8 U 8," which stops the machine when it is executed. This is why we must specify the starting point as immediately to the left of the first marked frame.[12] If instruction 1 encounters an unmarked frame, the machine will assume state 8, the Halt state. It assumes state 2 if it encounters a marked frame. Clearly then, the initial frame must be marked.

State 2 moves the tape to the right as long as the machine detects marked frames. When it encounters an unmarked frame, the machine moves left and erases the rightmost tape mark. It then assumes a series of states that move back to the left until it passes the starting point. It puts two marks on the tape at the first two unmarked frames it finds to the left of the starting point and then moves back to the starting point to repeat this cycle until it encounters no more marked frames to the right of the starting point. Each time through the cycle, it erases the rightmost mark until all marks are erased, at which point it halts.

The program starts from instruction 1 as shown in Fig. 2.38. The machine will halt when it executes the Halt instruction in instruction 8. There is no need to wait for the operator to become bored as with "Program 1" and "Program 2" because

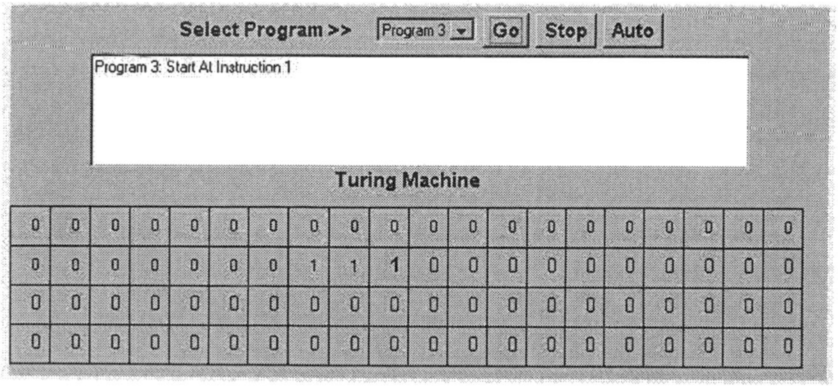

Figure 2.38. Program 3.

the Halt instruction prevents the machine from entering an endless loop. It is important to note that the Halt instruction is executed because it has been incorporated into the modified algorithm for this express purpose. It is not the case that the programs in "Program 1" and "Program 2" are wrong in any sense. As we shall see in our discussion of programming, programs do exactly what they are programmed to do, no more and no less. Many problems with programs arise because programmers fail to realize what it was exactly that they programmed. Turing machines require very precise data to operate properly. The machines will reject illegal input of any kind. It is important that the frames contain only one character, a "0" or "1." A cell containing "1"" or ""1" will be rejected as an incorrect entry as would an empty cell. Changing just one branching designation in the instruction table will produce unusual results.

It may seem a long way from a device that puts marks on tape to a modern computer. There were programmable devices like the Jacquard Loom and Babbage's Difference and Analytical Engines long before Turing developed his theory of computable numbers. Atanosoff, Zuse, Aiken, Mauchly, and Eckert were engineers who took pragmatic rather than theoretical approaches to the problem of programmable machine calculation. Turing's mathematical approach simply provided a theoretical model for their work much as Newton's *Principia* provided the theoretical underpinnings for the work of Kepler and Galileo. The Turing machine programs we have discussed here illustrate the basic principle of programmability. Their operations all turn on whether or not there is a mark in a frame and on the explicit alternatives that follow from its absence or presence. The next step is always contingent on the current one. As in a computer, what happens is determined by whether the switch of the moment is zero or one. Newton is the name to conjure with here. Turing's machine and its embodiment, the modern computer, are simulacrums of Newton's clockwork universe.

CHAPTER 3

The CPU as a Turing Machine

A VIRTUAL MACHINE

The Turing machine I have just described is the product of the thought experiment conceived by Alan Turing. The purpose of his experiment was to provide a context in which the concept of programmability could be subject to a formal analysis. In this chapter, I am going to propose another thought experiment, very similar to Turing's. In fact, my thought experiment is a variant Turing machine, designed to illustrate the basics of computer operation and programming. I refer to this thought experiment as a virtual CPU because it has only a mental reality. It is designed to provide explanations and specific examples of fundamental aspects of modern computers and no more. In this, it resembles the calculator we used in Chapter 2, which was designed not to calculate so much as to illustrate the idea of numerical bases. I have written a computer program in the JAVA programming language that illustrates the workings of this virtual CPU, just as I wrote the Turing machine program that illustrated the workings of the original Turing machine. My idea was to produce a model of a computer that illustrated, with a minimum of fuss, how a computer works. With the Turing machine, readers watched as a single bit in the frame under the aperture changed or didn't as the program directed. With the virtual CPU, readers get a direct view of the shifting binary patterns of cyberspace produced by multiple bit switches as they are thrown under the control of the CPU.

The CPU of a modern computer is a complex device, so complex in fact that any detailed description of its working tends to obscure its kinship to the relative simplicity of the Turing machine. It would take a book at least twice as long as this one to cover just the main features of the design and operation of a CPU such as the Intel Pentium. Rather than attempting anything so ambitious as this, I will describe a schematic version of the CPU as a way of illustrating how a device as simple in principle as a Turing machine may be extended to a device as complex as a modern CPU. The bewildering complexity of the Pentium CPU includes its three million transistor per square inch circuitry, its internal memory cache, and the interplay of a sixty-four bit data bus with a thirty-two bit address space, and its "look ahead" execution pipelines. (I don't expect readers to understand any of these terms; I use them to suggest to readers the technical complexity of devices like the Pentium microprocessor.)

In the course of running programs I have provided for this virtual CPU, readers will experience their first extended look into the realm of cyberspace as it appears to a programmer. Programming is the method by which programmers construct and manipulate cyberspace. In producing and running a program, programmers follow a four-step process:

1. Design the program and express the design in a suitable computer language such as JAVA. The resulting programming code, stored in a text file on the computer's disk, resembles a curious combination of natural language and mathematical notation.
2. Process the file containing the programming code with a translation program, called a compiler, that produces as its output a string of binary numbers containing the binary code for the program. This string of binary numbers is stored in another file on the disk. Because it contains a sequence of binary numbers that can be executed by the computer, this file is referred to as a binary or executable file. (The preferable term is executable file. All computer files are composed of binary numbers.) Users rarely see actual machine code. One purpose of the exercise with the virtual CPU is to enable readers to see machine code in operation.
3. Link the executable file to the operating system and load it into memory. All programs in a computer run under the supervision of the computer's operating system. Before machine code can be run, it must be connected to the operating system. It must also be loaded into memory beginning at some specific location because, in a von Neumann computer, programs must be placed in memory before being executed.
4. Execute the program by running the machine code.

In our discussion, I will provide programming code that the Virtual Machine will compile, link and load, and execute. Through this discussion, readers will come to understand the basic execution cycle of the computer in which data and instructions are moved from memory into the CPU, processed, and then returned to memory. The control and execution of this simple fetch and execute cycle are at the heart of any CPU, simple or complex.

At first glance, it may seem that the major difference between the Turing machine I have just described and the virtual CPU is that the Turing machine I postulated has separate memories for its instructions (the instruction table) and its data, the tape of infinite length. But as we have seen in our discussion of the historical development of the computer, once it became possible to build large capacity memories, the storing of data and instructions in memory represented a simplification of design.[1] It might also seem that the CPU's ability to handle numerical and text data is a significant difference between the CPU and the Turing machine. But again, as we have seen in our discussion of the Turing machine, the addition of extra move instructions such as the Halt instruction represent an extension of the Turing machine rather than a change in its nature. Such extensions may add to the complexity of the machine's components, but the payoff for this added complexity is that it also adds to the machine's practical usefulness. The CPU is an elaboration and extension of the Turing machine rather than an essentially different device. The same may be said of the relationship of the tape marking and scanning mechanisms of the Turing machine to the disks, printers, scanners, and pointing devices of the modern computer. In both cases, their operation comes down to whether the bit of the moment is zero or one.

Just as Blake's innocents "see a World in a Grain of Sand/ And a Heaven in a Wild Flower," programmers see cyberspace as a temporal sequence of bits changing from zero to one and back. The virtual CPU programs in this chapter are intended to communicate to readers a sense of the working of a CPU as it is experienced by a programmer. Plato divided the universe into the real world of ideas and the illusionary world of appearances. When I think of cyberspace in Platonic terms, I regard hardware as the realm of appearances and software as the realm of ideas. The ideas of software may be embodied in all types of material devices from clockworks to transistors. In Plato's famous parable of the cave, chained humanity can only see shadows of reality projected on the wall of the cave. It must be freed from its chains by Platonic dialectic so that it can turn to face reality. The exercises in this chapter may be thought of in terms of the parable of the cave. The virtual CPU provides readers with the dialectic needed to contemplate cyberspace not as it appears projected by a browser on the screen of a CRT but as it is in its binary austerity.

The CPU I have implemented in a JAVA program is a much simpler device than a Pentium microprocessor. This CPU is an example of what is termed a "virtual machine." Because every computer is a Turing machine, it is always possible to emulate one computer on another. The "Soft Windows" program that enables a Mac computer with its own unique hardware to run programs written for Windows computers that have entirely different hardware is an example of an elaborate virtual machine.[2] The main drawback to virtual machines is that they require a considerable amount of computing resource. Rather than simply doing something as it does when it executes an ordinary program, the computer, when executing a virtual machine program, must always pretend to itself that it is a virtual machine doing something. Inevitably, the pretense takes its toll. Software emulation runs more slowly than its hardware original. In Platonic terms, the virtual machine is like a work of art, an imitation of an imitation at three removes from reality.

But for our purposes, speedy execution is not a consideration. Not only can one emulate in software any existing hardware, but also one can, as is being done here, emulate a hypothetical piece of hardware. I suppose one might say that a hypothetical virtual machine like the one I will use in this chapter is four removes from reality. Our virtual machine program exists only as an idea expressed in a piece of JAVA software. When I refer, as I will, to its copying machine code from the disk of our virtual machine to its memory, what happens is that JAVA redraws the image on the screen of a Web browser. When I say that it is moving data or instructions to or from the computer's memory or CPU, it is copying the contents of one location in the table designated as memory to another location in another table designated as the CPU. And what appears to happen, as the screen displays the virtual machine, is that we are watching the changing of zeros to ones and ones to zeros, just as we watched the cells of the Turing machine's tape change. Both are ultimately in the nature of thought experiments. The display on the screen is arranged to mimic the appearance of a readout that would appear if actual hardware were in operation; but the appearance is in this case more real than the (imaginary) hardware of our virtual, hypothetical computer.

We should also keep in mind that JAVA software works on different computers—PCs, MACs, etc.—because the browsers on those machines include a JAVA virtual machine that makes it possible for the software to be "independent" of the computer on which it is running. The JAVA virtual machine is a computer program of the same type as the "Soft Windows" program for running Windows programs on MACs. It translates the binary code of the hypothetical JAVA computer to the binary code used by a MAC or Windows machine. To make JAVA work on any actual computer hardware, one must create or obtain a JAVA virtual machine program that is designed to make the translations required by the hardware. Our virtual CPU, then, is a virtual machine written to run on the JAVA virtual machine that runs on our real computer.

The cycle of our virtual CPU is designed to illustrate the basic operational cycle of an ideal CPU, not the minutiae of any actual one. For this reason its design has been greatly simplified. The addressing circuit of this computer works on words, not bytes. Its memory size is 120 words or 240 bytes. Addresses in this machine run from 0 to 119. There are nine locations in this CPU, each the same size as a memory location, but they are used very differently from memory locations. For this reason, they are referred to as "registers" rather than "locations." Each of these registers has a special purpose and holds a specific kind of data or specific part of a program instruction. In memory, program instructions and data are intermixed in accordance with the dictates of von Neumann architecture. When instructions and data are moved to the CPU, they are assigned different registers depending on whether they are instructions or data.

The nine registers that make up the virtual CPU are shown in Fig. 3.1. Humankind cannot bear too much reality, so I will show the registers as displaying their contents in decimal numbers rather than binary ones. But the virtual CPU program allows the virtual CPU to display the contents of its registers as decimal, binary, or hexadecimal numbers at the discretion of the user. In this it is like the display of the code ring whose numerical base could be changed at will. This ability to display numbers in different numerical bases is a function of the virtual machine's use as an instructional device. Registers in an actual CPU are composed of binary switches. I am using a decimal display because it is easier for readers unfamiliar with binary code to understand the numerical values contained in the memory and CPU of the virtual machine in decimal form. But in order to familiarize themselves with the binary nature of cyberspace, readers are encouraged to display the virtual machine's output as binary code as much as possible. The trace files in Appendix B contain binary representations of the contents of the CPU and memory.

There are two parts to our virtual CPU: a control section and a data section as shown in Fig. 3.1. The first five rows of this CPU diagram represent the control unit of the CPU. This is where instructions are stored when they are moved from memory to the CPU, where the computer keeps track of the location of the next instruction to be fetched from memory, and where arithmetical and logical operations are carried out. Each instruction takes three consecutive memory locations. When an instruction is moved from memory to the CPU, it is stored in the boxes labeled "Operation," "Operand 1," and "Operand 2." These three boxes, taken together, are the CPU's instruction register, which holds the three words that make up a machine instruction. The box labeled "Operation" specifies the operation the computer is to perform. The "Operand 1" and "Operand 2" boxes hold the data to be operated on by the operation. Row four of the CPU diagram, labeled "Location," is the CPU's location register, which is used to keep track of the memory location of the next machine instruction to be fetched from memory and executed. Remember that memory holds binary numbers. A binary number in memory is treated as

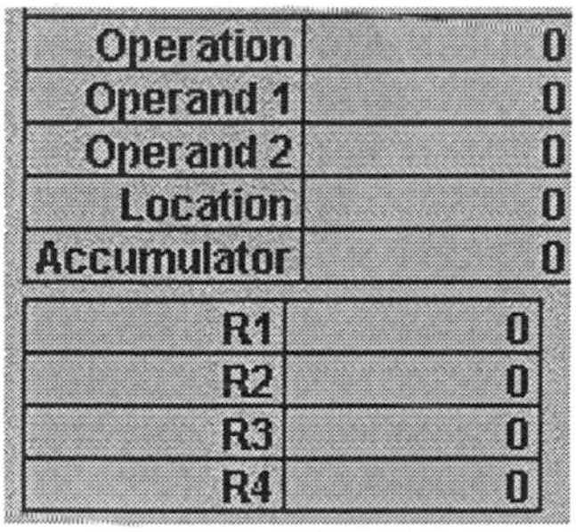

Operation	0
Operand 1	0
Operand 2	0
Location	0
Accumulator	0
R1	0
R2	0
R3	0
R4	0

Figure 3.1. Virtual machine CPU.

an instruction only when the memory address of the binary number is placed in the location register. It is the job of the programmer to organize the program so that only the addresses of instructions appear in the location register. The value stored in this register is the address from which instructions are fetched for execution. The location register is updated as part of the CPU execution cycle. The register marked "Accumulator," which is the register dedicated to the arithmetical and logical circuit of the computer, holds the result of any arithmetical or logical operation the CPU performs.

The last four rows of the CPU diagram make up the data section of the CPU. These are the locations in the CPU reserved for data, much as the first five rows are reserved for instructions and operations. There are four data registers in this CPU: "R1," "R2," "R3," and "R4." They hold any data that is moved from memory to the CPU. Machine instructions operate on the data in these registers. To change the value of data stored in memory, the CPU must move the new data value from one of these registers to memory. All this may seem very abstract but it will be illustrated and clarified—I hope—by the virtual CPU program. In the discussion of the virtual machine that follows I will try to give enough detail so that a reader who is not at a machine can follow the general drift of the presentation. Readers may refer to the trace files in Appendix B or run the virtual CPU program from the Web page.

The virtual CPU program is—shades of ENIAC—an electronic calculator that can be programmed to carry out sequences of arithmetical operations: addition, subtraction, multiplication, division, and exponentiation. There are machine instructions for each of these operations. The other machine instructions have to do with moving data to the CPU and back and with branching from one instruction to another as we have seen in the Turing machine. This computer's instruction set consists of twenty instructions as contrasted with the six instructions of the Turing machine (Right, Left, Halt, Erase, Mark, Unchanged). The names of the instructions make up what is termed the assembler language of the computer. These instructions are, therefore, called assembler instructions. There are instructions to start and stop the computer ("Go," "Stop"); arithmetical instructions ("Add," "Sub," "Mult," "Div," and "Exp"); instructions for copying data between the CPU and memory ("Move," "MoveA," "LoadR," "Store," "StoreC," and "StoreA"); branching instructions ("Jump," "JumpZ," "JumpP," and "JumpN"); a memory allocation instruction ("Dim"); an output instruction to display the intermediate and final results of a calculation ("Display"); and a so-called "compiler directive" ("End"). The assembler instructions and their operation codes as well as the function of these instructions are given in the table displayed in Fig. 3.2.

The assembler instructions refer to twenty specialized circuits in the CPU, one for each instruction. Any program it executes will be made up of some sequence of these twenty instructions. The order in which the operations will be performed is determined by the order in which program instructions are executed. The numerical operation codes run consecutively from one to twenty. In designing the CPU, I

Assembler instruction	Operation code	Function
Dim	1	Allocate memory.
Move	2	Move data to a data register.
MoveA	3	Move memory address to a data register.
Add	4	Add the contents of two data registers and store the result in the Accumulator.
Sub	5	Subtract the contents of two data registers and store the result in the Accumulator.
Mult	6	Multiply the contents of two data registers and store the result in the Accumulator.
Div	7	Divide the contents of two data registers and store the result in the Accumulator.
Exp	8	Raise the contents of a data register to the power stored in another data register and store the result in the Accumulator.
Jump	9	Place the address stored in a data register in the location register.
JumpZ	10	If the value in the Accumulator is zero, place the address stored in a data register in the location register.
JumpP	11	If the value in the Accumulator is greater than zero, place the address stored in a data register in the location register.
JumpN	12	If the value in the Accumulator is less than zero, place the address stored in a data register in the location register.
Stop	13	Halt execution of the program.
Go	14	Start execution of the program at this location.
Display	15	Display the values stored in consecutive memory locations.
Store	16	Store the value contained in a data register in a memory location.
StoreA	17	Store the address contained in a data register as the address of a variable.
StoreC	18	Store a constant in a memory location.
MoveR	19	Move the contents of one register to another register.
End	20	Mark end of compilation.

Figure 3.2. Assembler instructions and operation codes of virtual CPU.

followed what seemed to be an obvious way to go in assigning codes. Different types of actual CPUs use different codes for the same operation, so that the numerical operation code that means "ADD" in one computer probably means something else in another one. This is one reason why a program that works on one type of computer does not work on another type of computer. A program like Soft Windows that runs Windows programs on Apple hardware may be thought of as a table that gives the code equivalents for the Intel and Apple hardware.[3] In order to work properly, a CPU must have a unique operation code assigned to each operation but there is no need for these numbers to be consecutive.

The twenty operations given in Fig. 3.2 are the only instructions the virtual CPU can carry out because they are the only circuits the CPU has. Specifying operation code 21 is meaningless to the virtual CPU because it has only twenty operation codes, 1 through 20. The important thing to understand is that each instruction has a name and numerical value associated with that name. When one of these values is placed in the instruction register and executed, it turns on the circuit corresponding to the value in the same way that a telephone rings when its number is dialed.

Machine code provides the lowest level interface between the programmer and the machine. To program the earliest computers, programmers had to enter the numerical values corresponding to operation codes and data into memory. For example, programmers programmed ENIAC by wiring sequences of operation codes into circuit boards. Other early computers had slightly less tedious ways of entering programs, but they still required the manual input of sequences of essentially unintelligible numbers whose meaning was encoded beneath the numbers in the way that the Code Ring program hides the meaning of its message under its "secret" numerical code.

As programs grew longer and more complex, the possibility of making errors by entering the wrong numbers grew exponentially. The earliest solution to this problem was the invention of assembler language that substituted words for numbers. The vocabulary and syntax of these languages were kept simple to allow for a "translation" to machine code that involved little more than looking up the numerical equivalents of the words in various dictionary-like tables. Programs were then written to translate these words into the numerical operation codes the computer could execute. The programs for the virtual machine are written in an assembler language. The instructions for the assembler language—"Move," "Add," "Jump," etc.—are typical of assembler languages. With assembler languages, computer programming took its first step away from cabala and began to move in the direction of mathematical formalism and symbolic logic. Subsequent developments in computer interfaces led eventually to the development of the graphical user interface that is used on the World Wide Web.

SWAPPING VALUES IN MEMORY

The first assembler language program I will consider is a simple one that loads two values into memory, displays them, moves them to the CPU, returns them to memory in reversed locations, and displays them in now-reversed order. This program is intended to illustrate how the instruction cycle of a computer moves data between the CPU and memory. First the program must be compiled. The process of compilation translates English-like statements that programmers use to the binary machine code that the computer uses. Once it has been compiled, the machine code will be loaded into memory, linked to the operating system, and executed. The virtual machine, then, carries out a four-step process of compiling, linking, loading, and executing a program.

The code for this program is shown in Fig. 3.3. The assembler code looks very much like an instruction table for a Turing machine. I designed it to look this way to stress the idea that the computer is an elaborate form of Turing machine. Instructions are numbered sequentially in the first column. The second column is a machine instruction in the same way that the second column of a Turing instruction table is a tape move instruction. The third and fourth and columns are operands that specify what data is to be operated on, much as the operands of a Turing machine table operate on the contents of the tape frame.

Computer programs are usually divided into two segments, a data segment and a code segment. The data segment stores the data upon which the computer will operate and the code segment stores the instructions for operating upon the data. This division simplifies the programmer's task of making sure that the program keeps track of which numbers in memory are data and which are instruction codes.

0	Program	Swap	*
1	Dim	Location1	1:50
2	Dim	Location2	1:100
3	Go	*	*
4	Display	Location1	2
5	Move	Location1	R1
6	Move	Location2	R2
7	Store	R1	Location2
8	Store	R2	Location1
9	Display	Location1	2
10	Stop	*	*
11	End	*	*

Figure 3.3. "Swap" assembler program.

The first two rows of the "Swap" program define its data segment. Our assembler language uses the "Dim" statement to allocate memory and store values in the allocated memory. (The term "Dim" is short for "Dimension," the word used in FORTRAN, one of the earliest computer languages, to allocate memory.) The "Dim Location1 1:50" statement allocates a portion of memory and assigns it the name "Location1." It is good programming practice to give memory locations names that represent the contents of the location or the use of the data. In this program I use the names "Location1" and "Location2" because I want to show how data is moved from one memory location to another. I could have named these two locations "X" and "Y" or "Ken" and "Barbie" and the program would have worked as well if I had written it with, say, "Ken" for "Location1" and "Barbie" for "Location2." The "1:50" portion of the statement specifies the amount of memory to be allocated and the value stored in the allocated memory. The number before the colon designates the number of memory locations to be allocated and the number after the colon designates the value to be stored in the location or locations allocated. Each location in this machine is one word (or two bytes) long. Thus "1:50" allocates one word of memory and stores a value "50" in that word. Had this portion of the statement read "8:0," the computer would have allocated eight words of memory and stored zero in each of them.

I do not need to worry about the physical numerical address of "Location1." The computer keeps track of the numerical address and will supply it whenever the program uses that name. The statement "Dim Location2 1:100" allocates a portion of memory contiguous with "Location1" under the name "Location2." Its length and initial value are specified as "1:100," so it is one word long and contains a value "100."

Instructions three through ten are the code segment of the program. They are arranged in a simple, sequential list with a "Go" or start execution instruction at the top of the list and a "Stop" or halt execution instruction at the bottom. This list structure is the simplest form of organization for a computer program. The "Go * *" statement marks the start of program instructions. It designates the place at which the computer will start executing its instructions. By convention, it is the first statement in the code segment but in fact it can be placed wherever in the code segment the programmer wishes to begin execution. In this assembler language, asterisks are used to designate "null operands" in instructions that require less than two operands. The "Display Location1 2" instruction is used to display memory values on the Virtual Machine's screen. The first operand designates the memory location of the first value to be displayed. The second operand designates the total number of consecutive locations to be displayed. "Location1 2" specifies two locations, starting at "Location1." Since I have defined "Location2" as the memory location next to "Location1," the instruction will display the contents of these two locations.[4]

Data must be moved from memory to the CPU before the computer can operate on it. The two "Move" instructions accomplish this by copying the values in "Location1" and "Location2" to registers 1 and 2, respectively. It is traditional but slightly confusing to call this type of instruction a "Move" instruction. In ordinary usage, moving something from one location to another means that something is removed from the first location and relocated in the second. But as Negroponte points out in *Being Digital*, the digital world of cyberspace is made of bits of information, not atoms of matter. The rules of cyberspace are different than the rules of ordinary space. The basic principle of memory allows making as many copies of a location's value as we wish without in any way changing the value in the location we are copying. Moving something in cyberspace is like copying something in ordinary space, except that the copy is in no way distinguishable from the original except by its location. Without access to the program that placed them in memory, we cannot tell which is the original and which is the copy. In ordinary space, copying may carry connotations of cheating, degradation, devaluing, lack of imagination. In ordinary space, who would prefer a copy to an original?

The next two instructions, the "Store" instructions, copy values from the CPU to memory. "Store" has a much nicer ring to it than "Copy" or "Move." It sounds so prudential, if not retentive, and calls to mind the fable of the ant and the grasshopper. "Store R1 Location2" puts the value stored in register one into "Location2." "Store R2 Location1" puts the value stored in register two into "Location1." Since register one holds the original contents of "Location1" and register two holds the original contents of "Location2," execution of these two instructions reverses the order of the values in these locations.

The "Display Location1 2" instruction now displays "100 50" rather than "50 100" as did instruction 4. The "Stop" instruction halts execution. The Turing machine exercises have pointed out how important the provision of such an instruction is. The "End" instruction is a directive to the assembler to tell it that the assembly process is over. This simple program places data in memory, moves it to the CPU and then back to memory. In so doing, it illustrates the basic operation of any program.

These instructions are defined for the virtual CPU written in JAVA for this discussion. It is, as I have said, a thought experiment, not a real piece of hardware. The machine has four parts:

a CPU that executes the machine's instructions;

a memory of 120 words addressed as 0 through 119;

a disk file with the capacity to hold program input and data and compiled output;

a simple operating system that allows a user to compile a program into machine code, store the machine code on disk, load the code into memory, and execute it.

We run the virtual machine by double clicking on the "Virtual CPU" button on the book's dedicated Web Page:

Virtual CPU

Figure 3.4. Virtual machine link.

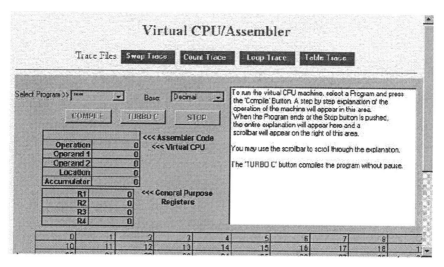

Figure 3.5. Virtual machine Web page.

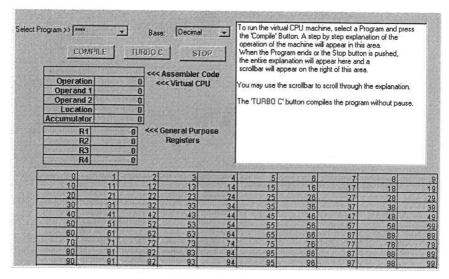

Figure 3.6. Virtual machine repositioned.

The virtual machine page now appears (Fig. 3.5).

This applet requires a bit more space than the right-hand frame allows initially. By using the scroll bar to the right of the CPU and by using the mouse to drag the border between the right and left frames to the left, one may reposition the application so that it is almost[5] completely visible (Fig. 3.6). The virtual machine program provides the user with a context sensitive interface. In other words, it gives the user only permissible selections in the course of its operation. For example, when it is first loaded, its display area contains instructions about operating the machine:

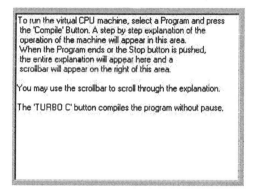

None of the buttons on its screen are enabled because a program has not been selected for compilation (Fig. 3.7). We select a program from the program selection box (Fig. 3.8), which offers us the choice of any of the four programs I will be discussing: the "Swap" program already mentioned as well as the "Count," "Loop," and "Table" programs I will be discussing after I finish with the "Swap" program.

We may also select the numerical base we want to display as we did with the code ring program in the previous chapter (Fig. 3.9). We will leave the base at its default setting of "Decimal" and select the "Swap" program (Fig. 3.10). This enables the buttons for the compiler and displays the "Swap" program in the text display area, which may be thought of as the monitor display for the virtual machine.

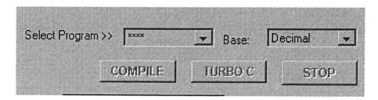

Figure 3.7. Program and base choice box and disabled buttons.

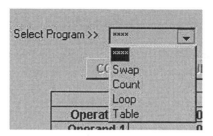

Figure 3.8. Available program choices.

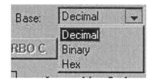

Figure 3.9. Numerical base selections.

The operating system of the virtual machine is designed to take users step by step through the process of compiling, loading, and executing assembler language programs. At each step, it provides in the text display area a running explanation of what is happening. When the program finishes execution, the entire history of compilation and execution is made available in the text display area, through which users may scroll. Listings of the operation of programs are also available in Appendix B, and on separate Web pages that may be examined by clicking on the links provided at the top of the Virtual CPU/Assembler Web Page (Fig. 3.11).

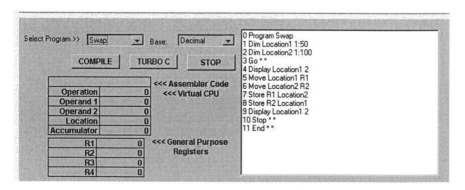

Figure 3.10. "Swap" program ready for compilation.

Virtual CPU/Assembler

Trace Files: | Swap Trace | Count Trace | Loop Trace | Table Trace |

Figure 3.11. Links to CPU/assembler trace files.

PROGRAM COMPILATION

The virtual CPU program provides three buttons to control the process of compilation by which the assembler instructions of the program are translated into machine codes:

a "COMPILE" button for step-by-step compilation;
a "TURBO C" button for automatic compilation;
a "STOP" button which halts step-by-step compilation.

The "Compile" button translates instructions one at a time until it reaches the "End * *" instruction, which marks the end of the compilation process. Each time the button is pushed, the contents of the CPU display, text display area, and disk file all change. The instruction to be compiled appears in the box above the CPU and in the text display area. The text display area also contains an explanation of what the assembler has done. The operation register of the CPU displays the numerical translation of the instruction. The translation is also written to the disk file from which it will be loaded into memory after completion of compilation. The first time the button is pushed, the locations in the disk file, which contain the numbers 0 through 119 representing the memory addresses of the compiled code, are all set to zero and the message "Clearing Disk/Memory" replaces the program listing in the text display area (Fig. 3.12). Subsequent pushes of the button compile machine code. The second push compiles the first "Dim" statement (Fig. 3.13). The box above the CPU now contains the assembler statement that has just been compiled and the text display area reads:

```
0000000000000000  0000000000000000  0000000000000000  0000000000000000  0000000000000000
0000000000000000  0000000000000000  0000000000000000  0000000000000000  0000000000000000
0000000000000000  0000000000000000  0000000000000000  0000000000000000  0000000000000000
0000000000000000  0000000000000000  0000000000000000  0000000000000000  0000000000000000
0000000000000000  0000000000000000  0000000000000000  0000000000000000  0000000000000000
0000000000000000  0000000000000000  0000000000000000  0000000000000000  0000000000000000
0000000000000000  0000000000000000  0000000000000000  0000000000000000  0000000000000000
0000000000000000  0000000000000000  0000000000000000  0000000000000000  0000000000000000
```

Figure 3.12. Cleared memory and binary file.

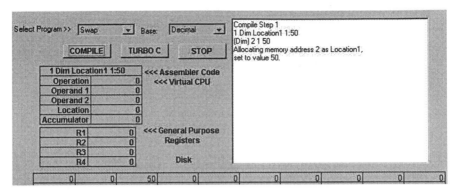

Figure 3.13. Compilation of "DIM" statement.

Compile Step 1
1 Dim Location1 1:50
(Dim) 2 1 50
Allocating memory address 2 as Location1,
set to value 50.

Memory location 2 on the disk now contains the value "50." (Memory locations 0 and 1 are reserved, as we shall see, for special purposes.)

Because "Dim" statements put data into memory rather than instructions, the instruction register is unchanged by a "Dim" statement. The "Dim Location2 1:100" instruction places the value "100" in memory location 3 just as the first instruction placed "50" in memory location 2. When the program's third instruction, "Go **," is compiled, both the CPU instruction register and memory change (Fig, 3.14). The text display area now reads:

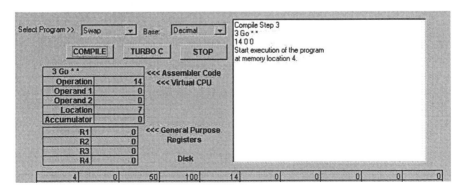

Figure 3.14. Compilation of "Go **" instruction.

Compile Step 3
3 Go * *
14 0 0
Start execution of the program
at memory location 4.

The CPU's instruction register now contains "14," "0," and 0" as do memory locations 4, 5, and 6. The location register now reads "7." It is pointing to the location at which the next machine instruction to be compiled will be placed in memory. Also, memory location 0 now contains the value "4." This memory location is reserved to contain the address of the first instruction of the program. When the program is loaded into memory, the first instruction to be fetched from memory into the CPU will be fetched from the address stored in memory location 0.

If we change the numerical base from decimal to binary, the virtual machine displays its values as binary numbers. For example, instruction 4 compiles as shown in Fig. 3.15. This shows us the actual bits of the virtual machine. The text display area gives the machine codes in both decimal and binary:

Compile Step 4
4 Display Location1 2
15 1 2
00001111 00000001 00000010
Display the values starting at Location1: 2 Locations.

Readers are encouraged to try compiling and running the virtual machine programs using different numerical bases. In particular, they should try the programs using binary to fix clearly in their minds the notion that computers operate on bits. The listing in Appendix B shows binary code. For purposes of our discussion, however, I will stick to decimal. The main point about these programs is to understand how code and numbers circulate and function in a computer.

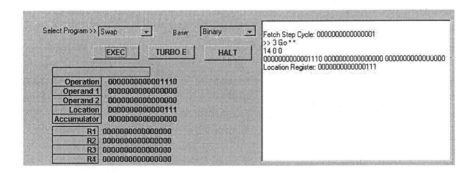

Figure 3.15. Virtual machine using binary numerical base.

The compilation continues step by step with each push of the "COMPILE" button until the "End" statement is reached. The text display area displays successively:

Compile Step 5
5 Move Location1 R1
2 1 1
00000010 00000001 00000001
Move the value of Location1 to R1.

Compile Step 6
6 Move Location2 R2
2 2 2
00000010 00000010 00000010
Move the value of Location2 to R2.

Compile Step 7
7 Store R1 Location2

16 1 2
00010000 00000001 00000010
Store the contents of R1 in Location2.

Compile Step 8
8 Store R2 Location1
16 2 1
00010000 00000010 00000001
Store the contents of R2 in Location1.

Compile Step 9
9 Display Location1 2
15 1 2
00001111 00000001 00000010
Display the values starting at Location1: 2 Locations.

Compile Step 10
10 Stop * *
13 0 0
00001101 00000000 00000000
Halt execution of the Program.

Compile Step 11
11 End * *
* * *
00001101 00000000 00000000
End of Assembler for Program Swap

When the "End" statement is reached, the disk contains the memory image of the machine code that will be loaded into memory for execution (Fig. 3.16).

Memory locations all contained 0 at the beginning of the compile step. The numbers now in memory are the data, operation codes, and operands that were

4	27	50	100	14	0	0	15	1	2
2	1	1	2	2	-2	16	1	2	16
2	1	15	1	2	13	0	0	2	3

Figure 3.16. Decimal base: disk memory image at end of compilation.

produced by the compiler. Memory location 1 now contains the value 27. (Memory addresses start at 0, so the second memory location has an address of 1.) This number is the offset in memory for the location of the variable pointer table. The virtual machine refers to variables by a number. The machine instruction "2 2 2" is a Move instruction because its operation code is "2," the operation code for a "Move." The variable it is to move is referred to as "2," which means that it is the second variable to be defined. The first variable is always assigned to memory location 2 by the virtual machine. But since the first variable may be defined as any number of locations, we cannot assume that the location of the second variable will be location 3. To find out the actual address of this location, the addressing circuit of the virtual machine adds the value stored in memory address 1 to the number of the variable. The result of this addition is 29 since $27 + 2 = 29$. It takes the value stored in location 29 as the address of variable 2. Because the Swap program is very short and uncomplicated, it turns out that the value in location 29 is "3" but it need not have been so. We will see that the use of a variable pointer table simplifies that handling of tables of numbers.

The reason why compiling assembly language is useful may be seen by examining the contents of the binary file produced by the compiler (Fig. 3.17). The program occupies 30 words (60 bytes) of memory and each memory location contains 16 bits. To enter this program into memory "by hand" would require setting 480 separate switches. Anyone who has tried to program a VCR will appreciate the difficulty of entering 480 switches correctly in sequence. A Hollerith card had 960 binary locations and so potentially could be punched 10^{288} different ways. The 480 bits containing the binary code of the swap program could be thrown in 10^{144} different ways, only one of which is the correct code for the program. The possibilities need not be infinite to be overwhelming. And this is a very simple program. The Windows operating system contains millions of bytes of language code and thus tens of millions of bits of binary code. Programmers use far more

0000000000000100	0000000000011011	0000000000110010	0000000001100100	0000000000001110
0000000000000000	0000000000000000	0000000000001111	0000000000000001	0000000000000010
0000000000000010	0000000000000001	0000000000000001	0000000000000010	0000000000000010
0000000000000010	0000000000010000	0000000000000001	0000000000000010	0000000000010000
0000000000000010	0000000000000001	0000000000001111	0000000000000001	0000000000000010
0000000000001101	0000000000000000	0000000000000000	0000000000000010	0000000000000011

Figure 3.17. Binary code for "Swap" program.

sophisticated computer languages and programming interfaces than simple assembler languages to produce today's typical JAVA or Windows program.

PROGRAM LOADING AND EXECUTION

When compilation finishes, the program has been translated into machine code and the translation has been written to a disk file. The next step is to link the program to the operating system and load this code from the disk into the computer's memory. The "COMPILE" button label changes to read "LOAD" (Fig. 3.18).

The "TURBO C" (explained below) and "STOP" buttons are now disabled and only the "LOAD" button is enabled. In other words, the virtual machine, having compiled a program to the end, insists that it be linked and loaded.[6] The text display area directs users to take the only option that will move the compile, load, execute cycle forward:

> Compile Step 11
> 11 End * *
> * * *
>
> End of Assembler for Program Swap
>
> Compilation completed; push 'Load' to continue.

Pushing the "LOAD" button reads the machine code from the (virtual) disk into (virtual) memory and prepares the CPU to fetch and execute instructions from memory starting with the "Go" instruction in location 4, the location value stored in memory location 0. This is a very simple operating system in which linking is accomplishing by fetching the starting address from memory location zero of the binary code (Fig. 3.19). The text display area now directs the user to push the "Fetch" button to proceed. The three buttons are now labeled "FETCH," "TURBO E," and "HALT," and the table at the bottom of the screen is now labeled "Memory" rather than "Disk" as it now represents the computer's memory rather than a disk file. The location register is set to "4," the location from which it will fetch the "Go" instruction that starts the execution of the program.

Program execution is a two-step process. Instructions are first moved to the CPU and interpreted, then executed. The button label of the first button will toggle

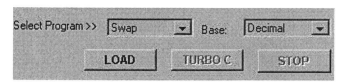

Figure 3.18. LOAD button.

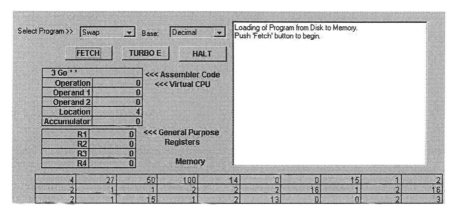

Figure 3.19. "Swap" program at start of execution.

back and forth from "FETCH" to "EXEC" as these steps are carried out. It takes two button pushes to complete the cycle for each instruction. As with the compilation phase, the instruction currently being executed will appear in the box above the CPU. It will also appear in the text display area along with a commentary explaining each step and recording the values stored in the CPU locations.

Instructions may alter the contents of the location register, the accumulator, and the general registers, as well as the contents of memory. The length of every instruction for the virtual machine is three words. Every time an instruction is fetched from memory, the first word is stored as the instruction register's operation code, the second as its operand 1, and the third as its operand 2. After fetching the instruction, the virtual machine adds three to the value stored in the location register so as to point to the next instruction. Computers execute their programs serially unless a branching instruction alters the contents of the location register. Branching instructions alter the contents of the location register so that the next instruction after the branching instruction is taken from the location value placed in the location register by the branching instruction. From that point, execution continues serially until the next branching instruction is encountered. We will see examples of the use of branching in the "Loop" and "Table" programs.

Pressing the "FETCH" button for the first time loads the "GO" instruction into the instruction register and increases the value in the location register by 3 (Fig. 3.20).

The text display records the fetch operation:

Fetch Step Cycle: 1
>> 3 Go * *
14 0 0

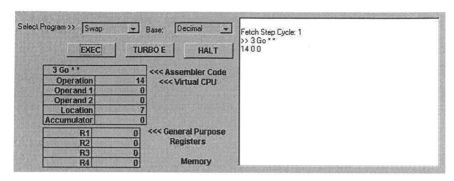

Figure 3.20. Initiating execution with "Fetch" button.

And the button label changes to "EXEC" in anticipation of the next step in the cycle. Pushing "EXEC" executes the instruction and produces an explanation of the start of execution in the text display area:

Exec Step Cycle: 1
Go instruction; starting execution at memory location 4.
Variable Pointer Table Offset = 27
Instruction Register: 14 0 0
Location Register: 7
Accumulator: 0
R1 = 0; R2 = 0; R3 = 0; R4 = 0

It also changes the label of the button back to "FETCH." The "Go" instruction is little more than a place keeper instruction used to initiate execution of the program and nothing else. It produces no changes in memory or in the general-purpose registers.

The next "FETCH" brings up a "Display" instruction, the function of which is to display values stored in memory in the text display area (Fig. 3.21). The "EXEC" step of this instruction produces the requested output as well as the explanation of the step:

4 Display Location 1 2	
Operation	15
Operand 1	1
Operand 2	2
Location	10
Accumulator	0

Figure 3.21. CPU during display instruction.

Exec Step Cycle: 2
Display 2 memory locations starting at Location1.

Program Output

50 100

Instruction Register: 15 1 2
Location Register: 10
Accumulator: 0
R1 = 0; R2 = 0; R3 = 0; R4 = 0

The purpose of this program is to show how memory values are changed. By executing this display instruction at the start of the program and an identical one at the close of the program, it shows users that the swap has occurred. Here it shows the values stored in variable "Location1" and "Location2" as they were set by the compiler. The second time, after the execution of the intervening instructions, this instruction will show the values in reverse order ("100 50" rather than "50 100").

The next instruction, a move instruction, will alter the contents of a register by placing a value stored in memory into the register. The "FETCH" step puts the move instruction into the CPU (Fig. 3.22) The "EXEC" step modifies the contents of the "R1" register, which now contains "50" (Fig 3.23). The explanation of the fetch and execute steps details the change in "R1":

Fetch Step Cycle: 3
>> 5 Move Location1 R1
2 1 1

Exec Step Cycle: 3
Move value (50) from Location1 to Register 1.
Instruction Register: 2 1 1
Location Register: 13

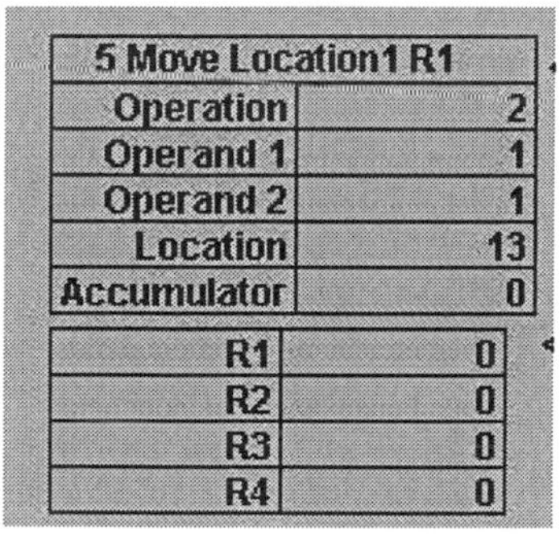

5 Move Location1 R1	
Operation	2
Operand 1	1
Operand 2	1
Location	13
Accumulator	0
R1	0
R2	0
R3	0
R4	0

Figure 3.22. "Fetch" step of move instruction.

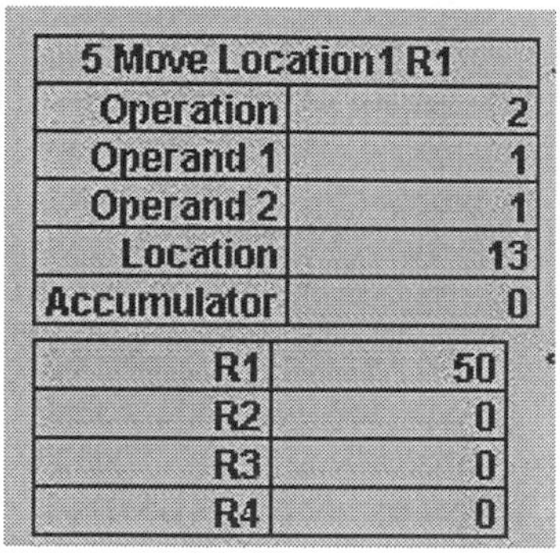

5 Move Location1 R1	
Operation	2
Operand 1	1
Operand 2	1
Location	13
Accumulator	0
R1	50
R2	0
R3	0
R4	0

Figure 3.23. Execute step of move instruction.

Accumulator: 0
R1 = 50; R2 = 0; R3 = 0; R4 = 0

Fetching and executing the next instruction alters "R2" in the same way that the previous one altered "R1" (Fig. 3.24). These two "Move" instructions illustrate the fact that values must be moved from memory to the CPU in order to be operated on.

The program alters the contents of memory with two "Store" instructions that are the reflex of the two "Move" instructions just executed. By moving the values stored in "R1" and "R2" back to memory, but to reverse locations, the values stored in "Location1" and "Location2" will be switched from "50 100" to "100 50". The effect of "Store" instructions is on memory, not on the CPU general registers. The first "Store" instruction produces the following explanation:

Fetch Step Cycle: 5
>> 7 Store R1 Location2
16 1 2

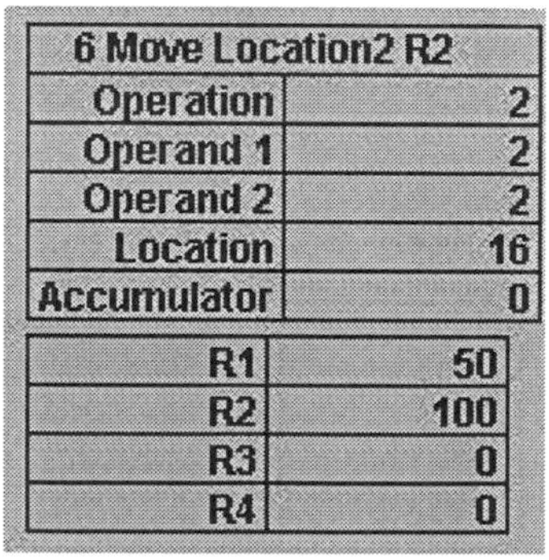

6 Move Location2 R2	
Operation	2
Operand 1	2
Operand 2	2
Location	16
Accumulator	0
R1	50
R2	100
R3	0
R4	0

Figure 3.24. Altered contents of R1 and R2.

Exec Step Cycle: 5
Store value (50) from Register 1
in memory variable Location2.
Instruction Register: 16 1 2
Location Register: 19
Accumulator: 0
R1 = 50; R2 = 100; R3 = 0; R4 = 0

It produces the following change in memory location 3 which now holds the value "50" rather than "100":

4	27	50	50	14	0	0	15	1	2
2	1	1	2	2	2	16	1	2	16
2	1	15	1	2	13	0	0	2	3

Figure 3.25. Memory location 3 altered.

The next "Store" instruction produces similar results:

Fetch Step Cycle: 6
>> 8 Store R2 Location1
16 2 1

Exec Step Cycle: 6
Store value (100) from Register 2
in memory variable Location1.
Instruction Register: 16 2 1
Location Register: 22
Accumulator: 0
R1 = 50; R2 = 100; R3 = 0; R4 = 0

It alters memory location 2 to contain the value "100" rather than "50:"

4	27	100	50	14	0	0	15	1	2
2	1	1	2	2	2	16	1	2	16
2	1	15	1	2	13	0	0	2	3

Figure 3.26. Memory location 2 altered.

With these two values reversed in memory, the display instruction executed in Cycle 7 produces output that is the opposite of Cycle 2:

Fetch Step Cycle: 7
>> 9 Display Location1 2
15 1 2
Location Register: 25

Exec Step Cycle: 7
Display 2 memory locations starting at Location1.

Program Output

100 50

Instruction Register: 15 1 2
Location Register: 25
Accumulator: 0
R1 = 50; R2 = 100; R3 = 0; R4 = 0

The final instruction in the program, a "Stop" instruction, brings the swap program to a close:

Fetch Step Cycle: 8
>> 10 Stop * *
13 0 0
Location Register: 28

Exec Step Cycle: 8
Stop instruction; halting execution.

Halt Step
Stop instruction; halting execution.

Instruction Register: 13 0 0
Location Register: 28
Accumulator: 0
R1 = 50; R2 = 100; R3 = 0; R4 = 0

The buttons are all disabled and the text display area now contains a complete listing of the compilation, loading, and execution of the program (Fig. 3.27).

Users may step through this program as many times as they feel it necessary for complete understanding simply by reselecting "Swap" from the list of programs. They should, of course, switch the numerical base of the display to binary to see how the changes in decimal values are reflected bit by bit. Or they may examine the trace file by scrolling through the contents of the text display area or by branching to the Web page that contains a list of the trace file.

Stepping through the compilation and execution of this program a few times should familiarize readers thoroughly with the cycle of compilation, loading, and execution that is at the heart of any computer process. An overall familiarity with the process will simplify understanding the rest of our discussion of the virtual machine. I will consider three more programs in this discussion. They demonstrate how computers count, branch, and calculate tables of numbers. In discussing them, I will focus on the new elements of computing they introduce rather than going over them step by step. The virtual machine and the trace listing in Appendix B or on the Web page should provide readers with the background familiarity they will need to understand the new elements I introduce.

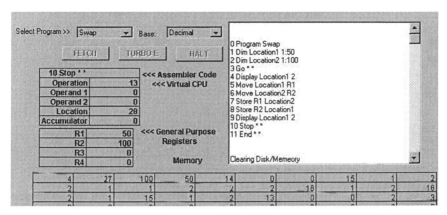

Figure 3.27. "Swap" program at end of execution.

HOW COMPUTERS COUNT

The next program I will discuss is a program called "Count," which shows how the arithmetical unit of our virtual machine works. In higher level languages like C or JAVA, counting is done by statements that read "Count++;" or "Count = Count + 1;". To those unfamiliar with such computer languages, the latter statement may seem to be either an algebraic absurdity or an insidious instruction from Big Brother. (In a café called The Spreading Chestnut Tree at the end of *1984*, Winston writes $2 + 2 = 5$ in the dust to show his submissive love of Big Brother.) But what this statement actually represents is a sequence of operations that direct the computer to move the value stored in memory location "Count" to the CPU, add 1 to it, and store the result in location "Count." This program is loaded by selecting "Count" from the program selection box of the virtual machine Web page (Fig. 3.28). In this program, the value "5" is stored at location "Count," displayed, and has one added to it. The result is stored back in location "Count," where it is displayed to show the new value. The program then stops.

Line 3 of the program, "StoreC 1 R1," is an instruction that was not used in the "Swap" program. "StoreC" stores the constant value of its first operand in the register designated by its second operand. Its first operand is always a numerical value as it is here. Such values are called "constants" because, unlike named memory locations, they are not referenced in the Variable Pointer Table and do not change value in the course of program execution. The assembler can distinguish between an operand that is a constant and one that is a named memory location or register because the machine operation code implies the type of each operand. The first operand of a "StoreC" instruction is always a numerical constant and the first operand of a "Move" instruction is always the name of a variable defined by a

1	Dim	Count	1:5
2	Go		
3	StoreC	1	R1
4	Display	Count	1
5	Move	Count	R2
6	Add	R1	R2
7	Store	AC	Count
8	Display	Count	1
9	Stop		
10	End		

Figure 3.28. Counter program.

previous "Dim" instruction. The assembler would balk at any attempt to use a variable name as the first operand of a "StoreC" or to use a constant value as the first operand of a "Move". (This is not so mystical as it may sound: location names must begin with a letter of the alphabet; constants must begin with a digit or a numerical sign and subsequent characters must all be digits. All the assembler does is check operands against these criteria to discriminate between variables and constants.) Line 3, "StoreC 1 R1," places the value "1" in R1. Lines 6 and 7 of the program illustrate how the computer does arithmetic. Values to be operated on must be stored in registers, in this case register one ("R1") and register two ("R2"). The results of any arithmetical operation ("Add R1 R2") are stored in the accumulator. This is why the "Store" instruction at line 7 uses the accumulator as the source of its data. The CPU after the execution of Cycle 2 contains:

3 StoreC 1 R1	
Operation	18
Operand 1	1
Operand 2	1
Location	9
Accumulator	0
R1	1
R2	0
R3	0
R4	0

Figure 3.29. Loading a constant into a register.

The text display area explains the fetch and execute steps of this cycle:

```
Fetch Step Cycle: 2
>> 3 StoreC 1 R1
18 1 1
Location Register: 9

Exec Step Cycle: 2
Store value 1 in Register 1.
Instruction Register: 18 1 1
Location Register: 9
Accumulator: 0
R1 = 1; R2 = 0; R3 = 0; R4 = 0
```

The CPU contents after the execution of the "Add R1 R2" instruction show the accumulator containing the result of the addition of the contents of "R1" and "R2":

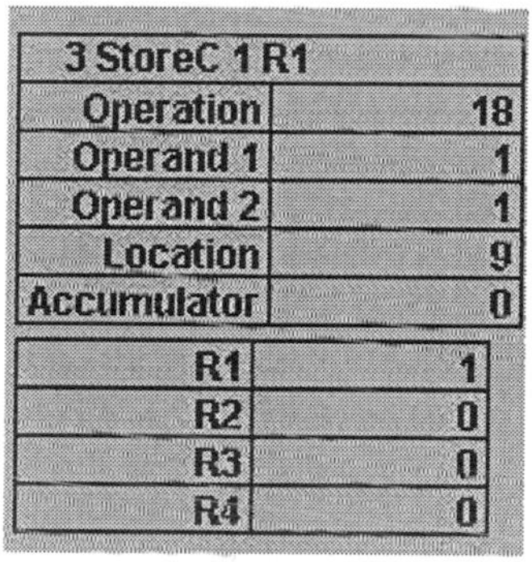

3 StoreC 1 R1	
Operation	18
Operand 1	1
Operand 2	1
Location	9
Accumulator	0

R1	1
R2	0
R3	0
R4	0

Figure 3.30. Accumulator holding result.

The explanation for this cycle is:

```
Fetch Step Cycle: 5
>> 6 Add R1 R2
4 1 2
Location Register: 18

Exec Step Cycle: 5
1 + 5 = 6
Instruction Register: 4 1 2
Location Register: 18
Accumulator: 6
R1 = 1; R2 = 5; R3 = 0; R4 = 0
```

"R1" contains "1," "R2" contains "5," and the accumulator holds the sum of "R1" and "R2": "6." The value contained in the accumulator is placed in memory location "Count" by the next instruction: "Store AC Count":

3	26	6	14	0	0	18	1	1	15
1	1	2	1	2	4	1	2	16	0
1	15	1	1	13	0	0	2	0	0

Figure 3.31. Store accumulator value in location "Count."

The next two instructions display the new value stored in "Count" and halt execution. These instructions operate in the same way as the "Store" and "Display" instructions in the "Swap" program and require no further explanation.

Readers should assemble and execute this program and use the trace file to answer any questions. The step-by-step mode of compilation is designed to allow an unhurried chase and unperturbed pace. The "TURBO C" and "TURBO E" buttons can be used whenever readers find "deliberate speed" is called for. They are used respectively to compile and execute the current program automatically without repeated button pushing. Any of the programs can be compiled, loaded, and executed by pressing in turn only three buttons: "TURBO C," "LOAD," and "TURBO E."

BRANCHING AND LOOPING

The two programs we have looked at so far both execute their instructions in sequential order. Computers are designed to execute instructions serially unless they encounter an explicit branching instruction. As we have seen with the Turing machine, branching is crucial to the operation of a programmable machine. The next program I examine, the "Loop" program, makes use of branching instructions. This is a very important topic and one whose complexity should be approached at an unhurried pace (Fig. 3.32).

This program's data section stores the value 5 in memory "Location1." Line 3 displays the value currently stored in "Location1" and line 4 loads the value just displayed into "R1." It repeats the sequence of instructions from line 3 to line 9 a total of five times. Each time it goes through this loop, instruction 6 subtracts 1 from the value stored in "Location1" and line 8 then stores the result in the accumulator in "Location1." Each pass through the loop produces a value in "Location1" that is 1 less than on the preceding pass. The instruction at line 9, "Jump 3," is an unconditional branching instruction which takes the program back to line 3,[7] where it resumes its sequential execution through the loop, displaying, loading, and decreasing by 1 the value stored in "Location1." It is line 7 ("JumpZ 10") that prevents the program from going into an endless loop. This instruction is a conditional branching instruction. It tests the value stored in the accumulator to determine whether to branch to line 10, the "Stop" instruction. "JumpZ" stands for

1	Dim	Location1	1:5
2	Go	*	*
3	Display	Location1	1
4	Move	Location1	R1
5	StoreC	1	R2
6	Sub	R1	R2
7	JumpZ	10	*
8	Store	AC	Location1
9	Jump	3	*
10	Stop	*	*
11	End	*	*

Figure 3.32. Loop program.

"Branch if the accumulator is zero." It branches only when the accumulator holds the value 0, which it will after five passes through the loop.

Readers should assemble the program using the "TURBO C" option, and step through the first one or two executions of the loop, paying particular attention to the way in which the "Jump" instruction changes the value in the location register and hence the sequence of instructions executed. When a "Jump" instruction is fetched from memory, the value in the location register is increased by three as it is with any instruction. Every instruction for our virtual machine takes up three memory locations. In adding three to the address of the instruction just fetched, the machine is assuming that its instructions are to be executed sequentially (Fig. 3.33).

The text display area for fetching and executing this instruction gives the relevant explanation:

```
Fetch Step Cycle: 8
>> 9 Jump 3 *
9 6 0
Location Register: 27

Exec Step Cycle: 8
Unconditional branch;
get the next instruction from memory location: 6
Instruction Register: 9 6 0
Location Register: 6
Accumulator: 4
R1 = 5; R2 = 1; R3 = 0; R4 = 0
```

The location register at the beginning of Cycle 8 contains the value "27" and at the end of Cycle 8 it contains the value "6." In the "Loop" program, the "Jump 3 *" instruction is stored at location 24. After it is fetched, the Location Register is set

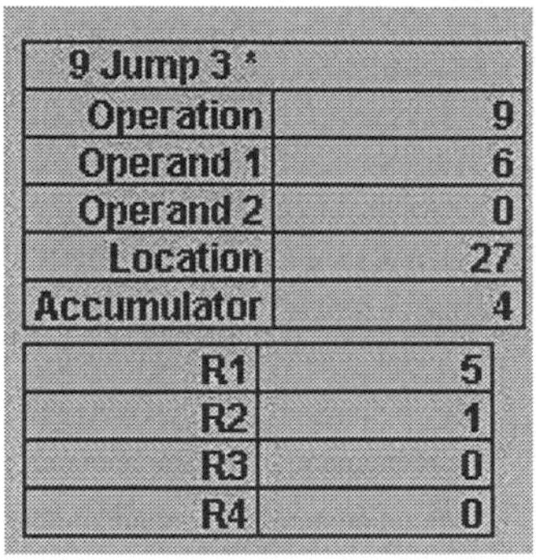

9 Jump 3 *	
Operation	9
Operand 1	6
Operand 2	0
Location	27
Accumulator	4
R1	5
R2	1
R3	0
R4	0

Figure 3.33. CPU fetching a "Jump" instruction.

to location 27 (see Fig. 3.33). But when it is executed, the Jump instruction changes the value of the Location Register to 6, the location of instruction 3 (Fig. 3.34). The next instruction executed is the one stored in memory location 6, "Display Location1 1," rather than the instruction stored at location 27.

The program will display the decreasing values stored in "Location1" as it loops through its instruction until subtracting 1 from the value in "Location1" places the value "0" in the Accumulator. The "JumpZ 10 *" at line 7 of the program will then transfer control to the "Stop" instruction and the program will halt. This occurs in Cycle 34, the trace file for which reads:

```
Fetch Step Cycle: 34
>> 7 JumpZ 10 *
10 27 0
Location Register: 21

Exec Step Cycle: 34
Branch if the accumulator is zero.
The accumulator is 0;
```

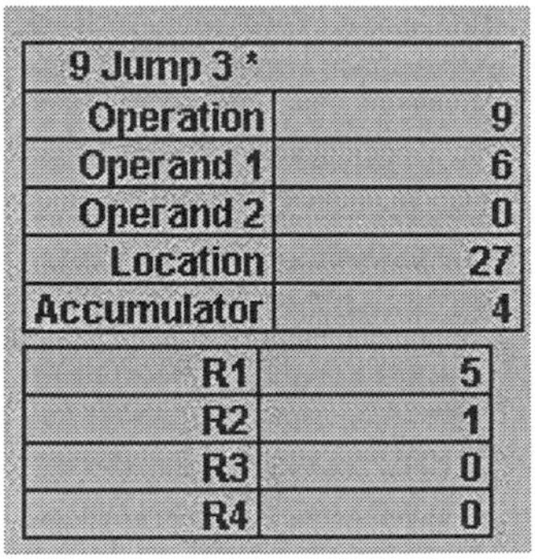

9 Jump 3 *	
Operation	9
Operand 1	6
Operand 2	0
Location	27
Accumulator	4
R1	5
R2	1
R3	0
R4	0

Figure 3.34. Effect of "Jump" instruction on location register asm31.

get the next instruction from memory location 27.
Instruction Register: 10 27 0
Location Register: 27
Accumulator: 0
R1 = 1; R2 = 1; R3 = 0; R4 = 0

Location 27 is where the "Stop" instruction is stored, so the program halts at the next cycle:

Fetch Step Cycle: 6
>> 7 JumpZ 10 *
10 27 0
Location Register: 21

Exec Step Cycle: 6
Branch if the accumulator is zero.
The value in the accumulator (4) is not 0;
get the next instruction from memory location 21.
Instruction Register: 10 27 0
Location Register: 21
Accumulator: 4
R1 = 5; R2 = 1; R3 = 0; R4 = 0

Fetch Step Cycle: 13
>> 7 JumpZ 10 *
10 27 0
Location Register: 21

Exec Step Cycle: 13
Branch if the accumulator is zero.
The value in the accumulator (3) is not 0;
get the next instruction from memory location 21.
Instruction Register: 10 27 0
Location Register: 21
Accumulator: 3
R1 = 4; R2 = 1; R3 = 0; R4 = 0

Fetch Step Cycle: 20
>> 7 JumpZ 10 *
10 27 0
Location Register: 21

Exec Step Cycle: 20
Branch if the accumulator is zero.
The value in the accumulator (2) is not 0;
get the next instruction from memory location 21.
Instruction Register: 10 27 0

Location Register: 21
Accumulator: 2
R1 = 3; R2 = 1; R3 = 0; R4 = 0
Fetch Step Cycle: 27
>> 7 JumpZ 10 *
10 27 0
Location Register: 21

Exec Step Cycle: 27
Branch if the accumulator is zero.
The value in the accumulator (1) is not 0;
get the next instruction from memory location 21.
Instruction Register: 10 27 0
Location Register: 21
Accumulator: 1
R1 = 2; R2 = 1; R3 = 0; R4 = 0

Fetch Step Cycle: 34
>> 7 JumpZ 10 *
10 27 0
Location Register: 21

Exec Step Cycle: 34
Branch if the accumulator is zero.
The accumulator is 0;
get the next instruction from memory location 27.
Instruction Register: 10 27 0
Location Register: 27
Accumulator: 0
R1 = 1; R2 = 1; R3 = 0; R4 = 0

Fetch Step Cycle: 35
>> 10 Stop * *
13 0 0
Location Register: 30

Exec Step Cycle: 35
Stop instruction; halting execution.

Fetch Step Cycle: 35
>> 10 Stop * *
13 0 0
Location Register: 30

Exec Step Cycle: 35
Stop instruction; halting execution.

Halt Step
Stop instruction; halting execution.

Instruction Register: 13 0 0
Location Register: 30
Accumulator: 0
R1 = 1; R2 = 1; R3 = 0; R4 = 0

Figure 3.35. Partial Listing of Loop Trace File

A partial listing of the trace file shows how the machine steps through the successive conditional and unconditional branching instructions (Fig. 3.35).

In programs containing looping and branching, a given instruction may be executed any number of times as determined by the program. At execution cycles 6, 13, 20, and 27, the value in the accumulator is not 0 so the next instruction is fetched from memory location 19. This causes the unconditional jump instruction to be executed at cycles 8, 15, 22, and 29. The unconditional jump sets the location register to memory location 6 so that the "Display" instruction stored there is the next instruction executed. At execution cycle 34, the value in the accumulator is 0 so the next instruction is taken from location 27, where the assembler stored the "Stop" instruction.

Readers may step through the loop once or twice to get an idea of the iterated execution of the instructions in the loop and then use the "TURBO E" button to make the program run uninterrupted to the end. They may then examine the trace record in the text display area to satisfy themselves about any points that remain unclear.

CALCULATING TABLES OF NUMBERS: HOMAGE TO CHARLES BABBAGE

The final assembler program we will consider in this discussion, the "Table" program, combines calculation and branching to produce a small table of numbers. In part, the program is homage to Charles Babbage whose original inspiration for his Difference Engine was to use it for the rapid and accurate calculation of tables of logarithms and navigational tables, which to date had to be laboriously calculated and checked "by hand."

1	Dim	Value	1:1
2	Dim	Power	1:8
3	Dim	HoldA	1:0
4	Dim	Results	8:0
5	Dim	Count	1:5
6	Go	*	*
7	MoveA	Results	R4
8	Store	R4	HoldA
9	StoreC	1	R1
10	Move	Power	R2
11	Display	Value	1
12	Set	Value	R3
13	Mult	R2	R3
14	Store	AC	Value
15	Store	AC	Results
16	MoveA	Results	R3
17	Add	R3	R1
18	StoreA	AC	Results
19	Move	Count	R3
20	Sub	R3	R1
21	JumpZ	24	*
22	Store	AC	Count
23	Jump	11	*
24	Move	HoldA	R1
25	StoreA	R1	Results
26	Display	Results	5
27	Stop	*	*
28	End	*	*

Figure 3.36. The "Calculate" program.

But the calculation of tables of numbers requires us to introduce a new and extremely useful concept, memory pointers, into our program. The "Table" program will produce a small table of the first five exponential powers of 8. This program is a much longer program than the ones we have looked at so far, with much expanded code and data sections. It also takes so many cycles to execute that it produces a listing that is much too long to be included in Appendix B. I include the parts of the program listing that relate to the new features of this program, especially the parts having to do with memory tables. Readers interested in the entire trace listing will find it on the web site.

The data segment of the program has five entries. The first entry sets aside one word of memory under the name "Value" and stores the value "1" in it. The program uses memory location "Value" to store the successive calculated values for the table. The second entry, "Power," will be used to hold the number by which "Value" will be repeatedly multiplied. Its "1:8" operand stores "8" in this location. The program, then, will calculate successive powers of 8. The third entry, "HoldA," will be used as a part of the memory pointer scheme. Its use will be explained below. The fourth entry, "Results," is used to hold the table. Eight successive words are set aside for this table, each with the initial value of "0." The fifth entry, "Count," is decreased by one at each pass through the program's loop and is used to control the number of iterations of the loop. Its initial value of "5" means that the loop will be executed five times as it assumes the successive values "4," "3," "2," "1," "0."[8] The number of times the loop is executed determines the number of entries (five) placed in the table.

The data segment of the program has five entries. As the assembler processes "Dim" statements, it builds a table of the locations that are allocated and their numerical address in memory. At the end of compilation, it writes this table at the end of the code segment and places the offset value to the table in memory location 1. The data segment is placed at the head of our assembler programs because the assembler program needs the information in this segment to assemble the code segment.[9] When the machine code references a variable, the addressing circuit of the CPU uses this table and the offset address to determine the memory address of the variable. It then fetches the value from the memory address it finds in the list. In other words, the table holds the addresses of the memory locations; the memory locations themselves hold the values. The table points to memory locations and is therefore called a table of memory pointers.

Like everything else in the computer, the contents of the memory pointer table are binary numbers. We can perform arithmetic on these numbers just as we could perform arithmetic on the binary numbers of ASCII code. I have made extensive use in the programs thus far of the "Move" and "Store" instructions to move data in and out of the CPU. To move addresses from memory to the CPU I use the "MoveA" instruction as in line 7 of the table program: "MoveA Results R4." This instruction moves the address pointer value associated with "Results" to register 4. Once it is in the CPU, I can perform arithmetic upon it. If its initial value is "3" and

I add "1" to it, the accumulator now holds the value "4." Using the "StoreA" instruction, I can put this value in the memory pointer table position for "Results" and references to "Results" are now to memory location 4, not memory location 3. Programmers must be careful when they do arithmetic with pointers. If by mistake "20" were added to the pointer for "Results," the pointer would reference a location within the code section of the program. If the program stored a value in this "out of bounds" location, it would raise havoc with the program's instructions and most likely cause the computer to crash much as the Turing machine would if it encountered an illegal tape mark.

In the table program, line 7 moves the address of "Results" to register four: "MoveA Results R4." The next line stores this value in memory location "HoldA" for future reference: "Store R4 HoldA." Later on in the program, the value of the address of "Results" will be changed by adding one to it each time the program's loop is executed. This is the way we store the result of each calculation in the table. At the end of the program, the contents of the entire table starting at the original location of "Results" are printed. To do this, the program restores the original value of the "Results" pointer. At line 24 it is moved from memory location "HoldA," where we stored it, to a CPU register ("Move HoldA R1"). At line 25 the contents of that register are stored in the pointer table location for results ("StoreA R1 Results"). The "Display" instruction at line 27 ("Display Results 5") will then begin its display of the results table starting at the original location of "Results":

Exec Step Cycle: 71
Display 5 memory locations starting at Results.

Program Output

8 64 512 4096 32768

Figure 3.37. Table output from Table program.

The program has displayed a one-line table of the first five powers eight, as shown in the highlighted portion of Fig. 3.37. The updating of the location within the program's loop is handled by instructions 16, 17, and 18:

16	MoveA	Results	R3
17	Add	R3	R1
18	StoreA	AC	Results

Figure 3.38. Updating memory reference "results."

A partial list of the trace file for execution cycles 11, 12 and 13 and 69 and 70 gives the details of the execution of these instructions (Fig. 3.39). In cycles 11

Fetch Step Cycle: 11
> 16 MoveA Results R3
3 4 3
Location Register: 47

Exec Step Cycle: 11
Move Address of Results (5) to Register 3.
Instruction Register: 3 4 3
Location Register: 47
Accumulator: 8
R1 = 1; R2 = 8; R3 = 5; R4 = 5

Fetch Step Cycle: 12
>> 17 Add R3 R1
4 3 1
Location Register: 50

Exec Step Cycle: 12
5 + 1 = 6
Instruction Register: 4 3 1
Location Register: 50
Accumulator: 6
R1 = 1; R2 = 8; R3 = 5; R4 = 5

Fetch Step Cycle: 13
>> 18 StoreA AC Results
17 0 4
Location Register: 53

Exec Step Cycle: 13
Store address value 6 from the Accumulator
as memory address of Results.
Instruction Register: 17 0 4

Location Register: 53
Accumulator: 6
R1 = 1; R2 = 8; R3 = 5; R4 = 5

…..

Fetch Step Cycle: 69
>> 24 Move HoldA R1
2 3 1
Location Register: 71

Exec Step Cycle: 69
Move value (5) from HoldA to Register 1.
Instruction Register: 2 3 1
Location Register: 71
Accumulator: 0
R1 = 5; R2 = 8; R3 = 1; R4 = 5

Fetch Step Cycle: 70
>> 25 StoreA R1 Results
17 1 4
Location Register: 74

Exec Step Cycle: 70
Store address value 5 from Register 1
as memory address of Results.
Instruction Register: 17 1 4
Location Register: 74
Accumulator: 0
R1 = 5; R2 = 8; R3 = 1; R4 = 5

Figure 3.39. Partial listing of the table trace file (emphasis added).

through 13, the pointer value is loaded into a CPU register, incremented by 1, and the result in the accumulator is then stored in the memory pointer table. In cycles 69 and 70, the original value of the "Results" pointer is retrieved from "HoldA" and restored to the memory pointer table. The address of "Results" is stored at memory location 83 in the variable pointer table. The value stored there changes after each iteration of the loop. It will begin with value "5," take on the successive values of "6," "7," "8," and "9" and then be reset to "5" before the display instruction that displays the table of values is executed. The program may be said to modify itself in this way as it executes. It provides an example of the typical program self-modification for a control function. Some researchers in artificial intelligence hope that this ability of programs to modify itself, seen here in the course of a routine control function, may be enhanced to the point that programs will be able to learn from experience and grow to consciousness.

VARIETIES OF CPUs

To conclude this discussion of the CPU, we will consider the relationship of our hypothetical, virtual machine to real hardware. Actual CPUs like the Intel Pentium contain not only their own unique set of machine instructions, but also the machine instructions of the earlier Intel CPUs going back to the 8086 that was used in the first PC. This is done to allow programs written for earlier CPUs to be "upwardly compatible" with them. Programs written for earlier CPUs in the 80x86 series will work on the Pentium, but any programs written for (the computer term is "optimized for") the Pentium will not work on earlier machines. This requirement of backward compatibility adds yet another order of complexity to the already complex Pentium.

CPUs are classified according to the complexity of their machine codes. Complex Instruction Set Computers (CISC) like the Intel Pentium have extensive instruction sets in which the lengths of different instructions vary from one to fifteen bytes in length. Reduced Instruction Set Computers (RISC) have fewer instructions that tend to be of uniform length. (According to this criterion, our virtual machine is obviously a RISC design.) Because of their simplified instruction sets, RISC machines can execute their instructions far more quickly than can CISC machines, but they may require more instructions to carry out an algorithm than do CISC machines. Whether CISC processors are inferior to RISC processors is a question of how they are evaluated. RISC machines obviously trade off faster execution of individual instructions against total instructions to be executed. The dispute between RISC and CISC advocates is something like the dispute between MAC users and PC users in which each side has its own favorite benchmark tests and other criteria for evaluation. In practice, there is a tendency to include many features of RISC design in CISC processors like the Pentium.

The most obvious difference between a modern CPU and a Turing machine is the enormous increase in the number of machine instructions for the CPU. This increase in instructions leads to the next important difference between the two, a difference in their execution cycles. What makes a Turing machine programmable is the fact that we can enter any number of instructions in any order into its table of instructions and still control the order in which instructions are executed and hence the operations of the mechanism. The three-step execution cycle of the Turing machine—Move, Mark, Branch—continues indefinitely until a Halt instruction is executed. A CPU has a similar, simpler two step cycle: it fetches an instruction from memory and executes it. As we have seen on our virtual machine, the CPU executes its instructions serially from the starting point, unlike the Turing machine whose every instruction contains a branching operation. Branching is accomplished on the CPU through explicit branching instructions.

The automatic determination of what to do next, however carried out, is the motive force that moves the machine along through its algorithmic steps, the Primum Mobile of cyberspace. Our virtual CPU has illustrated the way in which a CPU executes branch instructions. The CPU allows both unconditional branching at any point in a program as well as a full repertoire of conditional branching operations, controlled through its logical unit. It can branch depending on whether the values in two memory locations are equal to, greater than, or less than, equal to or greater than, or equal to or less than each other. It can also branch according to Boolean logical operations, whether two propositions are true, whether only one is true, or whether neither is true. So rich are the possibilities offered by the CPU for branching that programs can become unintelligible because of excessive branching. Branching instructions introduce considerable complexity, not to mention perplexity, into the operation of the programs run by the CPU. They also account for the power of computer programming in which a small number of steps can control a process of indeterminate, not to say infinite, length.

CHAPTER 4

The World According to Programmers

STRUCTURED, OBJECT-ORIENTED PROGRAMMING

One of the objects I keep on my desk is a small figurine of a shaman made by the American artist William Worrell (Fig. 4.1). Over the past few years, Worrell has produced a series of figures like this one, based stylistically on the cave paintings and petroglyphs of Southwest American Indian culture. I like this particular piece because it was much less elaborate than most of the works in this series, and because of the totem objects the shaman carries. At first glance, the stick and the circle suggest the binary digits. Also, the stick in the right hand is a Y-shaped stick,

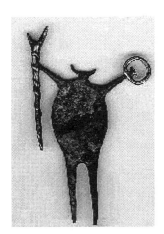

Figure 4.1. William Worrell figurine.

129

suggesting the listing and branching structures of many programs. The left-hand circle suggests the iterative loop as well as binary zero. The totems, then, can be construed as symbolizing both programming code and the data on which the code operates.

A sequential list of instructions is the simplest type of program structure. It is like simple recipes that begin with a box of cake mix, and lead step by step to a plate of rich-chewy-chocolate-frosted brownies. A branch, as we have seen, is a conditional command, to be executed only if a certain condition is satisfied. A recipe for brownies might have additional steps to be performed only if nuts were to be added. A loop is an iterative structure. The instructions in a loop are executed repeatedly until some condition is satisfied. For example, one could add a loop to our fudge brownie recipe that instructed us to repeat the recipe procedure until we had made at least six dozen brownies. The number of times we repeated the recipe would be determined by the cumulative yield of successive batches of brownies. (If something went wrong with the oven or if we ran out of brownie mix, we would never exit the loop.) To understand the world according to programmers, we need to make full use of the shaman's totems of zero, one, list, branch, and loop. With these totems, programmers construct and control cyberspace.

Programs are structured lists of machine instructions that the computer executes sequentially unless it encounters a branching instruction. The "Swap" and "Counter" assembler programs we examined in Chapter 3 are illustrations of this list structure. The canons of good programming style stipulate that the basic structure of every program be a list that reads from top to bottom. As we saw with the Loop and Table programs, computers have the ability to execute instructions in any desired order through the use of branching instructions. In our Turing machine, each instruction included a branch to the next machine state contingent on the contents of the current tape frame. It is, after all, the order in which instructions are carried out, not the order in which they are written down, that describes the procedure followed by the machine.

Every algorithm needs a starting point and an ending point but there is no need that they be respectively the first and last instructions on a list. The problem with excessive use of branching instructions becomes evident as soon as a typical program becomes longer than about thirty or forty instructions. Trying to follow the logical flow of control of a long program can become more an exercise in page flipping than in analysis. Programmers have coined the term "spaghetti code" to characterize the involuted sequence of instructions that poorly written programs follow in carrying out their algorithms.

To make program code easily intelligible, programmers invented and adopted the practice of structured programming ("*il dolce stil nuovo*," the sweet, new style), the first rules of which were to arrange instructions in sequential lists, to keep these lists as short as possible, and to avoid excessive use of branching instructions. Ideally, no list was to be longer than a page in length. Lengthy programs were to be broken up into shorter procedures. Programs were to consist of a main list that gave an overview of a program's algorithm followed by a series of subordinate lists that carried out the details of the algorithm. The purpose of this was to make structured programs much more comprehensible than their spaghetti code equivalents so that one programmer could readily understand and modify code written by another programmer. (If the CPU had a point of view about the style of the instructions it was given to execute, it would fall somewhere in the range between Olympian disdain and frigid indifference. The CPU takes things one at time, however they come.)

All of the programs discussed in this chapter will conform to the canons of structured programming. Because they are structured programs, they are far more intelligible than they would otherwise be. But this is not to say that they are self-explanatory or, to use the term preferred by programmers, self-documenting. Early in the history of software, program analysts realized that there was a real problem with the intelligibility of computer languages. Assembler languages, tied as they were to the specific hardware of different machines, were inherently opaque. They could not be understood in detail without extensive knowledge of the hardware they were designed to control. Early higher level languages like FORTRAN (short for Formula Translation) were somewhat better in this regard because they focused attention more on steps of the algorithm used to solve the problem at hand than on the step-by-step working of the CPU.[1]

Languages like COBOL, PL/I, and Pascal were designed to be "verbose" in the vain hope that this would make them intelligible to others—even nonprogrammers. Donald Knuth, whose contributions to Computer Science are in the same league as von Neumann's, developed his TEX system for computerized typesetting not only to provide high quality typesetting for mathematical and other technical material, but also to show how a complex program could be written to be self-documenting. None of these attempts proved successful in the sense that they have not ushered in an era of consistently self-documented code. Things became better after the widespread adoption of structured programming practices than they had been in the days of spaghetti code. But from the earliest days of programming, programmers have been notoriously bad at documenting their work, and no system as yet devised has made much of a change in this situation.[2] The current languages of choice for general-purpose programming are C, whose syntax is tersely mathematical, and its descendants C+ and C++, and JAVA, all of which share a similar syntax.

The practice of structured programming encouraged the development of increasingly complex programs. But as programs became more and more complex, they became more and more difficult to debug, maintain, and modify. Subtle interactions of instructions combined with unanticipated combinations of data led to bizarre, unreliable results as well as to program and system crashes. This was a paradoxical situation in which fundamental aspects of computing—branching, without which programmability does not exist, and von Neumann architecture, which was the blueprint for all modern digital computers—were as well at the heart of the problems that bedeviled programming. By controlling the tendency of programmers to use excessive branching, structured programming cleared up major problems in the surface structure of programs. But it left problems in the deep structure unaddressed. Von Neumann architecture mixed together the code and data in memory in a way that enabled any piece of code to modify any piece of data or code. Just as the computer's ability to use branching instructions in carrying out its programs had the unintended consequence of permitting spaghetti code, the storage of code and data in common memory had the unintended consequence of producing programs that tended to be operationally flawed.

This situation has been ameliorated by the development of object-oriented programming. In an object-orienting program, data and the program instructions that process the data are tightly bound together—the term for this is encapsulation—so that the data can be manipulated only by the specific program instructions with which it is bundled. Programs, as we have seen with the virtual CPU, are made up of data and program instructions. Object-oriented programs break programs down into encapsulated bundles of data and instructions. These bundles are called objects, hence the term object-oriented programs. Among the useful features of these objects is the fact that they can be easily moved from program to program, thus saving programmers the trouble of constantly reinventing the wheel.

Where structured programming divided programs into small modules for purposes of intelligibility, object-oriented programming divided programs into small modules for purposes of operational integrity. If there is a problem with the way a structured program responds to a mouse click, a programmer will first examine the code that specifically handles the mouse click. In a surprising number of cases, the mouse handling code will check out, and the problem will be traced to some other, unrelated piece of code that is jostling the code for the mouse in some unanticipated way. In object-oriented programming, a problem with the mouse is a problem whose cause will almost inevitably be found in the code specific to the mouse. Object-oriented programs construct "firewalls" around their modules so that potential problems are easily contained and controlled.

One way of thinking about object-oriented programming is to regard it as a way of creating a cyberspace model of parts of the real world that are amenable to representation and manipulation by computer. In object oriented programming, hierarchic classes of complex data structures are defined with properties that resemble aspects of real objects. The properties of objects selected for definition are the ones that the programmer wishes to manipulate. A library management system, for example, might have a class called "holdings" at the top of its hierarchy. Properties for the "holdings" class would include call number, shelf location, availability, and other things common to all library holdings. Derived or descended from this class in a parent–child relationship would be a number of classes for specific categories of holdings such as books, pamphlets, serials, manuscripts, films, photographs, CD-ROMs, etc. Physical attributes of the holdings, for example the weight or the condition and color of the binding of books, would not be defined as properties of their cyberspace simulacrums unless the programmer foresaw some specific need to include them. These derived classes would inherit the properties of the holding class, and have additional attributes for cataloguing bibliographical and other features unique to each derived class. These derived classes of data would have specific code associated with them so that the objects making up the class could be manipulated only by the associated code. The term "methods" is used to describe this code. Technically, object-oriented programming consists of manipulating the properties of objects by means of methods. For example, a manuscript or special collection holding could not be checked out using the method that checked out an ordinary book holding. The data for each specific holding, which would consist of the values for its properties, would thus be encapsulated with the methods that manipulated those properties so that only authorized methods could operate upon the encapsulated properties.

Object-oriented programming is a way of formalizing computer programs so that they are reliable as well as intelligible. The JAVA language we will be using in this discussion is designed to enable programmers to create two types of program objects: applications and applets. Application programs are just that: programs written to carry out some task on a system. Their great advantage is that they can run without change on different types of machines as long as the machine chosen to run them is equipped with a JAVA virtual machine. Applets are programs that are run from a Web page by means of a browser program like Netscape or Internet Explorer that come equipped with a JAVA virtual machine to run applets. Applets are potentially great sources of mischief since they enable the creator of a Web page to run any program she or he chooses on the computer accessing the Web page. This turns any JAVA applet into a potential virus that can steal, change, or trash anything on its host computer. Sun Microsystems, the developer of JAVA, has therefore gone to great lengths to encapsulate the JAVA applet class so that it cannot do anything harmful to its host. These precautions include obvious ones, such as not allowing an applet to access its host's file systems, to very subtle technical adjustments and restrictions that apply to JAVA applets but not to JAVA applications.

The Turing machine and virtual CPU programs are written as applets. An examination of their code, as provided by the book's dedicated Web page, reveals sections such as the following from the virtual CPU program, which is the code of the Swap program that it compiles and executes.

```
strProg1[0] = "0 Program Swap";
strProg1[1] = "1 Dim Location1 1:50";
strProg1[2] = "2 Dim Location2 1:100";
strProg1[3] = "3 Go * *";
strProg1[4] = "4 Display Location1 2";
strProg1[5] = "5 Move Location1 R1";
```

```
strProg1[6] = "6 Move Location2 R2";
strProg1[7] = "7 Store R1 Location2";
strProg1[8] = "8 Store R2 Location1";
strProg1[9] = "9 Display Location1 2";
strProg1[10] = "10 Stop * *";
strProg1[11] = "11 End * *";
```

If the virtual CPU program were rewritten as an application rather than an applet, it would not contain the programs it executed. They would be written as separate text files and, rather than selecting a program from a short list in a choice box, one would select a program from a standard menu "file/open" dialog.

The way in which object-oriented programming consists of methods applied to objects may be illustrated with a few lines of program code from the virtual CPU program. Readers will recall that the interface to this program contains three buttons whose label changes as the program proceeds from phase to phase. At the end of the compilation phase, the left-most button, which is the only one that is enabled at this point, is labeled "LOAD." The names assigned to these buttons, for reasons that need not concern us here, are, from left to right "IDOK," "IDCANCEL2," and "IDC_BUTTON1." To the programmer, each of these buttons is a "button" object with properties, among which are a label and a status that is either enabled or disabled. All the objects on the screen—the selection boxes, labels, text display area, etc.—are part of a Window object called "builder" out of which the screen display for the virtual CPU is built. We refer to the buttons on the "builder" window as "builder.IDOK," "builder.IDCANCEL2," and "builder.IDC_BUTTON1," thus assuring that it is the button on this screen and no other to which we refer. When we push the "LOAD" button, we use the "setLabel" and "enable" methods to change the labels on the three buttons and to enable the buttons now labeled "HALT" and "TURBO E".

```
builder.IDC_BUTTON1.setLabel("HALT");
builder.IDCANCEL2.setLabel("TURBO E");
builder.IDC_BUTTON1.enable();
builder.IDCANCEL2.enable();
...
builder.IDOK.setLabel("FETCH");
```

I will discuss object-oriented programming in detail in the next two sections.

PROGRAMMING A GRAPHICAL USER INTERFACE

A brief description of how an object like the builder Window is constructed, which will entail some explanation of its inner workings, illustrates how a Graphical User Interface (GUI) works. Constructing the object is a three-step process:

Draw the GUI object by placing controls in an empty dialog box;
Assign names and initial values to the properties of the controls;
Write code to integrate the object into the program.

I use a program development tool called Visual J++ to construct this window. Readers are not assumed to be using this program in the course of the discussion whose overall purpose is to explain how programming looks from a programmer's point of view. Visual J++ simplifies the process of laying out the window, of integrating with the program applet (in this case the virtual CPU), and testing its operation.

The Microsoft J++ Development Studio uses the term "project" to keep track of the files associated with developing a JAVA applet or application. It assigns a separate "workspace" or file directory for each project. The virtual CPU program for the Web page was named "VM2" because it was the second, applet version of this virtual machine, an earlier version of which, "VM1," was developed as an application. J++ provides the programmer with a graphical overview of the files in a project (Fig. 4.2).

In the left-hand window we see that there are four major pieces in this project: "DialogLayout.java," "IDD_DIALOG1.java," "vm2.java," and "vm2.rct." In the

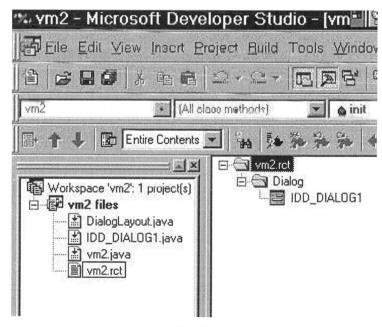

Figure 4.2. The VM2 directory workspace.

right-hand window, we see a breakdown of the contents of "vm2.rct." This break-down informs us that "vm2.rct" is a directory with a subdirectory called "Dialog" in which resides a file called "IDD_DIALOG1." J++ uses the term "Dialog" to refer to a window such as our builder window that provides a graphical user interface for a program. The term "dialog" reflects the fact that this window is a two-way window with which a user gets information from and provides information to the program.

J++ simplifies development of a JAVA program by automating the process of constructing the interface for a program. Of the four pieces of the VM2 project, the programmer writes only one, "vm2.java." This part of the project is what one thinks of as the program instructions. It contains the directions for compiling, loading, and executing the virtual machine programs. The programmer actually writes the code it contains line by line. The two other "java" files, "IDD_DIALOG1.java" and "DialogLayout.java," are generated automatically by J++ from the contents of dialog file "IDD_DIALOG1" in file "vm2.rct." This file contains a layout of the builder window, which the programmer draws with tools provided by J++.

Graphical user interfaces work on the principle that every object they display on a screen is itself a specialized window. A user tends to think of a window as a fairly large area on the computer's screen. But to the programmer, menu bars, buttons, etc. are windows as well, though in their case they are windows that are fixed in a specific size and location on what users think of as a window. Because JAVA was designed as a language in which its programs would have graphical user interfaces, it provides as part of its structure the standard interface controls with which users are familiar: text display and input areas, buttons, choice boxes, etc. But JAVA was also designed so that JAVA programs would run on a variety of machines running a variety of operating systems. This meant that the screen display functions for the objects it displayed were fairly abstract and complex entities. For every button attached at a particular location on a window, the programmer had to specify its size, caption, location, etc., as well as keeping track of its position, size, and alignment with every other object on the screen. For the programmer, this meant seemingly endless adjustments of various numerical parameters. J++ relieves the programmer of this chore by providing the means to layout the interface graphically.

At the beginning of the design process for a graphical interface, J++ provides a canvas in the form of a primitive dialog box containing two buttons and a palette with which to draw the interface (Fig. 4.3). The toolbox contains the standard Windows controls: command buttons, check boxes, radio buttons, scrollbars, dropdown boxes, text boxes, labels, etc. I place controls on the dialog box by selecting them one at a time from the toolbox with the mouse and dragging them to the positions we want them to occupy on the dialog box. Once a control is placed on the dialog box, it can be repositioned, relabeled, and resized. With some dragging, dropping, resizing and repositioning, I created the interface. This inter-face contains eight objects (Fig. 4.4). The objects on the window include three buttons, two labels, two choice boxes, and a text display area.

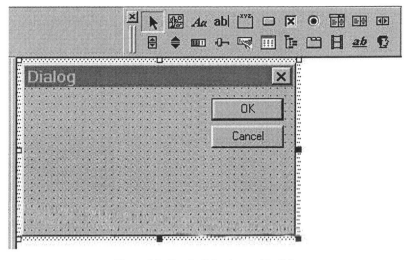

Figure 4.3. Empty dialog box and toolkit.

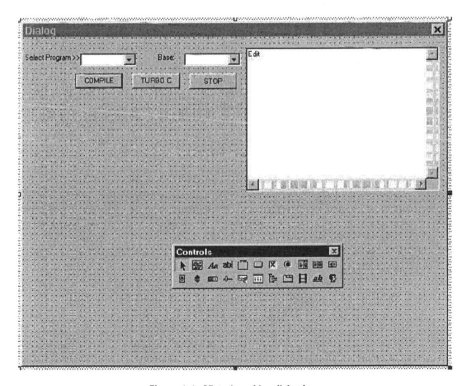

Figure 4.4. Virtual machine dialog box.

J++ assigns names and default properties to the objects placed in the dialog box. I can discover and alter these through the property window associated with each object. I call up the property window by selecting the object and clicking on it with the right-hand mouse button (Fig. 4.5). The "Styles" and "Extended Styles" tabs provide access to all the properties of this button object and their default settings. I can change these properties, as I have changed the caption property to read "COMPILE," by making entries on this screen. This sets the label on button "IDOK" to read "COMPILE" initially. As we have seen already, we can use the "setLabel" method to change this label as needed with program code.

Good programming practice requires that objects be given names descriptive of their content and usage rather than vague, general ones. A memory location used to hold the percentage discount would be called something like "PercentDiscount" rather than "p" or "d." We accept the very general names for these screen objects rather than renaming them with descriptive names, as good programming style requires, because this code is generated automatically by the J++ program, and the names themselves are all we really need to know. Toward automatically generated code, programmers generally observe a hands-off policy. The interface for the virtual CPU has five controls attached to its window. The dialog toolbox assigns them the names presented in Fig. 4.6. I will refer to these objects by the names thus assigned.

To generate program instructions that describe these objects, all that is necessary is that I save the dialog file and then select "Tools/JAVA Resource Wizard" from the J++ menu. This adds the two JAVA files necessary for the interface to our

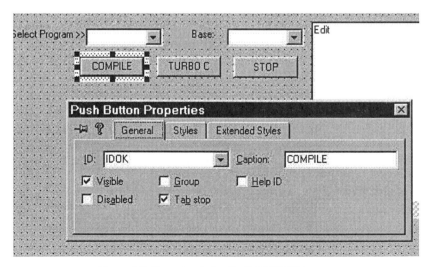

Figure 4.5. Property window for "COMPILE" button.

Object Name	Object Description
IDOK	Left Button
IDC_CANCEL2	Middle Button
IDC_BUTTON1	Right Button
IDC_COMBO1	Program Selection Dropdown Box
IDC_COMBO2	Numerical Base Selection Box
IDC_EDIT1	Text Display Area

Figure 4.6. Names of screen objects.

project. These files contain, for example, the following code that places the buttons, boxes, and labels, properly sized and shaped, exactly where we placed them on our window:

```
IDOK = new Button ("COMPILE");
m_Parent.add(IDOK);
m_Layout.setShape(IDOK, 55, 35, 50, 14);

IDC_COMBO1 = new Choice ();
m_Parent.add(IDC_COMBO1);
m_Layout.setShape(IDC_COMBO1, 60, 15, 60, 15);

IDC_COMBO2 = new Choice ();
m_Parent.add(IDC_COMBO2);
m_Layout.setShape(IDC_COMBO2, 170, 15, 60, 15);

IDC_STATIC1 = new Label ("Select Program >>", Label.RIGHT);
m_Parent.add(IDC_STATIC1);
m_Layout.setShape(IDC_STATIC1, 0, 15, 60, 10);

IDC_EDIT1 = new TextArea ("");
m_Parent.add(IDC_EDIT1);
m_Layout.setShape(IDC_EDIT1, 235, 10, 205, 140);

IDC_STATIC2 = new Label ("Base:", Label.RIGHT);
m_Parent.add(IDC_STATIC2);
m_Layout.setShape(IDC_STATIC2, 130, 15, 30, 15);

IDCANCEL2 = new Button ("TURBO C");
m_Parent.add(IDCANCEL2);
m_Layout.setShape(IDCANCEL2, 115, 35, 50, 14);

IDC_BUTTON1 = new Button ("STOP");
m_Parent.add(IDC_BUTTON1);
m_Layout.setShape(IDC_BUTTON1, 175, 35, 50, 15);
```

Readers won't understand the details of this code but should be able to appreciate the difficulty of getting the proper values for all the numerical parameters, which determine the size and position of each object on the screen. Any change in these numbers changes the position and size of an object on the screen. Getting all these parameters generated automatically and correctly is reason enough for programmers to be grateful for such tools.

We are now ready to examine how the code that was generated for the dialog box is integrated with the "vm2.java" code that implements the virtual machine. To connect the interface to the application, I wrote a procedure called an event or action handler that connects what happens on the dialog box to what happens in the virtual machine. The action handler for the virtual CPU reads as follows:

```
public boolean action(Event e, Object o)
{
  int i;
  if ("EXEC".equals((String)o)) ExecStep();
  else if ("STOP".equals((String)o)) HaltCompiler();
  else if ("TURBO C".equals((String)o)) TurboCStep();
  else if ("TURBO E".equals((String)o)) TurboEStep();
  else if ("COMPILE".equals((String)o)) CompileStep();
  else if ("LOAD".equals((String)o)) LoadStep();
  else if ("FETCH".equals((String)o)) FetchStep();
  else if ("HALT".equals((String)o)) HaltProg();
  else if (e.target == builder.IDC_COMBO2) repaint();
  else if (e.target == builder.IDC_COMBO1)
    {
    instruction = 0;
    iGoToggle = 1;
    strMsg = "";
    if (builder.IDC_COMBO1.getSelectedItem().equals("Swap"))
      {
      ProgLoad(strProg1);
      }
    else if(builder.IDC_COMBO1.getSelectedItem().equals("Count"))
      {
      ProgLoad(strProg2);
      }
    else if(builder.IDC_COMBO1.getSelectedItem().equals("Loop"))
      {
      ProgLoad(strProg3);
      }
    else if(builder.IDC_COMBO1.getSelectedItem().equals("Table"))
      {
      ProgLoad(strProg4);
      }
    }
    return false;
}
```

This procedure is a typical piece of structured program code. The left and right braces in this code function to parse the algorithm into distinct, nested steps when more than one line of code is needed to accomplish a particular step. In this code, only one instruction ("repaint()") takes care of the IDC_COMBO2 control, which causes the screen to be repainted when a user changes the numerical base of the display. Control IDC_COMBO1 is used to select the program to be compiled and run. To implement it requires four separate steps, one for each of the four programs. The use of indentations in this code emphasizes the divisions made by the brackets. These indentations are not necessary to the functioning of the code the way the braces are. Programmers indent the code to make the structure of the code readily apparent to anyone examining the code.

The event handler lays out the alternatives for each action to which the program is to respond through a sequence of "if...else" conditional branches that cover each action the program responds to, and puts the details of each event in a separate procedure of its own. The first eight conditions from "if("EXEC..." to "else if(Halt ... relate to button labels. They connect with the buttons by reading the label on the button as it is pushed. They work by giving each separate button label its own event method named for the program's response to the button that invokes it. Their names and functions are given in Fig. 4.7. Because the programmer is responsible for writing the instructions for these methods, their names are specific and descriptive, rather than simply unique. The other contingencies deal with the choice boxes that either change the numerical base of the display (IDC_COMBO2) or select the program to be run (IDC_COMBO1). Changing the numerical base causes the screen to be redrawn using the newly selected base. Picking a program name causes that program to be loaded for compilation.

Event Method Name	Button Label	Program Response
ExecStep()	**EXEC**	Execute the current Instruction
HaltCompiler()	**STOP**	Halt the compiler
TurboCStep()	**TURBO C**	Run compiler automatically
TurboEStep()	**TURBO C**	Run program automatically
CompileStep()	**COMPILE**	Compile the current instruction
LoadStep()	**LOAD**	Load program into memory
FetchStep()	**FETCH**	Fetch next instruction from memory
HaltProg()	**HALT**	Halt program execution

Figure 4.7. Button labels and methods.

The overall structure of this procedure, which is the control procedure for the entire virtual CPU program, is a closed loop, as may be seen from the flow chart of the procedure in Fig. 4.8. The branching points in the program are represented as diamond-shaped boxes with one entry point and two exit points ("Yes" and "No") illustrating the alternative branches. This loop appears at this level to be closed or infinite as it has no visible exit. In this it resembles our first Turing machine program which continued its relentless move to the right. But the program does have an exit point that is activated by the "HALT" button. A more detailed flow chart, which gives the methods associated with the labels of the three buttons, shows this (Fig. 4.9). In this diagram, the bottom-right "HALT" branch point links to the "HaltProg" method that is used to halt execution. This flowchart also makes clear the way in which the virtual CPU program is structured and object-oriented with encapsulated instructions for each object. A final flowchart (Fig. 4.10), showing the layout of the

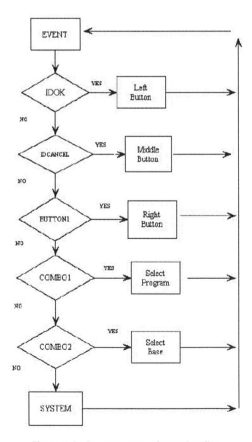

Figure 4.8. Loop structure of event handler.

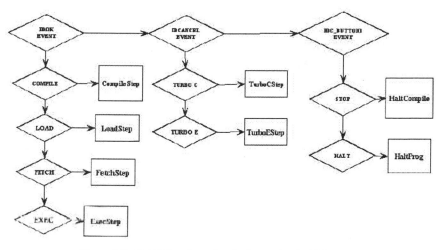

Figure 4.9. Detail flowchart of methods associated with buttons.

"Turbo E" button procedure, shows how objects are reused in building new methods. Here, the "FetchStep" and "ExecStep" methods are combined in a control loop that calls them in turn until a "Stop" instruction is executed.

The control section of any GUI program resembles the one for the virtual CPU program. When an event such as clicking a button occurs, it is first detected by the operating system. GUI operating systems like Windows keep track of such things as:

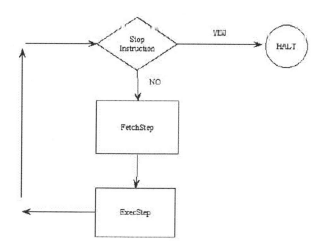

Figure 4.10. "Turbo E" procedure flowchart.

the position of the mouse,
every window that is currently open,
the size and position of every window on the screen,
what portion of a window is visible or hidden by another window,
the position of every control object on every window,
what application owns what window.

The Windows operating system regards each window as an object with its own set of properties, and each control as a special kind of window that is attached to and nested within the window that contains it. When an event like a mouse click occurs, the operating system determines the window on which the mouse is positioned when the click occurred. The operating system then sends a message to the application that owns the window informing it of the type of event (Click) and the location in x and y coordinates of the mouse at the time the click occurred. The application (in this case the JAVA virtual machine) determines from the x and y coordinates in the message on which of its control objects the mouse is positioned, and passes on the message to control object. The control object (vm2) determines which of its control objects (say a button labeled "COMPILE") is designated by the mouse position, and applies the method (CompileStep) designated by the event. The method "CompileStep" produces the desired result. We see here the object oriented model that makes modern graphical operating systems possible. There is a clear hierarchy of objects here—system, application, window, control—nested to whatever depth a given situation requires, with each level of the hierarchy defined by the windows, properties, and methods of its objects. The control is contained within the window, the window within the application, and the application within the system.

What happens when a command button is pushed is completely within the control of the program encapsulated within the object. If no code is supplied for an object, the operating system and application take the standard action defined for the object and event. With a command button, the standard action is to do nothing, since a command button is placed on a window in the expectation that some specific method is going to be encapsulated with it. To understand how the application responds to the event, one must first understand the concept of focus, which is a very important concept for understanding how a graphical user interface works. Though any number of windows may be opened on the screen of a graphical user interface, only one window can be active at a time, that is, capable of responding to a user's command. This is the window that is sometimes referred to as "on top." Also, within the active window, only one control at a time can be used. The currently active control on the currently active window is said to have the focus. When we are clicking a command button, the command button has the focus. When we are entering data into a text display area, the text area has the focus.

Graphical operating systems are event-driven rather than procedural. The programs for counting, swapping, looping, and calculating a table of values we have looked at in Chapter 3 are all procedural because they have a distinct beginning, middle, and end that is defined by the sequential list of their code and the data supplied to them at the start. In a procedural program, execution proceeds from start to end with the sequence of all its branches and loops predefined. The exact path of execution is determined by the data the program encounters as it executes. In graphical user interface programs, functions are distributed among subroutines bound to various controls and the order in which functions are carried out is up to the user. Using a procedural program is like playing a tune recorded on a player piano role. Using a graphical interface program is like improvising variations with the piano's keys.

ALGORITHMS + DATA STRUCTURES + INTERFACES = PROGRAMS

There are three things that programmers must think about in developing a program: the algorithmic steps that will process the data, the structure of the data, and the interface. In the preceding section, we saw how the J++ environment simplifies the development of a GUI. In this section, I will continue the discussion of how programmers look at data structures and algorithms through the lens of the J++ environment. I will show how the J++ environment enables programmers to step through JAVA programs one instruction at a time in the same way that we stepped through the Turing machine and virtual CPU programs in the preceding two chapters. They do this to insure that the program operates properly or to find the point at which a program misfires in some way. Readers are not expected to have access to the J++ environment. They will, however, run several JAVA applications as part of the exercises for this chapter. These are stand alone JAVA applications that run as separate programs rather than as "applets" on a Web page accessed with a browser program.

Programmers have always recognized the close connection between data and algorithms. One might even say that the von Neumann architecture, in intermixing data and code in memory, looked at this connection and found it good. Three decades ago, Nicklaus Wirth in his classic *Algorithms + Data Structures = Programs* put Algorithms first in his titular equation. But in his "Preface," as he traces the then current state of programming theory, he admits that thinking of algorithms before data structures is somehow counterintuitive: "...decisions about structuring data cannot be made without knowledge of the algorithms applied to the data and that, vice versa, the structure and choice of algorithms often strongly depend on the structure of the underlying data. In short, the subjects of program composition and data structures are inseparably linked...Yet, this book starts with a chapter on data structure for two reasons. First, one has an intuitive feeling that data precede algorithms: you must have some objects before you can perform operations." (Wirth's second reason is that his book is intended as an advanced text, the purpose of which was to build on the assumed familiarity of programmer readers with algorithms.) The step-by-step execution of JAVA code made possible by the J++ Development Suite enables programmers to observe the interaction of data and code as it occurs.

In quantum mechanics, physicists use a mathematical form of "doublethink" to manipulate the paradoxical wave/particle nature of events at the subatomic level. In programming, programmers use a bit of "triple-think" to manipulate the objects of a GUI. We have already seen how the J++ environment's dialog editor enables programmers to draw a program's GUI by dragging, dropping, and resizing controls on a canvas-like screen. The dialog editor provides the programmer with an "etch-a-sketch" that treats controls as graphical icons. We have also seen how programmers then link methods to these objects so that, for example, an event like the pushing of a button causes a method to be applied to an object's properties. But before drawing the GUI or attaching methods to objects, when programmers make the decision about which controls to use as opposed to where to place them on the screen, they consider the objects as data structures whose content will be used by a processing algorithm. The fact is that screen objects are complex data types with graphical, control, and data attributes. In learning to program, one learns the attributes of these objects and the appropriate contexts in which to reference and manipulate these attributes. I suggest that a new term be added to Wirth's equation: Algorithms + Data Structures + Interfaces = Programs.

The first JAVA program I will consider is a program that will read though a text file and count the number of occurrences of a word in the file. It is a word frequency program. Before considering an algorithm to count the frequency of a word in the text, the programmer must think about the information the program will need and the steps users will follow in operating the program. In working out these details, the programmer will in fact be developing the specifications for the data segment and interface controls of the program. Minimally, the program will need structures and controls for the following:

a control to input the name of the text
a structure to store the name of the text
a structure to hold individual lines from the text
a control to input the word to be counted
a structure to hold the word
a structure to hold the frequency count
a control to display the frequency count
a control to start the count
a control to reset of the program between words
a control to exit from the program

This list illustrates how "inseparably linked" in Wirth's phrase are the algorithm, data, and interface of a program. Any algorithm for determining the frequency of a word in a text manipulates three data structures: the text, the word, and the frequency count. But to enable the algorithm to manipulate these structures, the program must present the user with interface objects that enable the user to request the result and for the program to display it. Algorithms and data structures are inherently complex logical constructs whose formal properties fascinate mathematicians interested in theoretical Computer Science. But without interface structures of some kind, programs embodying algorithms and data structures are useless except as objects of contemplation and logical analysis by theorists. Programming is an applied science. As Quantum Mechanics must take account of the observer, it must take account of the user. The explosive transformation of the Internet into the World Wide Web triggered by the catalyst of a graphical interface browser illustrates how important the "Interface" term of the programming equation really is.

DESIGNING A GRAPHICAL USER INTERFACE

Nonprogrammers and beginning programmers may think of the design of a graphical interface in spatial terms analogous to drawing. Experienced programmers, on the other hand, do not think about placing data structures on an interface as a static and discrete exercise in spatial arrangement. Rather they think of it as part of all of a program's data structures in terms of their temporal as much as their spatial relationships. We have already seen how, for example, the numerical keys of the JAVA calculator reconfigure in accordance with the selection of a numerical base. This program has what is called a "context sensitive" interface and almost all of the programs we have used in this discussion have such interfaces. The important thing to realize is that to the programmer, the context is temporal and determined by a random sequence of temporal events, not spatial and determined by relative position in a list or hierarchy of some sort.

A static and spatial approach to designing the interface to a word frequency program would yield an interface something like that shown in Fig. 4.11. There is nothing "wrong" about this interface. One might argue that it is "intuitively obvious" how to obtain a word frequency count from a text with this program: type the file name and word into the designated boxes, press the "Frequency" button, and the word frequency will appear in the "Result" box.

A dynamic and temporal approach to the design of the interface produces a more compact look (Fig. 4.12). This interface has only two buttons rather than three as the first one, and the "Frequency" button is disabled when the program starts. This tells users that something has to be done before a frequency can be obtained. There is only one text display area on this interface and it contains directions users need to proceed. The "Enter File" box from the first interface has "morphed" into

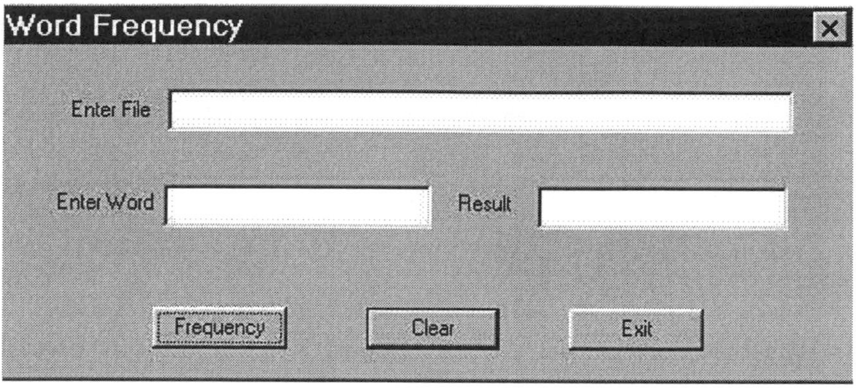

Figure 4.11. Static and spatial word frequency interface.

a File menu with "Open" and "Exit" options. One of the nice features of GUIs is that they free users from the error-prone need to type in file names.

A GUI provides standard file dialog boxes to open, close, save, rename, etc. files. This interface presents the user with a familiar option in its file menu. To select the file to be searched for the word, one uses the standard "File/Open" option. This will cause file "Open" dialog box to appear and allow the user to browse through the file system to locate the desired file. After the file has been selected, the "Frequency" button becomes enabled and the text area is cleared to accept input of the word. The program assumes that the user is capable of remembering and following the now-vanished directions. In the event that the user pushes the

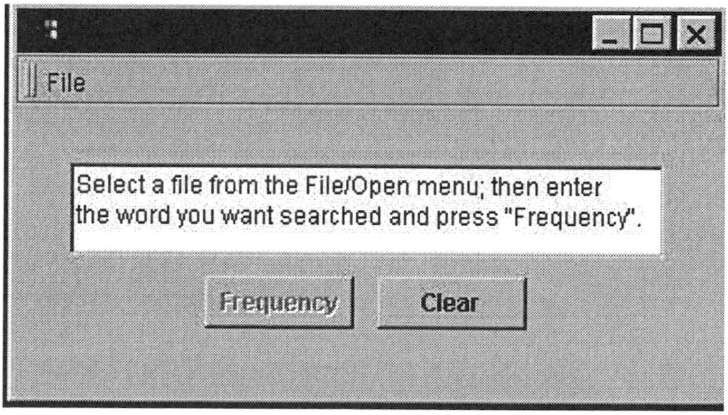

Figure 4.12. Dynamic and temporal word frequency interface.

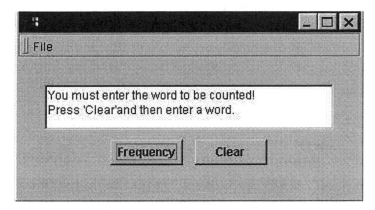

Figure 4.13. Dynamic user instruction.

"Frequency" button before entering a word, directions to enter a word will appear in the text area (Fig. 4.13).

DOWNLOADING JAVA PROGRAMS AND THE JRE

At this point, readers who are following along with a computer may wish to download the JAVA programs we will be using from the archive for Chapter 4 on the book's dedicated home page. After they have downloaded these programs, they must install the JAVA Runtime Environment (JRE) on their system. JRE is a JAVA virtual machine that runs under Windows. It is used in the same way to run JAVA programs under Windows that the Soft Windows program is used to run Windows programs on a MAC. JRE is a computer program whose function is to translate the binary code of JAVA program instructions into binary code that runs on an Intel Pentium or equivalent microprocessor. Every computer system that runs JAVA programs requires some equivalent of JRE. MAC computers use a program called Macintosh Runtime JAVA (MRJ) to run JAVA application programs. The JRE program for Windows and the MRJ program for MACs are complete versions of JAVA, designed to run complete JAVA applications. Readers may wonder why another JAVA machine is necessary when they can already run JAVA programs on Web pages. They need another version because the JAVA machines that come with browsers like Netscape and Internet Explorer are designed to run only JAVA "applets" on Web pages. These versions of JAVA are limited ones with extensive security provisions to protect users from predatory JAVA programs that might appear to be innocent parts of a Web page. The programs that use the browser version of JAVA are given the diminutive name "applets" to emphasize their restricted nature.

The archive is accessed from the "Archive" button:

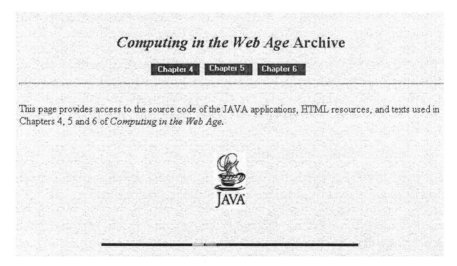

Figure 4.14. Archive button.

This will open the archive page (Fig. 4.15). The archive contains detailed instructions on how to download and install the material from the archive. The archives are compressed to minimize the time needed to download them (Fig. 4.16). The archive is divided into MAC and Windows sections because of the different ways in which MAC and Windows machines handle file compression and implement the stand-alone version of the JAVA virtual machine. I will continue the discussion of programming in the J++ environment as if readers had downloaded the JAVA programs in the Chapter 4 archive and the virtual machine for Windows, the Java Runtime Environment (JRE). JRE is used to run the JAVA programs I will be discussing. Detailed instructions for downloading programs, data, and JRE into Windows and MRJ for the MAC are given in the respective Windows and MAC portions of the Chapter 4 archive. Instructions for downloading and installing the JAVA programs and JRE for Windows 95 are also given in Appendix C (p. 315).

Computing in the Web Age Archive

Chapter 4   Chapter 5   Chapter 6

This page provides access to the source code of the JAVA applications, HTML resources, and texts used in Chapters 4, 5 and 6 of *Computing in the Web Age*.

JAVA

Figure 4.15. *Experiencing Information* archive.

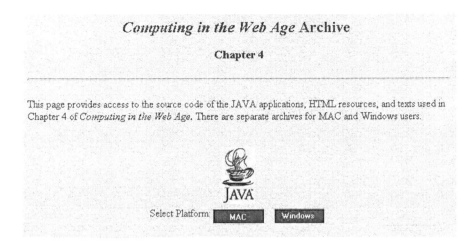

Figure 4.16. Chapter 4 archive.

THE WORD FREQUENCY PROGRAM

To run the word frequency program, we first must open the DOS window by selecting "MS-DOS Prompt" from the Start menu (Fig. 4.17). This opens the DOS window, in which we enter the command line to run the word frequency program on JRE (Fig. 4.18):

jre −cp /webinfo/wordfreq wordfreq

Pressing "Enter" loads "wordfreq" on the JRE (Fig. 4.19). We use the "File/Open" from the menu to display the "Search File" dialog box (Fig. 4.20).

A text of "Heart of Darkness" is included in a file in the "webinfo" directory in a subdirectory named "Conrad." These directories were created by the self-extracting archive we downloaded from the Web. This is the file we will search, so we highlight it and confirm our choice by pressing the "Open" button. The file dialog box then disappears and we type "devil" as our word selection in the text display area (Fig. 4.21). When we press the "Frequency" button, an informatory message displays in the text area (Fig. 4.22). As the search proceeds, a running total is displayed in the text area as a way of informing the user that the search is underway (Fig. 4.23). When the program terminates, a final result message is displayed (Fig. 4.24).

To obtain the frequency of another word in the text, one would press clear, enter the new word, and press "Frequency." To change to another file, one would

Figure 4.17. Starting MS-DOS from Windows.

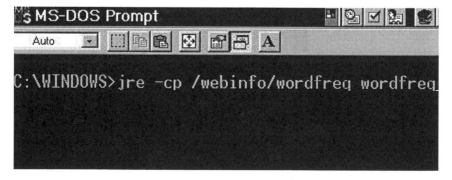

Figure 4.18. Running "wordfreq" from DOS prompt.

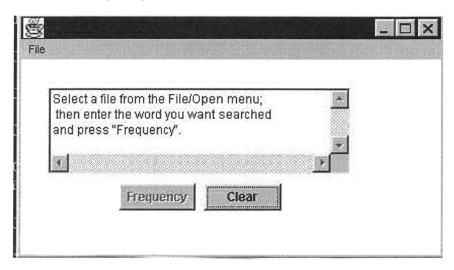

Figure 4.19. JRE executing the "wordfreq" program.

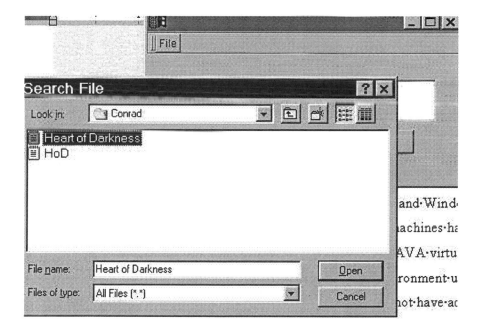

Figure 4.20. "Search File" dialog box.

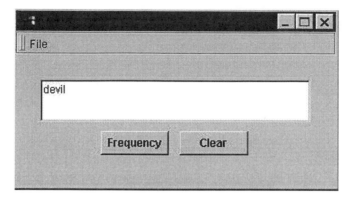

Figure 4.21. Enter word choice in text area.

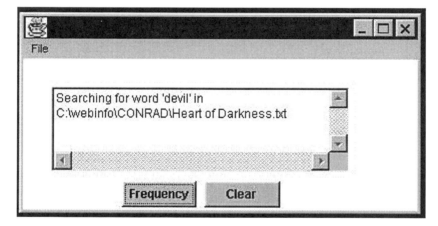

Figure 4.22. Informatory message from word frequency.

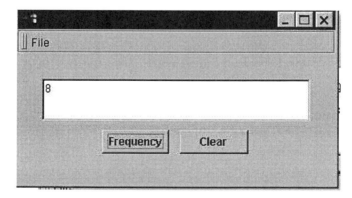

Figure 4.23. Running total display from word frequency.

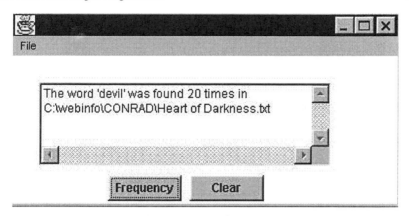

Figure 4.24. Final result from word frequency.

again select the "File/Open" menu. To close the program at any time one uses the "Exit" option on the File menu (Fig. 4.25).

The design of this interface takes into account each separate state of the process of program operation as well as the possible paths by which one arrives at each state. The result is an interface that changes over time in keeping with the direction of the user.

The JAVA++ environment enables the programmer to examine the inner workings of the program's code on various data structures at the same time that the interface is responding to the user. The algorithm for counting occurrences of words is embodied in a method named "wordcount()" that is linked to the "Frequency" button. Its code reads as follows:

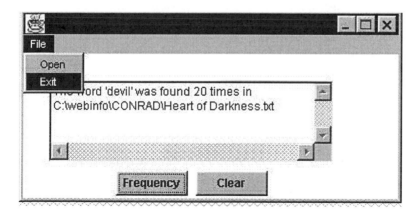

Figure 4.25. "Exit" option for word frequency.

```
public void wordcount()
{
//N.B.: The variables "count", "strSerachWord" and "strSearchFile" are globally defined
elsewhere.
```

// DATA SEGMENT

```
// memory locations used within method
int i = 0;
int j = 1;
String line; //data structure for current line of text
String strT1; // data structure used in final result display
```

// CODE SEGMENT

// initialization code

```
line = "Searching for word '" + strSearchWord + "' in\n" +
    strSearchFile; // construct informatory message
builder.IDC_EDIT1.setText(line); //put message in text area
show(); // display interface with updated text area
count = 0; // start count at 0
```

// main loop

```
// Read through file named in "strSearchFile" one line at a time
// The word to be searched is stored in "strSearchWord"
try {DataInput d =
    new DataInputStream(new FileInputStream(strSearchFile));
while((line = d.readLine()) != null) // loop to read file into line
{
    j = 0;
    while ((i = line.indexOf(strSearchWord,j)) != -1)
    {
        count++; // increment count by one
        builder.IDC_EDIT1.setText(String.valueOf(count));
        show(); // display count in text area
        j = i + strSearchWord.length(); // check for subsequent occurrences
    } // end of occurrences loop
} // end of loop through text
// read all lines from the text.
}
catch (IOException d) //system business
{
    i--;
}
```

// final result and exit.

```
if (count == 1) strT1 = " time in\n"; // "time" or "times"?
else strT1 = " times in\n";
line = "The word '" + strSearchWord + "' was found "
    + String.valueOf(count) + strT1 + strSearchFile;
builder.IDC_EDIT1.setText(line); // put final report in text area
show(); // display interface with updated text area.
```

```
    return; // end of method wordcount()
    }
```

The code is heavily commented so that readers can read through it to obtain a step-by-step account of its operation. In the JAVA programming language, a double slash indicates that everything beginning with the slashes is a comment supplied by the programmer to annotate and document the code. This method of commenting on code is standard practice among programmers. It is used, along with indentations and descriptive names, to make code comprehensible to human beings. The computer ignores these things.

The details of the code itself will be opaque to readers but the aim here is to follow what is in the programmer's mind as the code is written, not the details of how the code encapsulates the programmer's mental process. If the goal were to teach programming, explanation of these details would be essential. Before going through the narrative comments embedded in the code, readers should note the code's overall structure. It is divided into two parts, a data segment and a code segment, as were the assembler programs in the previous chapter. And for the same reason: all programs consist of "inseparably linked" data structures and the code that processes them. The code segment consists of three parts: the beginning, middle, and end, which in turn set up the data and state of the algorithm so that the algorithm will operate correctly, carry out the algorithm, and report the result. Taken together, the data and code segments embody the standard process created by programmers for programs: allocation of memory; initialization of the algorithm; computation of the result; and termination of the algorithm.

The J++ environment includes an interactive debugging program that enables programmers to step through the execution of a program one instruction at a time or to designate lines of code as "breakpoints" at which the program will halt execution and display the content of specific, designated data structures. These data structures are called "watch points" because the debugger enables programmers to watch the effect of successive lines of code on them. Programming is an exercise in control and programmers derive real pleasure from watching a program that executes exactly as they designed and hence predicted it would. They have an excellent idea of what memory should contain at any given point in the execution of a program. By observing crucial memory locations as code executes, programmers can usually spot problems arising from errors in their logic or unanticipated combinations of data. I will describe how the word frequency program runs under the control of the debugger to show how a programmer uses a debugger to analyze the operation of a program.

The heart of the word frequency program is contained in the eleven lines of code that read through a text line by line and check each line for the occurrence of the word. This is where the algorithm that counts occurrences is applied to the text under consideration:

```
while((line = d.readLine()) != null) // loop to read file into line
{
  j = 0;
  while ((i = line.indexOf(strSearchWord,j)) != -1)
  {
    count++; // increment count by one
    builder.IDC_EDIT1.setText(String.valueOf(count));
    show(); // display count in text area
    j = i + strSearchWord.length(); // check for subsequent occurrences
  } // end of occurrences loop
} // end of loop through text
```

These lines of code define two loops, an outer loop and an inner loop. The brackets on lines 2 and 11 define the outer loop, which reads through the text a line at a time. The brackets on lines 5 and 10 define the inner loop, which searches for multiple occurrences of the word in each line.

Of the total four hundred or so lines of code making up this program, less than twenty lines are used to code the algorithm. All the rest are used to create the interface for these twenty. This ratio underscores how, for the programmer, it is the case that Algorithms + Data Structures + Interfaces = Programs. Cyberspace, like the Ptolemaic universe, is configured as a hierarchy and this piece of code is a microcosm of the cyberspace macrocosm. The enclosed spheres of the Ptolemaic universe, it is frequently observed, provided a sense of security to the Classical and Medieval mind. The Primum Mobile was up there and the Underworld was down there and humanity was nested between the two. It was as logically absurd in Ptolemy's universe to ask what existed beyond the Primum Mobile's Unmoved Mover as it is to ask in Hawking's universe what happened before the Big Bang.

Cyberspace's hierarchies offer an analogous sense of orientation and security in the way they provide an overall context for the occurrence of seemingly random events. The structure of this code consists of two control (that word again!) loops. In the first loop, extending from lines 1 to 12, the controlling condition uses JAVA's readLine method to read lines of text as long as there is another line to be read from the file:

$$\text{while((line = d.readLine()) != null)}$$

This condition references a file. Files are conceptualized by the programmer as streams of bytes structured and interpreted in various ways. The bytes of program files, for example, are interpreted as binary numbers representing machine code; the bytes of an image file would be structured so as to represent a picture. The word frequency program uses the readLine() method, which operates on text files. Text files have a standard structure in which bytes are interpreted as character codes divided into lines by the occurrence of an end-of-line character. The control condition reads a text into memory location line and then checks to see whether the read operation actually transferred any bytes from the file to memory. If so, the loop continues; if not, the program drops through the loop and continues execution at the first instruction outside the scope of the loop. (This is the effect of the "!= null" condition. The notation "!=" is JAVA's way of expressing the logical condition "not equal to." The keyword "null" is JAVA's way of signifying an empty string, that is, one that contains no characters.)

In the inner loop, extending from lines 5 to 11, the controlling condition repeats a loop on any line containing an occurrence as long as there is another occurrence to count.

```
while ((i = line.indexOf(strSearchWord,j)) != -1)
```

This loop uses the indexOf() method to search the contents of a line for occurrences of the word to be counted in the line. When using the indexOf() method, the programmer thinks of the line as a sequence of characters to be referenced by their address relative to the first character in the string. The address of the first character in the string is 0, the address of the second character is 1, etc. The programmer supplies two parameters or pieces of information in applying the method to a line: the word to be searched, which in this case is stored in memory location strSearchWord; and the relative address at which the method is to start its search. This relative address is stored in memory location j, which has been allocated by the programmer for this purpose. There is a tradition among programmers that goes back to the early days of FORTRAN programming that one uses the names "i," "j," "k," "l," "m," and "n" for variables used to control iterative processes. The code here follows that tradition, using "i" and "j" as variables that control iterations in the inner loop.

The relative address for each successive line is initially set to 0 because the program must start each search at location address 0, the first character in the line. If the method finds an occurrence of the word within the line, it provides a number that is the relative address of the first character of the word for which it is searching the line. If the method does not find an occurrence of the word, it provides −1 as its numerical result. In either case, the method puts this relative address in memory location "i," whose successive values are used to determine whether the loop is to continue.

If an occurrence of the word is found, three events occur successively, as a result of instructions in lines six through nine. Memory location count is incremented by one ("count++") in line six to keep a running total of the number of occurrences. Lines seven and eight display this number in the text area. This is done to assure the user that the program is at work on its task. Finally, line nine resets the value of "j" to the value of "i," the relative address of the word within the string, plus a number equal to the number of characters in the word. The relative address in "j" now points to the first character beyond the occurrence of the word. The next time the indexOf() method is executed by the control sequence, the line will be searched starting there rather than at the start of the line. If "j" were not so incremented, the inner loop would become an infinite loop in which it found endlessly the same occurrence of the word. Such loss of control (gasp!) is the programmer's recurring nightmare.

The debugger program in the J++ environment enables the programmer to monitor a program's execution in order to maintain control over it. Debugger programs are a major feature of modern programming systems. The virtual CPU program in Chapter 3 would have the "look and feel" of a debugger program to a programmer. The J++ programming environment is designed for programmers and is much too complicated for casual or occasional use. I will describe its use here because I think it will help readers to understand what keyword searching is. It is important for readers to understand this because it is the technique that underlies all Web searching.

To observe the workings of the word frequency algorithm, we use the debugger to set a break point at instruction 9:

```
4.      while ((i = line.indexOf(strSearchWord,j)) != -1)
5.      {
6.              count++; // increment count by one
7.              builder.IDC_EDIT1.setText(String.valueOf(count));
8.              show(); // display count in text area
9.•             j = i + strSearchWord.length(); // check for subsequent occurrences
10.     } // end of occurrences loop
```

The bullet symbol "•" marks the location at which a breakpoint is set. Setting this instruction as a breakpoint means that the program will halt whenever it reaches this instruction in the course of execution. The breakpoint here means that the program will halt each time it finds an occurrence of the word. To see the state of memory at this point, we use the debugger to set up a table of watch points for the crucial memory locations in the program. When the program halts, the contents of the memory locations we wish to examine are displayed in this table. The first time the program halts, the watch point table reads as follows:

line	{"into. I've seen the devil of violence, and the devil of greed, and the devil of "}
count	1
strSearchWord	{"devil"}
strSearchFile	{"C:\wbinfo\CONRAD\Heart of Darkness.txt"}
i	20
j	0

From the table we can see

the location "line" in which the word was detected;

the location "count," which contains the current total;
the location "strSearchWord," which contains the word we are searching for;
the location "strSearchFile," which contains the name file we are searching;
the location "i," which contains the relative address of the word within "line";
the location "j," which contains the offset address at which the search began.

The values in the table indicate that the algorithm started searching at the beginning of "line" (offset address 0) and found the first occurrence of "devil" at offset address 20. The next time the program halts, the table contains different values for "count," "i," and "j";

Line	{"into. I've seen the devil of violence, and the devil of greed, and the devil of "}
Count	2
StrSearchWord	{"devil"}
StrSearchFile	{"C:\webinfo\CONRAD\Heart of Darkness.txt"}
I	47
J	25

On the second halt, the algorithm started at offset address 25—the sum of the first location of the word (20) and the word's length (5)—and found the second occurrence at location 47. At the third halt, "count" is 3, "i" is 71, and "j" is 52. The programmer can see from these successive readouts that the algorithm functions as designed, counting only lines of text that contain the specified word and, within the line, finding each occurrence. The contents of the table at the fourth halt show something else about the way the algorithm works:

line	{"hot desire; but, by all the stars! these were strong, lusty, red-eyed devils, "}
count	4
strSearchWord	{"devil"}
strSearchFile	{"C:\webinfo\CONRAD\Heart of Darkness.txt"}
i	70
j	0

The line does not contain the word "devil" but its plural form, "devils." What the algorithm really counts is not occurrences of the word "devil" but occurrences of the character sequence "devil." As it goes through the search of the entire file, it counts "devilry," "devil-god," and "devilish" as well as a few more plural forms in its total. The form does not occur capitalized in the text and would not have been counted if it did occur. As the code ring exercise in Chapter 2 made clear, the string

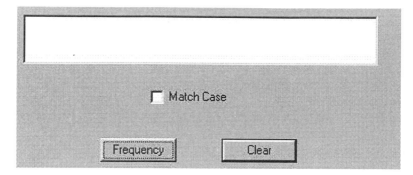

Figure 4.26. "Match Case" checkbox.

"devil" is coded in ASCII as "100 101 118 105 108," while the string "Devil" has as ASCII code of "68 101 118 105 108." The algorithm would not match "Devil" and "devil" because their ASCII representations do not match.

Tracing its execution through the file reveals that the algorithm counts too much and too little. It does not distinguish the designated form from derivative or related forms and it ignores capitalized forms altogether. The problem with the capitalized form is easily fixed by applying the toLowerCase() method to the line and to the search word. This method will put both the word and the line in lower case. Thus, it will insure that the algorithm will count all related forms by insuring that the search word code is "100 101 118 105 108" and that any occurrence of "68 101 118 105 108" in the line is converted to "100 101 118 105 108" before the search begins. Users would be given a choice of whether or not to make the count case sensitive or not by addition of a "Match Case" checkbox and related code (Fig. 4.26). The program would default to searches that ignored case, and users who wished to make case-sensitive searches would have to check the checkbox. The addition to the interface reflects the change in the algorithm, again illustrating the close connection between the two.

KEY WORD IN CONTEXT FILE SEARCH

Getting the algorithm to count only occurrences of "devil" and not related forms ("devils," "devilry," "bedeviled," etc.) is much more complicated than getting it to be case sensitive. Rather than having the program process the input text one line at a time, the programmer must break each line down into its constituent words, stripped of punctuation, and test each word individually. To do this, the programmer must embed the test loop within a loop that feeds words one at a time to the loop. The programmer must also add a "Whole Word" check box to the interface and the code to support that box in the program. This increases exponentially the amount of code needed to control the check boxes since two check boxes allow four possible settings: both checked, both unchecked, only one checked, and only the other checked. Further, only when the "Whole Word" option is checked is it necessary to consider words individually.

The second program we will consider is called "KWIC" for "Key Word In Context." The command line entry to run this program is "jre –cp /webinfo/kwic kwic." It is similar to the Word Frequency program but, rather than counting the occurrences of words, this program is a text retrieval program that produces a listing of every sentence in a text that contains a particular word. Its interface looks like the interface to the Word Frequency program with the check boxes added and an expanded text display area (Fig. 4.27). The text area of the interface has been made larger to allow for the listing of sentences. I have added code to the program that

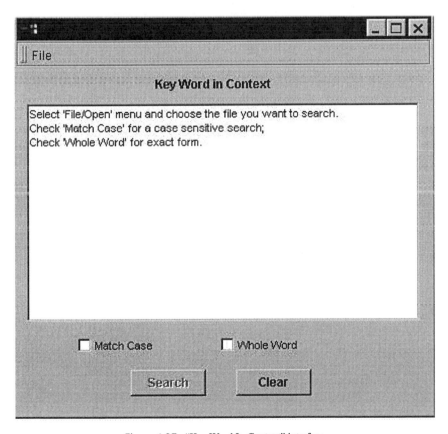

Figure 4.27. "Key Word In Context" interface.

constructs sentences from the words on the input line by adding each word it finds
to the sentence until it adds a word containing an exclamation point, question mark,
or period. Except for "Mr." the program takes any abbreviation or number containing a decimal point, exclamation point, or question mark as a sentence-ending word.
This is hardly a sophisticated sentence parser but it is adequate for the purposes of
this discussion.

The code required to implement the check boxes is found in a method called
"searchSentence()," which the program applies to every sentence as soon as it adds
the sentence-ending word to its constructed sentence. The method searches the
sentence for an occurrence of the word in accordance with the settings of the check
boxes. Its code is as follows:

```
public boolean searchSentence(String sentence, String word)
// if word is found in sentence, return true;
// otherwise return false.
{
int i, j, ipunc;
String strPunctuation;
strPunctuation = ".,;:\"?! ";
// Match Case True and Whole Word False
if ((builder.IDC_CHECK1.getState() == true)
   && (builder.IDC_CHECK2.getState() == false))
   {
   i = sentence.indexOf(word);
   if (i == -1) return false;
   else return true;
   }
// Match Case False
if (builder.IDC_CHECK1.getState() == false) // ignore case
   {
   // Translate word and sentence to lower case.
   sentence = sentence.toLowerCase();
   word = word.toLowerCase();
   }
// Whole Word False
if (builder.IDC_CHECK2.getState() == false)
   {
   // Search sentence without tokenizing.
   i = sentence.indexOf(word);
   if (i == -1) return false;
   else return true;
   }
// Whole word is True; tokenize sentence, eliminating punctuation.
StringTokenizer st = new StringTokenizer(sentence, strPunctuation, false);
while ( st.hasMoreTokens() == true)
   {
   if (word.equals((String) st.nextToken()) == true) return true;
```

```
    }
    return false; // no match found
} // end of method
```

"A mighty maze! but not without a plan;" all paths through this method lead to one "return" statement or another; and "return" statements provide exits to the maze. Since the method is a "Boolean" or logical type, each return statement is followed by a Boolean value, "true" or "false." The "return true" statements are the exits for sentences that satisfy the conditions specified on the interface; the "return false" statements are exits for statements that do not satisfy the interface conditions. If the search is to ignore case, the word and sentence are translated to lower case in lines 17 to 22. Rather than tokenizing every sentence, the algorithm tokenizes only those sentences for which "Whole Word" is checked. The tokenizing occurs in lines 32 to 36.

A subtle point to grasp about this method is that it operates on its own copy of the sentence and word. It changes this copy, not the original, which is still available to the overall program. Supplying copies of data to methods is termed "call by value." Sometimes, programmers write methods that can alter the original data that they are given. This is termed "call by reference," because the method receives the address of the value rather than the value itself to work with. We have used call by reference in the virtual CPU program that computed our table of values. In designing and using methods, programmers must be aware of whether they are using call by reference or call by value. Confusions between the two are a frequent cause of programming errors that can sometimes be very difficult to trace.

If we use the KWIC program to search our text of "Heart of Darkness" for the word "devil," leaving both the whole word and match case boxes unchecked, we obtain the following results:

Results of the search for the word 'devil' in file:

C:\CHAPTER 1\CONRAD\Heart of Darkness.txt

I've seen the devil of violence, and the devil of greed, and the devil of hot desire; but, by all the stars!

these were strong, lusty, red-eyed devils, that swayed and drove men -- men, I tell you.

But as I stood on this hillside, I foresaw that in the blinding sunshine of that land I would become acquainted with a flabby, pretending, weak-eyed devil of a rapacious and pitiless folly.

A neglected gap was all the gate it had, and the first glance at the place was enough to let you see the flabby devil was running that show.

'He is an emissary of pity and science and progress, and devil knows what else.

"He was becoming confidential now, but I fancy my unresponsive attitude must have exasperated him at last, for he judged it necessary to inform me he feared neither God nor devil, let alone any mere man.

'Yes,' answered the manager; 'he sent his assistant down the river with a note to me in these terms: "Clear this poor devil out of the country, and don't bother sending more of that sort.

He squinted at the steam-gauge and at the water-gauge with an evident effort of intrepidity -- and he had filed teeth, too, the poor devil, and the wool of his pate shaved into queer patterns, and three ornamental scars on each of his cheeks.

But the snags were thick, the water was treacherous and shallow, the boiler seemed indeed to have a sulky devil in it, and thus neither that fireman nor I had any time to peer into our creepy thoughts.

Why in the name of all the gnawing devils of hunger they didn't go for us -- they were thirty to five -- and have a good tuck-in for once, amazes me now when I think of it.

Don't you know the devilry of lingering starvation, its exasperating torment, its black thoughts, its sombre and brooding ferocity?

"The other shoe went flying unto the devil-god of that river.

-- he had withered; it had taken him, loved him, embraced him, got into his veins, consumed his flesh, and sealed his soul to its own by the inconceivable ceremonies of some devilish initiation.

He had taken a high seat amongst the devils of the land -- I mean literally.

I take it, no fool ever made a bargain for his soul with the devil; the fool is too much of a fool, or the devil too much of a devil -- I don't know which.

'At first old Van Shuyten would tell me to go to the devil,' he narrated with keen enjoyment; 'but I stuck to him, and talked and talked, till at last he got afraid I would talk the hind-leg off his favourite dog, so he gave me some cheap things and a few guns, and told me he hoped he would never see my face again.

Readers might try this search with and without checking the whole word box. They might also try similar searches on the word "dark" as well as any other words that pique their curiosity with and without checking the match case and whole word boxes.

KEY WORD IN CONTEXT DIRECTORY SEARCH

The KWIC program works well enough but it is not in the nature of programmers to leave well enough alone. They are as much kibitzers as they are control freaks. This goes back to Babbage whose endless kibitzing with the machinists executing his design of the analytical engine as well as his constant revisions of his design were among the reasons it never quite got finished. (Others, taking advantage of published accounts of his work, not only finished operational machines but also sold one to the British government that had funded Babbage's work.) The KWIC program, reflecting its origin as a word frequency utility, operates only on individual files. For short prose texts, this is perfectly acceptable. But for collections of related files, such as chapters of technical manuals, which tend to be recorded in multiple files, the program is tedious at best to work with. The usual way to handle works recorded in multiple files is to create separate directories for the works and place the constituent files in that directory. This is the way long works are placed on the Internet. By dividing a novel or collection of poems or a long technical manual, for example, into chapter-by-chapter or poem-by-poem files, providers of Web material enable users who want only portions of a text to get only what they need. This also simplifies downloading by breaking it down into easily handled chunks. If transmission is interrupted at any point, one needs to start retransmission at the beginning of a chapter rather than the beginning of the work. And because the Internet is the source from which one is likely to obtain files, it is likely as not that these files will contain HTML coding rather than simple ASCII text files.

To take care of the problems of multifile works and possible HTML coding, I developed an extension of the KWIC program called KWIC2 that is available in the archive. The command line program to run this program is "jre –cp /webinfo/kwic2 kwic2." This program, written to process a machine-readable version of the first edition of the *Poems of Gerard Manley Hopkins*, has several features not found in the KWIC program. This program handles all HTML tags contained in angle brackets by removing them from the text it displays. It handles tags beginning with an ampersand by substituting the appropriate ASCII character for the tag. Because line breaks are significant in poetry, I added code to indicate line divisions in the input text. Most importantly, it contains code that searches every file in the directory of the file selected by the users.

The program uses yet another loop to work its way through the files in the selected directory.

```
public void filesearch()
{
  int i = 0;
  int j = 1;
  File f1 = new File(strDir);
  String s[ ] = f1.list(); //get list of files and store in list s
  i = s.length; // get the number of files on the list
  for (j = 0; j  i; j++)
  {
    builder.IDC_EDIT1.setText(s[j]); // display the current file
    show();
    wordsearch(strDir, s[j]); // process each file in turn
  }
  builder.IDC_EDIT1.setText(strHistory); // display the entire list of files.
  show();
  return;
}
```

This method applies the list method to the directory object to obtain the list of the files in the directory. It then passes the file names to the wordsearch method, which is similar in structure and operation to the KWIC program. In effect, this executes a KWIC program for every file contained in the directory.

In substituting the character for the tag, it provides a classic example of a look up table, the code for which is as follows:

```
strSubsIn[0] = "&aacute;";strSubsOut[0] = "á";
strSubsIn[1] = "&eacute;";strSubsOut[1] = "é";
strSubsIn[2] = "&iacute;";strSubsOut[2] = "í";
strSubsIn[3] = "&oacute;";strSubsOut[3] = "ó";
strSubsIn[4] = "&uacute;";strSubsOut[4] = "ú";
strSubsIn[5] = "&Aacute;";strSubsOut[5] = "Á";
strSubsIn[6] = "&Eacute;";strSubsOut[6] = "É";
strSubsIn[7] = "&Iacute;";strSubsOut[7] = "Í";
strSubsIn[8] = "&Oacute;";strSubsOut[8] = "Ó";
strSubsIn[9] = "&Uacute;";strSubsOut[9] = "Ú";
strSubsIn[10] = "&egrave;";strSubsOut[10] = "è";
```

There are two tables involved here: strSubsIn, which holds the tags that occur in the text, and strSubsOut, which holds the character to be substituted for the tag.

The program defines a method called strLookup that checks every token beginning with an ampersand against its input table and, when it finds a match, returns the appropriate character:

```
public String strLookup(String strT1)
{
    int i;
    for (i = 0; i<11; i++)
    {
        if(strT1.equals(strSubsIn[i])) return strSubsOut[i];
    }
    return "[...]";
}
```

This is a String method and must return a String data structure. Its internal form is a counting loop that is executed as many times as there are entries in the table. The loop checks the eleven entries in the table and, if it does not find a match, returns a string containing the ellipsis marker "[...]". I have only defined the twelve strings found in the Hopkins text (the eleven in the table plus " ") in this program. A production program, as opposed to a demonstration one, would of course define all such tags and would also contain the code to format the text according to all the tags it contains.[3]

Searching for the word "God" in the Hopkins text produces the following (partial) output for poem 34:

```
Searching for the word 'god' in file:
C:\webinfo\HOPKINS\34.HTM
```

/ / Í say móre: the just man justices; / Kéeps gráce: thát keeps all his
goings graces; / Acts in God's eye what in God's eye he is-- / Chríst--for
Christ plays in ten thousand places, / Lovely in limbs, and lovely in
eyes not his / To the Father through the features of men's faces.

The input text of this particular find is as follows:

```
<p>
<dd>&Iacute; say m&oacute;re: the just man justices;
<dd>K&eacute;eps gr&aacute;ce: th&aacute;t keeps all his goings graces;
<dd>Acts in God's eye what in God's eye he is--
<dd>Chr&iacute;st--for Christ plays in ten thousand places,
<dd>Lovely in limbs, and lovely in eyes not his
<dd>To the Father through the features of men's faces.
```

The listing of all occurrences runs to several pages. Readers can reproduce it by running the KWIC2 program on the texts in the Hopkins subdirectory of the webinfo directory.

Of the making of a computer program there is no end. A number of possible extensions of KWIC2 suggest themselves. I could put the total occurrences in each text in a table that would be added to the occurrences file; note whether the match case and whole word boxes were checked or not; add code that would allow Boolean searching for passages containing collocations of words; etc. The step-by-step refinement of a computer program resembles the revision of a piece of prose. Good programming, like good writing, is not so much finished as abandoned under the pressure of a deadline. I began this discussion of programming with the description of a statue that suggested to me the intrinsic powers of the structured logic of programming. Now, we should be in a position to see that the perspectives of programmers on both the programs they write and the texts they process are

               ...not like statuary posed
For a vista in Louvre. They are things chalked
On the sidewalk so that the pensive man may see.

                        V

The pensive man...he sees that eagle float
For which the intricate Alps are a single nest.
Wallace Stevens   "Connoisseur of Chaos"

CHAPTER 5

Connections to the World Wide Web

NETWORKS: WHY AND HOW

From a mathematical point of view, all computers are Turing machines. From a social point of view, all computers are communications devices that provide users with powerful ways of copying and distributing information. It is sometimes observed by opponents of one or another government program that freedom of the press does not oblige the government to provide a printing press for every citizen. If there were such a constitutional requirement, the Web would go a long way toward meeting that obligation. In the former Soviet Union, it was necessary to get a government license to use a photocopy machine. During its last days, the Soviet Union was hopelessly behind in computer technology because it could not face up to the freedom of access to information inherent in computer technology. In China today, the government is trying to develop a modern, information-based economy while at the same time controlling the Internet the way the Soviets controlled photocopiers. Madness, it is said, is doing the same thing over and over and expecting different results. The Tiananmen Square uprising would not have happened without the ready access the student rebels had to fax machines. What does the Chinese government expect from students with access to the Web, however monitored and controlled? Computer security is an oxymoron. Building secure computer systems and networks is like making wheels with a bit of their circumference filed flat. It is true that the more one side is flattened, the more difficult it becomes to use the wheels on vehicles that can exceed the speed limit and it is exceedingly difficult to steal a car with a flat tire. But a slightly flattened tire is much more likely to be an inconvenience to the car's owner than it is to a potential thief.

171

The term "computer security" has two general meanings, one bad and one good. In the bad sense, computer security means the attempt to construct computer systems so as to place the control of and access to information on the systems in the hands of the systems' operators and administrators. It is a top down, authoritarian approach that attempts to compartmentalize information and users on a "need to know" basis. This type of security, encoded in the HAL 9000 computer of *2001: A Space Odyssey,* drove it to its homicidal schizophrenia. It offers security in the sense that it secures the power of the administrators over users' access to information. In the good sense, computer security begins with the premise that a computer file is the intellectual property of its creator who is responsible for its contents and for respecting the intellectual property rights of other computer users. It allows creators of computer files to determine who may read and copy them. System administrators and programmers in this type of computer security own and control files only in the sense that other users do. They provide services to the client users, not commands to the troops. Those who administer Web servers are properly regarded as existing to serve the needs of clients. In the hierarchy of Client/Server, the server exists for the client, not the other way around.

We all want computer security in the sense that we wish to control access to the information we place on computers. Personal information, medical records, financial transactions are examples that come immediately to mind of types of information that call for security in this sense. This gives rise to the need for encryption, for a way of scrambling information in files into a seemingly meaningless form that can be unscrambled only by those who have access to a secret decryption key. In our discussion of ASCII code, we used the example of a secret code ring as a way of explaining standard character encoding because encryption is encoding not understood. In our discussion of the development of modern computers, we pointed out that Turing spent World War II decrypting German military codes. The history of computing suggests that the involvement of computers in problems of encryption is likely to be a perennial one. On a modern network, the question of how to secure information encoded in ASCII is but one of many possible starting points for a discussion of security.

Various schemes of data encryption exist for securing computer files but none of them offer absolute protection. At their best, they offer practical as opposed to theoretical security for encrypted data. Given enough computer resources and time, a file that has been encrypted can most likely be decrypted by one or another combination of brute force computation and subtle hacking. Cryptographic literature is full of discussions of how much computer resource is required to crack various coding schemes. Such estimates are subject to being constantly downsized as the speed of computers increases. (When all else fails, steal the encryption key.) And the slower operation of the computer and the attendant personal inconvenience that encrypting entails make the great wheel of computing turn more slowly than it otherwise might.

Nothing is absolutely secure and no one claims to have an unbreakable encryption scheme. For example, users of RSA encryption, one of today's most widely used type of encryption, are warned that

> it has not been proven that the security of RSA relies solely on the mathematical difficulty of finding prime factors of large numbers. However, many of the other possibilities for finding [prime factors] given [a large number] have been shown to be of equivalent difficulty to factoring N [a large number]. One possibility is that an algorithm could be devised [that would operate] more easily than factoring N. Nevertheless, no such algorithm has been discovered so far, and RSA has withstood many attempts to crack it.

The possibility of a fresh mathematical insight is *le grand peut-être* for a properly skeptical user of any encryption scheme. With current encryption technology, information on computers can be made more secure than personal papers in a safety deposit box, which is to say that encryption offers pretty good privacy for most purposes.

Traditional encryption schemes, based on a single encryption key, have been superseded recently by so-called public/private or double key encryption schemes. In a public/private encryption scheme, a user gets not one but two encryption keys, one of which is public and made available to anyone from whom the user wishes to receive secure information, the other of which the user keeps secret so that only she or he knows it. To communicate secure information to a user whose public key is known, one uses that individual's public key and the file of information or "plain-text" one wishes to encrypt as input to an encryption program which produces a "cipher-text" file that can be decrypted only by someone who knows the private key. In two key systems, the public and private keys are mathematically related so that data encrypted by the use of one can only be decrypted by use of the other. There is no way, however, to derive the private key from the public one. If I encrypt a file using my private key, it can be decrypted by anyone who knows my public key. But that person knows that the file originated with me because I am the only one who knows the private key with which it was encrypted. This enables the receiver of the file to authenticate that the file is mine. If I wish to keep the information on the file from anyone but myself, I simply encode it with a private key and don't publish the public key. Similar methods are used to provide authenticated electronic signatures that can be attached to plain-text files in such a way that if the plain-text file is altered in any way, the signature is invalidated. Each use of the signature produces a uniquely encrypted signature so it is not possible to copy an electronic signature from one document to another.

Since June 1991, a public/private encryption scheme known as PGP (Pretty Good Privacy) has been available free of charge in the United States from the Massachusetts Institute of Technology. It was developed and published by Phil Zimmermann and has become the standard method of encryption for information on the Internet. PGP as published on the Internet makes encryption available to everyone. No encryption scheme can be more secure than the security of its key and the problem with any encryption key system is how to control access to the encryption key. With a single key system, control of the circulation of encryption keys is practical only within large governmental and other bureaucracies that can afford to build and maintain secure facilities and secure, private communication channels between them. With public/private key encryption, anyone with a pair of keys can publish a public key on a public medium such as the Internet and be sure that communications they receive over a public channel can be made safe from unauthorized access.

The story of how the U.S. government treated Zimmermann's publication of PGP illustrates the difference between academic Computer Science and its governmental and commercial analogs and the importance of maintaining not only academic freedom but also free speech and privacy rights for the Internet. Zimmermann based PGP on published academic work. What he did was to choose the best encryption methods available in the public domain and meld them into a useful suite of encryption programs. He then published both the programs and their source code. In all this he proceeded as a scholar publishing his work and subjecting it to open peer review. This way of proceeding is in complete contrast both to the way commercial program developers depend upon trade secret, copyright, and proprietary protections and to the secrecy that surrounds the work of the National Security Agency (NSA), the chief governmental organization concerned with computer security. To this day, no one knows whether the NSA has been able to crack PGP encryption.

The government has behaved as if NSA could not defeat PGP encryption. In 1992, Zimmermann was placed under investigation for violating the laws on export of munitions because computer encryption technology is on a list of technologies over which the government maintains import/export controls on national security grounds. For three years he was threatened with prosecution although it was unclear whether publication of PGP on the Internet, based as it was on publicly available and exportable information sources, legally constituted export of a controlled technology and whether, if it did, he was personally responsible for controlling access to the Internet by foreign nationals in foreign countries. The investigation of Zimmermann was eventually closed with the government deciding not to prosecute. Zimmermann was lucky enough to have the personal and institutional resources necessary to resist the investigation. However, one does not have to be a paranoid conspiracy theorist to believe that one result of the investigation of Zimmermann is a chilling effect on the work of others who might not be personally or institutionally so well situated as Zimmermann.

Zimmermann's experience does not represent an isolated instance of governmental interference with Internet users and attempts to monitor and control their activities. It continues today with ongoing attempts to control encryption technology through the "clipper chip," that would create in effect a third key, available to the government, to enable it to decode encrypted Internet traffic. There is also the attempt to regulate content of unencrypted Internet information in order to protect children from pornographic and other materials deemed by some to be subversive of "traditional family values." The Supreme Court has recently scotched this particular approach, holding that protecting children from unseemly material is not a reason to impinge upon the freedom of expression of adults. The 1984 view of the future, O'Brien tells Winston in the course of torturing him, is "a boot stamping on a human face—forever." The Internet originated with Defense Department attempts to make military command and control systems immune to disruption by nuclear attack, but it would appear to have developed into a complex system that is based on cooperation and that is beyond the control of any central authority.

Computer networks like Internet that integrate encryption technologies like PGP hold out the possibility of the development of an open society that leaves wide room for personal preference and eccentricity. They are a distinct stage in the evolution of the von Neumann architecture computer. Just as the development of the miniaturized disk enabled the computer to serve as a personal information retrieval system, the development of the computer network enables the computer to become as well a personal communication device.

As Nicholas Negroponte has pointed out so extensively, *Being Digital*[1] is our fate in the foreseeable future. The computer network blurs the distinctions between computers, publishing, television, and telephone as they all converge because they are digital rather than analog technologies. Digital technologies, based upon binary numbers and bits, are all candidates for the application of encryption. Television and radio, things that we are used to think of as broadcast media, may in the future be circulated on fiber optic cable. Computers and telephones, things that we are used to thinking of as connected by cable, may become wholly or in part connected via radio.[2] Using PGP technology, phone conversations can be transmitted over the Internet in an encrypted form that makes them as secure as the Moscow/Washington hot line.

The network builds on the basic fact that all computers are Turing machines. In practice, much of what we do in networking is designed to obviate the hardware and software incompatibilities between different types of computers. But networks are not simply ways of making incompatible systems compatible. If all computers had exactly the same hardware, operating systems, and software, so that no compatibility problems of any kind existed, we would still be eager to connect them in networks. Networks are sometimes justified on economic grounds because they make it possible for many computers to share expensive peripheral devices like printers, modems, scanners, and tape drives. While there may be some truth to these economic considerations, the main reason that computers get networked is that, when networked, they help gratify our human need to cooperate with each other in sharing information of mutual interest and concern.

INTERNET SOFTWARE

Network software enables users to share the cable which is the physical layer of the network to which the computers on the network are attached. The software divides large files of information into a sequence of smaller units called data packets for transmission across the network. Each packet includes addressing information that identifies the sender and the receiver as well as information about the place of the packet in the sequence. In a way that is analogous to the way that time sharing computer software allocates slices of the CPU's time to terminals connected to a single computer, the sender's network software allocates a slice of time sufficient to transmit a packet on the network cable, transmits the packet, and then waits until its turn comes round again to transmit the next packet. The packets making up a file need not all take exactly the same path across the network from the transmitting computer to the receiving computer. The network software insures that all the packets arrive at their destination and are reassembled in the correct sequence into a complete file.

Ethernet is one of the most widely used systems for controlling access to the network and a description of its workings gives the general flavor of all network access control schemes (Fig. 5.1). The full technical name of Ethernet is Carrier Sense Multiple Access/Collision Detection (CSMA/CD). When network software using Ethernet wants to transmit data across the network, it listens to the network for a carrier signal that indicates that the network is being used (Carrier Sense). As long as it detects the carrier, it does not transmit anything because the presence of the carrier indicates that the network is not available. When it does not detect a carrier, the absence of which indicates that the network is available, it begins transmitting while at the same time listening to the network. If the data it is receiving from the network does not match the data it is sending, a collision has occurred because some other station that also wanted to transmit has also not detected a carrier and has also begun to transmit data at about the same time (Collision

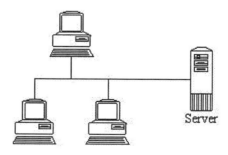

Figure 5.1. Ethernet network.

Detection). The station then stops transmitting data and transmits instead a jam signal, which interrupts data transmission on all stations currently transmitting data and causes each station to pause for a random interval of time before trying to resume transmission. Whichever station happens to get the shortest interval to pause will find the network available when it checks for the carrier, because all the other stations have also stopped transmitting when they received the jam signal but are still waiting for their pause interval to expire. The lucky winner of this little lottery resumes transmission and the other stations, when their time is up and they begin listening, now detect the winner's carrier and must wait their turn. Ethernet works remarkably well, as is evinced by its popularity, but as the number of stations seeking access to an Ethernet network increases, the network can get bogged down in mediating collisions rather than transmitting packets.

Other network access schemes are less sensitive than Ethernet to the volume of network traffic. For example, in Token/Ring schemes, stations are connected in a ring and pass a special packet called a token from one to another around the ring (Fig. 5.2). The stations play a game that resembles "Hot Potato." When the game begins, the token is marked as a free token, which means that the station holding the token is free to transmit data. The rule is that only the station currently holding the free token is allowed to initiate transmission. If it wishes to transmit, it marks the token as in use before passing it on and then transmits its data packet with appropriate addressing information. Each subsequent station recognizes the token as in use and checks the data to see if it is the addressee of the data. The stations that are not the addressee pass the token and the data on. When the data arrives at the addressee station, the addressee station accepts the data and marks the token as received before passing on the token and the data. Eventually, the token and the data make it back around the ring to the originating station, which then checks to see that the data has been marked as received and that the data has not been altered in the course of transmission. If the data has been received by the addressee

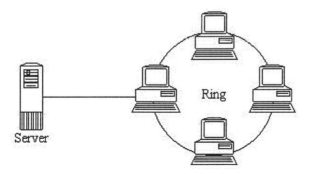

Figure 5.2. "Token/ring" network.

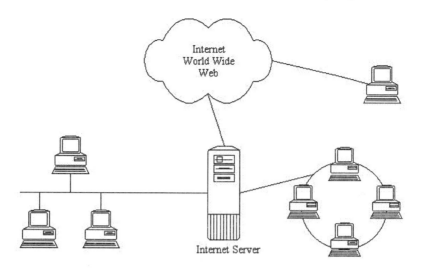

Figure 5.3. Internet server connecting Ethernet and "Token/Ring" networks.

somewhere around the circle and returned unaltered, the sender deletes the message from the ring and passes on a new free token, even if it has more packets to transmit. It waits until it receives a free token from the network before sending its next packet. In the event that it receives the packet back either altered or not marked as received, it takes appropriate action to correct the error. Token/Ring networks are more expensive that Ethernet networks but provide better service under heavy loads than Ethernet networks.

It is not unusual for an Internet server to connect a number of local networks, each with its own connection protocols, to each other as well as to the Internet. One advantage of the Internet is that it makes such connections invisible to the user. It makes no difference to users communicating on the network depicted in Fig. 5.3 whether they are communicating with someone in the same room or building, on the same or another local network, or on the Internet. All routings connect in cyberspace.

CLIENT/SERVER PROGRAMMING

The growth of the Internet was also fostered because of the development of TCP/IP (Transmission Control Protocol/Internet Protocol) communications protocol, which is the last aspect of the Internet's internal technology that I will describe. The protocol is a way of managing communications on the network by dividing the operations needed to communicate into five layers. The bottom layer refers to the

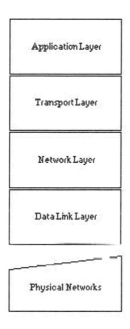

Figure 5.4. TCP/IP protocol stack.

actual networks that the Internet wishes to connect with each other. TCP/IP is designed to let these networks alone and manage only the interconnections between them. The other four levels are software levels that describe the steps by which data moves from the top or application layer to the physical network layer. (The application layer is the program that is using the Internet.) Data from the application layer of the transmitting station moves down the stack to the data link layer, where it moves across the Internet to the local network and then back up the stack to the application layer in the receiving station (Fig. 5.4).

As the data moves from level to level in transmission, information specific to each level is attached in front of the data. As it is received, information specific to each level is acted upon and then removed as the data moves up the stack. This wrapping and unwrapping process is called data encapsulation. The levels of TCP/IP protocol determine the order in which the information is to be presented to the network software and the sequence of the actions to be taken.

Data Link Header	Network Header	Transport Header	Application Data

Figure 5.5. Internet packet headers.

The devil is in the details of each layer and we will content ourselves with a general description of each layer and some specific examples.

At the application layer, the client and server sides of the application carry out their respective tasks as defined by the programmers of the application. The programmers decide which services the server is to provide and the way in which the client will request these services. The client and server are assigned a complimentary set of tasks and given a clearly defined set of conventions through which they communicate. In a client/server library cataloguing system, the server might hold all the information about the library's holdings in a large database and have the ability to search the database and retrieve information rapidly. The client would be responsible for formulating requests for information in a format the server understands and for displaying the results obtained from the server in a format that the user would find intelligible. This type of relationship between a database server and a client is a very common one. In such arrangements, the client is referred to as the front end and the database as the back end. There is a widely used database language called Structured Query Language (SQL), by means of which clients request information from database servers. The advantage of using SQL is that it makes a single client capable of working with a number of different SQL compliant databases.

Both servers and client workstations may run more than one client/server application at a time and a single client may be linked simultaneously to a number of servers. A server, by definition, is a network resource that any client on the network may use just as any client may request time for the transmission of a packet. A workstation client may have an E-mail program watching for incoming mail at the same time that it has another program sending a request for part of a file. The transport layer adds information that identifies a specific task on the client as associated with a specific task on a server to which many other workstations may be attached. The transport layer uses Transmission Control Protocol (TCP) to provide a "virtual circuit" or "socket" to link a specific program task on a server with a specific program task running on the client. It does this with a pair of two-part addresses that identify client and servers and the tasks running on each. It links task W on server X to task Y on server Z. The application layer is the locus of a communication link between a specific program running on the client and a specific program running on a server. The network layer manages the communication between the host servers of the Internet, which operate as a peer-to-peer network. The data link layer, which takes care of getting the data from the host server to the local area network that is attached to it, operates as a server-based network.

The conventions governing the communication at each layer of the network are called protocols; the conventions governing communications between a layer and the level immediately above or below it are called interfaces. When servers transfer files from the file system of one server to the file system of another server, they use a file transfer protocol because the file systems of hosts, as peers, are on the same logical level. On the other hand, when we use a program like Netscape to communicate between an Internet server and a workstation client, the program is called an interface because it connects file systems of logically different layers of the network. In each client/server pair, the corresponding protocol layers communicate with each other without regard to the other layers. They take care of their business and then pass the results to the layer above or below.

The network layer contains one of the most important and at the same time easily understood of protocols, the Internet Protocol (IP) address and its related domain name. As with computer memory where every location has a unique address, so with Internet locations, every one of which has a unique address. The immediately noticeable difference between an IP address and a domain name is that the IP address is a binary number and the domain name is a character string. Each IP address has a corresponding domain name so that the IP address and the domain name represent the same information encoded according to different conventions. They are stored in different formats because an IP address is for use by computers and the domain name is for use by people. A domain name is like the name of a programming constant. It gives a meaningful name to the numerical value of a location. (It is easier to think of "pi" than it is to think of 3.1417......) The Internet provides special servers called domain name servers that work like phone books (or decoder rings) with tables that relate each IP address to its domain name. The important difference between a phone book and domain server table is that every entry in the domain server table is made up of a unique IP address and a unique domain name. In a phone book, one name can be listed at several different numbers or several names can be listed at the same number. Neither of these situations would be allowed in a domain server table.

IP addresses have historically consisted of four bytes that designate uniquely each workstation on the Internet and the network to which the workstation is attached. These four bytes are written as decimal numbers separated by periods in what is called "dotted decimal" or "dotted quad" notation. A typical network IP address would look like

$$128.125.253.172$$

I do not know the origin of dotted quad notation. It is to me just one of those parts of the dialect of the tribe. I would have chosen to represent the four bytes of the IP address as a single hexadecimal number, which strikes me as clearer and more concise than dotted quad notation. Hexadecimal notation, as we shall see, is a convenient format for working with IP addresses. The conversion of dotted quad notation to hexadecimal can be done with the scientific calculator by entering the four decimal numbers one at a time and converting them one at a time to hexadecimal, taking note of each result. The decimal numbers must be entered one at a time because dotted quad notation is not the same as ordinary decimal notation. In our sample address, we use the scientific calculator to covert 128 to 80_{16}, 125 to $7D_{16}$,

253 to FD_{16}, and 172 to AC_{16}. This can then be written as a single hexadecimal number that represents the bit values of each of the four bytes that make up the address:

807DFDAC

In any form of notation we use, the notation expresses the underlying binary code, which, expressed in verbose binary notation, is closest to representing those actual bits that get transmitted across the network:

$$10000000011111011111110110101100_2$$

(The conversion is courtesy of the scientific calculator.) The important thing to which quad notation calls attention is that there are four distinct units that make up a traditional IP address. We will have to work with various ranges of these four bytes to understand how the Internet divides its four-byte address space into two parts, a network designator and a workstation designator.

The bytes of an IP address are divided into two parts, a network identifier and a workstation identifier, according to the size of the network:

- If the first byte of the IP address identifies a network, it is a large network and the last three bytes identify the workstation on the large network;
- If the first two bytes of the IP address identify a network, it is a medium-sized network and the last two bytes identify the workstation on the medium-sized network;
- If the first three bytes of the IP address identify the network, it is a small network and the last byte identifies the workstation on the small network.

This amounts to a zero sum game in which the number of networks of a given size is traded off against the number of workstations allowed on each network. Internet IP addresses are assigned by a private firm called InterNIC, which was designated by the National Science Foundation to be responsible for this function. Networks, not individuals, are members of Internet. InterNIC assigns the network designator portion of the IP address to organizations that want to put their networks on the Internet. The organizations are responsible for assigning the workstation designators to their workstations in accordance with Internet policy.

The Internet was founded before the explosion of networked personal computers that began in the nineteen-eighties. It soon became apparent that the Internet would run out of unique addresses sometime in the nineteen-nineties. To deal with this problem, a new IP addressing scheme has been developed (IPv6) which is based on a sixteen-byte address as contrasted with the current (IPv4) four-byte address. This new convention is designed to accommodate multimedia broadcasting and to provide an address space large enough for the foreseeable future. The Internet Protocol Next Generation (IPng) working group, which has overall responsibility for the design and implementation of IPv6, describes the size of this address space in rather striking terms:

> IPng supports addresses which are four times the number of bits as IPv4 addresses (128 vs. 32). This is 4 Billion times 4 Billion (2^{96}) times the size of the IPv4 address space (2^{32}). This works out to be:
>
> 340,282,366,920,938,463,463,374,607,431,768,211,456
>
> This is an extremely large address space. In a theoretical sense this is approximately 665,570,793,348,866,943,898,599 addresses per square meter of the surface of the planet Earth (assuming the earth surface is 511,263,971,197,990 square meters). In more practical terms the assignment and routing of addresses requires the creation of hierarchies which reduces the efficiency of the usage of the address space. Christian Huitema performed an analysis in which [he] evaluated the efficiency of other addressing architecture's (including the French telephone system, USA telephone systems, current internet using IPv4, and IEEE 802 nodes). He concluded that 128bit IPng addresses could accommodate between 8×10^{17} to 2×10^{33} nodes assuming efficiency in the same ranges as the other addressing architecture's. Even his most pessimistic estimate would provide 1,564 addresses for each square meter of the surface of the planet Earth. The optimistic estimate would allow for 3,911,873,538,269,506,102 addresses for each square meter of the surface of the planet Earth. [3]

IP addresses are paired, as we have seen, with domain names. InterNIC assigns domain names at the same time that it assigns IP addresses and in the same fashion; that is, it assigns a domain name to a network and it is then the responsibility of the network to assign workstation names. For example, my university, the University of Southern California, is assigned the Internet domain name "usc.edu," the first part of which is obviously an acronym for the institution. Its IP address is "128.125," which means that all IP addresses at USC begin with "128.125." Since no two domains can have the same name, the University of South Carolina is designated "sc.edu" and its IP addresses begin 129.125. The second part of these names, "edu," is the highest or generic level of these hierarchical names. Networks located in the United States usually use a three-letter generic designator. The "edu" stands for an educational institution. Other typical generic designators are "net" for internet service providers ("aol.net"), "org" for nonprofit organization ("c-span.org"), "com" for a commercial enterprise ("netscape.com") and "gov" for a government agency ("whitehouse.gov"). Other countries use different designators. For example, academic institutions in the United Kingdom all use "ac.uk" as the last part of their name. Oxford, for example, is "oxford.ac.uk." Unlike IP addresses, which are limited to four bytes, domain names can be quite long. The names are similar to file directory names. Each network maintains a unique list of its own host designator names and a pointer to the network above it in the hierarchy. There is, then, no central database of domain names and IP addresses. Rather these are distributed across the network with each network responsible for maintaining its own up-to-date list of workstations and for making it available to the network hierarchy.

THE INSCAPE OF NETSCAPE

With an enhanced understanding of what is going on in the background and with Negroponte's admonition not to mistake quantity for quality firmly in mind, we will now use the Web to obtain some bits (of information) we will need to carry out the exercises in this chapter and the next. The Web is a source of many types of information and we will be discussing how to obtain text, software, and images and how to configure Netscape to play sound and video files. The texts will serve as examples in our discussion of strategies for searching the Web and for our discussion of Hypertext Markup Language (HTML) in Chapter 6. The programs we obtain from the Web will assist us in developing HTML documents in the next chapter. They will include:

   a Zip program for the compression and decompression of files;
   an image viewer and editor to help us manipulate the graphic images we obtain
      from the Web;
   a file transfer protocol program that will simplify the transfer of files between
      our workstation client and our Web server; and
   a text editor which we will use to create and modify HTML documents.

All these programs are available free of charge on at least a trial basis and together they will provide a useful suite of programs for our HTML work. The images, sound, and video will provide the basis for our discussion of multimedia applications in research and instructions.

We will be using Netscape Navigator 3.0 as our interface between the Web and our workstation. Readers familiar with Netscape Communicator or Internet Explorer should have little difficulty following this discussion. MAC users should consult the MAC archive on the book's dedicated web site for programs equivalent to the Windows programs discussed here.

We have chosen to use Netscape over Microsoft's Internet Explorer because it currently has the advantage in market share over the Internet Explorer, although Internet Explorer is the technically superior product. Also the existence of two competing programs and the behavior of developers of each with regard to standards for the Internet provides an opportunity for the discussion of issues of official versus proprietary or *de facto* standards. The question of whether Internet Explorer or Netscape will ultimately dominate the field of Web browsers needn't concern us too much. When they asked J. P. Morgan whether the stock market would go up or down, he answered "Yes." But the effects of this marketplace competition to become the *de facto* standard must concern us. As Netscape and Microsoft add "enhancements" to their Web browsers that are not part of any official standard, the whole purpose of the Internet—universal access to information through standard protocols—is undermined. A user who adopts a proprietary standard on a Web page contributes to the fracturing of the Web.

I will give a brief overview of the functions of Netscape as they relate to the exercises in this book. A full treatment of the functions of this program is beyond the scope of this book and many excellent guides and introductions to Netscape are available. We will focus here, as elsewhere in this book, on those features that I think the majority of readers will find of particular interest and use. As does any complex program, Netscape frequently offers more than one way to accomplish a given task. In general, I will give only one way to accomplish each task, a way I hope makes clear to the reader what is being done and how it is being done. I will leave it to the knowledge and ingenuity of others to find other and better ways to accomplish the same end.

The main menu of Netscape certainly presents the user with many options and possibilities (Fig. 5.6). This is a typical home page that illustrates the ease of use of the Web. The two underlined phrases (Oakland University's and Virtual Software Library front desk at the Oak Repository) are called hyperlinks. By pointing to them with the mouse and then double clicking, one moves to a page pointed to by the link. Authors of Web pages design them with multiple links and pointers that allow readers of the page to use their own inclinations and interests to find their way through the page. Movement through the Web is associational and psychological

 OAK Software Repository

The OAK Software Repository (oak.oakland.edu) is a public service of Oakland University's Office of Computer and Information Services. OAK offers many collections of computer software and information to Internet users free of charge.

Virtual Software Library front desk at the OAK Repository
Search the OAK Repository and other popular archive sites for software.

Figure 5.6. Netscape main menu.

rather than linear and logical. The designer of a Web page must anticipate the interests of potential users and create the hypertext links to gratify these expectations.

We will describe now the Netscape options we will be using in the next chapter. Of the nine menu items on the menu toolbar we will be using only three: "File," "Bookmarks," and "Window":

Figure 5.7. Netscape menu bar.

We will use "File" to save on our client workstation HTML files displayed by Netscape; we will use "Bookmarks" to create our own personal map of the Web; and we will use "Window" in conjunction with the navigation buttons.

The navigation buttons enable us to page back and forth through the successive web sites we visit during a session on the Web:

Figure 5.8. Navigation buttons.

We always begin a Web session on a site we have designated as our home page but we usually go to a number of sites in the course of a session. Netscape maintains a list of site visits which the "Back" and "Forward" buttons allow us to visit sequentially by moving forward and back on the list. Each time in our session we

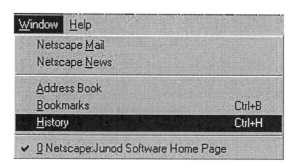

Figure 5.9. History option on Window menu.

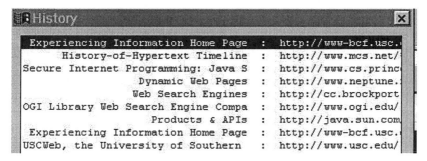

Figure 5.10. Netscape "History" page.

visit a site, Netscape adds the record of the visit to the top of the list. We can see this list of locations by selecting the "History" option on the "Window" menu (Fig. 5.9). This will bring up the History dialogue box (Fig. 5.10).

We can move at will to any of the locations we have visited by highlighting the location we want and pressing the "Go to" button. The list is a temporary list that exists only during our session. When we close Netscape, the list is discarded. However, Netscape maintains another list of visited sights, the "bookmark" list, which is permanent and so can be accessed from session to session. One way of adding a site on the history list to the bookmark stack is to highlight it and press the "Create Bookmark" button. One can examine the list of bookmarks by selecting the "Bookmarks" option from the "Windows" menu. One may select sites to visit from the bookmark list as one does from the history list.

The "Location:" field keeps track of where we are on the Web:

Figure 5.11. Location window and uniform resource locator (URL).

To succeed in the business of the Web, there are three things that are important: location, location, and location. The location field in Fig. 5.11 contains what is termed a *Uniform Resource Locator* or URL:

http://www.acs.oakland.edu/oak/oak.html

The concept of the URL is as fundamental to the Internet as binary code is to computers. "Locator" is the operative word in this term: the URL enables users of the Internet to know where things are on the net. All URLs are divided into three parts:

<Service Type>://<Machine IP Address>/<File Path Name>

The most common Service Type is "HTTP" which stands for HyperText Transfer Protocol. HTTP is the basic service provided by the Web and we will discuss it at length in the following pages. Other common types are "Gopher," which is used on the Internet by "Gopher" programs that simplify the transfer of text files, and "FTP," or File Transfer Protocol, which is used in peer-to-peer file transfers. We will confine our discussion to HTTP. Our sample URL begins "HTTP" and is therefore a part of the Web. The next part is the full IP address of the server we are accessing. The last part of the IP address, "oakland.edu," is the domain name of the Oakland University local network. The first part, "www.acs," is the name of the particular server at Oakland University that holds the file we wish to retrieve. The file path name, oak/oak.html, is the fully qualified path name of the file we are accessing on the server. A URL extends the domain name to specify a file name in the domain. The file system of a computer keeps track of the information on its disks by organizing it into hierarchies of directories, subdirectories, and files. The Internet provides an extension of the computer's file system to include files located on other machines. As the service type tells us the type of file we are accessing and the IP address identifies the network and machine on which the information sought is located, the file path tells us which specific file on the designated machine is to be accessed.

SEARCHING THE WEB

Most of the information on the Web is available without charge to anyone with access to the Web. This information may be retrieved through various Web search options we will be discussing in this section. There is, however, another class of information on the Web that may be retrieved only by those who have access to sites that are protected by passwords or other forms of restriction. Access to this information may require membership in some professional group or special class of users, purchase of a subscription, or payment of a direct charge for access. Colleges and universities frequently restrict access to course and library information to clients on their local networks. Other examples of restricted information include such things as the New York Times crossword puzzle; the Chronicle of Higher Education Internet Resources for the Humanities, Social Science, Science and Technology, and the Professions; and the OCLC FirstSearch Data Bases. Some people may express resentment at the idea of being charged for access to information on the Web. Their ideal Web would resemble a vast public library whose holdings are universally available without charge. Realistically, however, creating and maintaining large up-to-date databases of information requires the expenditure of considerable human intellectual capital. Compilers of dictionaries, bibliographies, and standard reference works such as *Books in Print* justly demand compensation for their work. Traditional public and university libraries compensated them for their efforts through institutional subscriptions and the purchase of their books. Library users paid these costs indirectly through taxes and tuition. As electronic publication supersedes traditional printing as the method of information distribution for their work, an electronic model of commerce will have to replace the traditional commercial one. We will limit our discussion of Web searching to sites with unrestricted information so that readers may carry out their exercises without entailing the cost of subscribing to online services over and above their subscription to an Internet Service Provider (ISP).

Netscape offers users six "Directory Buttons" to help in locating information on the Web. The button labeled "Net Search" is the one we use to gain access to Web search options.

| What's New? | What's Cool? | Destinations | Net Search | People | Software |

Figure 5.12. Netscape directory buttons.

Pushing the "Net Search" button brings us to the "Net Search" page provided by Netscape (Fig. 5.13). There are five major search options offered at the top of this page: Excite, Infoseek, Lycos, AltaVista, and LookSmart. The search option that is highlighted, in this case Infoseek, is the day's default search option. The default search option will vary from access to access and a user may select any of the others by pointing to it and clicking with the mouse. The default search option varies from day to day. Each of these options provides a way to find information stored at web sites. Each reflects the nature of the Web: dynamic, constantly growing and changing, and incomplete. Web sites by the thousands are added, moved, and removed on the Web each day and the distributed nature of the Web makes it

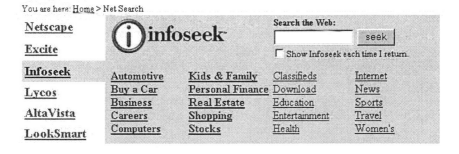

Figure 5.13. Top of Netscape search screen page.

impossible to know at any given instant the exact contents of the Web, composed as it is of elements that are "chalked on the sidewalk. . . . "

There are two types of search options available for Web searching. Some, like Yahoo! (http://yahoo.com), are similar to traditional library catalogues or reference works. They are compiled by humans from forms submitted to them by the creators of web sites and from visits made to web sites by the catalogue compilers themselves. Others, like Lycos and Infoseek, are called search engines. They use special software programs called web crawlers, robots, or spiders, which search the Web for new sites and analyze algorithmically the contents of sites they find. The results of their Web explorations are then stored in databases which users query in their search for information. For any query, the results returned by a search are based on matching keywords that supposedly characterize the contents of the site with keywords supplied by the search query.

Both directories and search engines, then, work by carrying out searches on keywords. The responses they give to users' queries are based on the words used in the queries, which become the keywords upon which they search. They rank the relevance of the sites they find by such things as the number and proximity of search keywords found at the site and the popularity of a site, a measure of the number of references to a site found on other sites. Some search all the text at a site for keywords, others focus on the title of the site as it appears at the top of the page and headings and titles contained on the site. Some search options—Excite, Lycos, HotBot (http://hotbot.com), and Yahoo!—are regarded as more generally useful and comprehensive than the others but all search methods return some results. Given the hit-and-miss way that the site keywords used as the targets of these searches are compiled and indexed, it is difficult to say for any topic what set of keywords and what search option is best. Users who want to do as thorough a search as is humanly possible must try every search method and be as inventive as possible in supplying synonyms of keywords on which to search. This part of Web searching is little different from searching the subject cards of a library catalogue.

In addition to the search options at the top of the page, the "Net Search" page gives a listing of many more options at the bottom (Fig. 5.14). Some of these services, for example the Electric Library, require users to pay for their services. Others are clearly commercial (AutoWeb.com) but are paid for through the sale of advertising. Another valuable place to get help, tips, and strategies for and information about finding things on the Web is the Yahoo! "How to" page (http://howto.yahoo.com), which is full of commonsense advice about Web searching (Fig. 5.15). Scrolling through the "How to" page provides an overview of the search options provided by Yahoo! For example, the "Art of Surfing" link on the "How to" page gives an excellent description of the whys and wherefores of Web searching. Figure 5.16 shows part of the opening page of this section. Readers are encouraged to investigate the links on the "How to" page before proceding further with the discussion of Web searching.

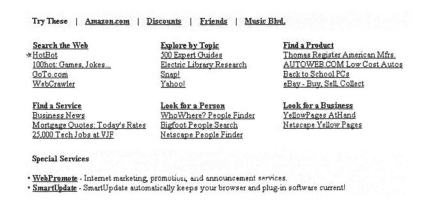

Figure 5.14. Additional search options.

In Chapter 1 of this book, I speculated about the future possible developments in the field of Artificial Intelligence. I will use Artificial Intelligence as the sample topic in the discussion of searching the Web. In this discussion, I will assume that readers are carrying out for themselves the searches I describe but I will try to give enough detail to enable readers who are not at a computer to follow the discussion.

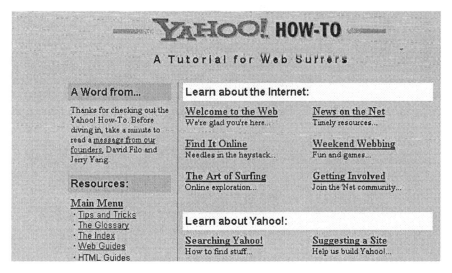

Figure 5.15. Yahoo! How to (partial listing).

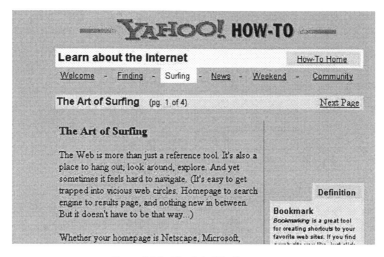

Figure 5.16. The Art of Surfing page.

There is a simple strategy that I usually follow in searching for information on the Web. I begin with the "Yahoo!" search because I have found it a generally useful search option and because it automatically submits any query I make to the other major search options. To begin our search, we enter "artificial intelligence" in the search keyword field and push the "Search" button. Readers should note that these searches are not case-sensitive and that the keyword area scrolls left to accommodate words and phrases that are too long for the display area on the screen (Fig. 5.17). The results returned from this search reflect the indexed nature of the Yahoo! database (Fig. 5.18). (Readers may note some discrepancies between the results they obtain from their search and the results shown here. This is a consequence of the shifting nature of the Web's content and should not be cause for alarm.). It should not surprise us that Yahoo! presents its categories in the context of a hierarchy of categories. Artificial Intelligence is one of its designated categories. For this search,

Figure 5.17. Initial search for "artificial intelligence."

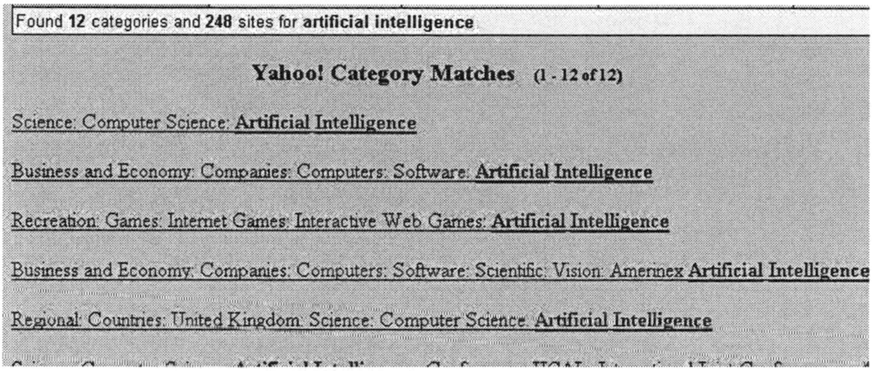

Found **12** categories and **248** sites for **artificial intelligence**

Yahoo! Category Matches (1 - 12 of 12)

Science: Computer Science: **Artificial Intelligence**

Business and Economy: Companies: Computers: Software: **Artificial Intelligence**

Recreation: Games: Internet Games: Interactive Web Games: **Artificial Intelligence**

Business and Economy: Companies: Computers: Software: Scientific: Vision: Amerinex **Artificial Intelligence**

Regional: Countries: United Kingdom: Science: Computer Science: Artificial Intelligence

Figure 5.18. Result of search on "artificial intelligence."

it matches the category of "Artificial Intelligence" with the categories it has determined are directly above it and below it in its hierarchy. It occurs as a subcategory of twelve categories including Computer Science, Business, Recreation, Conferences, and geographical areas.

The "Computer Science" category is a typical Yahoo! category (Fig. 5.19). At the top of the Computer Science: Artificial Intelligence category page is a search field that allows users to search for keywords within the category or across the entire Yahoo! database. The purpose of this search is to refine the results. Because Web keyword searches often return thousands of matches, refining results is a necessity in Web searching. In this page, we are offered 69 Institute sites, 55 Natural Language Processing sites, etc. as well as other categories for Artificial Life, Companies, Neural Networks, Ontology, Robotics, and Web-Based that may also contain information about Artificial Intelligence.

Yahoo!'s categories resemble wormholes in Web cyberspace. Entering one of these wormholes by clicking on its hyperlink leads us further into a honeycomb of sites and categories. Arriving at any site will most likely offer us, among its contents, yet another set of hyperlinks. Even if we try to restrain ourselves to pursue these links with unhurried chase and unperturbed pace, cyberspace scenery seems to flicker past our screens at seemingly relativistic velocity. The thing to do, as way leads on to way, is to make extensive use of the "Bookmarks/Add Bookmark" option to record a reference to any site that catches our attention while we take a way less traveled by. Who knows if we will ever come back to these sites, but memorializing with a bookmark our interest in a site is the only way to be certain that we will be able to find our way back to it. It's easy enough to delete entries from the bookmark list. See the cat! See the cradle!

Next on the category page is a link to "Indices," which are web sites that contain lists of links to sites related to the category. The sites listed in the indices are often

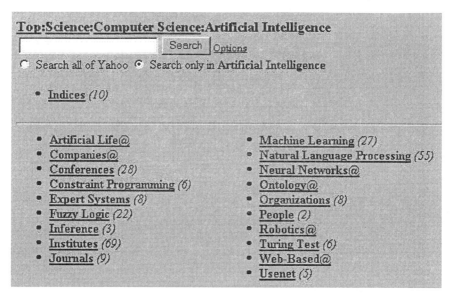

Figure 5.19. Yahoo! Computer Science: Artificial Intelligence category.

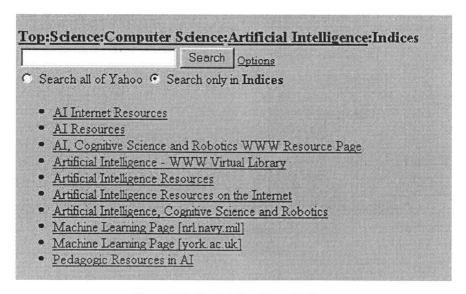

Figure 5.20. "Artificial Intelligence" indices.

compiled by interested parties: professionals in the field, professional organizations, etc. Frequently, these sites are the result of an expenditure of intellectual capital as much as that expended on sites with restricted access. Because trained individuals have had a hand in compiling them, they tend to be among the most useful sites and are prime candidates for recording with a bookmark.

The Indices for Artificial Intelligence are a good example of what is to be found in such listings (Fig. 5.20). "Pedagogic Resources in AI" is a rich source of information on courses on the topic. The "Artificial Intelligence—WWW Virtual Library" site provides a comprehensive list of ongoing research and organizations in the field. One should pay particular attention to the revision date of any Web page. The date for this last page, March 4, 1997, is about a year old at this writing. One hopes that it will be updated soon. More problematically, there is no guarantee that an index site will be there when we try to visit it. Just about anyone consulting the indices for Artificial Intelligence would be likely to take a look at the first entry, "AI Internet Resources." This turns out to be a dry hole rather than a wormhole, yielding only an all too familiar HTTP error message:

HTTP/1.0 404 Object Not Found

Figure 5.21. Missing hyperlink error message.

The time traveler in H. G. Wells's novel, *The Time Machine,* visits a library in the land of the Eloi where he finds nothing on the shelves but dust and the moldy remnants of bindings. In Wells's novel, the decay of knowledge is the work of ages. Things can vanish much more quickly in cyberspace and leave not a rack behind.

Beneath the categories on the result page for the search on "artificial intelligence" is a listing of 248 sites arranged in what appears to be helter-skelter order. Problems arise when one tries to examine the web sites on this list. Yahoo! breaks this list of sites into pages containing twenty entries each. This makes it difficult to deal with this list as a whole. There is no search option available on this list to refine it further. Yahoo! supposedly is listing its results "according to relevancy within each specific area" but I doubt that any user has the least idea what its definition of relevancy is.[4]

Another problem with the results of this search is that it seems to have yielded far fewer results than one would expect. Given the ongoing interest in Artificial Intelligence in fields of Philosophy, Neuroscience, Computer Science, Cognitive Science, etc., and the widespread use of the Web in all these fields, it would seem that there should be far more than 248 web sites devoted to the subject. When we try the "Alta Vista" option on the results page this number increases remarkably:

Figure 5.22. Alta Vista result of search for "artificial intelligence."

The discrepancy between 248 and 165199 needs some explanation. Cyberspace, I have pointed out, requires that we accustom ourselves to larger and smaller numbers than we usually use; but not to a large and small number simultaneously for the same quantity.

We can gain some insight about where these numbers come from by searching for "artificial intelligence" with the HotBot (http://hotbot.com) search engine (Fig. 5.23). We enclosed the words in quotation marks for this search. Enclosing a phrase in quotation marks is the notation in Web searching that means we are searching for a phrase, not for individual occurrences words making up the phrase.

In its search of the Web, HotBot finds 527,279 occurrences of the word "artificial," 768,180 occurrences of the word "intelligence," and 233,338 occurrences of the phrase "artificial intelligence." It is reporting the number of occurrences of the individual key words and the phrase, not, as does Yahoo!, the number of sites containing the key word. Repeating the Yahoo! search on the phrase makes a slight difference in the numbers reported:

look for [all the words   ▼]

["artificial intelligence"   ] (*SEARCH*)

(*NEW SEARCH*)   (*REVISE SEARCH*)

SEYBOLD NY **WEB PUBLISHER 98** CONFERENCE 16-18 March New York City
WIRED **BE THERE.**

Seybold/Wired Web Publisher '98: the one conference you can't afford to miss.

Returned: 233338 matches.

Breakdown: artificial: 527279, intelligence: 768180   1 - 10 ▶

Figure 5.23. HotBot search for "artificial intelligence."

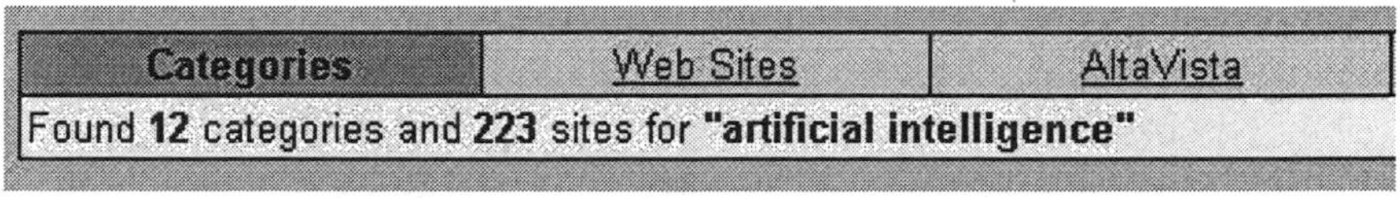

Categories	Web Sites	AltaVista
Found **12** categories and **223** sites for **"artificial intelligence"**		

Figure 5.24. Yahoo! search on phrase "artificial intelligence."

Searching on the phrase also produces some impact on the AltaVista findings as well:

Categories	Web Sites	AltaVista
Found **155660** AltaVista web pages for **"artificial intelligence"**		

Figure 5.25. AltaVista search on "artificial intelligence."

In our searches so far, we have asked Yahoo! to search the entire contents of each Web page. But it is also possible to search only the titles and headings on a page. This is a plausible limitation when we are looking for information on topics like Artificial Intelligence that are of a well-defined, institutional nature. Many sites dealing with Artificial Intelligence should include the phrase somewhere in their descriptive titles and headings. The way to restrict a search to titles is by prefixing "t:" to the phrase we are searching for: This has no effect on the number of categories for Artificial Intelligence but reduces the site count by more than half:

Categories	Web Sites	AltaVista
Found **12** categories and **104** sites for **t:"artificial intelligence"**		

Figure 5.26. Yahoo! title search for "artificial intelligence."

The AltaVista title search produces a much lower number than the unrestricted search:

Categories	Web Sites	AltaVista
Found **12** categories and **104** sites for **t:"artificial intelligence"**		

Figure 5.27. AltaVista title search for "artificial intelligence."

This number still strikes me as too low. A more realistic number is obtained from a title search on the acronym for Artificial Intelligence, "AI."

Categories	Web Sites	AltaVista
Found **17429** AltaVista web pages for **title:"ai"**		

Figure 5.28. AltaVista title search for AI.

If we add the number of AI sites to the number of Artificial Intelligence sites we come up with something over 20,000 total sites. Not all the sites with "AI" in the title have to do with Artificial Intelligence. "AI" is also an acronym for Amnesty International, whose reports on human rights are also posted on the Web. And there are many sites, for example those with "Neural Net" or other specialties within the field of Artificial Intelligence in their titles, not included in our total. The answer to the question of how many web sites deal with Artificial Intelligence is unanswerable. Searching the Web can be literally tantalizing.

What users get out of searching the Web is a function of what they bring to the search. Sophisticated users, well grounded in a subject area, will usually get more from the Web than will naïve novices. They will be able to formulate their queries with a precision that derives from their knowledge and experience. This can be illustrated with reference to searches in the area of Artificial Intelligence. A user with a philosophical interest in Artificial Intelligence would undoubtedly be following the discussions of Roger Penrose's two recent books on the subject, *The Emperor's New Mind* and *Shadows of the Mind.* Such a user, experienced as well in Web searching, would search the Web for Penrose's work on Artificial Intelligence with the following query:

Categories	Web Sites	AltaVista
Found **923** AltaVista web pages for **+"artificial intelligence" +penrose**		

Figure 5.29. Focused search for "artificial intelligence."

By prefixing both search terms with a plus sign, we immediately restrict the search only to sites containing both. A search on Penrose's name (+roger +penrose) produces 3900 matches, many of which have to do with Penrose's work in cosmology and quantum physics. The 923 matches of name and topic provide a solid list of sites from which readers may examine and catalogue with book marks.

Similar searches for others active in the field also yield extensive and useful results. John Searle appears on 1226 Web pages; Hubert Dreyfus on 353; and Daniel Crevier on 133.

The use of the plus sign as a part of the syntax of these queries leads to the topic of the syntax and options Yahoo! provides. There are a small number of symbols one may use to put various restrictions on Yahoo! searches. These include the minus sign, which eliminates sites containing a keyword; an asterisk, which provides for wild card searches; and a "u:" prefix that restricts a search to URLs just as the "t:" prefix restricted searches to titles. A full explanation of the syntax of Yahoo! queries is found at the "help" link at the bottom of any search result page:

Figure 5.30. Yahoo! help link.

This help is in addition to the help available on the "Tips" link (Fig. 5.15). For some reason, rather than offering a comprehensive list of help options up front, Yahoo! divides this information between before and after search pages. Readers should definitely consult the links offered by the "help" link next to the "options" link (Fig. 5.31).

Readers should also consult the "options" link to the left of the "help" link for still more ways to formulate Yahoo! searches (Fig. 5.32). The two groups of radio buttons at the top of this options page allow users to choose search method and search area and to place time limits on the scope of a search. Readers will have to form their own opinion about the intelligence of the "intelligent default" search method. And the caveat at the bottom about options not carrying over to other search engines is real and frustrating. For example, AltaVista searches launched from Yahoo! cannot be limited as to time.

Readers might want to try to search topics that interest them by starting with Yahoo! and branching out from there. But they should first search Yahoo! for

- How to use Yahoo! Search
- How Yahoo! Search Works
- Tips for Better Searching
- Query Syntax Options

Figure 5.31. Yahoo! help topics.

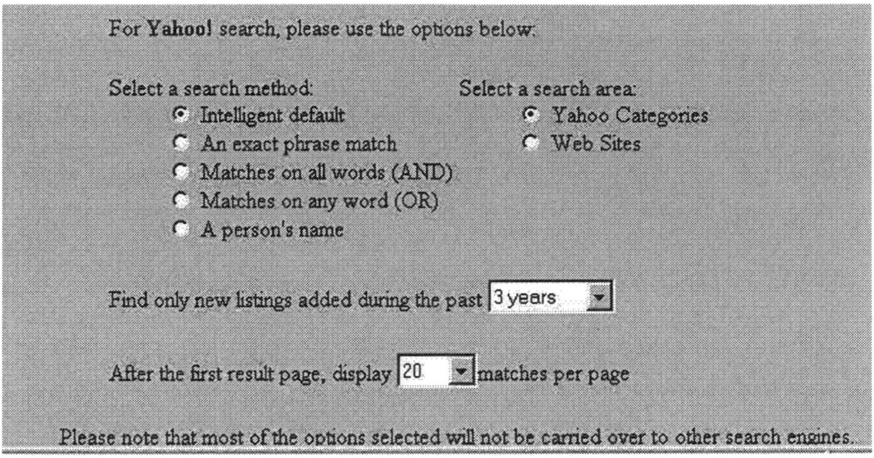

Figure 5.32. Yahoo! search options page.

artificial intelligence. The extent to which the results they obtain differ from the results published here will provide some measure of the transitory nature of information on the Web, which is by nature ephemeral. We could use the Latin phrase *in saecula saeculorom*, which translates roughly as "in cycles of cycles," [5] to express its transience if we remember that the computer's cycle of fetching and executing instructions is measured in nanoseconds, not years and decades.

The keyword searches carried out by Yahoo! *et al.* work best, in my experience, on the specialized vocabulary of technical literature, especially literature dealing with computer technology. (Try a search using the keywords "binary octal hexa-decimal.") For searches on topics relating to history, philosophy, and the arts, the results get very scattered. A search on "lyric epic dramatic" finds little poetry or theater beyond what is listed in some course syllabi. A search on "pity fear catharsis" gets us nowhere near Aristotle's Poetics or Sophocles' *Oedipus Rex*. To get to Aristotle's Poetics, one must be explicit and ask for "+aristotle + poetics." This search yields 2,372 web sites. Searching without the plus sign prefixes yields 18,348 matches.

Web searching with various options leaves me with an overall sense of the quirkiness of the procedure. The results returned by Web search options remind me of what Bokonon in *Cat's Cradle* calls a *karass*, a team that does God's will without ever discovering what it is doing:

In his "Fifty-third Calypso," Bokonon invites us to sing along with him:

> Oh, a sleeping drunkard
> Up in Central Park,
> A lion-hunter

In the jungle dark,
A Chinese dentist
And a British queen—
All fit together
In the same machine.

Nice, nice, very nice;
Nice, nice, very nice;
Nice, nice, very nice—
So many different people
In the same device.

. . .

Nowhere does Bokonon warn against a person's trying to discover the limits of his *karass* and the nature of the work God almighty has had it do. Bokonon simply observes that such investigations are bound to be incomplete.[6]

Results from Web searches, like inquiries into the purpose of a *karass*, must always be regarded as provisional. But I am surprised at the number of times I have found myself reading through the results of a search while quietly singing to myself, "Nice, nice, very nice. . . ." And the popularity of Web searching suggests that such responses are not atypical. Web searching is a problem that seems suited to the application of artificial intelligence technology, should it ever become generally available. In fact, it leads me to suggest a reformulated version of the Turing test: a machine should be judged intelligent if seventy percent of the time the results obtained from its Web searches are indistinguishable from the results obtained by a typical user.

I began our discussion of Web searching by comparing the keywords in Web searches to the subject headings in library catalogues. I will conclude by pointing to the similarity between searching the Web and browsing library stacks. No matter how many sites we bookmark for investigation, we cannot transform this index-learning into knowledge unless we read reflectively what we find on the sites we visit. The hyperspeed of hypertexts must eventually slow to the pace at which our human brains can absorb information. After searching the topic of Artificial Intelligence, I spent some time browsing, old style, at various sites and winnowing my bookmarks until I had come up with a list of sites that struck me as most generally useful or truly unusual. The full list is posted in the Chapter 5 archive of the book's dedicated Web page. It may be accessed by pressing the "AI" button on Chapter 5 archive (Fig. 5.33). Along with some excellent index sites, this list includes such things as Penrose's response to his critics, vigorous arguments pro and con for Artificial Intelligence, a sardonic fable about the implications of regarding human consciousness as a Turing machine, and some striking graphical images of Babbage's Difference Engine. Nice, nice, very nice.

This page provides access to the HTML resources and texts used in Chapter 5 of *Computing in the Web Age*. There are separate links for MAC and Windows users.

Figure 5.33. Chapter 5 archive.

SAVING INFORMATION FROM THE WEB

Saving information found on the Web is complicated by the fact that the Web usually retrieves results that are an amalgam of several different types of files, each of which must be saved in a different way. For example, suppose in the course of search on Charles Babbage, we come across the interesting graphic given below (Fig. 5.34). One way to "save" this textual information and the picture is to print it out by pushing Netscape's print button (Fig. 5.35). If we are fortunate enough to have a

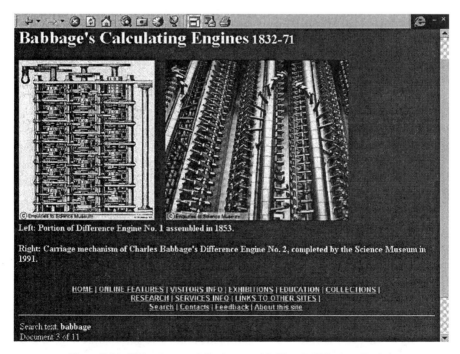

Figure 5.34. Web page containing images of Babbage's Difference Engine.

Figure 5.35. Netscape print button.

color printer, we would get a good copy of this page. More elaborate procedures are required to save the pictures in electronic form. In order to save a picture, image, or other graphic, one points to it with the mouse and clicks on the right mouse button. This brings up a dialog box that offers a number of options, of which the one we are to choose is "Save Image As" (Fig. 5.36). Choosing the "Save Image As . . ." option will open the standard file "Save As" dialog box. We will save this file in the "\webinfo\AI directory" as the "diffeng1." We then click with the right-hand mouse button on the other image to save it as "diffeng2" in the same directory.

As was explained in our discussion of HTML coding in Chapter 4, information of the Web contains embedded code to direct a browser program in displaying the information. We can view this encoded form of the page by selecting the "View/Frame Source" option from the Netscape menu (Fig. 5.37). We will be discussing HTML code in Chapter 6. This code may be saved with Netscape's

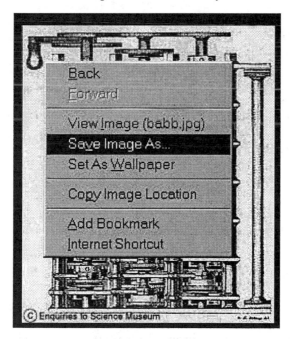

Figure 5.36. Saving image of Difference Engine.

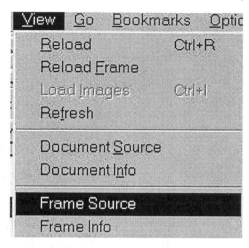

Figure 5.37. Netscape view/frame source menu.

"File/Save Frame As" menu command. The code for this page is found in the "\webinfo\AI" directory as file "babb2."

This page is taken up by its graphics and contains no text worth saving. It is possible to save the text of the file without its HTML coding through use of the Windows clipboard. For example, suppose we wanted to save the text of John Reilly's story "The Stopping Problem," the sardonic tale listed in the Chapter 5 AI archive. We would open the page containing the story with Netscape. To move the text of the story to the clipboard, we use in turn Netscape's "Edit/Select All" and "Edit/Paste" menu commands. These two commands move the text—without embedded codes—to the clipboard. We could then open a word processor such as Word or a text editor program such as Notepad and use its "Edit/Paste" menu command to move the text from the clipboard to the program, where we could then save it as we would any text file or word processing document. The "\webinfo\ai\" archive contains a text of this story saved as a text document. Readers may view this text by using the Wordpad program that is supplied with Windows 95. After opening the text, readers should set the word wrap option found on the "View/Options" menu selection to "Wrap to ruler." Text and images are only two of the many types of information accessible on the Web. We will discuss multimedia in Chapter 6.

DOWNLOADING SOFTWARE

Our final topic in this chapter is how to download software from the Web. Among the pieces of software we will be downloading will be an image file viewer that will enable us to display and edit the image files we obtain from the Web.

Figure 5.38. Archive page.

All the software we need to download for this chapter and the next may be found in Oakland University's Oak Software Repository. To access this archive, we first must load Netscape and connect it to the book's dedicated home page on the Web. We then push the "Archive" button on the left panel to bring up the archive page (Fig. 5.38). The Chapter 5 button takes us to the Chapter 5 Archive (Fig. 5.39). MAC users will find a parallel discussion in the MAC portion of the archive. We will follow the Windows branch for our discussion (Fig. 5.40).

Shareware is a method of distributing software that bypasses commercial distribution channels. Programmers using Shareware make their programs available on a trial basis. If users of the program decide to keep the program after trying it, they pay a small licensing fee to the programmer, usually less than fifty dollars.

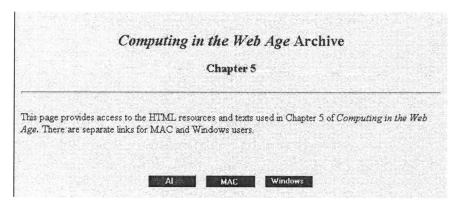

Figure 5.39. Chapter 5 archive.

Software Download Sites

OAK Software Repository

SHAREWARE.COM Shareware Archive

Chapter 5

Figure 5.40. Windows software download.

Programs obtained from Shareware are usually complete programs, but they sometimes contain extra code to remind users that the program is being used on a trial basis. When the users purchases the program, they receive a "licensed" version that omits the trial notifications. The programs we are about to download are all Shareware programs. The use of these programs for the exercises in this book constitutes a trial use. Readers who wish to use these programs beyond the trial period must register them. The programs all contain explicit directions for doing so. Readers looking for useful software will find both the Oak and Shareware archives to be valuable resources.

Clicking on the "Oak Software Repository" connect us to the archive (Fig. 5.41). The first program we are going to retrieve from the archive is a file compression and decompression program for Windows 95 called "PKZIP." File

 OAK Software Repository

The OAK Software Repository (oak.oakland.edu) is a public service of Oakland University's Office of Computer and Information Services. OAK offers many collections of computer software and information to Internet users free of charge.

Virtual Software Library front desk at the OAK Repository
    Search the OAK Repository and other popular archive sites for software.

Walnut Creek CDROM Simtel.Net ® Mirror
    Keith Petersen's world-wide distribution site for MS-DOS, Windows, and Windows 95 software.

Figure 5.41. Oak Repository home page.

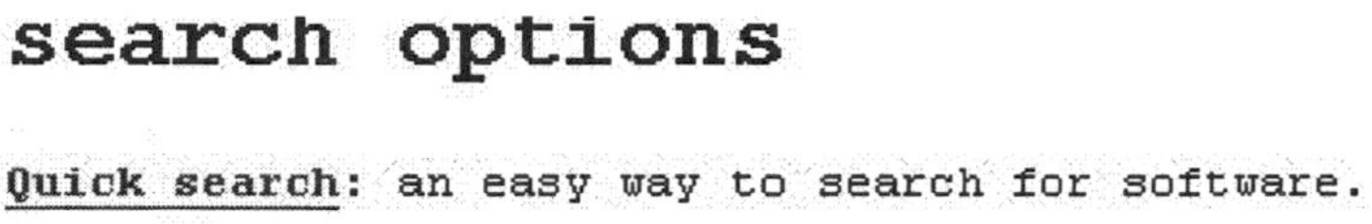

search options

Quick search: an easy way to search for software.

Figure 5.42. Quick search option.

compression, as we explained in Chapter 1, is one of the basic techniques used to increase network performance. Almost all the programs in the archives are compressed in one way or another. The PKZIP program enables us to decompress them so that we can install them on our workstations. We now click of the "Virtual Software Library front desk" and scroll down to the search options (Fig. 5.42). The option we select is "Quick search" (Fig. 5.43).

We select "MS-Windows95" for our search category, enter "PKZIP" as the first search word, and push the "start search" button. After a few minutes, the results of the search are displayed. The program we want is "pk250w32.exe" (Fig. 5.44). When we click with the mouse on this file, we are offered a selection of sites from which to download this file. The Oak Repository keeps track not only of the files in its archive but also of the locations of other copies of the files. This enables users to download files from locations near to them, thus minimizing network traffic. It turns out that for me, the nearest site is the Oak Repository (Fig. 5.45).

When I select this site, the "Save As . . ." dialogue box appears. We will download all the files from the Oak Repository into directory "\webinfo\shareware" which has been created when we extracted the JAVA programs from their archive but left empty for this purpose (Fig. 5.46). When the "Save" button is pushed, Netscape's "Saving Location" dialog appears (Fig. 5.47). This enables users to monitor the progress of their down loading.

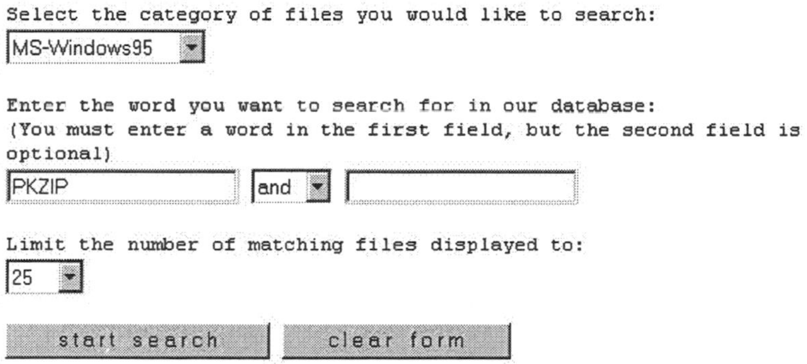

Select the category of files you would like to search:
MS-Windows95 ▾

Enter the word you want to search for in our database:
(You must enter a word in the first field, but the second field is optional)
PKZIP   and ▾ [   ]

Limit the number of matching files displayed to:
25 ▾

start search   clear form

Figure 5.43. Search for PKZIP.

```
Files found in sim-win95 archive as of Nov 20,1996:

pk250w32.exe new
        file size: 661 K (676444 bytes)
        file date: Nov 12,1996
        path: compress/

        PKZIP for Windows, version 2.50 - 32 bit

Files found in 3com-mswin archive as of Nov 20,1996:
```

Figure 5.44. Search result for PKZIP search.

USA

```
* pk250w32.exe [661 K]  from ftp.hkstar.com
* pk250w32.exe [661 K]  from ftp.cdrom.com
* pk250w32.exe [661 K]  from ftp.digital.com
* pk250w32.exe [661 K]  from uiarchive.cso.uiuc.edu
* pk250w32.exe [661 K]  from ftp.bu.edu
* pk250w32.exe [661 K]  from oak.oakland.edu
* pk250w32.exe [661 K]  from ftp.rge.com
* pk250w32.exe [661 K]  from ftp.ou.edu
* pk250w32.exe [661 K]  from ftp.orst.edu
* pk250w32.exe [661 K]  from ftp.cyber-naut.com
```

Figure 5.45. Downloading sites for PKZIP in USA.

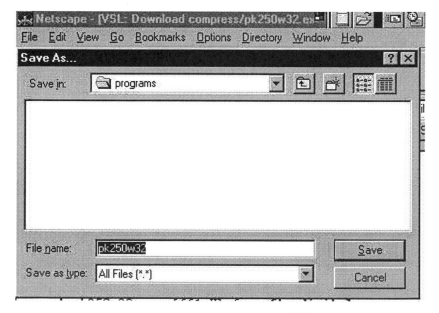

Figure 5.46. "Save As" dialog box for PKZIP.

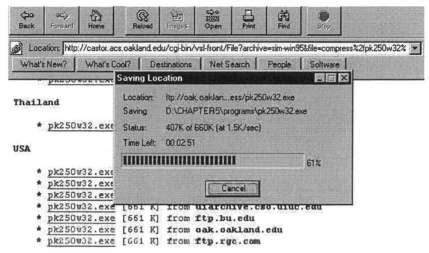

Figure 5.47. Save location for PKZIP.

When the PKZIP file has finished downloading, we return to the "quick search" page to retrieve the "LView" graphics editor and viewer program. We use the same basic procedure for this file as we did with the "PKZIP" program, except that we specify "LView" and "Graphics" as our search words (Fig. 5.48). The file we are seeking this time is called "lview1d2.zip." Because it is a "ZIP" file, Netscape displays an "Unknown File Type" dialog when we begin to unload it (Fig. 5.49). All we need do is push the "Save File . . ." button and the "Save As . . ." dialog appears. We then proceed as with the PKZIP file.

```
Select the category of files you would like to search:
MS-Windows95  ▼

Enter the word you want to search for in our database:
(You must enter a word in the first field, but the second field is
optional)
LVIEW          and  ▼  Graphics

Limit the number of matching files displayed to:
25  ▼

    start search        clear form
```

Figure 5.48. Quick search for LView.

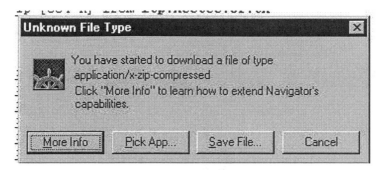

Figure 5.49. "Unknown File Type" dialog.

Once this file has downloaded, we download the text editor program and the FTP utility, both of which we will be using in Chapter 6. These files are downloaded in the same way as the "LView" file. The search words for the text editor are "PFE" and "Editor." The file we want to download for the text editor is "pfe0601i.zip." The single search word for the FTP utility is "ws_ftp32" and the file to be downloaded is "ws_ftp32.zip."

These four files each take about five to ten minutes to download through a 28.8K Baud modem, less than a minute through an ethernet or other high speed connection. When they have all been downloaded, the contents of the "\webinfo\share-ware" directory will be as shown in Fig. 5.50. We are now ready to install these programs so that we may make use of them.

The first program we will install is the PKZIP program. Although it is already a program, it is not the program we use to decompress the other files. Rather, it is what is called a "self-extracting archive." As was pointed out in our discussion of networks, data compression is one of the standard tactics used to increase the capacity of networks to transmit data. A self-extracting archive is a program file that contains in its data segment a compressed version of the data file or files containing its archival material, and in its code segment the instructions for decompressing the archive. When it arrives at its destination, it can reconstitute its archival material, without needing any other software. This makes self-extracting archives very convenient and they are widely used to distribute software both on networks and on disks. Their one drawback is that they are usually somewhat larger than compressed file archives that are not self-extracting.

To decompress the files in the PKZIP program "pk250w32" we select the "Run" option from the "Start" button on the Windows 95 task bar (Fig. 5.51). This starts the installation dialog which allows us to designate the place on our disk where we want the program to be installed (Fig. 5.52). When we push the "Extract" button, the program installs itself and creates the "Pkware" Icon group (Fig. 5.53). This icon group is placed with other such groups on the "Programs" menu, where

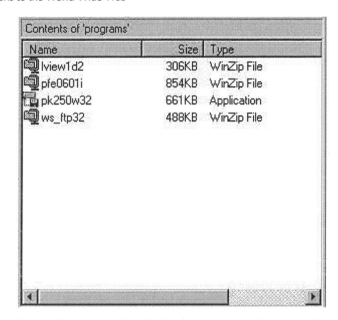

Figure 5.50. Contents of the \Ch4\shareware directory after downloading.

it can be referenced as needed (Fig. 5.54). Those who are interested in using this
program beyond its trial period should follow the instructions in the "License Info"
and "Order Form" sections of this menu. As part of our trial period, we will use the
program to install the other three programs.

To install the LView program, we run PKZIP and, using PKZIP's File/Open
menu, we select its ZIP version from "\webinfo\shareware" (Fig. 5.55). When we
push the open button, PKZIP displays a screen detailing the contents of
"lview1d2.ZIP" (Fig. 5.56).

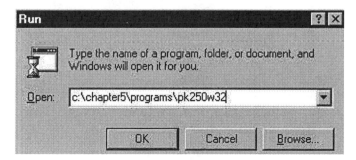

Figure 5.51. Running program PK250W32.

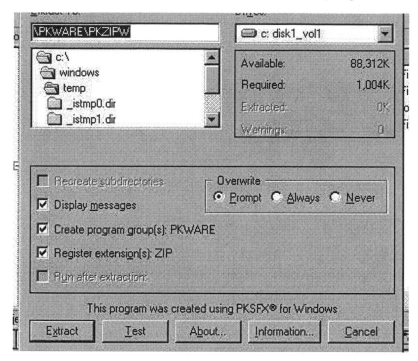

Figure 5.52. PKZIP installation screen.

Figure 5.53. PKware icons.

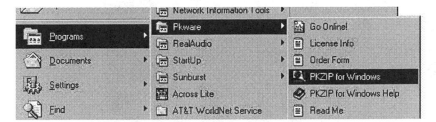

Figure 5.54. Selecting PKZIP from "Programs" folder menu.

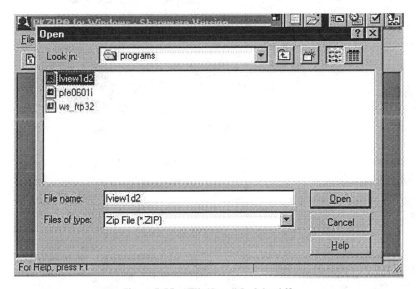

Figure 5.55. "File/Open" for lview1d2.

	Filename	Date	Time	Orig Size	Comp Size
1	CHANGES.TXT	7/17/96	2:00:48 am	13,791	5,204
2	IREGISTR.TXT	7/18/96	12:17:16 am	2,077	862
3	LVIEWPRO.EXE	8/29/96	5:56:00 am	502,784	244,493
4	LVIEWPRO.HLP	8/26/96	6:50:16 am	81,132	59,742
5	README.TXT	7/21/96	7:41:00 pm	2,675	1,258
6	SREGISTR.TXT	7/16/96	9:02:00 pm	2,553	978

Figure 5.56. Contents of lview1d2.zip.

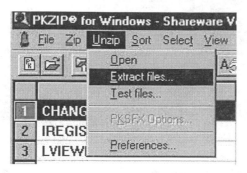

Figure 5.57. Selecting "Unzip/Extract" from menu.

Readers will note the difference in size between the compressed and uncompressed versions of the files. To extract these files, we select "Unzip/Extract" from PKZIP's menu bar (Fig. 5.57). PKZIP now displays the Extract dialog box so that we may decide where to place the extracted files. If the directory we designate does not exist, PKZIP will create it for us (Fig. 5.58).

In this example, we designate directory "C:Lview" as the destination directory but the files may be placed anywhere. It is good practice, however, to place them in a directory of their own with a meaningful name. When we press the "Extract" button, the files will be decompressed and placed in the designated directory. PKZIP

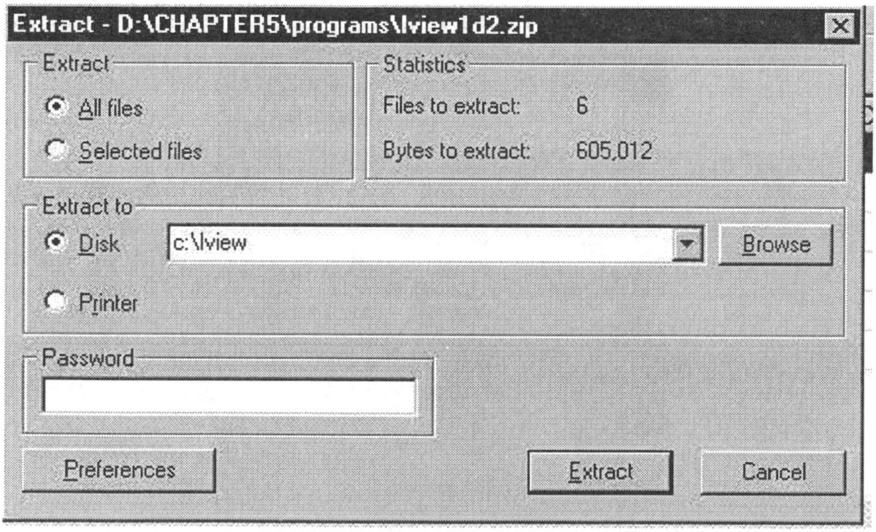

Figure 5.58. Extract dialog box.

Extract / Test Zip

Zip File: D:\CHAPTER5\programs\lview1d2.zip

Progress

Filename: c:/lview/CHANGES.TXT

File #: 6 of 6   Progress: **100%**

Extracting: c:/lview/LVIEWPRO.HLP - OK
Extracting: c:/lview/README.TXT - OK
Extracting: c:/lview/IREGISTR.TXT - OK
Extracting: c:/lview/SREGISTR.TXT - OK
Extracting: c:/lview/CHANGES.TXT - OK
Done.

Warnings: 0   [Done]

Figure 5.59. PKZIP report screen.

will then display a screen reporting the results of its operation (Fig. 5.59). The extraction was successful and LView has been installed in directory "C:\LView."

We can test LView by executing it from the "Run" option (Fig. 5.60). We may then use "File/Open" to view the image of "diffeng2" we downloaded earlier and stored in directory "Ch4/AI" (Fig. 5.61).

We will be using this program and the others we have downloaded in the next chapter. The text editor and FTP utility are installed in much the same way as LView

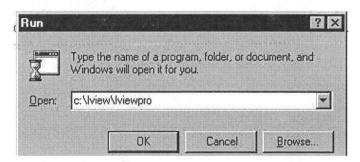

Figure 5.60. Running LView.

Figure 5.61. Image of Difference Engine displayed by LView.

using PKZIP to extract their contents to a directory and then following any instructions to complete the installation.[7] With these tools, we will be able to place information on the Web as well as download it from the Web. And judging by what we have seen so far, there are wonderful things lurking in the jungle of the Web. And if it is a jungle, intellectually responsible users may help it come to be, with less irony than Conrad's jungle in *Heart of Darkness,* "an exotic Immensity ruled by an august Benevolence.

CHAPTER 6

HTML Programming and Web Publishing

FROM PRINT TO HYPERTEXT

This chapter takes the next step in understanding and using the Web by showing how to create web sites and place information on the Web. It begins by showing how to take an ordinary text file and transform it into a hypertext document suitable for publication on the Web. Drawing on the work with programming in earlier chapters, this chapter explains how to program using HyperText Markup Language (HTML). The basic "tags" and conventions for laying out Web documents are introduced as well as the way in which documents are organized on the Web. The concept of the Uniform Resource Locator (URL) and the use of relative and absolute addressing on web sites is covered in detail. URLs are used to track where and how things are located on the Web. The use and placement of images on files and the methods HTML provides for displaying them on Web pages are covered as part of a general discussion of Web applications for multimedia information. The way in which helper applications are used to enhance the capabilities of Web browsers and how these applications are obtained from the Web are part of the topic of multimedia. Both video and audio applications are covered. Finally, the basics of the UNIX operating system are introduced as part of the explanation of how and where to place hypertext material on a Web server for access on the Web.

In the *New York Times* for January 21, 1996, there appeared an article entitled "Where to Browse for Art on the Web" that listed the growing number of museums, galleries, auction houses, and artists with established professional presences on the Web. This article struck me as a real find, one of those rare articles that instruct the ignorant and edify the instructed. For those taking an active part in connecting the art world to the World Wide Web, the article is a public acknowledgment of the successful fruition of their efforts. For those active on the Web but not familiar with the work in the field of art, it holds out the prospect of many sessions of delightful Web surfing. For those interested in art but as yet uninitiated in the mysteries of the Web, it gives practical advice about what they need to get started on the Web as well as a motive to do so. The article gives the Web addresses (URLs) for an impressive array of museums, auction houses and galleries, publications, individual art and artist sites, and generally useful home pages, directories, tools, and search engines. Accompanying each entry in this skillfully organized compilation of addresses is a succinct description of its content. Web searching will be a mature technology when it becomes possible to obtain search results whose quality and usefulness approach the level of this article's contents.

When the article appeared, the *New York Times* was not yet available as the *Cybertimes*. To get this article in machine-readable form as an ASCII text file while avoiding the tedious task of retyping, it was first scanned with optical character recognition software. It was then copy edited to remove the mistakes made by the optical character recognition program. Readers are encouraged to read the article before proceeding further in this chapter. It is a short article, the gist of which can be gleaned in five or ten minutes of personal page scanning. The article is available in the archive downloaded from the Web as "\webinfo\html\NY Times January 21, 1996.txt" and may be opened with the Notepad accessory program of Windows.

In order to introduce readers to the fundamental concepts and procedures of HTML coding, we will use the article as a sample of a printed text to be converted to a hypertext document by the insertion of appropriate HTML tags in its text. There are two versions of this file in the \webinfo\html\directory: an ASCII text version named "artweb.txt;" and an HTML version of the file named "artweb.html." The ASCII text and HTML files are byte for byte identical copies of the output from the optical character recognition software with no other codes added. The difference between them is that the operating system has been told to regard the first as an ASCII text file and the second as an HTML source file. This was done by saving the first file with a ".txt" file-type extension and the second with an "html" file-type extension. Despite their identical content, Netscape displays them in entirely different formats, as readers may verify by clicking on the links to them. The extension given to a file is very important in Web programming because browsers use file extensions to determine the basic way to display a file.

In Chapter 4, we made use of HTML encoded text of Hopkins's poetry. Our main concern then was to get rid of this coding as expeditiously as possible. It is now time to begin to explain HTML coding in detail. The opening section of "The Wreck of the Deutschland" down to the end of the first stanza reads as in Fig. 6.1. We see here the text of the poem interspersed with HTML tags. It is in a form intelligible to Web browsers but hopelessly cluttered for readers. The purpose of HTML tags is to add to the text of the poem the specifications for the format in which text is to be presented to a reader. The HTML tags in this example are used

```
<html>
<title>Hopkins, Gerard Manley. 1918. Poems: The Wreck of the Deutschland.</title>
<body bgcolor="#ffffff" text="#000020"
LINK="#000050" VLINK="#000050" ALINK="#000050">
<p>
<center><font size="+2"><b>4</b>
<br><a href="103.html#4">The Wreck of the Deutschland</a></font>
<p><i>To the
<br>happy memory of five Franciscan Nuns
<br>exiles by the Falk Laws
<br>drowned between midnight and morning of
<br>Dec. 7th. 1875</i></center>
<p>
<dl>
<center><font size="-1">PART THE FIRST</font>
<p>1</center>
<dd>                 T<font size="-1">HOU</font> mastering me
<dd>              God!
giver of breath and bread;
<dd>        World's strand, sway of the sea;
<dd>            Lord of
living and dead;
<dd>    Thou hast bound bones and veins in me, fastened me flesh,
<dd>    And after it almost unmade, what with dread,
<dd>        Thy doing: and dost thou touch me
afresh?
<dd>Over again I feel thy finger and find thee.
<p>
```

Figure 6.1. HTML encoded text of "The Wreck of the Deutschland."

as formatting instructions by HTML-aware programs like Netscape. There are two types of HTML tags: those like "<TITLE>" enclosed within less than and greater than signs; and those like " " beginning with an ampersand and ending with a semicolon. The tags delimited by the less than and greater than signs tend to occur in pairs that together mark the scope of a particular formatting feature. The "<TITLE>" tag, for example, marks the start of the text of the title and the "</TITLE>" tag marks the end of the text of the title. In HTML, a tag beginning "</" is an end tag, used to mark the end of a feature. A tag set composed of a pair of start and end tags is called a content tag because it is a container for some part of the text. Not all tags are defined as content tags; those that are not are called empty tags. Empty tags usually introduce a specific feature into the document. For example, the "<HR>" tag puts a horizontal rule across the page and the "<BR>" tag forces a line break at the point of its occurrence. Neither of these tags has a companion closing tag because neither of them requires one. Tags like " " which are delimited by the ampersand and semicolon represent special typographical characters. This tag is a "non-breaking space" tag, which introduces a blank space in the text as long as the space does not cause a line break. These special character tags allow for the encoding of characters with diacritical signs and other special symbols that are assumed not to be available for displaying and printing on all computer systems or to have a standard encoding across different computer systems.[1] These tags are HTML's way of getting around the 256 character limitation of ASCII that we discussed in Chapter 2. In the long term, the adoption of Unicode will eliminate the need for this type of tag.

HTML-aware programs interpret these tags in ways compatible with the computer hardware they have available to produce a plausibly formatted version of the text. In effect, the tag says that some formatting or special character occurs at this point in the text and leaves it up to the HTML software to decide how that formatting or special character is to appear. HTML programs like Netscape and Internet Explorer are called "browsers" in part because they take arcane HTML coding and allow it to be read easily by people rather than computers. If we open file "04.htm"[2] in the \webinfo\html\ directory with Netscape's "File/Open" menu choice, we will see on our screen a text of "The Wreck of the Deutschland" whose typographical layout resembles closely that of the first edition of Hopkins's poems. Readers should keep in mind that Netscape can view HTML files wherever they are located, either on a Web server or on their own PC or MAC.

Our main goal here is to understand how HTML works by learning the fundamentals of producing a hypertext document. Knowledge of HTML tags is essential for this understanding. We are going to use a text editor to add HTML tags "by hand" in this chapter. If our goal was only the production of a hypertext document, we might be tempted to use an HTML editor that would allow us to create an HTML page in the same way we would create a formatted text with a word processor. What HTML editors are designed to do is to insert HTML tags automatically into texts and thus to obviate the need to know about the tags, which remain invisible to the user as the internal codes of a word processor. They keep tags from view in the same way that a browser does when it displays a document. The latest version of Word, Word97, includes the capability of saving documents as HTML files rather than in word processor format. There are add-on products that turn standard word processors into HTML editors and the version of Netscape known as Netscape Communicator comes with an HTML editor.[3] Most readers will probably use HTML editors in the future when they wish to create hypertext documents "from scratch." A real benefit of understanding HTML tags is that this understanding is of great help in learning to use HTML editors, so learning about them here should prove useful in the future. After we add our tags to the file and save it on our workstation's hard disk with an "HTML" file extension, we may use Netscape to view the tagged document.

Browser programs can display many types of text, image, sound, and video files. They rely on the operating system to identify the type of a file they are to display. They rely on a list of the types of files they can display and the method they are to use in displaying them. These file types are technically called "mime types." "MIME" stands for "Multipurpose Internet Mail Extension." As their name implies, the Internet treats different mime types as files containing different classes of mail. The Internet's popularity was initially based on its E-mail function. At first, E-mail was restricted to text only but it soon because possible to attach all types of files to messages. Mime extensions are the Web's way of keeping track of the various types of E-mail files. The "Helpers" tab of Netscape's "Options/General Preferences" menu item gives a list of the mime types this installation of Netscape is configured to handle(Fig. 6.2). Each entry in this list consists of three columns: a file type, an action, and a file extension. The file type consists of two parts, a type and a subtype. There are two subtypes of "text" files on the portion of the list visible in Fig. 6.2, "html" and "plain;" and two subtypes of images, "GIF" and "jpeg." The action for all of them is "Browser" which means that Netscape has a built-in capacity to handle these types of files. The extensions column lists the various extensions associated with each type/subtype: txt and text for "text/plain;" htm and html for "text/html," etc. Mime types are defined on both the client and the server. If the client or server asks for a mime type that is unknown to the other, the file in question is assumed to be a text file and displayed as such.

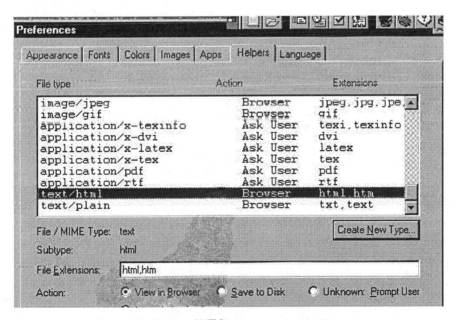

Figure 6.2. Display of MIME types recognized by Netscape.

Where to Browse for Art on the Internet from The New York Times, January 21, 1996
OCR by Wordscan 4.0, HERE IS A LIST OF SOME OF THE INTERESTING, USEFUL
and eccentric art sites and their addresses on the World Wide Web. Minimum
equipment required: a PC computer with a 486 processor or an equally fast Macintosh.
You'll need a modem, prefer- ably running at 28.8 kilobits per second or faster, and
access to the In- ternet from a provider, Most sites are created for viewing with
Netscape's browser, which enables you to see the more sophisticated graphics and
layouts. The address, always beginning with http://, is typed into the browser or clicked
on to take you to a site. Be patient; it often takes time for connections to be made. Have
a nice time! MUSEUMS Art Tower Mito, http://www.soum.co.jp/mito/art-e.html Current
exhibitions and gallery talks, in English and Japanese. California Museum of
Photography, University of California, Riverside, http://www.cmp.ucr.edu Historical and
contemporary photography exhibitions, including use of the very cool "Virtual
Magnifying Glass," which allows users to zoom in on details of images. Dia Center for
the Arts, http://www.diacenter.org Works from the permanent collection, program

Figure 6.3. Netscape display of HTML file.

The action column may contain the name of a program that Netscape is to
launch as a "helper" application to display files of the type/subtype given in the
"File type" column. Netscape has defined an application program interface which
allows it to launch standard Windows programs like the Excel spreadsheet program
or the PowerPoint presentation manager or special purpose programs to support
multimedia sound and video. This feature allows Netscape to extend its capacity to
handle new mime types as they come into use. Other common action column entries
include the "Ask User" entry which allows the user to define the helper program to
be used for a file type at the time the file arrives at the PC; and the "Save" entry,
used with file extensions like "exe" (binary program code) and "zip" (compressed
files). This option is designed to facilitate file downloading from server archives as
we did in Chapter 5.

The way in which mime-type specifications affect the way a file is handled by
Netscape is illustrated by displaying in turn the HTML and text versions of the New
York Times article. The HTML version of the article, though so designated by the
Windows 95 operating system, contains no HTML tags of any kind. Lacking any
instructions, Netscape displays it as one chunk of undifferentiated content (Fig.
6.3). The browser ignores the line breaks and spacing of the input file and divides
the text into lines according to its own algorithm. On the other hand, if we display
the text version of the file, which is byte for byte identical with the HTML version,
we get the following, very different display presented in Fig. 6.4.

The reason for the differently formatted file displays is that Netscape treats text
files as a mime type already divided into lines and displays them preserving the line
breaks they contain. The format of a document determines in large measure its
usefulness for particular purposes. By adding HTML tags to the HTML version of

```
Where to Browse for Art on the Internet
from The New York Times, January 21, 1996
OCR by Wordscan 4.0,

HERE IS A LIST OF SOME OF THE INTERESTING, USEFUL
and eccentric art sites and their addresses on the World Wide
Web. Minimum equipment required: a PC computer with a 486
processor or an equally fast Macintosh. You'll need a modem, prefer-
ably running at 28.8 kilobits per second or faster, and access to the In-
ternet from a provider, Most sites are created for viewing with
Netscape's browser, which enables you to see the more sophisticated
graphics and layouts. The address, always beginning with http://, is
typed into the browser or clicked on to take you to a site. Be patient; it
often takes time for connections to be made. Have a nice time!

MUSEUMS
```

Figure 6.4. Netscape display of text file.

the article, we can transform it from an almost useless blob of reading material to a hypertext document useful in browsing art sites on the Web. In so doing, we will also become familiar with the basic elements of HTML programming and become able to create our own hypertext documents.

The purpose of the encoding of the opening of "The Wreck of the Deutschland" given in Fig. 6.1 is to control the appearance of the text. Generally speaking, it is not a good idea to attempt to control precisely the appearance of an HTML document because any specific display of a document is a function of three things: the HTML tags, the browser software, and the computer hardware of the displaying workstation. The encoder has control over only the first of these. An important point that is sometimes overlooked about HTML tagging in documents is that tagging describes at least in part the logical structure of documents much more than their physical appearance. Paragraphing, titles, subheadings, line divisions in poetry, etc., as well as the words of the text contribute to the meaning of a document. Bibliographers and editors pay attention to these aspects of the text in hope of distinguishing the substantive intentions of the author from the accidentals introduced in the process of publication and transmission.

HTML coding imposes a conventional structure upon documents and the first step in turning the article's text into hypertext is to encapsulate it within this conventional form. The form divides the text into two parts, the heading and the body. The tags to accomplish this are displayed in Fig. 6.5. The tags in this figure are shown as indented to emphasize the nested structure of an HTML file. The nested hierarchy of the HTML document embodies the same structure as the nested loops of a program. Tags are not indented in this way when used in an HTML. Because HTML files are ASCII files, one can use any text editor or word processor to add the tags to the HTML article file. I prefer to use the PFE32 text editor that was downloaded in Chapter 5 for this purpose because it is a multifile editor that

```
<HTML>
  <HEAD>
    <TITLE>
      title text
    </TITLE>
    heading tags and text
  </HEAD>
  <BODY>
    body tags and text
  </BODY>
</HTML>
```

Figure 6.5. Structure of an HTML document.

simplifies coordinating files and copying text from file to file. It also is capable of handling very large files, an important consideration in preparing long prose works as HTML files. But for the task at hand one could as well use the Windows 95 accessory NotePad or WordPad or, for MAC users, the Simpletext program. Whatever editor is used, it is important to save the file as an HTML file.

With these added codes, the opening of the file now reads:

```
<HTML>
<HEAD>
<TITLE>Where to Browse for Art on the Internet</TITLE>
</HEAD>
<BODY>
from The New York Times, January 21, 1996
..........
```

and the end of the file now reads:

```
.............
Another major directory, Yahoo! has an excellent art section, with
summaries of what many sites offer.
</BODY>
</HTML>
```

I will divide the texts into paragraphs by replacing blank lines with the paragraph tag, "<p>." This is done in the PFE32 editor by searching for all occurrences of the sequence "\n\n" and replacing them with the sequence "\n<p>\n." The "\n" annotation is the symbol the PFE32 uses for a line break. Thus "\n\n" means a line followed immediately by a blank line which is to be replaced by a "\n<p>\n," that is, the blank line is to be replaced by a line containing the paragraph tag, "<p>." This puts a number of "<p>" tags at appropriate points in the text (Fig. 6.6).

The paragraph tags, though they are content tags that divide the text into paragraphs, are used without corresponding "</p>." This ending tag can be omitted

```
........
<p>
MUSEUMS
<p>
Art Tower Mito,
http://www.soum.co.jp/mito/art-e.html
Current exhibitions and gallery talks, in English and Japanese.
<p>
California Museum of Photography,
University of California, Riverside,
http://www.cmp.ucr.edu
Historical and contemporary photography exhibitions, including use of
the very cool "Virtual Magnifying Glass," which allows users to zoom
in on details of images.
<p>
........
```

Figure 6.6. Article with paragraph tags inserted.

because the paragraph tag has been defined so that its occurrence closes any currently open paragraph before opening a new one. In other words, a paragraph by definition cannot be nested within another paragraph. Paragraphs are defined in this way for the convenience of HTML programmers. The "<p>" tag is probably the most frequently used of all HTML tags and defining it in this way saves the trouble of having to add the "</p>" tag at the end of each paragraph followed by the "<p>" tag to start the next. Encoding, it should be observed, is tedious enough under the best of circumstances.

A version of the article with the basic and paragraph tags added is saved in the \webinfo\html directory as "NYT1.HTML." When we use Netscape to browse this file, we see a much improved version (Fig. 6.7). The title bar contains the title of the article which is a good description of its contents,[4] and the body of the text is now divided into paragraphs. The underlying HTML coding may be examined with the Netscape "View/Document Source" menu selection.

The article contains the URL of each site it discusses as may be seen in the "nyt1.html" display. The reader will recall from our discussion of programmability in Chapter 2 that the ability to jump from one sequence of instructions to another is at the heart of the operation of programmable devices. The use of URLs as jump addresses is but an extension of this general technique to jump from file to file rather than from memory location to memory location. To make the article into a hypertext document, the URLs it contains must be activated so that clicking on the name of the site will connect to it. These URLs are pointers to other locations and may be selected or not in whatever order the user chooses at the time of browsing. To

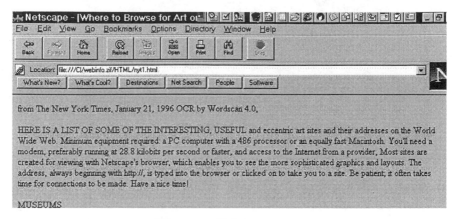

Figure 6.7. HTML file, version 1.

activate a hypertext link, the name of each site must be enclosed in a set of link or anchor tags:

"<A href="URL">......</A>,"

where "URL" is the Web address of the site to which the link is to be made. The anchor tag must be a text container because it must specify not only the site to which it offers a link but also the text to be clicked on in order to visit that site. The "Art Tower, Mito" entry becomes an HTML link when it is encapsulated within such tags:

```
...
<p>
<A href= "http://www.soum.co.jp/mito/art-e.html"> Art Tower Mito, </A>
http://www.soum.co.jp/mito/art-e.html
Current exhibitions and gallery talks, in English and Japanese.
<p>
.......
```

The name of the site will appear as a link in a blue colored, underlined font that is the default for links in HTML:

MUSEUMS

Art Tower Mito, http://www.soum.co.jp/mito/art-e.html Current exhibitions and gallery talks, in English and Japanese.

Figure 6.8. Article with hypertext links inserted.

File "nyt2.html" has in place the links for all the sites and is thus a fully activated hypertext document.

The encoding in file "nyt2.html" describes its contents as a series of paragraphs of running prose. There is nothing wrong about this especially, if the point of encoding the article is simply to transform it to hypertext. One could, perhaps, add heading tags to mark out the subsections of the article. HTML offers six heading tags, "<H1>...</H1>" through "<H6>...</H6>." So we might encode the divisions of the article as

> <H1>Where to Browse for Art on the Internet</H1>[5]
>
> ......
>
> <H2>AUCTION HOUSES, ART GALLERIES AND ART MALLS</H2>

Readers may view the coding for the six types of heading and the way Netscape formats that coding by viewing file "headings.html" in the \webinfo\html\ directory. But HTML offers other structures that would describe its structure more accurately than as a string of paragraphs. The article begins by saying "HERE IS A LIST OF SOME OF THE INTERESTING, USEFUL and eccentric art sites and their addresses on the World Wide Web;" and the structure of the article is not so much a single list as a collection of lists, with an outer list that corresponds to the section headings and inner lists of the sites nested within each section. There are two types of lists in HTML that we may use in specifying the nested list structure of our document: ordered lists tagged by "<OL>...</OL>;" and unordered lists tagged by "<UL>...</UL>". Ordered lists are numbered; unordered ones are not. Individual list items are tagged as "<LI>" and nested within the tags that open and close the list. As with the "<p>" tag, the "<LI>" tag need not be balanced with an "</LI>" tag.

Unlike paragraphs, lists may be nested within lists. As we saw in our discussion of programming in Chapter 4, the nesting of structures such as loops within loops is a standard part of structured programming style. Nested structures are widely used in all sorts of computer applications. Nested structures require explicit ways to mark their scope. Since HTML lists may be nested one within another, it is necessary to tag the end of an ordered or unordered list explicitly. Netscape handles the numbering of ordered lists automatically. It also indents lists nested within lists. We can encode the article as ordered outer list and a series of inner, unordered ones, each nested below an element of the ordered list (Fig. 6.9). Netscape presents this coding in a way that emphasizes the organization of the article's material with the "nyt3.html" link in the \webinfo\html\ (Fig. 6.10).

HTML allows control of the style of numbering in ordered lists, which can be Arabic numbers, upper- or lower-case letters, or upper- or lowers-case Roman numbers.. The "type" attribute is used for this purpose. If an ordered list begins with the "<UL type="A">" tag, the elements of the list will be identified with upper-case letters. The other options are "a" for lower-case letters, "i" for lower case Roman,

```
......
<HTML>
<HEAD>
<TITLE>Where to Browse for Art on the
    Internet</TITLE>
</HEAD>
<BODY>
<H1>Where to Browse for Art on the
    Internet</H1>
....
HERE IS A LIST OF SOME OF THE
    INTERESTING, USEFUL
....
<p>
<OL>
<LI>MUSEUMS
<UL>
<LI><A href="http://www.soum.co.jp/mito/
    art-e.html">Art Tower Mito, </A>
...
<LI>
<A href="http://www.cmp.ucr.edu">
California Museum of Photography,
....
<p>
</UL>
<LI>AUCTION HOUSES, ART GALLERIES
    AND ART MALLS
<UL>
<LI>
<A href="http://www.artscope.com/
    index.html">
Artscope, </A>
.....
<p>
</UL>
<LI>
PUBLICATIONS
<UL>
<LI>
<A href="http://www.thing.net/jca">
....
<p>
</UL>
<LI>
ARTISTS' WORKS AND ARTIST SITES
<UL><LI>
<A href="http://adaweb.com">
ada 'web, </A>
....
<p></UL>
<LI>
GENERAL WEB DIRECTORIES, ARTIST
INFORMATION AND ART HISTORICAL
TOOLS
<UL><LI>
<A href="http://www.uky.edu/Artsource/
    general.html">
Artsource, </A>
...
</UL>
</OL>
</BODY>
</HTML>
```

Figure 6.9. Article encoded as nested loops.

and "I" for upper-case Roman. Omitting the "type" attribute or setting it to "1" produces a list with Arabic numerals. The starting number of a list need not be one; the "start=n" attribute will start numbering at the nth element. The tag "<OL type="A" start=24>" produces a list whose first element is "X." A type attribute may also be used with the unordered list tag, "<UL>," to change the type of bullet for the list. The choices are "disc," "circle," and "square." The tag "<UL type="square">" would mark the start of each element in the list with a square bullet. The "clear" attribute, as in "<UL clear>," specifies a nonbulleted unordered list.

○ WebMuseum, Paris, http://sunsite.unc.edu/wm This superb site includes
  special exhibitions as well as the "Famous Paintings Exhibition," which
  covers Gothic art through modern works and provides a glossary of painting
  styles.
○ Whitney Museum of American Art, http: //www.echonyc.com/~whitney The
  Whitney's ambitious virtual museum covers all the bases, with current
  shows, works from the permanent collection, essays, library information and
  up-to-the-minute web art projects sponsored by the museum.

2. AUCTION HOUSES, ART GALLERIES AND ART MALLS
○ Artscope, http://www.artscope.com/index.html A mall that can keep visitors
  indoors for some time, with many New York and California galleries to
  browse through, Portfolios by artists, offerings of print editions and auction
  prices.
○ Christie's, http://www.christies.com/Christie.htm Far less sophisticated than
  Sotheby's site this is nonetheless thorough in covering the forthcoming

Figure 6.10. Display of nested lists.

We have been working to modify a version of this article to make it into a
hypertext document. It is the case, however, that the article is also available through
the "CyberTimes," the *New York Times* web site,[6] by using the site's search function
to search on the terms "museum," "Internet," and "browse." Unfortunately, there
is an error in the HTML coding for this entry[7] that makes most of the text of the
article unreadable (Fig. 6.11). The CyberTimes version is listed as "cyber-
times.html" in the \webinfo\html\ directory, complete with the encoding error.

MUSEUMS

Art Tower Mito
Current exhibitions and gallery talks, in English and Japanese.

California Museum of Photography, University of California, Riverside
Historical and contemporary photography exhibitions, including use of the ver

Dia Center for the Arts
Works from the permanent collection, program schedules and artists' web pr

Los Angeles County Museum of Art
On-line catalogues of exhibitions, artist interviews, current shows and sample

Louvre Museum

Figure 6.11. CyberTimes version of article.

FONTS, TEXT ALIGNMENT, AND SPECIAL CHARACTERS

Browsers are designed to display information on computer screens, not as typesetting programs. The typical laser printer today has a resolution of 600 dpi or 360,000 dots per square inch; a computer screen with a resolution 1024 by 768 dots for the entire display area has a resolution of less than 100 dpi or less than 10,000 dots per square inch. The low resolution of computer screens as contrasted with laser printing translates into a much narrower range of typographical choices in HTML. Even the typeface in which a page is displayed, that most basic of typographical design features, is left up to the browser software since the page designer has no way of knowing in advance what fonts will be available on client machines across the Web.[8] The Netscape menu's "Options/General Preferences" selection allows users to select two fonts, one a proportional font and one a fixed length font (Fig. 6.12). Text is usually displayed in the proportional font. Text to be displayed in the fixed font is enclosed in "<TT>...</TT>" tags. Fixed fonts have the appearance of a typewriter font like Courier.

Fonts come in seven progressively larger sizes, numbered one through seven, but there is no correspondence between these numbers and point size or any other standard fixed measure. Font size is set with the size attribute of the "<FONT>" tag. To set font size at four, one uses a "<FONT size=4>" tag. By convention, size three is the default or normal size. The font size may be set in terms relative to the current size. A "<FONT size=+1>" tag increases the font size by one level; a "<FONT size=-2>" tag decreases the font size by two levels. The scope of a font change of any kind is limited to the text between the "<FONT size=...>....</FONT>" tags. The table in Fig. 6.13 lists the tags that affect the appearance of the displayed font.

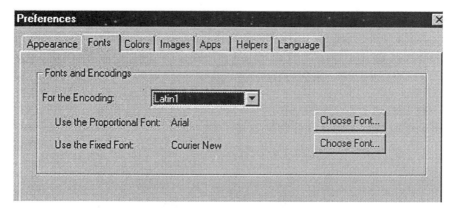

Figure 6.12. Font selection for Netscape.

The logical styles supposedly relate to the content of the text they contain while the physical styles relate to their appearance. The "<CITE>" tag identifies the title of a cited work, usually by placing it in italics; the "<CODE>" tag identifies computer programming code by observing line breaks as in ASCII text and by using a fixed font; the "<EM>" tag is for emphasis, usually by italics; the "<KBD>" tag identifies text supposedly entered from the keyboard, by using the fixed font; the "<SAMPLE>" tag allows users to give samples of HTML coding by passing through the literal representation of any character; the "<STRONG>" tag marks strong emphasis by putting it in a bold font. There is no way to tell the difference between a file tagged for emphasis and a file tagged for italics without examining the HTML source code. Programs might be written to take advantage of these tags in their analysis.

Font tags may be nested within other font tags to produce a cumulative set of font changes:

<I>Italic <B> Bold <BIG> Big <U> Underlined </I></B></BIG></U>

will produce:

Physical Styles	
<B>...</B>	Bold
<BIG>...</BIG>	Increase Font Size
<I>...</I>	Italic
<S>...</S>	Strikethrough
<SMALL>...</SMALL>	Decrease Font Size
_{...}	Subscript
^{...}	Superscript
<TT>...</TT>	Teletype (fixed)
<U>...</U>	Underline
Logical Styles	
<CITE>...</CITE>	Citation
<CODE>...</CODE>	Programming Code
<EM>...</EM>	Emphasis
<KBD>...</KBD>	Text typed by user
<SAMP>...</SAMP>	Sample
<STRONG>...</STRONG>	Strong Emphasis

Figure 6.13. Type formatting code.

Italic **Bold** ***Big*** <u>***Underlined***</u>

It is good programming practice to close nested structures in the order in which they are opened. Netscape will produce the same effect with the end tags in the nesting example in any order as long as they follow the word "Underlined." The end tags mark the end of the scope of the formatting specified by the opening tags. If the "</BIG>" tag is placed immediately after the word "Big," a different effect is produced because the scope of the "<BIG>" tag applies only to the word "Big":

<I>Italic <B> Bold <BIG> Big </BIG><U> Underlined </I></B></U>

This produces:

Italic **Bold** ***Big*** <u>*Underlined*</u>

File "formats.html" in the \webinfo\html\ directory contains examples of each single and nested tag. (Netscape's "View/Document Source" menu selection displays the unformatted HTML encoded version of these files.) The way in which nested font formatting can be cumulative should alert HTML users to the potential hazards associated with careless nesting of tags. Often when a text does not appear to be formatted correctly, the problem is the result of incorrect nesting.

We have already seen the HTML paragraph tag "<p>," which is used to divide text into paragraphs. There are two attributes for the paragraph tag that are worth noting, "align" and "clear." The "align" attribute has three possible values, "left," "center," and "right" which determine the line justification of the paragraph. The "<p align="center"> tag causes the paragraph's lines of text to be centered on the screen. Specifying "align="left" " sets the paragraph's line flush left (the default); "align="right" " sets them flush right. There is some recognition that a "Justify" option might also be useful but is not available in the version of Netscape we are using. (It may be available in readers' versions.) The "clear" attribute is used to position text in relation to images that are positioned to the left or right on the page. The "left/right/all" options move a paragraph down until the specified margin or margins are empty. It is also possible to specify a vertical space before the paragraph. The tag <p clear="20pixels"> will leave twenty pixels of space blank before the text of the paragraph. (A pixel is small dot on a CRT screen. Pictures are drawn with pixels.) The "<p>" tag usually does not indent a paragraph. The usual practice is to use single or multiple occurrences of the special character " " to indent at the beginning of a paragraph, as is done in the text of "The Wreck of the Deutschland" quoted at the beginning of this chapter.

The line break tag, "
," which causes a line break at the point of its occurrence, is sometimes used as if it were interchangeable with the paragraph tag. It is, however, an "empty" tag and does not have a corresponding end tag or any attributes as does the paragraph tab. HTML ignores line breaks in its source file, so this tag is used to divide text into meaningful chunks that are not to be taken as separate paragraphs. It might be used for things like marking the line ends of an address within a paragraph. It is also used to add blank space within a text. The sequence "

" would add a blank line to a text display. (For an example of this usage, see the HTML coding for file "formats.html" which uses a "

" to separate the examples of the different formats.) Its effect on the layout is visually the same as that of the paragraph tag, "<p>," used without any attributes, which explains its use as an alternate to the paragraph tag. It is good practice, however, to distinguish between these two tags so that the HTML coding of a text represents its structure as closely as possible.

There are four more tags that I need to mention in this brief discussion of text alignment. The first two are used to control the division of text into lines. The "<PRE>...</PRE>" tag is used for pre-formatted text. Text within this container is presented with the line breaks of the input text. The "<NOBR>...</NOBR>" tag suspends line divisions so that text within its scope is placed in a single line without breaks irrespective of the length of the resulting line. The effect it produces may be seen in Figure 6. 11, the CyberTimes version of the article, where the omission of a right angle bracket from the "<IMG>" tag at the end of line twenty caused Netscape to ignore the closing "</NOBR>" tag. The "<CENTER>...</CENTER>" tag is used to center headings and other text that is not regarded as a paragraph. Finally, the "<DIV>...</DIV> tag is used to group successive paragraphs and longer sections of text into larger divisions. The "<DIV>" tag has the same "align" and "clear" attributes as the paragraph tag. Paragraphs contained within the scope of a "<DIV align="right">...</DIV>" would all be set flush right. Netscape's facilities for dividing text in ways that describe the structure of the content of its files is ad hoc at best. HTML originally contained about thirty tags and there are only about one hundred tags available in its current release. HTML has developed under the pressure of contradictory user demands for simplicity and comprehensiveness. As HTML editors that require no knowledge of HTML tags come into use, HTML tags will undoubtedly increase in number and complexity because the tags will be generated with and through software rather than by human encoders, who will be free to concentrate on the elements of page design rather than the minutiae of coding.

MULTIMEDIA: COLORS, IMAGES, SOUND, AND VIDEO

The first thing that strikes most people about a hypertext document is not its hypertext links to other documents but its color. Rather than the puritanical black on white of the printed page, the hypertext computer screen is awash with colors and images in quantities reminiscent of medieval illuminated manuscripts. One monastery of Benedictine monks, the Monastery of Christ in the Desert in the Sangre de Cristo Mountains north of Santa Fe, New Mexico, has established an electronic scriptorium[9] to cultivate the design of hypertext pages *Ad Majorem Dei Gloriam* in much the same way that monks in the Middle Ages explored the artistic possibilities of manuscript illumination. No one would mistake the typical Web page for a leaf from the Lindisfarne Gospel but a discussion of the use of Web multimedia should begin with a discussion of the way in which the Web handles colors and images.

All colors and images in HTML are digitized because that is the way in which computer hardware handles colors and images. The process of digitization may be compared to a child's paint by the numbers game. To digitize an image is, in effect, to place a fine grid over it and to measure the color within each square of the grid. The fineness of the grid determines the resolution of the image. The color within each grid is represented by a number, and the magnitude permitted to the number representing the color determines the color depth of the image. Color depth, in other words, corresponds to the number of different paints on the paint by numbers pallet. Although images displayed on a screen appear to be solidly analog representations, they are actually composed of discrete points called pixels to which a numerical value is assigned. An image on a screen is represented in memory as a series of numbers. The resolution of the image is a function of the number of pixels of which it is composed.

HTML divides the colors it displays into red, green, and blue components. This form of color encoding is called RGB color. The technique is the same as is used with color film and television. It is based on the way the human eye sees colors with rods that are sensitive to three bands of wavelengths. HTML specifies a color's components as three bytes. Since each byte has 256 possible values, HTML can in theory specify 16,777,216 different and distinct colors ($256 \times 256 \times 256$). The content of these bytes is expressed in hexadecimal numbers. The value 000000_{16} specifies black, the absence of all color; the value $FFFFFF_{16}$ specifies white, an equal mix of all. Shades of gray are expressed by colors that have the same value for each component. Values like 202020_{16} or $A0A0A0_{16}$ would be differing shades of gray with the former much darker than the latter. There are, then, 256 shades of gray. Not all display screens or graphics devices are capable of displaying the full range of sixteen million plus colors. Even with devices capable of the full range of colors, a color with the same red, green, and blue components may appear differently on different machines depending on the physical characteristics of the screen. An HTML color specification should be regarded as the expression of a wish rather than the issuing of a command. As with the actual appearance of a type face, the browser software will make the determination of the color displayed based upon the graphics capability of the client workstation.

The resolution of an image is measured in dots per inch (dpi), which increases as the square of the number. A 600 dpi picture requires four times as much memory as a 300 dpi picture. The color resolution of the image also affects the amount of memory needed to store an image. A one inch square image at 600 dpi requires

360,000 pixels. The lowest graphics resolution used today is four bits per pixel.[10] At this resolution, each byte (8 bits) can hold the information for two pixels so this low resolution, black and white image would require 180,000 bytes for storage of a one inch square image. The same image stored as a high resolution color image with 3 bytes per pixel to represent its RGB color components would require 1,080,000 bytes, more than six times as much memory. A three-by-five photograph would have a size of over 16,000,000 bytes at this resolution and color depth.

HTML allows users to specify colors for the background and for fonts through attributes of the "<BODY>" tag. These attributes distinguish four types of fonts: "text" for ordinary text; "link" for hypertext links; "vlink" for a hypertext link that has been "visited," i.e., selected in the past; and "alink" for an activated hypertext link, i.e., for the color a link will take on momentarily when it is selected. Setting these attributes in the "<BODY>" tag will determine these colors for the entire page. The "<FONT>" tag has a "color" attribute with which the global settings of the "text" and "link" attributes of the "<BODY>" tag may be overridden. Background color is specified with the "bgcolor" attribute of the "<BODY>" tag, so there are a total of five color attributes for the "<BODY>" tag.

Colors are specified for these attributes by specifying three hexadecimal numbers in a string whose syntax is "#RRGGBB," where "RR" in the value of the color's red component, "GG" is the value of the color's green component, and "BB" is the value of the color's blue component. For example, a "<BODY bgcolor="#e9967a" text="x8b4513" link="xFFEFD5" vlink="FF6347" alink="#FFE7BA">" will set the specification of the background color of the document to a salmon color, the text to chocolate, the links to papaya, the visited links to tomato, and the active links to wheat. File "nyt4.html" in the \webinfo\html\ directory is identical with "nyt3.html" except for the "<BODY>" tag which specifies this particular set of colors. Readers are encouraged to experiment with different RGB specifications for these attributes.[11] In any event, the results one sees will be a product of one's hardware and software as well as of the contents of the HTML file.

It is difficult to guess in advance what the effect of particular RGB combinations will be or to know what particular set of hexadecimal values will produce a rich chewy chocolate or cherry Garcia color. There is, however, a web site that can simplify color selection. This is the ColorServe JAVA site.[12] The software at this site enables one to choose in turn the color of each attribute from a color wheel, to observe the effect of the selection, and to get a readout of the hex values of the color wheel selection. The software also allows one to enter hex values for attributes and see the colors the hex values produce. Spending some time at this site exercising its various functions is the way to become familiar with the workings of RGB color specifications in HTML. File "htmlprog.html" in the \webinfo\html\ directory is an HTML file with links to this site and to other sites containing information and software useful for HTML programming.

The ability of HTML to translate RGB color specifications into actual colors on a screen, important though it is for typeface and background colors, becomes crucial when dealing with images. As we have seen, the overriding constraints on all color displays are their dpi resolution and color depth. Images can be digitized at very high density and color depth if one is prepared to deal with the very large resulting files.[13] Commercial photographers deal in files that are tens and hundreds of millions bytes in size. HTML, which allows for a twenty-four bit color depth, can specify over sixteen million different colors and call for their display. But when it comes to displaying the colors specified in HTML, Hotspur's repost to Glendower's claim that he could "call spirits from the vasty deep" should be kept in mind: "Why, so can I, or so can any man;/ But will they come when you do call for them?" (I Henry IV, Act 3 Scene 1). Images that look acceptable on a high resolution monitor can seem washed out when displayed on a screen with an RGB projector.

CAPTURING WEB IMAGES FROM THE COMPUTER SCREEN

When an image is captured by a scanner, displayed on a screen, or sent to a printer, it is in bitmap form. This means that there is a one-to-one correspondence between the pixels that produce the image and a location in memory that contains the numerical color value associated with the pixel. The graphical devices that display images work by establishing a link between each specific pixel and each specific memory location. This link insures that the pixel's color corresponds to the value in memory that is dedicated by the operating system to the display device. Images are changed by changing the numerical values in memory. The speed with which a screen can be repainted is the speed with which the values in this dedicated memory can be changed. Graphics display devices usually have their own CPUs that are dedicated to managing this memory because in this way images on the screen can be updated quickly. This gives the user a faster response time than if the screen updating is handled by the computer's main CPU, which has a large number of other tasks to juggle. The size of each graphics memory location is determined by the number of bits of color depth the device can handle. As we have seen, HTML color specifications require three bytes per pixel for color depth, one byte each for the red, green, and blue values of the composite color. The number of graphics memory locations is equal to the total number of pixels on the device.

There are two ways to capture an image from a Web page: screen capture and downloading. (We have discussed downloading in Chapter 5.) Windows 95 PCs have a key labeled "Print Screen" which can be used to capture the image of whatever is currently displayed on the screen. When this key is pressed, the system copies the current screen image to the system's clipboard from which it may be pasted into an image editing program like LviewPro, the image editor we downloaded from the Web in Chapter 5. Suppose, for example, that I am browsing on the Web and come across an image of the famous tourist attraction Tintern Abbey that I decide I would like to save for a presentation on legacy systems (Fig. 6.14). I would press the "Print screen" button, load the LviewPro program that was downloaded in Chapter 5, and copy the screen image from the clipboard to the program by using its "Edit/Paste" menu selection. One would then crop the screen image so that it contained only what one wanted to save, the picture of Tintern Abbey (Fig. 6.15).

The screen image illustrations used throughout this book were produced in this way and copies of the images referenced in this chapter are found in the \webinfo\images directory. An image screen captured in this way is a bitmap image whose resolution and color density correspond to the resolution and color density of the computer screen. The other way to download an image from the screen—say a picture, icon, button, or decoration—is to point to it with the mouse and click the right mouse button as we did in Chapter 5. The advantage of this method is that we get the image, without cropping or other fuss, at the density it was stored on its server, not at the density it was displayed by our workstation. This produces a drop down list menu from which I can select the "Save Image As" option which brings up a standard save file dialog box (Fig. 6.17). One may save the image wherever

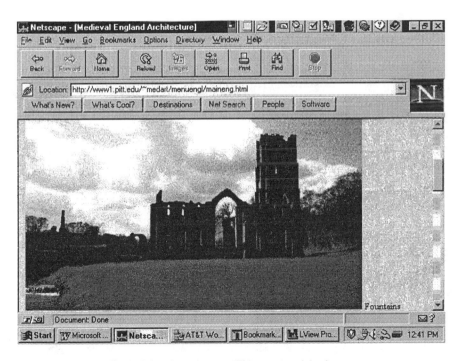

Figure 6.14. Screen capture Web page containing image.

Figure 6.15. Image cropped from screen image.

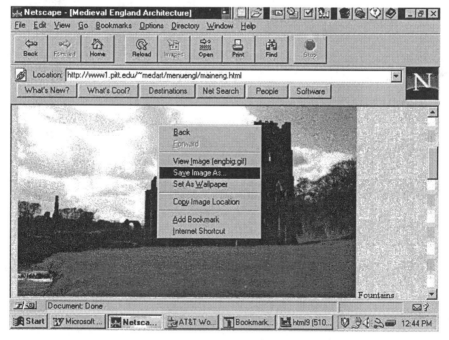

Figure 6.16. "Save Image As" selection of properties menu.

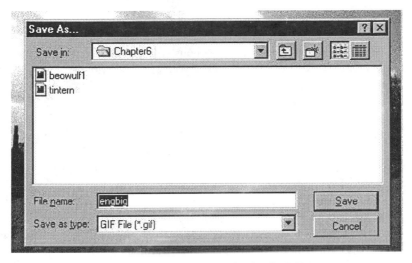

Figure 6.17. Save file dialog box for downloaded image.

one chooses on the disk under whatever name one wishes. In doing this, one may
not change the file type. A "GIF" file must be saved with a "gif" extension; a JPEG
file with a "jpg" or "jpeg" extension.

COMPRESSING IMAGES

Images are not stored on servers or transmitted over the Web in bitmap form because
bitmap images are too large. Before being made available on the Web, images are
compressed to save space and decrease the amount of time needed to transmit them.
Images are made up of irregularly shaped areas of the same color. When they are
digitized, they become represented by a two-dimensional array of numbers with as
many rows and columns as are necessary to contain a value for each pixel. Within
this array, there are numerous contiguous rows and columns that hold the same
value. For example, an area in an RGB image of the same color blue (232375_{16})
might be 47 pixels long and 83 pixels high. In bitmap form, this requires 47×83
$\times 3$ or 11,703 bytes of storage. But we could also encode this in eleven bytes, where
the first four bytes are the x and y coordinates of the rectangle on the screen, the
next four hold the area's length and width in pixels ($2F_{16} \times 53_{16}$), and the last three
hold the actual RGB value (232375_{16}). This is a simple example of a large
rectangular area and it is only meant to show that breaking the image down into
contiguous pixels offers the possibility of substantial reductions in the amount of
storage needed to represent the image. The more complex the image, the smaller

are the contiguous areas. There are complications about transitional areas and sharp and fuzzy edges that different image compression techniques solve with better or worse success. Our example of the contiguous rectangular area is an example of "lossless" compression, because the original values of the bitmap can be restored byte for byte from the compressed image. There are also "lossy" compression techniques that greatly increase the amount of compression at the price of loss of some of the original bitmap values. Compressed images must be decompressed back into a bitmap form to be displayed. The saving in Web traffic overhead resulting from the transmission of compressed images is paid for in part by the extra burden on software or the cost of extra hardware used in decompression.

There are two standard types of compressed image files used on the Web, GIF (Graphics Information Format) files and JPEG (Joint Photographic Experts Group) files. JPEG is the name of a compression technique, not a file format. What is referred to as a "JPEG" file is properly termed a "JFIF" file (JPEG File Interchange Format). GIF was developed and popularized by CompuServe, one of the commercial predecessors of the Web. It allows for image sizes of $65,536 \times 65,536$ pixels and for a color depth of up to 8 bits. It uses a general-purpose numerical compression algorithm called LWZ to reduce the size of the image. GIF is a very popular image format for which there is viewing software available on a large number of systems. GIF files are identified on the Web by a "GIF" extension. The JPEG compression method used by JFIF files is a much more sophisticated compression technique than the LWZ compression used by a GIF file. It is a "lossy" technique based on the way the human eye responds to color, not on the simple additive scheme of RGB. The human eye is much more sensitive to the relative brightness of an image than to gradations of color. JPEG compression works by preserving relative brightness at the expense of gradations of color. When using JPEG compression, one can adjust for the quality of the color gradation in an image. The higher one sets this value, the less color gradation is lost. But this also leads to a decrease in the amount by which an image is compressed. JFIF files of the Web are identified by a "JPG" or "JPEG" file extension.

Unlike GIF which is limited to 8 bits of color depth or 256 different colors, JFIF files can handle 24-bit color. JFIF is particularly well suited for complex images that contain many transitional areas. This means that JFIF is used for photographs of natural objects and art works. It is not so effective for images generated by computer that contain sharply delineated areas of color separated by sharp edges. It will tend to blur or "dither" these edges. GIF is much more suitable than JFIF for this type of image. Also, because JFIF is a "lossy" compression method, repeated applications of it will produce increasing degradation of the image. JFIF is a way to archive or transmit files over the Web. Bitmap images are suited to editing and other software manipulations. Only when an image is in its final form is it appropriate to compress it via JFIF.

JFIF files are used when high quality images are required. When JFIF files are included on a Web page, the implied assumption is that users of the page will use a machine equipped for high resolution color. GIF files, which as we have seen are not capable of extended color depth, tend to be smaller and to give a consistent effect over a wide range of graphical hardware setups. Therefore, GIF files are used for backgrounds, logos, buttons, icons, and controls on Web pages. We could make use of a GIF image as the wallpaper background for a hypertext document. We might use "\images\beachsand.gif" for this purpose. Backgrounds are specified by using the "background" attribute of the "<BODY>" tag instead of the "bgcolor" attribute. The tag would now read "<BODY backround=beachsand.gif" text="x8b4513" link="xFFEFD5" vlink="FF6347" alink="#FFE7BA">." File "nyt5.html" in the \wcbinfo\html\ directory is a version of our article with the beach sand background wallpaper.

The "beachsand.gif" file is an image about one inch square, the size that is typically used for wallpaper images. One can use images of any size for this purpose. The "Edit/Resize" option of LviewPro enables one to shrink a larger image so that it may be used as a thumb nail or wallpaper (Fig. 6.18). LviewPro does a

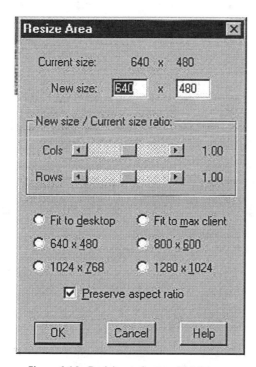

Figure 6.18. Resizing an image with lviewpro.

good job of shrinking images. When it comes to expanding them, the results vary with the resolution of the image to be expanded. Readers should open files "\webinfo\images\robot.jpg" and "\webinfo\ images\minirobot.jpg" with Lview-Pro to view a pair of files that illustrate the way LviewPro can be used to resize images. File "robot.jpg" measures 216×394 pixels while "minirobot.jpg" measures 84×153 pixels. The smaller file was produced by reducing the column size of the larger file by sixty percent with the "Preserve aspect ratio" option checked and saving it as "minirobot.jpg."

POSITIONING AND SIZING IMAGES ON WEB PAGES

The "<IMG src="URL"...>" tag is the general tag used to put images on pages. It is an empty tag since its "src" attribute identifies the location of the image to be displayed. Its attributes are many and serve a variety of purposes (Fig. 6.19). The "width" and "height" attributes cause Netscape to resize the image to the dimensions they specify. The appearance of the image can be distorted by inappropriate specifications of these parameters. When the "lowsrc" attribute is specified, the image specified by the "lowsrc" attribute is loaded immediately while the larger "scr" image is loaded in the background.

  Readers should open the file "album.html" in the \webinfo\html\ archive to see what effect each of the attributes of the "<IMG>" tag has on the image the tag displays. This file displays the "robot" and "minirobot" images from the resizing

Attribute	Function
align= "..."	"top/bottom/middle" placement relative to surrounding text "left/right" placement relative to screen margins
alt= "..."	text to be displayed in lieu of image on text only browsers
border=n	n is the width in pixels of border
height=n	n is the height in pixels of image
hspace=n	n is width in pixels of empty space to left and right of image
lowsrc= "URL"	source of low resolution image to be used until image in "src" is being loaded
src= "URL"	specify location of image source
vspace=n	n is width in pixels of empty space above and below image
width=n	n is the width in pixels of image

Figure 6.19. <IMG> tag attributes.

example above without using any attributes except the "src" attribute to identify the image to be displayed and then a series of the "minirobot" images with various attributes set. Each image displayed is labeled with the text of the "<IMG>" tag that produced it. For example, the image using the "border" attribute is coded in "album.html" as

```
<BR>
<IMG src="images/minirobot.jpg" align="center" border=10>
&lt;IMG src="images/minirobot.jpg" align="center" border=10>
<BR>
```

The line beginning "<IMG ..." is the image tag with the "border" attribute set to ten pixels. The line beginning "<IMG..." is a line of text that is identical with the tag except that it uses the special character tag "<" instead of the actual less than character, "<", so that it will be taken as a line of text rather than as an HTML tag. This produces the image displayed in Fig. 6.20.

In viewing this file, readers should note the use of the "width" and "height" attributes to resize the "minirobot.jgp" to a smaller size and to the dimensions of "robot.jpg":

```
<IMG src="minirobot.jpg" align="center" width=50 height=75>
&lt;IMG src="minirobot.jpg" align="center" width=50 height=75>
<br>
<BR>
<BR>
<IMG src="minirobot.jpg" align="center" width=216 height=394>
<BR>
&lt;IMG src="minirobot.jpg" align="center" width=216 height=394>
```

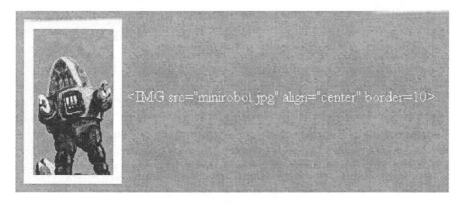

Figure 6.20. Image and tag from file "album.html."

The smaller image is quite presentable while the larger one shows the general effect of the "lossy" JPEG compression algorithm. What the results of the various codings on this page shows is that Netscape treats images inline with text as though they were large, decorative capital letters analogous to the decorative capitals of illuminated manuscripts.

The value given for "src" attribute, "minirobot.jpg," requires some comment. The "src" attribute of this tag, like the "href" and "background" attributes of "<A>" and "<BODY>" tags, calls for a URL or Web address to locate the file to be used. For the anchor tags in our article we gave the complete, so-called *absolute address*, of the file, "http://www.soum.co.jp/mito/art-e.html" for Art Tower Mito, etc. We did this because the files we wanted were located in disparate parts of the Web. For the "<BODY>" and "<IMG>" tags, we gave only partial, so-called *relative addresses*, for the files we wanted, "salmon.gif" and "minirobot.jpg." These locations are specified relative to the directory in which the html file containing these tags is stored. Because it is a file name given with no additional specifications, "salmon.gif" is taken to be located in the same directory ("\html") as the HTML file ("\html\nyt5.html"). On the other hand, the "minirobot.jpg" file is preceded by a directory name, "images/." The file specification "images/minrobot.jpg" identifies the location of file "minirobot.jpg" in directory images, which is a subdirectory of the directory holding the "album.html" file. Unless the full URL or absolute address for a file is given, Netscape will look for it to be located in the HTML file's directory or in a location that is designated as relative to the HTML file's directory. We will return to the topic of relative and absolute addressing of Web files when we discuss Web publishing in the next section of this chapter.

In the examples we have seen so far in this chapter, a link to another document is made by clicking on a portion of text identified by its color and underlining as a link, a portion of text contained within the scope of an "<A>...</A>" tag. But images, buttons, and icons, alone or in conjunction with text, can be the locus of a link as well. This is done by including whatever one wished to serve as the link identifier within the link tag. We could use the scaled down version of "minirobot.jpg" as a link to my home page with the following code:

```
<A href="http://www-bcf.usc.edu/~dilligan/">
<IMG src="images/minirobot.jpg" align="center" width=50 height=75>
</A> Click on Robot for Bob Dilligan's Home Page
<BR>
```

Readers will find this code implemented in the next to last example at the bottom of file "album.html." The robot is outlined with a blue border to indicate that it is a link. The text, if so desired, could have been included in the link, as it is in the final example in the file:

```
<A href="http://www-bcf.usc.edu/~dilligan/">
<IMG src="images/minirobot.jpg" align="center" width=50 height=75>
```

Click on Robot for Bob Dilligan's Home Page </A>

Coded this way, the text is underlined and colored blue as would be any default link identifier.

OBTAINING IMAGES FROM THE WEB

Though it is an easy thing, as we have seen, to download images, buttons, icons, and backgrounds, one should be responsible in doing so. Intellectual honesty and respect for the intellectual property of others are as much responsibilities on the Web as they are in traditional scholarship. The cooperative and collaborative nature of the Web may sometimes seem to dull this fact, but it is as important to keep track of the provenance of the images one downloads as it is to keep track of the source of any quoted or cited material. That said, it is the case that the Web provides numerous resources of public domain material useful for designing Web pages. In my estimation the best single site for Web programming resources is the "Nuthin' but Links" home page,[14] which is to Web programming what "Where to Browse for Art on the Internet" is to the art world.

The "Links" referred to in its title are links to a wealth of information organized in four main sections, "New This Month," "HTML Links," "Internet/Computers," and "Miscellaneous." Its "HTML Links" section is an easily browseable compendium covering what seems to be just about everything useful on the topic that is available on the Web. Its "Web Page Graphics" category provides access to sites containing icons, bullets, buttons, horizontal rules, and other useful graphics. Among the notable sites in this category is the one for "Background Textures." Its "Backgrounds Index"[15] provides over 700 different background textures for downloading. The "Read more here!" link on this page contains an excellent and intelligent explanation of the conditions of use of these background textures. The "Color Selectors" category connects not only with ColorServ Pro but also with over a dozen different sites that provide facilities for all sorts of manipulation of RGB color. For example, the "Using Color"[16] link gives the names of 140 different colors that are recognized by Netscape and may be used in lieu of "xRRGGBB" hexadecimal notation to specify colors. Anyone wishing to experiment with an HTML editor will find its "HTML Editor" category invaluable. There they will find a broad selection of public domain, shareware, and commercial HTML editors, most of which, including the commercial software, is available for downloading on at least a trial basis.

With the knowledge of HTML tags obtained from this chapter as background, readers should be able to explore and evaluate the HTML editors offered at this site. Readers should also be aware of its "HTML Tutorial" and "Advanced Topics" categories, which provide extensive documentation and instruction for all levels of

HTML programming from the introductory to the most sophisticated. With the information available on the Web, readers will be able to develop their skills in HTML page design to whatever level of sophistication they desire. Readers who still feel baffled by HTML tags might want to take a look at the " Crash Course in HTML"[17] link. Readers interested in information on different browsers and helper applications or in creating their own home page with a "fill-in-the-blanks" form should examine the "Home Page Creation Center" link.[18] The links to the sites mentioned here are all found in file "\webinfo\html\htmlprog.html" for easy reference, but readers should familiarize themselves with the wide resources of the "Nuthin' but Links" site.

There are a number of aspects of HTML programming—some of which, like the division of Web pages into separate, independently scrollable screens called "frames" or the use of JAVA applets, are fairly straightforward though detailed; others of which, like developing JAVA applets, using JAVA Script and Cgi-bin, require extensive developmental programming and system programming experience—that we have omitted from our discussion of HTML programming in the interests of focusing on the underlying principles of HTML rather than attempting a comprehensive treatment of every tag available. I hope that with this introduction, readers will be able to discuss HTML programming intelligently with experienced HTML programmers and will have taken for themselves the first steps in the direction of becoming experienced HTML programmers. But there are two topics, namely, the use of video and sound, that I need to touch upon, if only briefly, before concluding this introduction.

WEB VIDEO AND SOUND APPLICATIONS

The first thing to be noted about the use of video and sound is that they require, for their successful implementation, specialized hardware and software on both clients and servers. Producing original sound and video material for the Web, even something so mundane as the taping of a presentation or lecture, requires not only professional audio and video facilities and equipment—video cameras, tape editors, sound recording, and editing devices—but also digitizing equipment to convert video and audio tape to digital form for the Web. Web workstations need to be equipped with sound cards, speakers, high speed video display cards and CRTs, and very powerful CPUs if they are to be capable of receiving sound and full video from the Web. So severe is the load that full video puts on a computer that the very latest models of Intel's Pentium chip are designed with MMX ("MultiMedia eXtension") capabilities. Web servers are likewise challenged by the demands of providing video and sound to their clients. It is usually the case that web sites dedicate servers exclusively to providing sound and video. There are many "server side" software packages for this purpose and servers require massive amounts of high speed disk storage to allow, on demand, multiple access to their video and sound files. We need not get into technical details of bandwidth for readers to appreciate the problems involved in transmitting large sound and video files across the net. A typical video file recorded in 256 colors at 15 frames per second, half the number of frames of today's television, and with an image size of 320×240 pixels, half the size of the lowest screen resolution, will require the delivery to the client of about ten million bytes per minute. High quality music requires at least one million bytes per minute. A popular site might have to service a hundred or more clients at a time, which conceivably could require it to deliver one billion bytes per minute to the Web.

There is no clear favorite file or mime type for audio and video analogous to JPEG and GIF for images. Different companies have invented their own proprietary file formats for audio and video and provide would-be users with free viewing or listening software. These programs are written to use Netscape's application program interface (API) and so are compatible with the already installed version of Netscape software. Users are expected to download this viewing or listening software and install it as a helper application on their browsers.[19] Readers whose computers are equipped with a sound card and speakers may get some idea of the quality of sound on the Web by installing the RealAudio 5.0 Player software on their computer. This software enables a browser to play and display a number of different types of audio and video files.They may obtain this software without charge from the RealAudio Home Page.[20] The directions provided on the site are quite easy to follow. The program that is downloaded is a self-installing executable program. It will install the RealAudio player automatically and add audio and video mime types to the list of helper applications on the Netscape browser. Once the player software is installed, readers may select from a wide range of sites listed at the RealAudio 5.0 Sites Directory that provide many different music, sports, and talk sites for listening and viewing.

The quality of the sound delivered over the Web is determined by three things: the sound card and speakers installed on the client, the speed of the connection to the Web, and the amount of traffic on the Web. As with the effect of the monitor and graphics card on color, the absolute limit of sound quality is determined by the quality of the sound card and speakers. Just as 24 bit color is lost on an 8-bit system, 16- or 32-bit sound is lost on an 8-bit sound card. And the best sound card is crippled, as any audiophile will confirm, by a poor set of speakers. The amount of sound information that can be delivered in real time to the client is limited by the speed of the client's network connection. RealAudio promises "FM Stereo" quality with a 28.8 kb modem and "near CD-ROM" quality with an ISDN or Ethernet connection. But sound card, speakers, and connection are all at the mercy of the volume of network traffic. The source of the sound file is located at some arbitrary place on the Web and the speed of the connection of the client to the Web is more accurately described as the speed of the connection between the client and its host server. No matter how stable and uncluttered that connection may be, the host server's connection to the server holding the sound file is subject to all the vagaries of general network traffic. What this produces, in my experience, are annoying gaps in the reception of sound. For music, they remind me of the skips produced by a scratch in a phonograph record. For talk, they are less annoying than for music but still are irritating, the effect being similar to listening to a lecturer with a case of occasional hiccups.

I have not noticed this problem on the few occasions when I have used the Web's ability to transmit sound as a telephone connection. There are other applications that use the Web for sound-dependent applications with some success. One of these is for teaching foreign languages. A number of sites on the Web offer conversational language lessons. One of the sites I have referred people to is the "Learn to Speak Italian" page,[21] where Professor Antonio offers colloquial Italian lessons in a family setting:

> "One day, maybe you'll grow up to be a Pope!"
> *Un giorno, forse diventarai Papa!*
>
> "Be a brave man and change little Mario's diaper, OK?"
> *Sii un uomo corraggioso e cambia i pannolini di piccolo Mario.*
>
> "Can you take out the garbage, my love?"
> *Amore mio, puoi tirare la spazzatura fuori?*
>
> "You're not fat. Those are just love handles."
> *Non sei grasso. Sono solamente le maniglie dell'amore.*

This site offers sound in four different sound file formats. Whether or not readers find the contents of this page useful, they should find its form instructive. It is an example of the type of sound application that works well on the Web: an application that can segment its sound into sound bytes that can be downloaded completely in a few seconds before playback.

Audio applications from the Web, given the current state of the Web and of this technology, may be of some marginal use to most readers. I find it much more difficult to find any use for current video applications on the Web. It is easy to imagine the potential usefulness of video applications on the Web. Readers interested in any of the performing arts—music, opera, theater, film, television, etc.— would benefit greatly from on demand video from some vast Web library of performances. They would want not only the ability to download entire performances but also the ability to download parts of performances—passages, arias, scenes, sound bites—to be played in any order dictated by the logic of an analysis, presentation, or discussion. The quality of sound should be comparable to CD stereo sound and the quality of the video should be that of high definition television. But applications at this level await not only the solution of technical issues related to bandwidth, connection speed, compression, and file format, but also the solution of complex legal issues relating to copyright, intellectual property, and royalties. Of course, what everyone would like from the Web is the simulacrum of God's infinite universe forever to delight themselves with. With much more realistic hope, I suspect that the first generally useful video applications will be delivered on Digital Video Disk (DVD) technology, not on the Web.

What video on the Web offers today is the ability to decorate a web site with some attention-grabbing snippets. Such decorative animation can also be produced by other means such as JAVA and JAVA script, which have the advantage of not being so dependent as video upon the bandwidth available to connect the client to the Web. Anything more than this is simply beyond the capacity of clients attached by 28.8 kb modems with which it can take ten or more minutes to download a 30-second clip recorded at 15 frames per second. The downloading times are better with 10-megabit Ethernet, with which brief scenes of four or five minutes can be downloaded in two or three minutes. This makes possible so called "streaming" in which a viewer starts playing a clip while it is still being received. But streaming

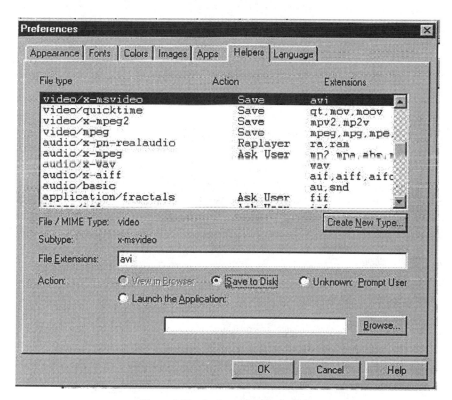

Figure 6.21. Saving video files to disk.

applications are subject to the vagaries of network traffic. And even when they work, streaming applications deliver small, relatively low quality video images and sound. I agree with most forecasts that video applications in the foreseeable future will result in a convergence of the currently separate technologies of television broadcasting, VCR, CD-ROM, and computer networks. But only time will tell the exact configuration of this future convergence.

My own approach to video applications on the Web is to configure Netscape to save incoming video files to disk. This is easily done with the "Helpers" tab of the Netscape "Options/General Preferences" menu selection (Fig. 6.21). I have also downloaded from the Web a number of different video viewing programs. Readers can find these viewers on the "Movie Viewers for Windows 95" page.[22] At the very least, one should download Apple computer's "Apple QuickTime Movie Viewer for Windows 95,"[23] which is the most widely used of video viewers. Sample Quick-Time video files can be found by searching the Web. Netscape, when configured as in Fig. 6.21, saves these samples to disk in a designated directory after which one may view them by launching the QuickTime viewer, "Play32.exe." Files are viewed by opening them with "File/Open" menu selection of the viewer program and then pushing a start button. Following this procedure, readers can experience for themselves both the ratio of the time it takes to download a file versus the time it takes to view it and the quality of the video and sound provided by the Web. They will then be in a position to decide for themselves whether this particular game is worth it.

PUBLISHING ON THE WEB: FTP AND A TOUCH OF UNIX

So far in this chapter, we have discussed how to create an HTML page, how to save it on our PC disk drive, and how to view it with Netscape. In this section we will discuss how to "publish" the pages we create by making them available on the Web. All it takes to make something available on the Web is to copy it from a directory on our PC disk drive to a directory on a disk drive on a Web server. To copy a file to a server, one must be authorized to do so by the organization that runs the server. Academic institutions, nonprofit organizations, governmental agencies, and commercial Web providers are among the places that may provide access to a Web server. (Individuals may also own and operate their own servers, but this entails technical proficiency far beyond the scope of this book.) For purposes of this discussion, I will assume that readers have obtained authorization to use a Web server that they will be sharing with other Web users and that they are in possession of four crucial pieces of information without which they will be unable to proceed:

1. The Internet name of the server to which they will copy their files;
2. The URL of their web site;

3. Their user name;
4. Their password which enables them to log on to their server.

All this information should be obtained from the entity that authorizes users to have a site on the Web. We will use the WS_FTP program we downloaded in the previous chapter to accomplish this copying. The WS_FTP program uses the File Transfer Protocol (FTP) to link the file system of our PC and the file system of the server on a peer-to-peer basis.

Most Web servers run the UNIX[24] operating system and an understanding of some of the basics of UNIX, especially its file system, will enable readers to understand what is involved in transferring files from their machine to their server. The UNIX file system resembles the DOS file system that underlies Windows because DOS's file system was originally designed to resemble UNIX's. They share the same hierarchic, tree structure in which directories may be nested within other directories. The principal difference between the DOS and UNIX file systems is that DOS is designed as a single user system while UNIX is designed to be used by many users at the same time. UNIX, consequently, must provide a way to allow users to share disks and files without disturbing each others' work. UNIX does this by designating an owner for each directory and also by giving each user a "home" directory, which is the directory to which the user will be attached automatically upon logging on. A user owns her or his home directories and any subdirectories that descend from the home directory. It is the "home" directory that most concerns Web users.

When a UNIX user tries to read from or write to a data file or execute a program file, UNIX will check to see whether or not the user is authorized to carry out the operation and allow only authorized operations. Owners are the ones who give permission to access their files, either on a directory-by-directory or file-by-file basis. They may, for example, deny themselves permission to alter a file they own in order to prevent themselves from accidentally changing a file they wish to preserve. They may designate a group of users to whom they may grant or withhold permission on a group basis. This might be done for groups collaborating on a project, seminars, classes, etc. And they may make a file a public one by allowing anyone with access to the system to read and/or write the file. (Usually, public permission is for "read only" access but file owners may do with their files as they wish.)[25]

UNIX uses the slash character, "/," rather than the backslash character, "\," to delimit directory names. UNIX file names are case-sensitive while DOS file names are not. In DOS, both "Images" and "images" refer to the same file or directory; in UNIX, "Images" and "images" refer to different ones. For this reason, it is good HTML programming practice to name all files in lower case and to be careful to create the names of UNIX directories in lower case. "<IMG>" tags reading "<IMG src="Images/robot.jpg">" and "<IMG src="images/robot.jpg">" will refer to the same file as long as they are on a DOS client, but will refer to two different files (one or the other of which may not exist) when transferred to a UNIX server. In UNIX, the period, ".", refers to the current directory and two dots refer to the parent directory of the current directory. A reference to "./letters/mary" refers to file "mary" in directory "letters," which is a subdirectory of the current directory; a reference to "../letters/mary" refers to file "mary" in directory "letters," which is a subdirectory of the parent directory of the current directory. The double dot annotation may be concatenated: "../../" refers to the parent of the parent of the current directory. The tilde, "~", is an abbreviation for the home directory of a user. A reference to "/~mary/" is a reference to the home directory of user "mary."

The DOS file system is hierarchic only within the confines of its disk volumes, each of which has its own root directory. The UNIX file system, by contrast, is completely hierarchic. There is a single root directory for the entire file system, "/," and users move from one part of the file system to another without any concern about what physical or logical disk volume they are on. They must of course have the appropriate permissions to access various parts of the system. Users share access to some directories, for example the "/usr" directory, which has subdirectories such as "/usr/bin" that contains system utilities and "/usr/games" that contains game programs. User home directories are all placed in a directory called "/home." My home directory would be "/home/dilligan/" (or "/~dilligan/"). The root directory, "/," is the home of the "superuser." Access to this directory is very carefully controlled because the "superuser" has complete control over the computer's resources.

To use the WS_FTP program, we must first make sure we are connected to the Internet. When we load the program, the first screen it presents us with is a log on screen (Fig. 6.22). On this screen we fill in our own "Host Name," "User ID," "Password," and "Local PC" fields and set the "Host Type" to "Automatic detect" and push the "OK" button to log on. The screen shown in Fig. 6.22 is filled in with my information. The "Host Name" is the Internet FTP name of our Web server. The Web, one should recall, is part of the larger Internet, servers for which have a unique name called an "FTP" name because it is the name used with the FTP command to initiate a connection with a server. The "User ID" is our user name on the server and the "Password" is the password for the "User ID." The "Local PC" field contains the full path name of the directory from which we are going to copy files to the server. In this case we plan to copy from the "d:\chapter6" directory. The "Host Type" field is used to identify the type of computer of the server. Usually, the program can detect this automatically so that "Automatic detect" is the default setting. Some servers, however, may require explicit type identification. This field is a drop down box which allows users to select a server type from the list of types recognized by the program. The "Save" button on this screen enables us to save this information under the name we enter in the "Profile Name" field. The "New Button"

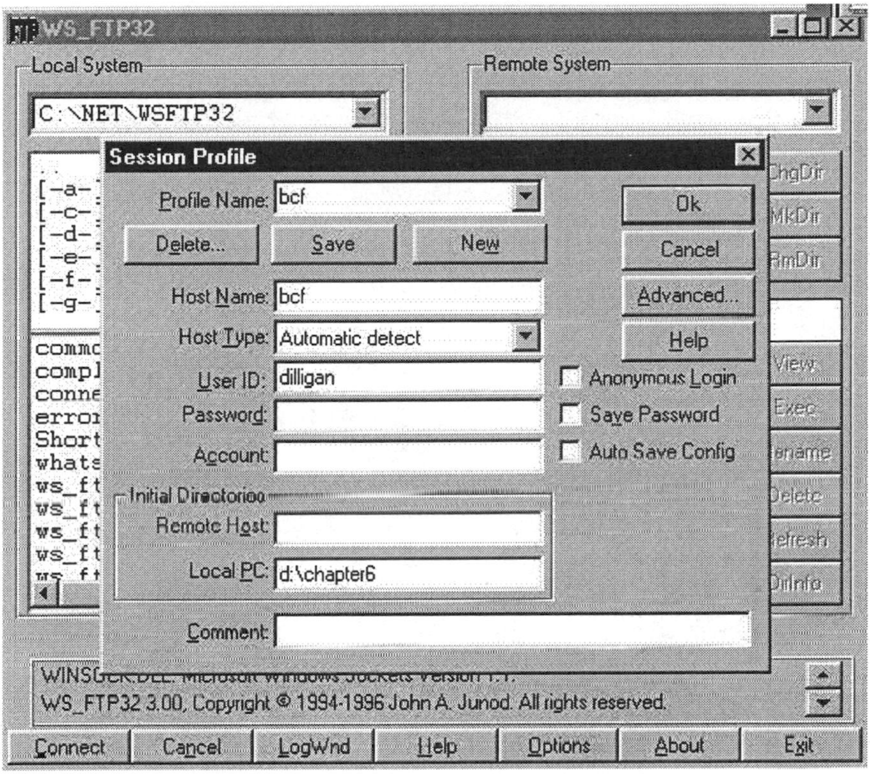

Figure 6.22. WS_FTP log on screen.

clears all fields so that we may enter the profile of another server to which we have access. The "Delete" button deletes the information saved under a profile name.

When the log on procedure we initiated by pressing the "OK" button is complete, the log on screen vanishes and we now have access to the FTP screen (Fig. 6.23). The FTP program has established a link between a directory on my workstation (D:\chapter6) and my UNIX home directory (/~dilligan/), as is seen in Fig. 6.23. This is a very complex screen, but it can be easily understood by dividing it into its functional parts. The purpose of the screen is to manage copying of data between two systems. The bottom of the screen contains a multiple line field that scrolls as commands and responses are exchanged across the Internet. The "Remote Host" field of the log on screen was left empty so that we would be attached to the default host directory, which is our home directory on the host. We use the scroll button of this field to scroll through the messages until we reach the message that gives us the full path name of our home directory on the host:

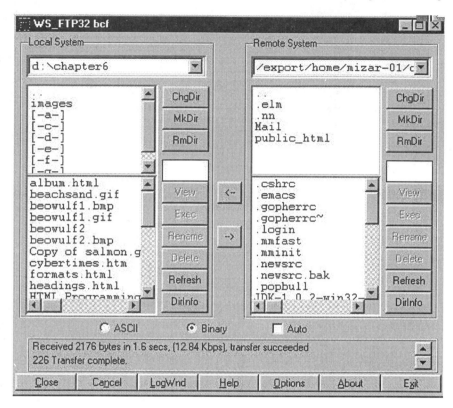

Figure 6.23. FTP screen.

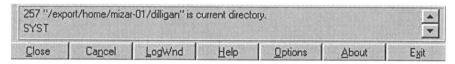

Figure 6.24. Internet messages area showing home directory.

The two buttons on the bottom of the screen that concern us are the "Close" and "Exit" buttons. The "Close" button closes the connection between the two computers. When it is pushed, it ends the connection and changes into a "Connect" button with which we may connect to another host. The "Exit" button is used to end the program.

The upper right part of the screen is labeled "Remote System." This area contains the screens and controls that give us access to the file system of the host

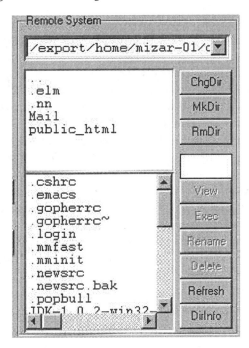

Figure 6.25. Remote system area of FTP screen.

(Fig. 6.25). The top half of this area shows the subdirectories of the current directory, which is my home directory. Of the five entries in this screen the ".." entry refers to the parent directory of this directory. To examine the contents of this directory, we would double click on the ".." entry. The ".elm," ".nn," and "Mail" directories need not concern us. The "public_html" directory, however, is the single most crucial directory for Web programming because this is the parent directory for any material we wish to put on the Web. Anything we put in this directory or any subdirectory descended from it is accessible to other Web servers simply by virtue of its presence there. The lower portion of the "Remote System" area lists the files contained in the current directory. By using the scroll bar to the right of this area, we may scroll through all the files in the directory.

There is an important convention associated with all directories accessible by the Web which can be illustrated with the URL of my home page, "http://www-bcf.usc.edu/~dilligan/." The last part of this URL, "/~dilligan/," identifies the directory of this URL as the home directory of user "dilligan" on the "www-bcf" server of my university's domain, "usc.edu." My home page is in this directory in a file called "index.html." If no file name is given for a Web directory, the Web browser will display the contents of the file "index.html" if it exists. The address of my home page relative to my user directory on my server is therefore dilli-gan/public_html/index.html. Web software takes care of figuring out where exactly a directory or file is located. All Web users need to know is how to address them relative to the "public_html" directory.

The upper left side of the screen is labeled "Local System" and this area gives us access to our PC's file system (Fig. 6.26). The directory area shows the parent directory of the "chapter6" directory as the ".." entry, an images subdirectory, and a list of the disk drives attached to this PC. One can move to any of these by double clicking on it. The lower part of this area lists the files in the "\webinfo\html" directory.

The left and right arrow buttons in the center of the screen are file transfer buttons (Fig. 6.27). To transfer a file from the PC to the remote host, one would highlight the file to be transferred by clicking on it once and then copying it to the directory on the remote system by clicking on the right arrow. To transfer a file from the remote host to the PC, one highlights it and then clicks the left arrow. The name of the transferred file will appear in the file list of the directory receiving the transfer and a message confirming the transfer will appear in the Internet messages area at the bottom of the screen. Both ASCII and Binary file transfers may be made in this

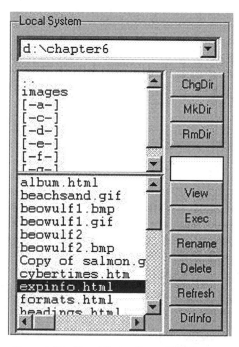

Figure 6.26. "Local System" area of FTP screen.

Figure 6.27. File transfer buttons.

way. The file-type buttons below the "Local System" area are used to specify the type of the file to be transferred:

Figure 6.28. File-type radio buttons.

Image files are binary files and HTML files are ASCII files. It is a good idea, however, to make all file transfers as binary files because in binary transfers the file that arrives will always be a byte-for-byte copy of the transmitted file. Neither ASCII files nor image files are altered in any way by transferring them as binary files. In ASCII transfers, bytes that contain values above 127 will be altered. An image file inadvertently transferred as an ASCII file will arrive altered.

The overall process of creating and publishing a Web page is given in Fig. 6.29.

We will now carry out an exercise that will explain step by step the details of moving a file from a PC to a Web directory. The objective of the exercise will be to move the "htmlprog.html" from the "\webinfo\html" directory of our PC to a directory on our server. We will set up a directory structure that would enable us to move all the HTML files associated with this book to the Web.

The first thing we do is to log in to the server, which attaches us to our user home directory. We then will move to the "public_html" subdirectory by highlighting it (Fig. 6.30). We are now in the "public_html" directory which has two subdirectories ("images" and "software") and a number of files, among which is "index.html," my home page, as well as a number of directories for courses I have taught and for the Web material for this book in directory "expinfo" (Fig. 6.31). To create the "web_age" directory, we used the "MkDir" button which brings up a dialog box in which we supply the name of the new directory (Fig. 6.32). The URL of this directory is "http://www-bcf.usc.edu/~dilligan/web_age/." This will add "web_age" to the directory listing of the "Remote System" area (Fig. 6.33).

To create the subdirectories for this directory, we highlighted "web_age" and changed to that directory by pushing the "ChgDir" button. We then created the

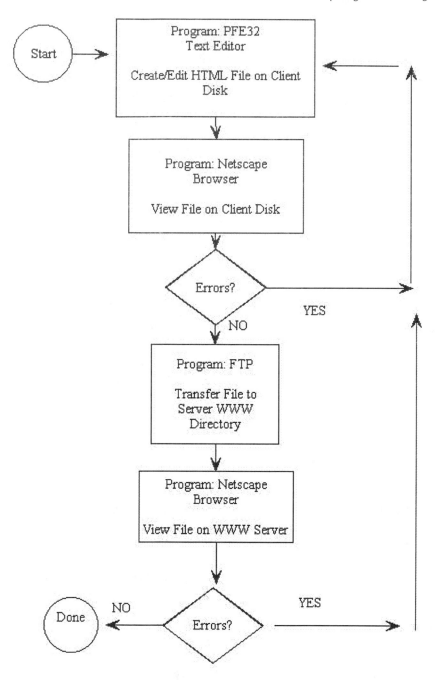

Figure 6.29. Overview of HTML programming.

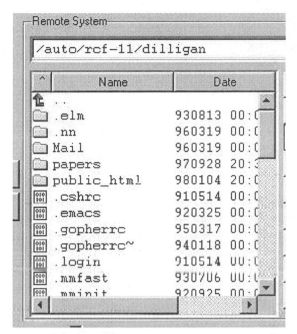

Figure 6.30. Contents of user home directory.

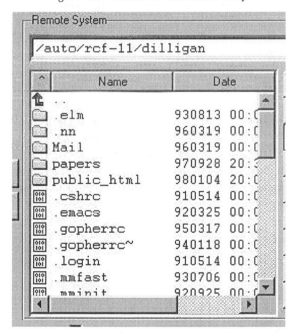

Figure 6.31. Contents of user's Web home directory.

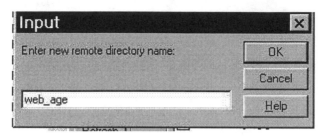

Figure 6.32. Dialog box for creating a Web directory.

various subdirectories for this page and transferred files to them. To transfer a file
to the Web, we highlight its name in the "Local System" area, as is seen in Fig. 6.34,
and copy it to directory "web_age" by pushing the right arrow button. The URL of
this file is http://www-bcf.usc.edu/~dilligan/web_age/ or one of its subdirectories.
Before we use this page, we need to copy two image files into it: "shaman.jpg,"
which is the graphic image on the page; and "back_19.jpg," which is the background image for the page.

Our plan is to organize the files on the server in the same way as we have done
on the PC. We use the "MkDir" button to create a number of directories that
correspond roughly to the navigation buttons on the Web page (Fig. 6.35). If we
use the URL of the "expinfo" alone by typing "http://www-bcf.usc.edu/~dilli-
gan/web_age/source" into the Netscape's location field and pressing "Enter," the
Web will display the contents of the directory (Fig. 6.36). We could then display
the contents of the various directories of the book's dedicated home page by double
clicking on their names in this listing. Readers are encouraged to explore the layout
of this home page by using this technique.

Four of the buttons to the right of the file listing of the "Remote System" area
are used frequently in Web publishing. They all work by highlighting the file on
which one wishes to carry out an operation and then by pushing the button for the
desired operation. The "Delete" button deletes the highlighted file from the system.
The "Rename" button allows one to rename a file. This is particularly useful in

```
images          970830  00:0
software        960825  00:0
web_age         980123  05:2
abg56.htm       970916  00:0
anatomy.pdf     971007  06:4
anatomy.ppt     970930  07:4
anatony.log     971007  06:4
```

Figure 6.33. Contents of public_html directory.

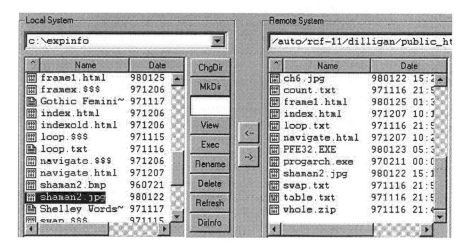

Figure 6.34. Transferring "shaman.jpg" to the Web.

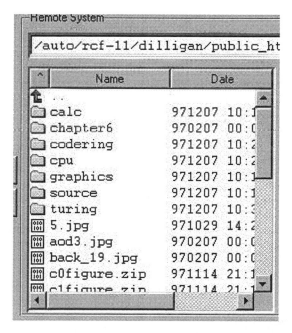

Figure 6.35. Contents of "web_age" Web directory.

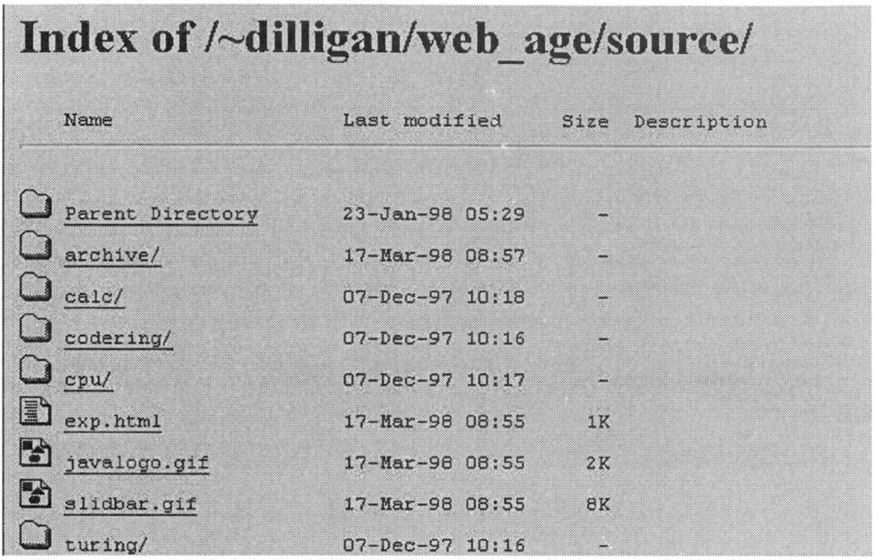

Index of /~dilligan/web_age/source/

Name	Last modified	Size	Description
Parent Directory	23-Jan-98 05:29	-	
archive/	17-Mar-98 08:57	-	
calc/	07-Dec-97 10:18	-	
codering/	07-Dec-97 10:16	-	
cpu/	07-Dec-97 10:17	-	
exp.html	17-Mar-98 08:55	1K	
javalogo.gif	17-Mar-98 08:55	2K	
slidbar.gif	17-Mar-98 08:55	8K	
turing/	07-Dec-97 10:16	-	

Figure 6.36. Web display of "expinfo/source" URL.

correcting upper/lower case mistakes in file names and for designating a file as the "index.html" file. The "Refresh" button updates the directory and file listing if these are not done automatically when a file or directory is changed in some way. The "DirInfo" button provides a list of all files and subdirectories along with their current permission status. Pushing this button for the "web_age/source/archive" directory produces a screen with the following listing:

```
total 28
drwxr-xr-x    2 dilligan m-engl     512 Jan 24 19:33 ch4
-rw-r--r--    1 dilligan m-engl    1333 Dec  7 11:10 ch4.jpg
drwxr-xr-x    2 dilligan m-engl     512 Jan 20 16:37 ch5
-rw-r--r--    1 dilligan m-engl    1335 Dec  7 11:10 ch5.jpg
drwxr-xr-x    2 dilligan m-engl     512 Jan 22 15:28 ch6
-rw-r--r--    1 dilligan m-engl    1358 Dec  7 11:10 ch6.jpg
-rw-r--r--    1 dilligan m-engl     680 Dec 13 06:37 exp.html
-rw-r--r--    1 dilligan m-engl    1027 Dec 13 06:31 mac.jpg
-rw-r--r--    1 dilligan m-engl    1310 Dec 13 06:31 windows.jpg
```

This screen gives an overview of the ownership and permissions of the files and subdirectories in the current directory. It is a rather cryptic display of the sort that only a UNIX system programmer could love. The third column from the left gives the user name of the owner of the file. UNIX keeps an owner name for each file because it is a multi-user system. The rightmost column gives the names of the files in the directory. The leftmost column contains a sequence of ten characters. If the first character is "d," the name refers to a directory name; if it is "-," the name refers to a file. The next nine characters show UNIX divides user permissions into three classes of three characters each: owner, group, and other. The letters used are "w" for write permission, "r" for read permission, "-" for permission denied, and "x" for execute permission. The "x" is used only for program files. In the notation for "ch4," drwxr-xr-x, "d" means that the name is a directory, "wrx" means that the owner can read, write, and execute any file in the directory; the first "r-x" means that the group (as defined by the owner) can read and execute but not write the directories; the second "r-x" gives the same permissions to all other users as was given to the group. Permissions may be changed by the owner. The most sensitive permission is write permission, because that allows those to whom it is granted to alter the contents of files. Material published on the Web usually gives "r-x" permission to all users and restricts "w" permission to the owner.

In the opening chapter of *A Portrait of the Artist as a Young Man*, Stephen Dedalus, before embarking on his explorations of the mazes of self and culture through which he will ultimately "go to encounter for the millionth time the reality of experience and to forge in the smithy of [his] soul the uncreated conscience of [his] race," orients himself within an enclosing nest of conventional reference:

Stephen Dedalus
Class of Elements
Clongowes Wood College
Sallins
County Kildare
Ireland
Europe
The World
The Universe

Stephen engages here in an extreme form of "absolute" addressing. The process of Web publishing we have described here is a process by which we place material for the Web in a series of nested references:

The client work station
PFE32
WS_FTP
The Internet
The local Web server
The UNIX user directory (/~username/)
The home page directory in the user directory (public.html)
The home page file in the home page directory (index.html)
The World Wide Web

Though it may seem at times to be a Dedalian conundrum where we find ourselves "in wandering mazes lost," the organizing metaphor of the worldwide network is a Web of home pages, not an imprisoning maze, because of its nested structure. Equipped with a browser like Netscape and a knowledge of HTML programming, we may not only encounter the millions of possibilities extant on the Web but also forge for ourselves new links in the pattern of its constantly evolving culture.

Glossary

Accumulator: the register in CPU that is used to hold the results of arithmetical and logical operations.

Advanced Research Projects Administration (ARPA): an agency of the United States government charged with sponsoring scientific research projects on advanced technology at institutions of higher education, corporations, and think tanks.

AI: acronym for Artificial Intelligence.

Algorithm: a finite series of steps that will produce a specified output from a specified input.

American Standard Code for Information Interchange (ASCII): the most widely used coding scheme for recording text material for computer processing.

Analog Computer: a nonprogrammable computer the output of which provides the solution to a specific equation or group of equations.

Analog Data: data that is recorded as a continuous stream that is proportional to the information being recorded. Tape recorders and phonograph records are examples of devices that use analog data.

Analytical Engine: a programmable, mechanical calculator invented by the nineteenth century mathematician Charles Babbage as an improvement on his earlier invention, the Difference Engine.

Applet Program: a computer program written in the JAVA programming language to be run from a Web page.

Application Program: a computer program that carries out some task under the supervision of the computer's operation system.

ARPA: see Advanced Research Projects Administration.

ARPANET: the original name for the Internet, sponsored by the federal government's Advanced Research Projects Administration (ARPA).

Artificial Intelligence: the field of computer research devoted to the development of computer programs and systems that replicate the capabilities of human intelligence.

ASCII: see American Standard Code for Information Interchange.

Assembler Language: a low level computer programming language that is specific to a single type of central processing unit.

Bandwidth: in computer networking, the capacity of a network cable or physical layer, measured either in bits per second or frequency (Hertz), to carry information.

Base Address: the location at which the first byte of a program is loaded into memory.

Base Eight Number: a number expressed in a number system that counts in powers of eight and that is written with the digits 0 through 7.

Base Sixteen Number: a number expressed in a number system that counts in powers of sixteen and that is written with the digits 0 through 9 and A through F.

Base Ten Number: a number expressed in a number system that counts in powers of ten and that is written with the digits 0 through 9.

Base Two Number: a number expressed in a number system that counts in powers of two and that is written with the digits 0 and 1.

Binary Code: the information in any part of a computer represented as binary numbers.

Binary File: a file that contains a computer program written in binary code.

Binary Number: see Base Two Number.

Bit: a binary switch whose on state is represent by 1 in binary code and whose off state is represented as 0 in binary code.

Bitmap: an uncompressed image file whose size is a function of the color depth of the image.

Borg: an aggressive species of beings in *Star Trek* who are cyborgs, that is, part computer and part biological and whose goal is to assimilate all cultures into their own collective consciousness.

Branch Structure: a Boolean fork in a computer program that directs a program to carry out one set of instructions if a specified condition is true and another set of instructions if the specified condition is false.

Branching Instruction: a machine language instruction that may change the contents of a CPU's location register. Branching Instructions are used to create a Branching Structure in a program.

Browser: an application program that formats the contents of information on the Web so as to allow users to examine it in an easily readable form.

Byte: a unit of eight consecutive bits that provides the basic addressing scheme of computer memory.

Byte Aligned: binary code that is stored in a way that observes the byte divisions of memory. C: a high level programming language with a terse mathematical syntax developed for the UNIX operating system but widely used throughout the computer industry.

C++: an advanced version of the C computer language that is designed for the development of object-oriented programs.

Call by Reference: a way of passing the address of a piece of data to a method or subroutine so as to allow the method of subroutine to modify the data stored at that address.

Call by Value: a way of passing a copy of piece of data to a method or subroutine so that the method or subroutine can use the data in its computation without modifying the original copy of the data.

Carrier Sense Multiple Access/Collision Detection (CSMA/CD): the technical name for the method used by Ethernet to control the exchange of information on a computer network.

Carrier Signal: the signal used by Ethernet to indicate that the network is busy and to prevent access to the network while it is busy.

Central Processing Unit (CPU): the main operation part of a computer where instructions are carried out and data is modified.

Checkbox: an icon on a graphical user interface that allows a user to turn an option on or off.

CISC: see Complex Instruction Set Computer.

Client: In Client/Server computing, the workstation which requests operations from the network server.

Client/Server Computing: a form of computing designed to minimize network traffic by dividing computation tasks between two computers, the Client and the Server.

Clipper Chip: a scheme whereby the government or anyone possessing the proper codes can decrypt supposedly confidential information on a page.

Code Page: the use of the ASCII codes ranging from 128 to 255 to represent the glyphs of alphabets such as Hebrew, Cyrillic, and Arabic.

Code Segment: the part of a computer program that holds the binary code of the program's instructions.

Color Depth: the number of bits used to record or display the colors of a graphic image. It may range from four bits (sixteen possible colors) to twenty-four bits (over sixteen million colors).

Compiler Directive: an instruction in a computer program whose purpose is to control the process of compiling a program rather than to provide an instruction for the program being compiled.

Compiling: the process of translating the instructions of a computer program written in text by a programmer into the binary code that will be used by the computer to carry out the instructions.

Complex Instruction Set Computer (CISC): a computer whose CPU is capable of operations that are many and elaborate.

Compression: the application of numerical techniques to binary code in order to reduce the number of bytes needed to represent the information contained in the code.

CPU cycle: the sequence of fetching, interpreting, and executing a program instruction.

CPU Register: a location in the computer's CPU used to hold either machine instructions or data.

CPU: see Central Processing Unit.

CRT: a computer terminal that displays information on a cathode ray tube.

CSMA/CD: see Carrier Sense Multiple Access/Collision Detection.

Cyberpunk: a Science Fiction genre set in a highly computerized, MTV-like future dealing with the adventures of its protagonists in cyberspace.

Cyberspace: the metaphor used by our culture to conceptualize the interactions of humans with computer data and programs, especially on the Word Wide Web.

DARPA: see Defense Advanced Research Projects Administration.

Data Bus: the addressing circuit of a computer that provides the channels through which data is passed between memory, peripheral devices, and the CPU.

Data Compression: see Compression.

Data Packets: the parcels containing network addresses and information into which network software divides large files of information for transmission over a network.

Data Segment: the part of a computer program containing the binary code of the data on which the program will operate.

Decimal Number: see Base Ten Number.

Deep Blue: the IBM chess playing computer.

Defense Advanced Research Projects Administration (DARPA): the central research and development organization for the Department of Defense.

Dialog Box: a window displayed by a program to provide information to or obtain information from the user.

Difference Engine: the first mechanical calculating machine invented by Charles Babbage.

Digital Computer: a computer that uses discrete numerical quantities to express its data and code.

Digital Data: information that is recorded as a sequence of discrete numerical values rather than as a continuous one.

Digital Video Disk (DVD): a CD-ROM disk containing video information such as a television show or film recorded at a very high density (4 billion bytes or more).

Digitize: to record data in digital format or to convert data from analog format to digital format.

Directory: a named subdivision of the file system hierarchy in which are stored computer files and other directories that are called subdirectories.

Disk Drive: a storage device that records information on a disk-shaped platter so that it can be readily accessed.

Document Type Definition (DTD): the part of an SGML document that specifies, according to the rules of a formal grammar, the structure and encoding of a class of SGML documents.

DOS Window: the Windows 95 display screen used to provide a DOS command line interface for programs that do not have a Graphical User Interface.

Dotted Quad Notation: the decimal notation for IP addresses made up of four numbers ranging from 0 to 255 separated by three decimal points, e.g., 128.125.243.116.

Doubleword: a binary number recorded in four consecutive bytes.

Drag and Drop: the process of relocating an item on a graphics screen by selecting it with a mouse, moving the mouse, with a button held down, to the point at which you wish to relocate the item, and placing it there by releasing the button.

Dropdown Box: A standard Window control that displays a list of options from which the user chooses.

DTD: see Document Type Definition.

DVD: see Digital Video Disk.

EDVAC: Electronic Discrete Variable Computer; a computer designed by John von Neumann in 1946 that embodied the principles of von Neumann computer architecture.

Encapsulation: the bundling of data and program instructions that is characteristic of object-oriented programs.

Encryption: the process of applying mathematical transformations to computer data so as to render it unintelligible.

Encryption Key: a number, analogous to a lock combination, that is used to render encrypted data intelligible.

ENIAC: the Electric Numerical Integrator And Calculator; a computer developed during World War II that was regarded as the first modern computer.

Ethernet: a method of connecting workstations on a network and managing the communications between them.

Event Handler: the object-oriented programming method or subroutine that is used to process commands from a graphical user interface.

Executable File: a file containing binary program code.

Execute Step: the step in the CPU cycle that executes an instruction.

Execution Cycle: see CPU cycle.

Execution: the process of running a computer program.

Fetch Step: the step with which the CPU moves a machine instruction from memory to the CPU.

File Transfer Protocol (FTP): the Internet protocol used to transfer files from one Internet server to another.

Floppy Disk Drive: a small disk drive that is easily inserted or removed from a computer.

Flowchart: a diagram of the logical steps followed by a computer algorithm or program.

Focus: the currently selected control on the currently active window of a graphical user interface.

FORTRAN: a portmanteau composed of *form*ula *trans*lation; an early computer language designed for numerical computation.

FTP: see File Transfer Protocol.

General Purpose Register: a location in the CPU used to hold data.

GIF: Graphical Information Format; a method of encoding graphic information to be displayed on Web pages and computer screens generally.

Gigabit: one billion bits.

Gigabyte: one billion bytes.

Graphical User Interface (GUI): a method of passing information to and obtaining information from a computer program that uses windows, icons, and a pointing device (mouse) as the primary means of communication.

GUI: see Graphical User Interface.

HAL: an Artificial Intelligence computer in Stanley Kubrick's film *2001: a Space Odyssey*.

Halfword: a byte of computer memory used to hold a numerical value.

Hard Drive: a computer disk drive that is permanently attached to a computer.

HDTV: high definition television, based on digital technology.

Helper Application: a program that works in conjunction with a browser program to enable the browser to display a special type of file format.

Hexadecimal Number: see Base Sixteen Number.

Hollerith Card: a card used to hold computer data recorded by holes punched in the card.

Home Directory: the directory owned by a UNIX user.

Home Page: the first page on a web site; a Web page dedicated to information about a person, business, school, governmental organization, or other entity.

HTML: HyperText Markup Language, the coding scheme used to indicate the layout of Web pages.

HTML Tag: an HTML command designating a formatting feature.

HTTP: HyperText Transfer Protocol: the communication protocol used to transmit information on the Web.

Hypertext: a text that is designed to be read in multiple ways rather than simply from start to end.

Hypertext Link: a point in a hypertext document that provides for a branching to another location on the document containing the link or to another document.

Image File: a computer file holding a graphical image.

Infinite Loop: a condition that occurs when a computer program keeps repeating the same instructions over and over with no means of stopping the repetitions.

Instruction Register: the locations in the CPU that hold the operation code and operands of a computer instruction.

Instruction Table: the location in the control unit of a Turing machine that holds program instructions.

Internet Explorer: the Web browser program marketed by Microsoft Corporation.

Internet Protocol (IP): the addressing scheme of the internet by which each workstation and server on the internet is assigned a unique numerical address.

Internet Service Provider (ISP): an organization, usually a for-profit one, that provides access to the Internet for its subscribers.

Internet: the information superhighway; the world wide network of computer networks open to anyone.

Internic: the organization designated by the National Science Foundation to issue Internet addresses.

IP: see Internet Protocol.

IP Address: the unique numerical address assigned to an Internet workstation or server.

Ipv4: the original Internet addressing scheme, consisting of four bytes of information.

Ipv6: the new Internet addressing scheme, consisting of sixteen bytes of information.

ISO: International Standards Organization; an intergovernmental group charged with setting international standards for computers and other technologies.

ISP: see Internet Service Provider.

Jacquard Loom: a nineteenth century automated weaving machine, one of the first practical programmable devices.

JAVA: a computer programming language developed by Sun Micro systems and designed to run on any computer system.

JAVA Runtime Environment (JRE): the JAVA virtual machine used to translate JAVA's binary program instructions into binary computer instructions for Intel microprocessors running the Windows 95 operating system.

JFIF: JPEG File Interchange Format.

JPEG: Joint Photographic Experts Group: a format for storing compressed images.

JPG: see JPEG.

JRE: see JAVA Runtime Environment.

Jump Instruction: a computer instruction that alters the contents of the CPU location register, causing the computer to take the next instruction from the location specified by the Jump instruction.

Keypunch Machine: a data entry device that records data on Hollerith cards.

Killer-app: an extraordinarily successful computer program that alters the way in which tasks are usually performed.

Kilobit: 1000 or 1024 bits. $1024 = 2^{10}$, the power of two nearest to 1000.

Kilobyte: 1000 or 1024 bytes. $1024 = 2^{10}$, the power of two nearest to 1000.

Linking: the process whereby binary computer instructions of an application program are integrated with the computer's operating system.

Liquid Crystal Display (LCD): an output display device, used on many electronic products from digital watches to computers.

List Structure: a sequence of computer instructions that are executed one after the other with no branching.

Loading: the process whereby binary computer instructions are copied from the computer's disk to the computer's memory.

LocalTalk: a networking scheme made popular by Apple computer to connect Apple computers.

Location Register: the CPU register that contains the address of the instruction to be fetched next from memory and loaded into the CPU instruction register.

Logic Loop: see Infinite Loop.

Loop Structure: a sequence of computer instructions that executes repeatedly until some condition is satisfied.

Lossless Compression: a method of compressing digitized data that allows the data to be uncompressed without any loss of information.

Lossy Compression: a method of compressing digitized data that allows the data to be uncompressed with some loss of information.

LWZ Compression: a method of compressing color images that preserves the relative brightness of different colors.

Machine Code: the binary numbers that the computer executes.

Machine Instruction: a sequence of binary numbers that make up the operation code and operands of a computer instruction.

Machine State: the current contents of the CPU registers and memory of a computer; for Turing machines, the number of the instruction currently being executed.

Machine Tape: a tape of infinite length, divided into frames which contain either a single 0 or a single 1; a part of the Turing machine.

Macintosh JAVA Runtime (MJR): the JAVA virtual machine used to translate JAVA's binary program instructions into binary computer instructions for Apple micro-processors running the Apple operating system.

Magnetic Tape: a data storage device on which data is recorded by the presence or absence of magnetism.

Mainframe Computer: a large, multi-user computer with extensive memory, disk storage and processing capacity; the type of computer most popular from the 1950s to the 1970s.

Mark I: an electromechanical calculator developed at Harvard during Word War II.

Megabit: 1,000,000 bits or 1,048,576 bits; $1,048,576 = 2^{20}$, the power of two nearest to 1,000,000.

Megabyte: 1,000,000 bytes or 1,048,576 bytes; $1,048,576 = 2^{20}$, the power of two nearest to 1,000,000.

MEMEX: a hypothetical personal information storage device, proposed by Venaver Bush; a forerunner of the idea of hypertext.

Menu Command: a standard type of instruction given to a computer program by selecting the instruction from a menu.

Method: in object-oriented programming, a module of program instructions encapsulated with data as part of a program object.

Microprocessor: a single computer chip containing all the circuits of a CPU.

Microsecond: one thousandth of a second.

Millisecond: one millionth of a second.

MIME type: Multipurpose Internet Mail Extension, a class of Internet E-mail distinguished by a specific data format.

MJR: see Macintosh JAVA Runtime.

MMX Technology: Multimedia Extensions; special machine instructions on the more recent versions of the Intel Pentium processor, designed to facilitate the processing of audio, video, and other types of multimedia files.

Modem: Modulator Demodulator; a device that converts binary data to sound tones (modulate) and sound tones to binary data (demodulate), used to connect computers to networks over phone lines.

Moore's Law: a rule of thumb proposed in 1965 by Gordon Moore to the effect that computer memory and processing capacity doubles every eighteen months.

Mouse: a computer pointing device invented by Xerox as part of a graphical user device.

Nanosecond: one billionth of a second.

National Security Agency (NSA): the agency charged with maintaining computer security for the federal government.

Nested Structure: an arrangement of files, directories, computer window screens, computer code, program objects, or other entities related to the computer that are arranged in a hierarchical order.

Netscape: a Web Browser developed and marketed by Netscape Corporation; the most widely used Web browser.

Nibble: a sequence of four bits used by computer programmers for the mental conversion of hexadecimal numbers to binary numbers.

NSA: see National Security Agency.

Numerical Base: the number of digits in a number system, the number by powers of which we count in a number system.

Object-Oriented Programming: a modern technique for enhancing the operational integrity of a computer program by dividing it into tightly organized hierarchies of data and machine instructions called program objects so that the data may be manipulated only by the machine instructions with which it is bundled.

Octal Number: see Base Eight Number.

Open Standards: specifications for some aspect of computing that is developed and published by a professional organization, governmental body, or international consortium and available to users without charge.

Operand: the portion of a machine instruction that specifies the data to be operated on by the operation code of the instruction.

Operating System: the supervisor program of the computer that integrates its components into a functioning whole and controls access by application programs to the computer's resources

Operation Code: the portion of a machine instruction that specifies the operation to be performed on the data designated by the operands of the instruction.

PARC: Palo Alto Research Center; a research facility of the Xerox Corporation at which were developed the concepts of graphical user interfaces, networking, and object-oriented programming later popularized by Apple Computer.

Pentium: the fifth generation of Intel's 8086/8088 microprocessors; currently the most widely used microprocessor because PCs built around this processor provide the hardware for the Microsoft's Windows operating system.

Peripherals: input/output devices such as keyboards, terminal, printers, disk drives, and the like that are attached to a computer.

PGP: see Pretty Good Privacy.

Pixel: a small, phosphorescent point on a CRT screen. The size, shape, and number of pixels determines the resolution of the screen.

PKZIP: a popular DOS and Windows file compression program.

Point and Click: the process of selecting an item on a graphics screen by positioning the mouse on it and pushing a mouse button.

PostScript: a file format for communicating information to a printer, invented by the Adobe Corporation and popularized by Apple Computers.

Pretty Good Privacy (PGP): a suite of data encryption programs widely used on the Word Wide Web that uses a double key method of encryption.

Private Encryption Key: the PGP encryption key kept secret by the owner of the key for encrypting messages the owner originates and for decrypting messages encrypted with the owner's public key.

Program Code Segment: see Code Segment.

Program Compilation: see Compilation.

Program Data Segment: see Data Segment

Program Execution: see Execution.

Program Linking: see Linking.

Program Loading: see Loading

Property: in object-oriented programming, the name of a piece of data that is part of an object.

Proprietary Standards: specifications for some aspect of computing that is the property of a computer manufacturer, available to users either free of charge or for payment of a licensing fee.

Public Encryption Key: the encryption key in a double key encryption scheme that is made available by others for decryption of messages from the owner encrypted with the owner's private key and for encryption of messages to the owner.

Public_HTML Directory: the name of the directory on a Web server that is a subdirectory of a Web user's home directory into which the user places information that she or he wishes to make available on the Web. All information on the Web must be in this directory or a directory that is a subdirectory of this directory.

Quick Time: a file format for storing video information invented by Apple Computers and widely used on the Web.

Radio Button: a button on a graphical user interface that allows users to select from a number of mutually exclusive options.

RAM: see Random Access Memory

Random Access Memory (RAM): the place where data and program instructions are stored in a computer so that they are available to the CPU.

Recording Medium: the material used to record data on a computer.

Register: a location in the CPU used to hold program instructions or data.

Relative Addressing: designating the location in memory in relation to the location of another location in memory. In relative addressing, one address is called the base address and assigned the value of 0. The other address is then specified as so many units of memory plus or minus from the base address.

Replicant: In the film *Blade Runner,* an artificial, biological computer closely resembling a human being.

RGB Color: a method of encoding colors by breaking them down into their Red, Green and Blue components.

RISC Processor: a Reduced Instruction Set Computer, designed to carry out relatively simple machine instructions at a very high rate.

Scientific Notation: numbers expressed as a value followed by a power of ten, e.g., $12 \; ' \; 10^{24}$.

Search Engine: a computer program used in keyword searching of the Web.

Self-Extracting Archive: a computer program that contains compressed data in its data segment and the program instructions to decompress the data.

Server: in Client/Server computing, a large computer designed to provide services and information over a network to client workstations.

SGML: see Structured General Markup Language.

Socket: in Client/Server computer applications, the connection between the part of an application running on a client and the part of the application running on the server.

Spaghetti Code: program instructions that are difficult for a programmer to understand because of their excessive and unstructured use of branching instructions.

SQL: see Structured Query Language.

Strong AI: the claim that human intelligence is an algorithm that can be programmed into a computer.

Structured General Markup Language (SGML): a method of encoding data, usually of a textual nature, that insures that the data encoded is in the correct order, that it contains all required codes, and that all the codes it contains are legal and placed in the proper order.

Structured Programming: the organization of program code into discrete modules consisting of list, loop, and branch structure that are read from top to bottom.

Structured Query Language (SQL): a computer language designed to formulate queries for database access and processing.

Subdirectory: a directory that is stored within another directory and a lower element of the file system's hierarchy.

Tape Mark Instruction: in a Turning machine, an instruction that writes a 1 on the current frame.

Tape Move Instruction: in a Turing machine, an instruction that moves the tape one frame to the left or right, or halts the machine.

TCP/IP: Transfer Control Protocol/Internet Protocol; the basic communication protocol of the Internet.

Text Area: see Text Display Area.

Text Display Area: the portion of graphical user interface window that is used to enter or display textual information.

Text File: a file containing textual data encoded in ASCII divided into lines of text by the carriage control and new line character.

Throughput: the amount of data a computer can actually process in a given time.

Token/Ring: a method of transmitting data on a network whose workstations are connected in a ring.

TrueType Fonts: a method used by the Windows operating system for encoding, printing, and displaying text in different fonts.

Turing Machine: a hypothetical machine invented by Alan Turing that provides the underlying mathematical model of all computers.

Turing Number: a number that can be computed with an algorithm.

Turing Test: a test, proposed by Alan Turing, to judge whether or not a computer is intelligent by human standards.

Unicode: A method of encoding the glyphs which make up writing systems that uses two consecutive bytes to represent each glyph.

Uniform Resource Locator (URL): the notational convention used to designate the location of a hypertext document on the Web.

UNIX: a multi-user computer operating system that was used for the development of the Internet. Many Web servers use this operating system today.

Upper ASCII: the ASCII codes between 128 to 255. The ASCII codes below this number are fixed to specific Roman alphabet glyphs and never reassigned; the codes above 127 are sometimes assigned to glyphs needed for specific application but not otherwise available.

URL: see Uniform Resource Locator.

UTP: Untwisted Pairs; the name for standard copper telephone wire, used for both telephone and data communication.

Virtual Machine: a hypothetical device or thought experiment used to examine the formal properties of an idea or hypothesis.

Virtual Memory: the use of storage on the computer's disk in conjunction with the computer's memory to allow a computer to run multiple programs at the same time and to run computer programs that are too large to fit into memory.

Von Neumann Architecture: the basic layout of a modern computer promulgated by John von Neumann. The main points of this architecture are that data and program instructions are stored in the same memory and that data and instructions must be moved from memory to the CPU to be processed.

Web: see World Wide Web.

Web Page: a hypertext document viewable on the Web.

Webmaster: the person responsible for maintaining a Web page and/or a server.

Windows 95: Microsoft's operating system designed with a graphical user interface for Intel Pentium microprocessors; the dominant PC operating system.

Word: two consecutive bytes used to hold a numerical value.

World Wide Web: the portion of the Internet that uses HTTP, usually with a graphical user interface.

WORM Drive: Write Once, Read Many times; a CD-ROM disk drive that allows data to be recorded permanently on it by writing only once but that allows this data to be retrieved many times.

WYSIWYG: What You See Is What You Get; the requirement that a Word Processor print its documents exactly as they appear on the screen.

X-Windows: a version of the UNIX operating system that has a graphical user interface.

Yahoo!: a Web search option built around a database catalogue of web sites and information compiled by humans.

Z1, Z2, Z3: digital computers, based on mechanical telephone switches, built in Germany in the late 1930s by Konrad Zuse.

Zip File: see PKZIP.

APPENDIX A

Turing Machine Trace Files

TURING MACHINE PROGRAM 1 OUTPUT

0	0	0	0	1	1	1	0	0	**0**	0	0	0	0	0	0	0	0	0	0

Initial Tape Setting

```
Program 1: Start At Instruction 1
1 R U 1 E 2
2 L M 3 U 2
3 L M 4 U 3
4 R U 1 U 4
END


Program 1: Start At Instruction 1

Step 1: State: 1 R U 1 E 2
Move the tape RIGHT; the current frame is unmarked (0);
the branching instruction is U 1:
Leave the current frame unchanged and assume state 1.

Step 2: State: 1 R U 1 E 2
Move the tape RIGHT; the current frame is unmarked (0);
the branching instruction is U 1:
Leave the current frame unchanged and assume state 1.

Step 3: State: 1 R U 1 E 2
Move the tape RIGHT; the current frame is marked (1);
the branching instruction is E 2:
Erase the current frame by setting it to '0' and assume state 2.

Step 4: State: 2 L M 3 U 2
Move the tape LEFT; the current frame is unmarked (0);
```

the branching instruction is M 3:
Mark the current frame by setting it to '1' and assume state 3.

Step 5: State: 3 L M 4 U 3
Move the tape LEFT; the current frame is unmarked (0);
the branching instruction is M 4:
Mark the current frame by setting it to '1' and assume state 4.

Step 6: State: 4 R U 1 U 4
Move the tape RIGHT; the current frame is marked (1);
the branching instruction is U 4:
Leave the current frame unchanged and assume state 4.

Step 7: State: 4 R U 1 U 4
Move the tape RIGHT; the current frame is unmarked (0);
the branching instruction is U 1:
Leave the current frame unchanged and assume state 1.

Step 8: State: 1 R U 1 E 2
Move the tape RIGHT; the current frame is marked (1);
the branching instruction is E 2:
Erase the current frame by setting it to '0' and assume state 2.

Step 9: State: 2 L M 3 U 2
Move the tape LEFT; the current frame is unmarked (0);
the branching instruction is M 3:
Mark the current frame by setting it to '1' and assume state 3.

Step 10: State: 3 L M 4 U 3
Move the tape LEFT; the current frame is marked (1);
the branching instruction is U 3:
Leave the current frame unchanged and assume state 3.

Step 11: State: 3 L M 4 U 3
Move the tape LEFT; the current frame is marked (1);
the branching instruction is U 3:
Leave the current frame unchanged and assume state 3.

Step 12: State: 3 L M 4 U 3
Move the tape LEFT; the current frame is unmarked (0);
the branching instruction is M 4:
Mark the current frame by setting it to '1' and assume state 4.

Step 13: State: 4 R U 1 U 4
Move the tape RIGHT; the current frame is marked (1);
the branching instruction is U 4:
Leave the current frame unchanged and assume state 4.

Step 14: State: 4 R U 1 U 4
Move the tape RIGHT; the current frame is marked (1);

the branching instruction is U 4:
Leave the current frame unchanged and assume state 4.

Step 15: State: 4 R U 1 U 4
Move the tape RIGHT; the current frame is marked (1);
the branching instruction is U 4:
Leave the current frame unchanged and assume state 4.

Step 16: State: 4 R U 1 U 4
Move the tape RIGHT; the current frame is unmarked (0);
the branching instruction is U 1:
Leave the current frame unchanged and assume state 1.

Step 17: State: 1 R U 1 E 2
Move the tape RIGHT; the current frame is marked (1);
the branching instruction is E 2:
Erase the current frame by setting it to '0' and assume state 2.

Step 18: State: 2 L M 3 U 2
Move the tape LEFT; the current frame is unmarked (0);
the branching instruction is M 3:
Mark the current frame by setting it to '1' and assume state 3.

Step 19: State: 3 L M 4 U 3
Move the tape LEFT; the current frame is marked (1);
the branching instruction is U 3:
Leave the current frame unchanged and assume state 3.

Step 20: State: 3 L M 4 U 3
Move the tape LEFT; the current frame is marked (1);
the branching instruction is U 3:
Leave the current frame unchanged and assume state 3.

Step 21: State: 3 L M 4 U 3
Move the tape LEFT; the current frame is marked (1);
the branching instruction is U 3:
Leave the current frame unchanged and assume state 3.

Step 22: State: 3 L M 4 U 3
Move the tape LEFT; the current frame is marked (1);
the branching instruction is U 3:
Leave the current frame unchanged and assume state 3.

Step 23: State: 3 L M 4 U 3
Move the tape LEFT; the current frame is unmarked (0);
the branching instruction is M 4:
Mark the current frame by setting it to '1' and assume state 4.

Step 24: State: 4 R U 1 U 4
Move the tape RIGHT; the current frame is marked (1);

```
the branching instruction is U 4:
Leave the current frame unchanged and assume state 4.

Step 25: State: 4 R U 1 U 4
Move the tape RIGHT; the current frame is marked (1);
the branching instruction is U 4:
Leave the current frame unchanged and assume state 4.

Step 26: State: 4 R U 1 U 4
Move the tape RIGHT; the current frame is marked (1);
the branching instruction is U 4:
Leave the current frame unchanged and assume state 4.

Step 27: State: 4 R U 1 U 4
Move the tape RIGHT; the current frame is marked (1);
the branching instruction is U 4:
Leave the current frame unchanged and assume state 4.

Step 28: State: 4 R U 1 U 4
Move the tape RIGHT; the current frame is marked (1);
the branching instruction is U 4:
Leave the current frame unchanged and assume state 4.

Step 29: State: 4 R U 1 U 4
Move the tape RIGHT; the current frame is unmarked (0);
the branching instruction is U 1:
Leave the current frame unchanged and assume state 1.
Program Halted!
```

TURING MACHINE PROGRAM 2 OUTPUT

0	0	0	0	1	1	1	0	0	**0**	0	0	0	0	0	0	0	0	0	0

Initial Tape Setting

```
Program 2: Start At Instruction 4
1 R U 4 U 1
2 L M 1 U 2
3 L M 2 U 3
4 R U 4 E 3
END


Program 2: Start At Instruction 4

Step 1: State: 4 R U 4 E 3
Move the tape RIGHT; the current frame is unmarked (0);
```

the branching instruction is U 4:
Leave the current frame unchanged and assume state 4.

Step 2: State: 4 R U 4 E 3
Move the tape RIGHT; the current frame is unmarked (0);
the branching instruction is U 4:
Leave the current frame unchanged and assume state 4.

Step 3: State: 4 R U 4 E 3
Move the tape RIGHT; the current frame is unmarked (0);
the branching instruction is U 4:
Leave the current frame unchanged and assume state 4.

Step 4: State: 4 R U 4 E 3
Move the tape RIGHT; the current frame is unmarked (0);
the branching instruction is U 4:
Leave the current frame unchanged and assume state 4.

Step 5: State: 4 R U 4 E 3
Move the tape RIGHT; the current frame is marked (1);
the branching instruction is E 3:
Erase the current frame by setting it to '0' and assume state 3.

Step 6: State: 3 L M 2 U 3
Move the tape LEFT; the current frame is unmarked (0);
the branching instruction is M 2:
Mark the current frame by setting it to '1' and assume state 2.

Step 7: State: 2 L M 1 U 2
Move the tape LEFT; the current frame is unmarked (0);
the branching instruction is M 1:
Mark the current frame by setting it to '1' and assume state 1.

Step 8: State: 1 R U 4 U 1
Move the tape RIGHT; the current frame is marked (1);
the branching instruction is U 1:
Leave the current frame unchanged and assume state 1.

Step 9: State: 1 R U 4 U 1
Move the tape RIGHT; the current frame is unmarked (0);
the branching instruction is U 4:
Leave the current frame unchanged and assume state 4.

Step 10: State: 4 R U 4 E 3
Move the tape RIGHT; the current frame is marked (1);
the branching instruction is E 3:
Erase the current frame by setting it to '0' and assume state 3.

Step 11: State: 3 L M 2 U 3
Move the tape LEFT; the current frame is unmarked (0);

the branching instruction is M 2:
Mark the current frame by setting it to '1' and assume state 2.

Step 12: State: 2 L M 1 U 2
Move the tape LEFT; the current frame is marked (1);
the branching instruction is U 2:
Leave the current frame unchanged and assume state 2.

Step 13: State: 2 L M 1 U 2
Move the tape LEFT; the current frame is marked (1);
the branching instruction is U 2:
Leave the current frame unchanged and assume state 2.

Step 14: State: 2 L M 1 U 2
Move the tape LEFT; the current frame is unmarked (0);
the branching instruction is M 1:
Mark the current frame by setting it to '1' and assume state 1.

Step 15: State: 1 R U 4 U 1
Move the tape RIGHT; the current frame is marked (1);
the branching instruction is U 1:
Leave the current frame unchanged and assume state 1.

Step 16: State: 1 R U 4 U 1
Move the tape RIGHT; the current frame is marked (1);
the branching instruction is U 1:
Leave the current frame unchanged and assume state 1.

Step 17: State: 1 R U 4 U 1
Move the tape RIGHT; the current frame is marked (1);
the branching instruction is U 1:
Leave the current frame unchanged and assume state 1.

Step 18: State: 1 R U 4 U 1
Move the tape RIGHT; the current frame is unmarked (0);
the branching instruction is U 4:
Leave the current frame unchanged and assume state 4.

Step 19: State: 4 R U 4 E 3
Move the tape RIGHT; the current frame is marked (1);
the branching instruction is E 3:
Erase the current frame by setting it to '0' and assume state 3.

Step 20: State: 3 L M 2 U 3
Move the tape LEFT; the current frame is unmarked (0);
the branching instruction is M 2:
Mark the current frame by setting it to '1' and assume state 2.

Step 21: State: 2 L M 1 U 2
Move the tape LEFT; the current frame is marked (1);

the branching instruction is U 2:
Leave the current frame unchanged and assume state 2.

Step 22: State: 2 L M 1 U 2
Move the tape LEFT; the current frame is marked (1);
the branching instruction is U 2:
Leave the current frame unchanged and assume state 2.

Step 23: State: 2 L M 1 U 2
Move the tape LEFT; the current frame is marked (1);
the branching instruction is U 2:
Leave the current frame unchanged and assume state 2.

Step 24: State: 2 L M 1 U 2
Move the tape LEFT; the current frame is marked (1);
the branching instruction is U 2:
Leave the current frame unchanged and assume state 2.

Step 25: State: 2 L M 1 U 2
Move the tape LEFT; the current frame is unmarked (0);
the branching instruction is M 1:
Mark the current frame by setting it to '1' and assume state 1.

Step 26: State: 1 R U 4 U 1
Move the tape RIGHT; the current frame is marked (1);
the branching instruction is U 1:
Leave the current frame unchanged and assume state 1.

Step 27: State: 1 R U 4 U 1
Move the tape RIGHT; the current frame is marked (1);
the branching instruction is U 1:
Leave the current frame unchanged and assume state 1.

Step 28: State: 1 R U 4 U 1
Move the tape RIGHT; the current frame is marked (1);
the branching instruction is U 1:
Leave the current frame unchanged and assume state 1.

Step 29: State: 1 R U 4 U 1
Move the tape RIGHT; the current frame is marked (1);
the branching instruction is U 1:
Leave the current frame unchanged and assume state 1.

Step 30: State: 1 R U 4 U 1
Move the tape RIGHT; the current frame is marked (1);
the branching instruction is U 1:
Leave the current frame unchanged and assume state 1.

Step 31: State: 1 R U 4 U 1
Move the tape RIGHT; the current frame is unmarked (0);

the branching instruction is U 4:
Leave the current frame unchanged and assume state 4.

Step 32: State: 4 R U 4 E 3
Move the tape RIGHT; the current frame is unmarked (0);
the branching instruction is U 4:
Leave the current frame unchanged and assume state 4.

Step 33: State: 4 R U 4 E 3
Move the tape RIGHT; the current frame is unmarked (0);
the branching instruction is U 4:
Leave the current frame unchanged and assume state 4.

Step 34: State: 4 R U 4 E 3
Move the tape RIGHT; the current frame is unmarked (0);
the branching instruction is U 4:
Leave the current frame unchanged and assume state 4.

Step 35: State: 4 R U 4 E 3
Move the tape RIGHT; the current frame is unmarked (0);
the branching instruction is U 4:
Leave the current frame unchanged and assume state 4.

Step 36: State: 4 R U 4 E 3
Move the tape RIGHT; the current frame is unmarked (0);
the branching instruction is U 4:
Leave the current frame unchanged and assume state 4.

Step 37: State: 4 R U 4 E 3
Move the tape RIGHT; the current frame is unmarked (0);
the branching instruction is U 4:
Leave the current frame unchanged and assume state 4.

Step 38: State: 4 R U 4 E 3
Move the tape RIGHT; the current frame is unmarked (0);
the branching instruction is U 4:
Leave the current frame unchanged and assume state 4.

Step 39: State: 4 R U 4 E 3
Move the tape RIGHT; the current frame is unmarked (0);
the branching instruction is U 4:
Leave the current frame unchanged and assume state 4.
Program Halted!

TURING MACHINE PROGRAM 3 OUTPUT

| 0 | 0 | 0 | 0 | 0 | 0 | 0 | 0 | 0 | **0** | 1 | 1 | 1 | 0 | 0 | 0 | 0 | 0 | 0 | 0 |

Initial Tape Setting

```
Program 3: Start At Instruction 1
1 R U 8 U 2
2 R U 3 U 2
3 L U 5 E 4
4 L U 5 U 4
5 L M 6 U 5
6 L M 7 U 6
7 R U 1 U 7
8 H U 8 U 8
END
```

Program 3: Start At Instruction 1

Step 1: State: 1 R U 8 U 2
Move the tape RIGHT; the current frame is marked (1);
the branching instruction is U 2:
Leave the current frame unchanged and assume state 2.

Step 2: State: 2 R U 3 U 2
Move the tape RIGHT; the current frame is marked (1);
the branching instruction is U 2:
Leave the current frame unchanged and assume state 2.

Step 3: State: 2 R U 3 U 2
Move the tape RIGHT; the current frame is unmarked (0);
the branching instruction is U 3:
Leave the current frame unchanged and assume state 3.

Step 4: State: 3 L U 5 E 4
Move the tape LEFT; the current frame is marked (1);
the branching instruction is E 4:
Erase the current frame by setting it to '0' and assume state 4.

Step 5: State: 4 L U 5 U 4
Move the tape LEFT; the current frame is marked (1);
the branching instruction is U 4:
Leave the current frame unchanged and assume state 4.
Step 6: State: 4 L U 5 U 4
Move the tape LEFT; the current frame is marked (1);
the branching instruction is U 4:
Leave the current frame unchanged and assume state 4.

Step 7: State: 4 L U 5 U 4
Move the tape LEFT; the current frame is unmarked (0);
the branching instruction is U 5:
Leave the current frame unchanged and assume state 5.

Step 8: State: 5 L M 6 U 5

Move the tape LEFT; the current frame is unmarked (0);
the branching instruction is M 6:
Mark the current frame by setting it to '1' and assume state 6.

Step 9: State: 6 L M 7 U 6
Move the tape LEFT; the current frame is unmarked (0);
the branching instruction is M 7:
Mark the current frame by setting it to '1' and assume state 7.

Step 10: State: 7 R U 1 U 7
Move the tape RIGHT; the current frame is marked (1);
the branching instruction is U 7:
Leave the current frame unchanged and assume state 7.

Step 11: State: 7 R U 1 U 7
Move the tape RIGHT; the current frame is unmarked (0);
the branching instruction is U 1:
Leave the current frame unchanged and assume state 1.

Step 12: State: 1 R U 8 U 2
Move the tape RIGHT; the current frame is marked (1);
the branching instruction is U 2:
Leave the current frame unchanged and assume state 2.

Step 13: State: 2 R U 3 U 2
Move the tape RIGHT; the current frame is marked (1);
the branching instruction is U 2:
Leave the current frame unchanged and assume state 2.

Step 14: State: 2 R U 3 U 2
Move the tape RIGHT; the current frame is unmarked (0);
the branching instruction is U 3:
Leave the current frame unchanged and assume state 3.

Step 15: State: 3 L U 5 E 4
Move the tape LEFT; the current frame is marked (1);
the branching instruction is E 4:
Erase the current frame by setting it to '0' and assume state 4.

Step 16: State: 4 L U 5 U 4
Move the tape LEFT; the current frame is marked (1);
the branching instruction is U 4:
Leave the current frame unchanged and assume state 4.

Step 17: State: 4 L U 5 U 4
Move the tape LEFT; the current frame is unmarked (0);
the branching instruction is U 5:
Leave the current frame unchanged and assume state 5.

Step 18: State: 5 L M 6 U 5

Move the tape LEFT; the current frame is marked (1);
the branching instruction is U 5:
Leave the current frame unchanged and assume state 5.

Step 19: State: 5 L M 6 U 5
Move the tape LEFT; the current frame is marked (1);
the branching instruction is U 5:
Leave the current frame unchanged and assume state 5.

Step 20: State: 5 L M 6 U 5
Move the tape LEFT; the current frame is unmarked (0);
the branching instruction is M 6:
Mark the current frame by setting it to '1' and assume state 6.

Step 21: State: 6 L M 7 U 6
Move the tape LEFT; the current frame is unmarked (0);
the branching instruction is M 7:
Mark the current frame by setting it to '1' and assume state 7.

Step 22: State: 7 R U 1 U 7
Move the tape RIGHT; the current frame is marked (1);
the branching instruction is U 7:
Leave the current frame unchanged and assume state 7.

Step 23: State: 7 R U 1 U 7
Move the tape RIGHT; the current frame is marked (1);
the branching instruction is U 7:
Leave the current frame unchanged and assume state 7.

Step 24: State: 7 R U 1 U 7
Move the tape RIGHT; the current frame is marked (1);
the branching instruction is U 7:
Leave the current frame unchanged and assume state 7.

Step 25: State: 7 R U 1 U 7
Move the tape RIGHT; the current frame is unmarked (0);
the branching instruction is U 1:
Leave the current frame unchanged and assume state 1.

Step 26: State: 1 R U 8 U 2
Move the tape RIGHT; the current frame is marked (1);
the branching instruction is U 2:
Leave the current frame unchanged and assume state 2.
Step 27: State: 2 R U 3 U 2
Move the tape RIGHT; the current frame is unmarked (0);
the branching instruction is U 3:
Leave the current frame unchanged and assume state 3.

Step 28: State: 3 L U 5 E 4
Move the tape LEFT; the current frame is marked (1);

the branching instruction is E 4:
Erase the current frame by setting it to '0' and assume state 4.

Step 29: State: 4 L U 5 U 4
Move the tape LEFT; the current frame is unmarked (0);
the branching instruction is U 5:
Leave the current frame unchanged and assume state 5.

Step 30: State: 5 L M 6 U 5
Move the tape LEFT; the current frame is marked (1);
the branching instruction is U 5:
Leave the current frame unchanged and assume state 5.

Step 31: State: 5 L M 6 U 5
Move the tape LEFT; the current frame is marked (1);
the branching instruction is U 5:
Leave the current frame unchanged and assume state 5.

Step 32: State: 5 L M 6 U 5
Move the tape LEFT; the current frame is marked (1);
the branching instruction is U 5:
Leave the current frame unchanged and assume state 5.

Step 33: State: 5 L M 6 U 5
Move the tape LEFT; the current frame is marked (1);
the branching instruction is U 5:
Leave the current frame unchanged and assume state 5.

Step 34: State: 5 L M 6 U 5
Move the tape LEFT; the current frame is unmarked (0);
the branching instruction is M 6:
Mark the current frame by setting it to '1' and assume state 6.

Step 35: State: 6 L M 7 U 6
Move the tape LEFT; the current frame is unmarked (0);
the branching instruction is M 7:
Mark the current frame by setting it to '1' and assume state 7.

Step 36: State: 7 R U 1 U 7
Move the tape RIGHT; the current frame is marked (1);
the branching instruction is U 7:
Leave the current frame unchanged and assume state 7.

Step 37: State: 7 R U 1 U 7
Move the tape RIGHT; the current frame is marked (1);
the branching instruction is U 7:
Leave the current frame unchanged and assume state 7.

Step 38: State: 7 R U 1 U 7
Move the tape RIGHT; the current frame is marked (1);

the branching instruction is U 7:
Leave the current frame unchanged and assume state 7.

Step 39: State: 7 R U 1 U 7
Move the tape RIGHT; the current frame is marked (1);
the branching instruction is U 7:
Leave the current frame unchanged and assume state 7.

Step 40: State: 7 R U 1 U 7
Move the tape RIGHT; the current frame is marked (1);
the branching instruction is U 7:
Leave the current frame unchanged and assume state 7.

Step 41: State: 7 R U 1 U 7
Move the tape RIGHT; the current frame is unmarked (0);
the branching instruction is U 1:
Leave the current frame unchanged and assume state 1.

Step 42: State: 1 R U 8 U 2
Move the tape RIGHT; the current frame is unmarked (0);
the branching instruction is U 8:
Leave the current frame unchanged and assume state 8.

Step 43: State: 8 H U 8 U 8
Halt Tape; the current frame is unmarked (0);
the branching instruction is U 8:
Leave the current frame unchanged and assume state 8.
Program Halted!

APPENDIX B

Assembler Program Execution Trace Files

PROGRAM SWAP TRACE FILE

0 Program Swap
1 Dim Location1 1:50
2 Dim Location2 1:100
3 Go * *
4 Display Location1 2
5 Move Location1 R1
6 Move Location2 R2
7 Store R1 Location2
8 Store R2 Location1
9 Display Location1 2
10 Stop * *
11 End * *
Clearing Disk/Memeory

Compile Step 1
1 Dim Location1 1:50
(Dim) 2 1 50
0000000000000000 0000000000000000 0000000000000000
Allocating memory address 2 as Location1,
set to value 50.

Compile Step 2
2 Dim Location2 1:100
(Dim) 3 1 100
0000000000000000 0000000000000000 0000000000000000
Allocating memory address 3 as Location2,
set to value 100.

Compile Step 3
3 Go * *
14 0 0
0000000000001110 0000000000000000 0000000000000000
Start execution of the program
at memory location 0000000000000100.

Compile Step 4
4 Display Location1 2
15 1 2
0000000000001111 0000000000000001 0000000000000010
Display the values starting at Location1: 2 Locations.

Compile Step 5
5 Move Location1 R1
2 1 1
0000000000000010 0000000000000001 0000000000000001
Move the value of Location1 to R1.

Compile Step 6
6 Move Location2 R2
2 2 2
0000000000000010 0000000000000010 0000000000000010
Move the value of Location2 to R2.

Compile Step 7
7 Store R1 Location2
16 1 2
0000000000010000 0000000000000001 0000000000000010
Store the contents of R1 in Location2.

Compile Step 8
8 Store R2 Location1
16 2 1
0000000000010000 0000000000000010 0000000000000001
Store the contents of R2 in Location1.

Compile Step 9
9 Display Location1 2
15 1 2
0000000000001111 0000000000000001 0000000000000010
Display the values starting at Location1: 2 Locations.

Compile Step 10
10 Stop * *
13 0 0
0000000000001101 0000000000000000 0000000000000000
Halt execution of the Program.

Compile Step 11

11 End * *
* * *
0000000000001101 0000000000000000 0000000000000000
End of Assembler for Program Swap
Compile Step 11
11 End * *
* * *
0000000000001101 0000000000000000 0000000000000000
End of Assembler for Program Swap
Compilation completed; push 'Load' to continue.

Compile Step 11
11 End * *
* * *
0000000000001101 0000000000000000 0000000000000000
End of Assembler for Program Swap
Compilation completed; push 'Load' to continue.
End of compilation

Fetch Step Cycle: 0000000000000001
>> 3 Go * *
14 0 0
0000000000001110 0000000000000000 0000000000000000
Location Register: 0000000000000111

Exec Step Cycle: 0000000000000001
Go instruction; starting execution at memory location 0000000000000100.
Variable Pointer Table Offset = 0000000000011011
Instruction Register: 0000000000001110 0000000000000000 0000000000000000
Location Register: 0000000000000111
Accumulator: 0000000000000000
R1 = 0000000000000000; R2 = 0000000000000000;
R3 = 0000000000000000; R4 = 0000000000000000

Fetch Step Cycle: 0000000000000010
>> 4 Display Location1 2
15 1 2
0000000000001111 0000000000000001 0000000000000010
Location Register: 0000000000001010

Exec Step Cycle: 0000000000000010
Display 0000000000000010 memory locations starting at Location1.
Program Output
 0000000000110010 0000000001100100

Instruction Register: 0000000000001111 0000000000000001 0000000000000010
Location Register: 0000000000001010
Accumulator: 0000000000000000
R1 = 0000000000000000; R2 = 0000000000000000;
R3 = 0000000000000000; R4 = 0000000000000000

Fetch Step Cycle: 0000000000000011
>> 5 Move Location1 R1
2 1 1
0000000000000010 0000000000000001 0000000000000001
Location Register: 0000000000001101

Exec Step Cycle: 0000000000000011
Move value (0000000000110010) from Location1 to Register 0000000000000001.
Instruction Register: 0000000000000010 0000000000000001 0000000000000001
Location Register: 0000000000001101
Accumulator: 0000000000000000
R1 = 0000000000110010; R2 = 0000000000000000;
R3 = 0000000000000000; R4 = 0000000000000000

Fetch Step Cycle: 0000000000000100
>> 6 Move Location2 R2
2 2 2
0000000000000010 0000000000000010 0000000000000010
Location Register: 0000000000010000

Exec Step Cycle: 0000000000000100
Move value (0000000001100100) from Location2 to Register 0000000000000010.
Instruction Register: 0000000000000010 0000000000000010 0000000000000010
Location Register: 0000000000010000
Accumulator: 0000000000000000
R1 = 0000000000110010; R2 = 0000000001100100; R3 = 0000000000000000; R4 =
0000000000000000

Fetch Step Cycle: 0000000000000101
>> 7 Store R1 Location2
16 1 2
0000000000010000 0000000000000001 0000000000000010
Location Register: 0000000000010011

Exec Step Cycle: 0000000000000101
Store value (0000000000110010) from Register 0000000000000001
in memory variable Location2.
Instruction Register: 0000000000010000 0000000000000001 0000000000000010
Location Register: 0000000000010011
Accumulator: 0000000000000000
R1 = 0000000000110010; R2 = 0000000001100100;
R3 = 0000000000000000; R4 = 0000000000000000

Fetch Step Cycle: 0000000000000110
>> 8 Store R2 Location1
16 2 1
0000000000010000 0000000000000010 0000000000000001
Location Register: 0000000000010110

Exec Step Cycle: 0000000000000110

Store value (0000000001100100) from Register 0000000000000010
in memory variable Location1.
Instruction Register: 0000000000010000 0000000000000010 0000000000000001
Location Register: 0000000000010110
Accumulator: 0000000000000000
R1 = 0000000000110010; R2 = 0000000001100100;
R3 = 0000000000000000; R4 = 0000000000000000

Fetch Step Cycle: 0000000000000111
>> 9 Display Location1 2
15 1 2
0000000000001111 0000000000000001 0000000000000010
Location Register: 0000000000011001

Exec Step Cycle: 0000000000000111
Display 0000000000000010 memory locations starting at Location1.
Program Output
 0000000001100100 0000000000110010

Instruction Register: 0000000000001111 0000000000000001 0000000000000010
Location Register: 0000000000011001
Accumulator: 0000000000000000
R1 = 0000000000110010; R2 = 0000000001100100;
R3 = 0000000000000000; R4 = 0000000000000000

Fetch Step Cycle: 0000000000001000
>> 10 Stop * *
13 0 0
0000000000001101 0000000000000000 0000000000000000
Location Register: 0000000000011100

Exec Step Cycle: 0000000000001000
Stop Instruction; halting execution
Accumulator: 0000000000000000
R1 = 0000000000110010; R2 = 0000000001100100; R3 = 0000000000000000; R4 =
0000000000000000

PROGRAM COUNT TRACE FILE

0 Program Count
1 Dim Count 1:5
2 Go * *
3 StoreC 1 R1
4 Display Count 1
5 Move Count R2
6 Add R1 R2
7 Store AC Count
8 Display Count 1

9 Stop *
10 End * *
Clearing Disk/Memeory

Compile Step 1
1 Dim Location1 1:50
(Dim) 2 1 50
0000000000000000 0000000000000000 0000000000000000
Allocating memory address 2 as Location1,
set to value 50.

Compile Step 2
2 Dim Location2 1:100
(Dim) 3 1 100
0000000000000000 0000000000000000 0000000000000000
Allocating memory address 3 as Location2,
set to value 100.

Compile Step 3
3 Go * *
14 0 0
0000000000001110 0000000000000000 0000000000000000
Start execution of the program
at memory location 0000000000000100.
Compile Step 4
4 Display Location1 2
15 1 2
0000000000001111 0000000000000001 0000000000000010
Display the values starting at Location1: 2 Locations.

Compile Step 5
5 Move Location1 R1
2 1 1
0000000000000010 0000000000000001 0000000000000001
Move the value of Location1 to R1.

Compile Step 6
6 Move Location2 R2
2 2 2
0000000000000010 0000000000000010 0000000000000010
Move the value of Location2 to R2.

Compile Step 7
7 Store R1 Location2
16 1 2
0000000000010000 0000000000000001 0000000000000010
Store the contents of R1 in Location2.

Compile Step 8
8 Store R2 Location1

16 2 1
0000000000010000 0000000000000010 0000000000000001
Store the contents of R2 in Location1.

Compile Step 9
9 Display Location1 2
15 1 2
0000000000001111 0000000000000001 0000000000000010
Display the values starting at Location1: 2 Locations.

Compile Step 10
10 Stop * *
13 0 0
0000000000001101 0000000000000000 0000000000000000
Halt execution of the Program.

Compile Step 11
11 End * *
* * *
0000000000001101 0000000000000000 0000000000000000
End of Assembler for Program Swap

Compilation completed; push 'Load' to continue.

Fetch Step Cycle: 0000000000000001
>> 2 Go * *
14 0 0
0000000000001110 0000000000000000 0000000000000000
Location Register: 0000000000000110

Exec Step Cycle: 0000000000000001
Go instruction; starting execution at memory location 0000000000000011.
Variable Pointer Table Offset = 0000000000011010
Instruction Register: 0000000000001110 0000000000000000 0000000000000000
Location Register: 0000000000000110
Accumulator: 0000000000000000
R1 = 0000000000000000; R2 = 0000000000000000; R3 = 0000000000000000; R4 = 0000000000000000

Fetch Step Cycle: 0000000000000010
>> 3 StoreC 1 R1
18 1 1
0000000000010010 0000000000000001 0000000000000001
Location Register: 0000000000001001

Exec Step Cycle: 0000000000000010
Store value 0000000000000001 in Register 0000000000000001.
Instruction Register: 0000000000010010 0000000000000001 0000000000000001
Location Register: 0000000000001001
Accumulator: 0000000000000000

R1 = 0000000000000001; R2 = 0000000000000000;
R3 = 0000000000000000; R4 = 0000000000000000

Fetch Step Cycle: 0000000000000011
>> 4 Display Count 1
15 1 1
0000000000001111 0000000000000001 0000000000000001
Location Register: 0000000000001100

Exec Step Cycle: 0000000000000011
Display 0000000000000001 memory locations starting at Count.
Program Output
0000000000000101

Instruction Register: 0000000000001111 0000000000000001 0000000000000001
Location Register: 0000000000001100
Accumulator: 0000000000000000
R1 = 0000000000000001; R2 = 0000000000000000;
R3 = 0000000000000000; R4 = 0000000000000000

Fetch Step Cycle: 0000000000000100
>> 5 Move Count R2
2 1 2
0000000000000010 0000000000000001 0000000000000010
Location Register: 0000000000001111

Exec Step Cycle: 0000000000000100
Move value (0000000000000101) from Count to Register 0000000000000010.
Instruction Register: 0000000000000010 0000000000000001 0000000000000010
Location Register: 0000000000001111
Accumulator: 0000000000000000
R1 = 0000000000000001; R2 = 0000000000000101;
R3 = 0000000000000000; R4 = 0000000000000000

Fetch Step Cycle: 0000000000000101
>> 6 Add R1 R2
4 1 2
0000000000000100 0000000000000001 0000000000000010
Location Register: 0000000000010010

Exec Step Cycle: 0000000000000101
0000000000000001 + 0000000000000101 = 0000000000000110
Instruction Register: 0000000000000100 0000000000000001 0000000000000010
Location Register: 0000000000010010
Accumulator: 0000000000000110
R1 = 0000000000000001; R2 = 0000000000000101;
R3 = 0000000000000000; R4 = 0000000000000000

Fetch Step Cycle: 0000000000000110
>> 7 Store AC Count

16 0 1
0000000000010000 0000000000000000 0000000000000001
Location Register: 0000000000010101

Exec Step Cycle: 0000000000000110
Store value (0000000000000110) from the Accumulator
in memory variable Count.
Instruction Register: 0000000000010000 0000000000000000 0000000000000001
Location Register: 0000000000010101
Accumulator: 0000000000000110
R1 = 0000000000000001; R2 = 0000000000000101;
R3 = 0000000000000000; R4 = 0000000000000000

Fetch Step Cycle: 0000000000000111
>> 8 Display Count 1
15 1 1
0000000000001111 0000000000000001 0000000000000001
Location Register: 0000000000011000

Exec Step Cycle: 0000000000000111
Display 0000000000000001 memory locations starting at Count.
Program Output
0000000000000110

Instruction Register: 0000000000001111 0000000000000001 0000000000000001
Location Register: 0000000000011000
Accumulator: 0000000000000110
R1 = 0000000000000001; R2 = 0000000000000101;
R3 = 0000000000000000; R4 = 0000000000000000

Fetch Step Cycle: 0000000000001000
>> 9 Stop *
13 0 0
0000000000001101 0000000000000000 0000000000000000
Location Register: 0000000000011011

Exec Step Cycle: 0000000000001000
Stop Instruction; halting execution

PROGRAM LOOP TRACE FILE

0 Program Loop
1 Dim Location1 1:5
2 Go * *
3 Display Location1 1
4 Move Location1 R1
5 StoreC 1 R2
6 Sub R1 R2

7 JumpZ 10 *
8 Store AC Location1
9 Jump 3 *
10 Stop * *
11 End * *
Clearing Disk/Memeory

Compile Step 1
1 Dim Location1 1:50
(Dim) 2 1 50
0000000000000000 0000000000000000 0000000000000000
Allocating memory address 2 as Location1,
set to value 50.

Compile Step 2
2 Dim Location2 1:100
(Dim) 3 1 100
0000000000000000 0000000000000000 0000000000000000
Allocating memory address 3 as Location2,
set to value 100.

Compile Step 3
3 Go * *
14 0 0
0000000000001110 0000000000000000 0000000000000000
Start execution of the program
at memory location 0000000000000100.

Compile Step 4
4 Display Location1 2
15 1 2
0000000000001111 0000000000000001 0000000000000010
Display the values starting at Location1: 2 Locations.

Compile Step 5
5 Move Location1 R1
2 1 1
0000000000000010 0000000000000001 0000000000000001
Move the value of Location1 to R1.

Compile Step 6
6 Move Location2 R2
2 2 2
0000000000000010 0000000000000010 0000000000000010
Move the value of Location2 to R2.

Compile Step 7
7 Store R1 Location2
16 1 2
0000000000010000 0000000000000001 0000000000000010

Store the contents of R1 in Location2.

Compile Step 8
8 Store R2 Location1
16 2 1
0000000000010000 0000000000000010 0000000000000001
Store the contents of R2 in Location1.

Compile Step 9
9 Display Location1 2
15 1 2
0000000000001111 0000000000000001 0000000000000010
Display the values starting at Location1: 2 Locations.

Compile Step 10
10 Stop * *
13 0 0
0000000000001101 0000000000000000 0000000000000000
Halt execution of the Program.

Compile Step 11
11 End * *
* * *
0000000000001101 0000000000000000 0000000000000000
End of Assembler for Program Swap
Compilation completed; push 'Load' to continue.

Fetch Step Cycle: 0000000000000001
>> 2 Go * *
14 0 0
0000000000001110 0000000000000000 0000000000000000
Location Register: 0000000000000110

Exec Step Cycle: 0000000000000001
Go instruction; starting execution at memory location 0000000000000011.
Variable Pointer Table Offset = 0000000000011101
Instruction Register: 0000000000001110 0000000000000000 0000000000000000
Location Register: 0000000000000110
Accumulator: 0000000000000000
R1 = 0000000000000000; R2 = 0000000000000000;
R3 = 0000000000000000; R4 = 0000000000000000

Fetch Step Cycle: 0000000000000010
>> 3 Display Location1 1
15 1 1
0000000000001111 0000000000000001 0000000000000001
Location Register: 0000000000001001

Exec Step Cycle: 0000000000000010

Display 0000000000000001 memory locations starting at Location1.
Program Output
 0000000000000101

Instruction Register: 0000000000001111 0000000000000001 0000000000000001
Location Register: 0000000000001001
Accumulator: 0000000000000000
R1 = 0000000000000000; R2 = 0000000000000000;
R3 = 0000000000000000; R4 = 0000000000000000

Fetch Step Cycle: 0000000000000011
>> 4 Move Location1 R1
2 1 1
0000000000000010 0000000000000001 0000000000000001
Location Register: 0000000000001100

Exec Step Cycle: 0000000000000011
Move value (0000000000000101) from Location1 to Register 0000000000000001.
Instruction Register: 0000000000000010 0000000000000001 0000000000000001
Location Register: 0000000000001100
Accumulator: 0000000000000000
R1 = 0000000000000101; R2 = 0000000000000000;
R3 = 0000000000000000; R4 = 0000000000000000

Fetch Step Cycle: 0000000000000100
>> 5 StoreC 1 R2
18 1 2
0000000000010010 0000000000000001 0000000000000010
Location Register: 0000000000001111

Exec Step Cycle: 0000000000000100
Store value 0000000000000001 in Register 0000000000000010.
Instruction Register: 0000000000010010 0000000000000001 0000000000000010
Location Register: 0000000000001111
Accumulator: 0000000000000000
R1 = 0000000000000101; R2 = 0000000000000001;
R3 = 0000000000000000; R4 = 0000000000000000

Fetch Step Cycle: 0000000000000101
>> 6 Sub R1 R2
5 1 2
0000000000000101 0000000000000001 0000000000000010
Location Register: 0000000000010010

Exec Step Cycle: 0000000000000101
0000000000000101 - 0000000000000001 = 0000000000000100
Instruction Register: 0000000000000101 0000000000000001 0000000000000010
Location Register: 0000000000010010
Accumulator: 0000000000000100
R1 = 0000000000000101; R2 = 0000000000000001;

R3 = 0000000000000000; R4 = 0000000000000000

Fetch Step Cycle: 0000000000000110
>> 7 JumpZ 10 *
10 27 0
0000000000001010 0000000000011011 0000000000000000
Location Register: 0000000000010101

Exec Step Cycle: 0000000000000110
Branch if the accumulator is zero.
The value in the accumulator (0000000000000100) is not 0;
get the next instruction from memory location 0000000000010101.
Instruction Register: 0000000000001010 0000000000011011 0000000000000000
Location Register: 0000000000010101
Accumulator: 0000000000000100
R1 = 0000000000000101; R2 = 0000000000000001;
R3 – 0000000000000000; R4 = 0000000000000000

Fetch Step Cycle: 0000000000000111
>> 8 Store AC Location1
16 0 1
0000000000010000 0000000000000000 0000000000000001
Location Register: 0000000000011000

Exec Step Cycle: 0000000000000111
Store value (0000000000000100) from the Accumulator
in memory variable Location1.
Instruction Register: 0000000000010000 0000000000000000 0000000000000001
Location Register: 0000000000011000
Accumulator: 0000000000000100
R1 = 0000000000000101; R2 = 0000000000000001;
R3 = 0000000000000000; R4 = 0000000000000000

Fetch Step Cycle: 0000000000001000
>> 9 Jump 3 *
9 6 0
0000000000001001 0000000000000110 0000000000000000
Location Register: 0000000000011011

Exec Step Cycle: 0000000000001000
Unconditional branch;
get the next instruction from memory location: 0000000000000110
Instruction Register: 0000000000001001 0000000000000110 0000000000000000
Location Register: 0000000000000110
Accumulator: 0000000000000100
R1 = 0000000000000101; R2 = 0000000000000001;
R3 = 0000000000000000; R4 = 0000000000000000

Fetch Step Cycle: 0000000000001001
>> 3 Display Location1 1

15 1 1
0000000000001111 0000000000000001 0000000000000001
Location Register: 0000000000001001
Exec Step Cycle: 0000000000001001
Display 0000000000000001 memory locations starting at Location1.
Program Output
0000000000000100

Instruction Register: 0000000000001111 0000000000000001 0000000000000001
Location Register: 0000000000001001
Accumulator: 0000000000000100
R1 = 0000000000000101; R2 = 0000000000000001;
R3 = 0000000000000000; R4 = 0000000000000000

Fetch Step Cycle: 0000000000001010
>> 4 Move Location1 R1
2 1 1
0000000000000010 0000000000000001 0000000000000001
Location Register: 0000000000001100

Exec Step Cycle: 0000000000001010
Move value (0000000000000100) from Location1 to Register 0000000000000001.
Instruction Register: 0000000000000010 0000000000000001 0000000000000001
Location Register: 0000000000001100
Accumulator: 0000000000000100
R1 = 0000000000000100; R2 = 0000000000000001;
R3 = 0000000000000000; R4 = 0000000000000000

Fetch Step Cycle: 0000000000001011
>> 5 StoreC 1 R2
18 1 2
0000000000010010 0000000000000001 0000000000000010
Location Register: 0000000000001111

Exec Step Cycle: 0000000000001011
Store value 0000000000000001 in Register 0000000000000010.
Instruction Register: 0000000000010010 0000000000000001 0000000000000010
Location Register: 0000000000001111
Accumulator: 0000000000000100
R1 = 0000000000000100; R2 = 0000000000000001;
R3 = 0000000000000000; R4 = 0000000000000000

Fetch Step Cycle: 0000000000001100
>> 6 Sub R1 R2
5 1 2
0000000000000101 0000000000000001 0000000000000010
Location Register: 0000000000010010

Exec Step Cycle: 0000000000001100
0000000000000100 - 0000000000000001 = 0000000000000011

Instruction Register: 0000000000000101 0000000000000001 0000000000000010
Location Register: 0000000000010010
Accumulator: 0000000000000011
R1 = 000000000000100; R2 = 0000000000000001;
R3 = 000000000000000; R4 = 0000000000000000

Fetch Step Cycle: 0000000000001101
>> 7 JumpZ 10 *
10 27 0
0000000000001010 0000000000011011 0000000000000000
Location Register: 0000000000010101

Exec Step Cycle: 0000000000001101
Branch if the accumulator is zero.
The value in the accumulator (0000000000000011) is not 0;
get the next instruction from memory location 0000000000010101.
Instruction Register: 0000000000001010 0000000000011011 0000000000000000
Location Register: 0000000000010101
Accumulator: 0000000000000011
R1 = 000000000000100; R2 = 0000000000000001;
R3 = 000000000000000; R4 = 0000000000000000

Fetch Step Cycle: 0000000000001110
>> 8 Store AC Location1
16 0 1
0000000000010000 0000000000000000 0000000000000001
Location Register: 0000000000011000

Exec Step Cycle: 0000000000001110
Store value (0000000000000011) from the Accumulator
in memory variable Location1.
Instruction Register: 0000000000010000 0000000000000000 0000000000000001
Location Register: 0000000000011000
Accumulator: 0000000000000011
R1 = 000000000000100; R2 = 0000000000000001;
R3 = 000000000000000; R4 = 0000000000000000

Fetch Step Cycle: 0000000000001111
>> 9 Jump 3 *
9 6 0
0000000000001001 0000000000000110 0000000000000000
Location Register: 0000000000011011

Exec Step Cycle: 0000000000001111
Unconditional branch;
get the next instruction from memory location: 0000000000000110
Instruction Register: 0000000000001001 0000000000000110 0000000000000000
Location Register: 0000000000000110
Accumulator: 0000000000000011

R1 = 0000000000000100; R2 = 0000000000000001; R3 = 0000000000000000; R4 = 0000000000000000

Fetch Step Cycle: 0000000000010000
>> 3 Display Location1 1
15 1 1
0000000000001111 0000000000000001 0000000000000001
Location Register: 0000000000001001

Exec Step Cycle: 0000000000010000
Display 0000000000000001 memory locations starting at Location1.
Program Output
0000000000000011

Instruction Register: 0000000000001111 0000000000000001 0000000000000001
Location Register: 0000000000001001
Accumulator: 0000000000000011
R1 = 0000000000000100; R2 = 0000000000000001;
R3 = 0000000000000000; R4 = 0000000000000000

Fetch Step Cycle: 0000000000010001
>> 4 Move Location1 R1
2 1 1
0000000000000010 0000000000000001 0000000000000001
Location Register: 0000000000001100

Exec Step Cycle: 0000000000010001
Move value (0000000000000011) from Location1 to Register 0000000000000001.
Instruction Register: 0000000000000010 0000000000000001 0000000000000001
Location Register: 0000000000001100
Accumulator: 0000000000000011
R1 = 0000000000000011; R2 = 0000000000000001;
R3 = 0000000000000000; R4 = 0000000000000000

Fetch Step Cycle: 0000000000010010
>> 5 StoreC 1 R2
18 1 2
0000000000010010 0000000000000001 0000000000000010
Location Register: 0000000000001111

Exec Step Cycle: 0000000000010010
Store value 0000000000000001 in Register 0000000000000010.
Instruction Register: 0000000000010010 0000000000000001 0000000000000010
Location Register: 0000000000001111
Accumulator: 0000000000000011
R1 = 0000000000000011; R2 = 0000000000000001;
R3 = 0000000000000000; R4 = 0000000000000000

Fetch Step Cycle: 0000000000010011
>> 6 Sub R1 R2

5 1 2
0000000000000101 0000000000000001 0000000000000010
Location Register: 0000000000010010

Exec Step Cycle: 0000000000010011
0000000000000011 - 0000000000000001 = 0000000000000010
Instruction Register: 0000000000000101 0000000000000001 0000000000000010
Location Register: 0000000000010010
Accumulator: 0000000000000010
R1 = 0000000000000011; R2 = 0000000000000001;
R3 = 0000000000000000; R4 = 0000000000000000

Fetch Step Cycle: 0000000000010100
>> 7 JumpZ 10 *
10 27 0
0000000000001010 0000000000011011 0000000000000000
Location Register: 0000000000010101

Exec Step Cycle: 0000000000010100
Branch if the accumulator is zero.
The value in the accumulator (0000000000000010) is not 0;
get the next instruction from memory location 0000000000010101.
Instruction Register: 0000000000001010 0000000000011011 0000000000000000
Location Register: 0000000000010101
Accumulator: 0000000000000010
R1 = 0000000000000011; R2 = 0000000000000001;
R3 = 0000000000000000; R4 = 0000000000000000

Fetch Step Cycle: 0000000000010101
>> 8 Store AC Location1
16 0 1
0000000000010000 0000000000000000 0000000000000001
Location Register: 0000000000011000

Exec Step Cycle: 0000000000010101
Store value (0000000000000010) from the Accumulator
in memory variable Location1.
Instruction Register: 0000000000010000 0000000000000000 0000000000000001
Location Register: 0000000000011000
Accumulator: 0000000000000010
R1 = 0000000000000011; R2 = 0000000000000001;
R3 = 0000000000000000; R4 = 0000000000000000

Fetch Step Cycle: 0000000000010110
>> 9 Jump 3 *
9 6 0
0000000000001001 0000000000000110 0000000000000000
Location Register: 0000000000011011

Exec Step Cycle: 0000000000010110

Unconditional branch;
get the next instruction from memory location: 0000000000000110
Instruction Register: 0000000000001001 0000000000000110 0000000000000000
Location Register: 0000000000000110
Accumulator: 0000000000000010
R1 = 0000000000000011; R2 = 0000000000000001;
R3 = 0000000000000000; R4 = 0000000000000000

Fetch Step Cycle: 0000000000010111
>> 3 Display Location1 1
15 1 1
0000000000001111 0000000000000001 0000000000000001
Location Register: 0000000000001001

Exec Step Cycle: 0000000000010111
Display 0000000000000001 memory locations starting at Location1.
Program Output
0000000000000010

Instruction Register: 0000000000001111 0000000000000001 0000000000000001
Location Register: 0000000000001001
Accumulator: 0000000000000010
R1 = 0000000000000011; R2 = 0000000000000001;
R3 = 0000000000000000; R4 = 0000000000000000

Fetch Step Cycle: 0000000000011000
>> 4 Move Location1 R1
2 1 1
0000000000000010 0000000000000001 0000000000000001
Location Register: 0000000000001100

Exec Step Cycle: 0000000000011000
Move value (0000000000000010) from Location1 to Register 0000000000000001.
Instruction Register: 0000000000000010 0000000000000001 0000000000000001
Location Register: 0000000000001100
Accumulator: 0000000000000010
R1 = 0000000000000010; R2 = 0000000000000001;
R3 = 0000000000000000; R4 = 0000000000000000

Fetch Step Cycle: 0000000000011001
>> 5 StoreC 1 R2
18 1 2
0000000000010010 0000000000000001 0000000000000010
Location Register: 0000000000001111

Exec Step Cycle: 0000000000011001
Store value 0000000000000001 in Register 0000000000000010.
Instruction Register: 0000000000010010 0000000000000001 0000000000000010
Location Register: 0000000000001111
Accumulator: 0000000000000010

R1 = 0000000000000010; R2 = 0000000000000001;
R3 = 0000000000000000; R4 = 0000000000000000

Fetch Step Cycle: 0000000000011010
>> 6 Sub R1 R2
5 1 2
0000000000000101 0000000000000001 0000000000000010
Location Register: 0000000000010010

Exec Step Cycle: 0000000000011010
0000000000000010 - 0000000000000001 = 0000000000000001
Instruction Register: 0000000000000101 0000000000000001 0000000000000010
Location Register: 0000000000010010
Accumulator: 0000000000000001
R1 = 0000000000000010; R2 = 0000000000000001;
R3 = 0000000000000000; R4 = 0000000000000000

Fetch Step Cycle: 0000000000011011
>> 7 JumpZ 10 *
10 27 0
0000000000001010 0000000000011011 0000000000000000
Location Register: 0000000000010101

Exec Step Cycle: 0000000000011011
Branch if the accumulator is zero.
The value in the accumulator (0000000000000001) is not 0;
get the next instruction from memory location 0000000000010101.
Instruction Register: 0000000000001010 0000000000011011 0000000000000000
Location Register: 0000000000010101
Accumulator: 0000000000000001
R1 = 0000000000000010; R2 = 0000000000000001;
R3 = 0000000000000000; R4 = 0000000000000000

Fetch Step Cycle: 0000000000011100
>> 8 Store AC Location1
16 0 1
0000000000010000 0000000000000000 0000000000000001
Location Register: 0000000000011000

Exec Step Cycle: 0000000000011100
Store value (0000000000000001) from the Accumulator
in memory variable Location1.
Instruction Register: 0000000000010000 0000000000000000 0000000000000001
Location Register: 0000000000011000
Accumulator: 0000000000000001
R1 = 0000000000000010; R2 = 0000000000000001;
R3 = 0000000000000000; R4 = 0000000000000000

Fetch Step Cycle: 0000000000011101
>> 9 Jump 3 *

9 6 0
0000000000001001 0000000000000110 0000000000000000
Location Register: 0000000000011011

Exec Step Cycle: 0000000000011101
Unconditional branch;
get the next instruction from memory location: 0000000000000110
Instruction Register: 0000000000001001 0000000000000110 0000000000000000
Location Register: 0000000000000110
Accumulator: 0000000000000001
R1 = 0000000000000010; R2 = 0000000000000001;
R3 = 0000000000000000; R4 = 0000000000000000

Fetch Step Cycle: 0000000000011110
>> 3 Display Location1 1
15 1 1
0000000000001111 0000000000000001 0000000000000001
Location Register: 0000000000001001

Exec Step Cycle: 0000000000011110
Display 0000000000000001 memory locations starting at Location1.
Program Output
 0000000000000001

Instruction Register: 0000000000001111 0000000000000001 0000000000000001
Location Register: 0000000000001001
Accumulator: 0000000000000001
R1 = 0000000000000010; R2 = 0000000000000001;
R3 = 0000000000000000; R4 = 0000000000000000

Fetch Step Cycle: 0000000000011111
>> 4 Move Location1 R1
2 1 1
0000000000000010 0000000000000001 0000000000000001
Location Register: 0000000000001100

Exec Step Cycle: 0000000000011111
Move value (0000000000000001) from Location1 to Register 0000000000000001.
Instruction Register: 0000000000000010 0000000000000001 0000000000000001
Location Register: 0000000000001100
Accumulator: 0000000000000001
R1 = 0000000000000001; R2 = 0000000000000001;
R3 = 0000000000000000; R4 = 0000000000000000

Fetch Step Cycle: 0000000000100000
>> 5 StoreC 1 R2
18 1 2
0000000000010010 0000000000000001 0000000000000010
Location Register: 0000000000001111

Exec Step Cycle: 0000000000100000
Store value 0000000000000001 in Register 0000000000000010.
Instruction Register: 0000000000010010 0000000000000001 0000000000000010
Location Register: 0000000000001111
Accumulator: 0000000000000001
R1 = 0000000000000001; R2 = 0000000000000001;
R3 = 0000000000000000; R4 = 0000000000000000

Fetch Step Cycle: 0000000000100001
>> 6 Sub R1 R2
5 1 2
0000000000000101 0000000000000001 0000000000000010
Location Register: 0000000000010010

Exec Step Cycle: 0000000000100001
0000000000000001 - 0000000000000001 = 0000000000000000
Instruction Register: 0000000000000101 0000000000000001 0000000000000010
Location Register: 0000000000010010
Accumulator: 0000000000000000
R1 = 0000000000000001; R2 = 0000000000000001;
R3 = 0000000000000000; R4 = 0000000000000000

Fetch Step Cycle: 0000000000100010
>> 7 JumpZ 10 *
10 27 0
0000000000001010 0000000000011011 0000000000000000
Location Register: 0000000000010101
Exec Step Cycle: 0000000000100010
Branch if the accumulator is zero.
The accumulator is 0;
get the next instruction from memory location 0000000000011011.
Instruction Register: 0000000000001010 0000000000011011 0000000000000000
Location Register: 0000000000011011
Accumulator: 0000000000000000
R1 = 0000000000000001; R2 = 0000000000000001;
R3 = 0000000000000000; R4 = 0000000000000000

Fetch Step Cycle: 0000000000100011
>> 10 Stop * *
13 0 0
0000000000001101 0000000000000000 0000000000000000
Location Register: 0000000000011110

Exec Step Cycle: 0000000000100011
Stop Instruction; halting execution

APPENDIX C

Downloading JAVA Programs for Windows

This page is used to download the Windows programs, data, and the JAVA Runtime Environment. It is divided into three sections:

1. Downloading the Self-Extracting Archive containing the JAVA programs and data;
2. Installing the JAVA Runtime Environment on your system.
3. Running JAVA applications using the JAVA Runtime Environment on your system.

SOFTWARE ACCESS AND INSTALLATION

The JAVA programs we will be using in this book are accessible through the World Wide Web at the *Computing in the Web Age* web site:

http://www-rcf.usc.edu/~dilligan/web_age

Readers may access this site as they would any site on the Web by typing this address into the "netsite" or "Address" field of their browser and pressing the "Enter" key.

To use these programs, you must have a PC or MAC computer that is connected to the Web with an up-to-date Web browser program such as Netscape 3.0 or Netscape Communicator 4.0 or above or Internet Explorer 4.0 or above. (We will use both Internet Explorer and Netscape in our discussions. Both are available at no cost to the reader. *Pace* Janet Reno and the Justice Department Antitrust Division.) Directions for running the programs are included on their respective Web pages. Some of the programs run while connected to the Web. Others are run on

Computing in the Web Age:
A Web-Interactive Introduction

@Robert Dilligan 1996, 1997, 1998

This home page is designed to be used in conjunction with the text of *Computing in the Web Age*. Site visitors should refer to the text for details concerning this page.

You can e-mail me at: *dilligan@bcf.usc.edu*

the local machine after being downloaded from the Web as archive files. The *Computing in the Web Age* site provides instructions for downloading various pieces of MAC and PC software.

DOWNLOADING THE SELF-EXTRACTING ARCHIVE

To make this process clear to the reader, we will now describe how to download and use a Windows archive from the Web. Once our computer is attached to the web site, we go to the archive by pushing the button labeled "Archive" on the left side of the screen. This brings up the main archive page:

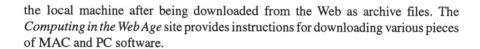

Computing in the Web Age Archive

Chapter 4   Chapter 5   Chapter 6

This page provides access to the source code of the JAVA applications, HTML resources, and texts used in Chapters 4, 5 and 6 of *Computing in the Web Age*.

JAVA

We push the button labeled "Chapter 4" to get us to the archive for this chapter:

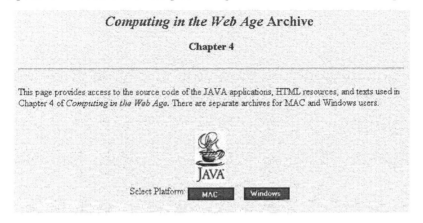

We push the button labeled "Windows" and download the archive for Windows by clicking on the appropriate link:

Self-Extracting Archive

Download the Self-Extracting Archive "webinfo.exe" by clicking on this link.

Netscape displays a file dialog box with which one can specify the directory into which the archive is to be downloaded:

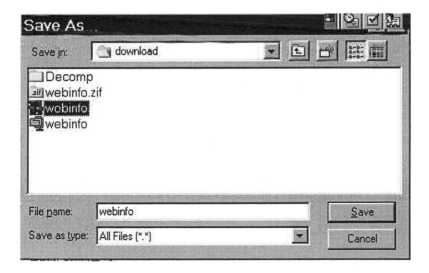

The files downloaded from the *Computing in the Web Age* site are so-called "self-extracting" archives. This means they are themselves computer programs that hold data in compressed form. When these programs are run, they extract the data they contain and put it on the computer's disk as standard computer files. These programs are run as any other application is run: either by double clicking on its icon or by using the "Run" option of Windows. To run the "webinfo.exe" archive program, one would first select the Windows "Run" option:

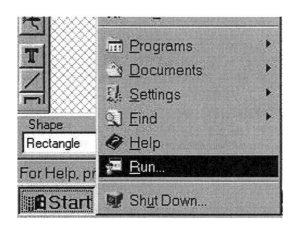

Select "Run" from Start Menu and enter "webinfo.exe" as the program you want to run from the directory into which you have placed it.

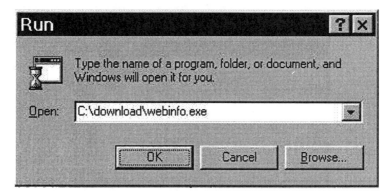

(In this example, the archive has been downloaded to a directory called "download" on the C drive. You may, however, download this program to any directory or drive on your system.) Push the "OK" button and the following screen appears:

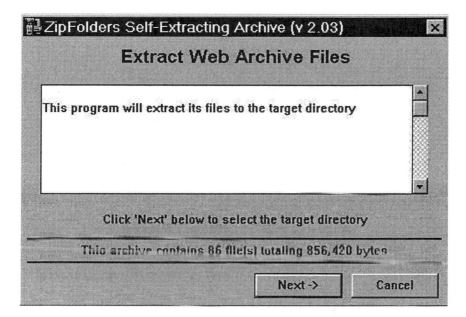

Push "Next" to continue installation. By default, the program will install the directories in the directory of the "webinfo" in the root directory of the current drive.

You may enter any valid drive and directory name in place of "\ch4." For example, entering "D:\" will install the files on the root directory of the D drive. The programs may be installed on any directory of the selected drive. When you push the "Next" button, the programs will be installed on the designated drive. The following screen appears as files are extracted:

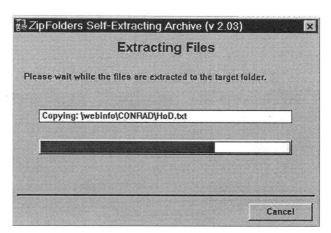

When the extraction process is complete, the following screen appears:

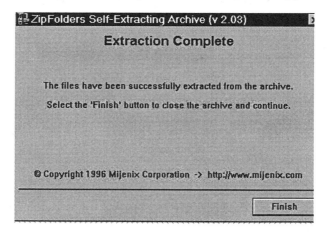

Push the "Finish" button to end the extraction program. The files extracted from the archive are now ready for use. Directions for downloading and extracting MAC archive material is provided in the *Computing in the Web Age* site's archive section.

The extraction process will create the "webinfo" directory on your hard disk. "webinfo" is a default name for this directory. The extraction process will allow you to give this directory any name you wish.

There are eight sub directories in the "webinfo" directory:

1. "Conrad" containing an ASCII text of "Heart of Darkness;"
2. "Hopkins" containing texts of Hopkins's Poetry;
3. "Wordfreq" containing the JAVA source and executable files for the "word-freq" word frequency program;
4. "KWIC" containing the JAVA source and executable files for the KWIC program;
5. "KWIC2" containing the JAVA source and executable files for the KWIC2 program;
6. "AI" to hold files downloaded from the Web in Chapter 5;
7. "Shareware" to hold programs downloaded from the Web in Chapter 5;
8. "Images" to hold LViewPro files discussed in Chapter 6.

DOWNLOADING AND INSTALLING JAVA RUNTIME ENVIRONMENT (JRE)

What follows are detailed instructions for installing JRE and running JAVA applications using JRE. A link to the web site from which JRE is downloaded is provided at the end of these instructions. Sun Computers is the developer of JAVA. JRE is downloaded from their products and api Web page at

  http://java.sun.com/products/index.html:

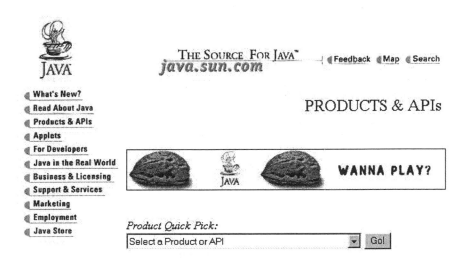

The first thing one does is select JRE as the product to be downloaded and push the "Go!" button:

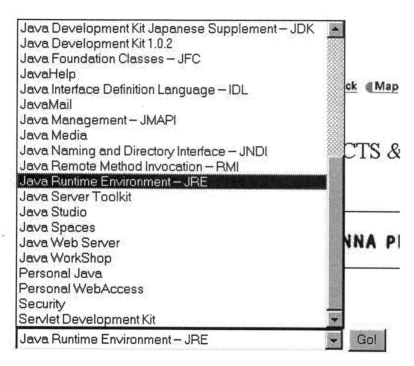

One then selects Windows 95 as the desired operating system and pushes the "Continue" button:

1. Download JRE 1.1.5 software

The Windows version of JRE 1.1.5 is intended for use on Windows 95 and Windows NT 4.0. This JRE will not work on Windows NT 3.51.

To find out more about this software, read:
README   CHANGES   LICENSE and DISTRIBUTION

This displays the JRE license agreement for which one pushes the "Agree" button:

THE SOURCE FOR JAVA™
java.sun.com | ◀Feedback ◀Map ◀Search

License & Export for JDK - Java Runtime Environment 1.1.5

Downloading FAQ

d

[Agree] [Disagree]

JRE is stored in a self-extracting archive named "jrc115-win32.exe." You are now ready to begin downloading the three million plus bytes that comprise JRE by pushing the FTP download button:

download size of jre115-win32.exe is 3,397,603 bytes.

ftp download:

[FTP download jre115-win32.exe]

http download:

[HTTP download jre115-win32.exe]

You must specify a directory location in which to store the archive. It takes approximately twenty minutes to download the archive. In this example, the archive is downloaded to a directory called "download."

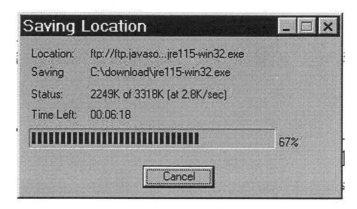

Once the archive is downloaded, you run it as you did the "webinfo.exe" archive, either by clicking on its icon or by using the Windows "Run" option. The program informs you that it is about to install JRE on your computer.

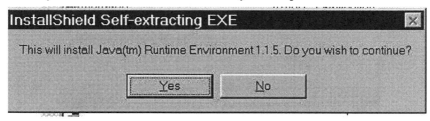

You then follow the instructions of the installation program, which will inform you of the directory in which it is installing JRE. It is important to take note of the directory in which JRE is installed. You may accept its default location or specify a location of your own choosing. In this example, we have installed JRE in the root of drive C in a directory named "javajre." Once the installation has completed, one must alter the path statement of file "autoexec.bat" to include the name of this directory.

> PATH=C:\NETCOM;c:\javajre\bin;C:\JDK1.1.4\BIN;

The path command reads "c:\javajre\bin;" because the main JRE program is always located in the "bin" sub-directory.

RUNNING JAVA APPLICATIONS USING THE
JAVA RUNTIME ENVIRONMENT

Before running JRE, the computer must be restarted. JRE is run in the DOS Window. Including the name of this directory in the path statement insures that JRE can be run from any directory. JRE's interface is a very old fashion character-based command line interface. To run a JAVA application with JRE, one must start up Windows' MS-DOS box and type a command at the DOS prompt. This is the way all DOS programs were run when DOS was first introduced. To run the word frequency program, the command line must read:

jre -cp /webinfo/wordfreq wordfreq

To run the word KWIC program, the command line must read:

jre -cp /webinfo/kwic kwic

To run the KWIC2 program, the command line must read

jre -cp /webinfo/kwic2 kwic2

These commands are case sensitive. Readers should also note that the directory name separator is the forward slash "/", not the back slash "\" one might expect in a DOS environment.

Notes

CHAPTER 1

[1] Let me say a word about diction. This book is full of abbreviations and acronyms because these are a distinguishing feature of the dialect of the tribe when it comes to computers. Developers of computer technology seem to take a particular pride when the initials used to designate their work are also a catchy acronym. The most extreme example of this that I know of is the abbreviation/acronym used for optical scanner technology: TWAIN. This is not a reference to Samuel Clemens or any other person named TWAIN who had a hand in its development. It stands for "Technology Without An Interesting Name." I will try to keep this technobabble to a minimum and to define and illustrate any technical terms I introduce. I have included a glossary of technical terms to aid the reader.

[2] See Brooks, Frederick, *The Mythical Man-Month: essays in software engineering,* Anniversary Edition (Reading, Mass.: Addison-Wesley Publ. Co., 1995).

[3] The point is often made that the dictionary definition of "computer" before World War II was a person who carries out arithmetical calculations with the aid of a calculator. Many people, usually female, were hired by banks and insurance companies for this purpose.

[4] The British developed a computer they named Colossus which enabled them to read the German Enigma code. Alan Turing, regarded as the founder of theoretical Computer Science, worked on this project and made contributions to it that remain classified to this day.

[5] Bolter, J. David, *Turing's Man: western culture in the computer age* (Chapel Hill: University of North Carolina Press, 1984), p. 8. My argument here is an extension of his that regards the development of the World Wide Web as a defining technology distinct from, though obviously based on, the computer.

[6] For a full account of the technical development of early computers, see Ceruzzi, Paul, *Reckoners:* the prehistory of the digital computer, from relays to the stored program concept: 1935–1945 Westport, Conn: Greenwood Press, 1983. I am indebted to Ceruzzi for many of the technical details mentioned in this section.

[7] Turing's article has been reprinted in Feigenbaum, E. A. and J. Feldman, eds., *Computers and Thought* (New York: McGraw-Hill, 1963).

[8] The *Experiencing Information* web site provides a link to the Loebner Prize site in the "AI" section of its Chapter 5 archive, the method of access to which is explained in Chapter 5.

[9] For a translation of the letter, see Randell, Brian, *The Origins of Digital Computers: selected papers* (Berlin, Heidelberg, New York: Springer-Verlag, 1973), pp. 167–169.

[10] Burk, Alice R., *The First Electronic Computer: the Atanasoff story*, p. 14, recounts how Atanasoff used capacitors as the basis of his memory because vacuum tubes were too expensive. The problem with a capacitor, which is a device to store an electrical charge, is that the charge gradually leaks until it is all gone. To solve this problem, he developed a way to recharge his memory capacitors periodically. This is the first example of dynamically refreshed memory that is the modern DRAM (Dynamic Random Access Memory) technology.

[11] Larson, Earl R., "Findings of Fact, Conclusions of Law, and Order of Judgement," File No. 4-67 Civ. 138, Honeywell, Inc., vs. Sperry Rand Corporation and Illinois Scientific Developments, U.S. District Court, District of Minnesota, Fourth Division.

[12] ENIAC also had a read only memory of one hundred numbers to hold numerical tables and twenty constants that were set by throwing switches.

[13] These are Babbage's terms for the processor and memory.

[14] Binary numbers are written with a training subscripted 2 to indicate the numerical base two as opposed to the numerical base ten of decimal numbers. Binary numbers are explained at length in Chapter 2.

[15] See, for example, the West Semitic Research Project web site at http://www.usc.edu/dept/LAS/wsrp/ for an example of the use of modern digital technology for text analysis.

[16] The problem many organizations face today because of software that can't deal with dates after 1999 because they record only the last two digits of the year in their dates is symptomatic of early concerns about using as little system resource as possible in solving a problem. It was this concern, not the frequently cited theory that the developers of systems with this problem assumed that their programs would be obsolete and superseded long before the year 2000, that led to this problem. These developers knew, as does any programmer, the difference between data structures and algorithms. This problem arises because of a decision about how to store data, not how to process it, decisions about which can be made only after the decision about data storage. COBOL (Common Business Oriented Language) was the computer programming language favored by business at this time. Many dialects of this language allowed numbers to be stored in a format known as packed binary coded decimal. In this format, an eight bit byte can hold two decimal digits, each digit requiring four bits ($2^4 = 16$), enough to encode the ten decimal digits. Thus the last two digits of a year can be stored in one byte and manipulated as a decimal digit. The other problem that exacerbates the 2000 C.E. problem is the lack of documentation for programs and file structures. It is frequently difficult to know exactly which byte holds the year and what code manipulates it. The dialect of the tribe refers to this situation, somewhat inaccurately, as the Y2K problem (Y for year, 2K for two kilobytes). Two kilobytes is actually 2048 bytes.

[17] Http://www.sil.org/sgml/general.html

[18] Modern systems handle these problems with device drivers in a way that resembles general markup. The operating system writes a generic description of what it wants from a peripheral device and the driver for the device translates this description into the specific instructions that carry out the task.

[19] Pynchon, Thomas, *The Crying of Lot 49* (New York: Harper & Row, 1986), p. 24.

[20] See http://ww.sil.org/sgml/sgmlhist0.html for Goldfarb's account of the development of SGML from GML.

[21] These organizations are cited again and again as examples of the success of SGML. Neither, it should be noted, has a particularly distinguished reputation for developing or identifying important new technologies. Pope said it a long time ago: "Whatever is, is right."

[22] See Barger, Jorn, "The History Of Hypertext Timeline" at http://www.mcs.net/~jorn/html/net/time-line.html

[23] Burke (see note 24) points out that Bush saw his work on document retrieval as providing a necessary service to the scientific elite but that early on many scientists felt that he exaggerated the difficulties of keeping abreast of current work in their fields.

[24] See Burke, Colin, *Information and Secrecy: Vannevar Bush, Ultra, and the other Memex* (Metuchen, N.J.: Scarecrow Press, 1994) for a full account of Vannevar's place in the history of Information Science and of his work on the Rapid Selector and Comparator.

[25] See http://www.boardwatch.com/mag/95/jun/bwm1.htm for Jack Rickard's account of the development of Internet from a DARPA project to the Web. Rickard argues that the Internet as a generally available resource dates from about 1989.

[26] http://www.forthnet.gr/forthnet/isoc/short.history.of.internet

[27] The intellectual debt of Apple to Xerox PARC is so massive that I have always regarded Apple's claims to originality and its lawsuits over its rights to "the look and feel" of MAC software as tainted with intellectual dishonesty, whatever the legalities of the situation.

[28] The basic measure of the capacity of a network is the speed with which it can transfer bits. LocalTalk has a speed of 230,000 bits per second, Ethernet a speed of 10,000,000 bits per second. Both are considerably faster than the 28,800 bits per second modems used to access the Web.

[29] This program is available as freeware from a number of program archives on the Web. We will discuss how to download a version of it in Chapter 5.

[30] *Being Digital*, p. 28.

[31] Some have argued that the law does not quite stand up to its reputation as a predictor of the rate of technological change. See *New York Times*, August 14, 1996, "The Demise of Moore's Law Signals the End of Digital Frontier," by Ashley Dunn. Dunn points out that there is some fudging in the exact statement of the doubling period of the law and what exactly it covers. She chides defenders of the law for using tactics akin to "Stalinesque revisionism" in computing the numbers predicted by the law. She likens debating its efficacy to medieval debates about the number of angels that could dance on the head of a pin. I accept the law symbolically as a statement of the dizzying rush of computer development.

[32] See *New York Times*, September 17, 1997, "New Chip May Make Today's Computer Passé," by John Markoff. The development discussed in the Intel announcement is a way of making transistor switches that can assume more than the two states of the traditional on/off computer bit with no loss of speed and no increase in size. Markoff says these developments rejuvenate a quickened version of Moore's Law. Dunn's report of the law's demise is premature according to Markoff.

[33] Crevier, Daniel, *AI: the tumultuous history of the search for artificial intelligence* (New York: Basic Books, 1993), p. 303.

[34] *The Emperor's New Mind: concerning computers, minds, and the laws of physics* (New York, Oxford: Oxford University Press, 1989).

[35] *Shadows of the Mind: a search for the missing science of consciousness* (Oxford, New York: Oxford University Press, 1994).

[36] Searle, John R., "Minds, Brains and Programs," *Behavioral and Brain Sciences* 3 (3 [1980]): pp. 417–458.

[37] (New York: Harper & Row, 1972). He continues his discussion in a revised edition (New York: Harper & Row, 1979), Mind over Machine: the power of human intuition and expertise in the era of the computer (New York: The Free Press, 1986) and *What Computers Still Can't Do: a critique of artificial intelligence* (Cambridge, Mass: MIT Press, 1992).

[38] Hermam, Arthur, *The Idea of Decline in Western History* (New York: Free Press, 1997), p. 8.

CHAPTER 2

[1] We get this by adding the order of magnitude of the atoms in the sun to the order of magnitude of the number of suns in the universe: $57 + 22 = 79$. Emiliani implies that the matter of interstellar gas,

planets, comets, etc. is negligible compared to the matter contained in suns; and he does not consider the possibility of "dark" matter.

[2] There was also provision made for "unsigned" numbers; an unsigned byte could have values from 0 to 255.

[3] This scheme works fine as long as the computer is dealing with data one byte at a time. The situation is a little more complicated when it is dealing with words and double words. Suppose we wanted to store the number 1 in a "word" because we were going to be counting something we anticipated would be in the range of ±32,768. We could write this in binary digits "naturally" as 0000000000000001. But some computers would store this number in a word as 0000000100000000, putting the least significant byte first, while others would store it as 0000000000000001, putting the least significant byte last. One of the major functions of software is to shield users from perplexing hardware details like this one. There may be deep and subtle reasons why hardware designers decide to place the most significant byte to the left or to the right but I have never heard a satisfactory explanation for the choice. In the days when mainframes dominated the field of computers, computer manufacturers not only took no steps to make their machines compatible with each other but also used machine incompatibility as a marketing strategy. Once a purchaser had committed to a particular brand of computer, the manufacture's interest was served by making a change to another brand as difficult and expensive as possible. Anything that was compatible with the machines of other manufacturers was a potential reason in favor of change of manufacturers. Hardware was very expensive in those days and IBM attained its market dominance with a corporate culture built around "selling iron." So when I think about the problem of placement of the most significant byte, I am reminded of the fierce disputes in Swift's Lilliput between the Little Endians and the Big Endians, all generated from a sacred text that abjured the faithful always to break their eggs on the appropriate end. In the world of computing, in fact, computers based on the Intel 80x86 processors (the PC for example) are Little Endians, putting the least significant byte first, and Macs based on the Motorola 68000 processor are Big Endians, putting the least significant byte last.

[4] The programs only appear to operate simultaneously. A computer can execute only one instruction at a time. The appearance of simultaneity arises because the computer executes instructions and switches program to program so rapidly.

[5] To simplify keeping track of what is used for what, computer programs usually are divided by the computer into two parts: the data segment which contains the data to be processed; and the code segment which contains the program instructions. But these segments can be loaded anywhere in memory that has enough room for them to fit. A byte of memory may contain data or instructions at any given time.

[6] These cards were then usually read onto a magnetic tape which in turn was read into the computer.

[7] Nadine Kano and Asmus Freytag in "The International Character Set Conundrum: ANSI, Unicode, and Microsoft Windows," *Microsoft Systems Journal* Vol. 9, No. 11, p. 55, begin their discussion of character sets with the following lament: "Most developers of international Windows-based programs have at some point banged their heads against the wall trying to come to grips with character encoding. As if by deliberate cruelty on the part of designers, the mish-mash of standards makes it hard for users to share data and for programmers to create worldwide software. Some standards are 7-bit, others are 8-bit. Single-byte character sets come in several flavors, as do double-byte standards, which are also called multibyte because they are really a mix of single-byte and double-byte character codes. Trying to pass data from different character encodings across networks or between operating systems involves a gauntlet of mappings, conversions, fonts, and general headaches."

[8] Texts that require a single character set of 256 characters or less could in many circumstances be translated into one byte representation for transmission over the Web in a way comparable to the way image files are compressed for transmission over the Web.

[9] See Chapter 1 for an account of Turing's life and contributions to computing.

[10] If a machine has 6 operations and a table of 15 instructions, its instructions may specify any of 91,125 ($3 \times 3 \times 15 \times 3 \times 15 \times 15$) states.

[11] If we regard any contiguous group of marked frames as a binary number, the value of the number is 2^n-1 where n is the number of marks in the group. The algorithm might be adapted, then, to generate binary representations of the powers of two minus one: 1, 3, 7, 15, etc.

[12] Actually, the program will work as long as there is an unmarked frame to the right of the starting position. We could start at any point within a sequence of marked frames except the last.

CHAPTER 3

[1] In von Neumann's design, memory is memory, available for whatever the need is. What the programmer doesn't use for program instructions is available for data. With separate memories for programs and data, there would be problems with programs that needed disproportionate amounts of memory for data or instructions.

[2] Strictly speaking, a virtual machine generates the same numbers as does its hardware counterpart. Its actual output is limited by the machine on which it is running. For example, a virtual machine could produce the sequence of numbers needed to display a color picture but it could not display the color picture unless it had the hardware to display it, in this case a CRT capable of displaying a color picture at the required resolution.

[3] Of course, the Soft Windows program has to do a lot more than just substitute one number for another because Apple and Intel microprocessors differ in ways more profound than simply using different codes for the same operations. There is no one-to-one correspondence between their operations.

[4] Programmers usually do not need to know where memory is located in the machine. But they do need to know the locations of one portion of memory relative to another.

[5] The last line of the memory table may not be visible on some CRT screens. But this line of memory is not used in the exercises for this chapter.

[6] At this point one can always use the program choice box to select or reselect a program. This option, which resets the virtual machine, is always available.

[7] More precisely, the program branches back to the memory location where the assembler placed the machine code for instruction 3. The line numbers symbolize the location of code instructions in the same way that names symbolize the location of data.

[8] The place at which the program checks the recalculated value of "Count" determines the number of iterations of the loop. If the calculation and check is made at the start of the loop, as it was in the "Loop" program, the number of iterations is equal to the initial value of "Count" minus 1. If it is done at the end of the loop, the number of iterations will be equal to the initial value of "Count." Circumstances determine whether it is better to make the check at the start or the end of the loop. If it is not made until the end of the loop, the loop will always be executed once, irrespective of the initial value of "Count."

[9] The assembler program is called a "one pass" assembler for this reason. Other, more elaborate assemblers and computer language compilers are "multi-pass" programs and can place the data segment anywhere in the program. In a one pass assembler, a variable must be defined in the data segment before it can be referenced in the code segment.

CHAPTER 4

[1] Recall, for example, the "Counter" program from Chapter 3. It is much easier to understand that "Count = Count + 1" is an instance of counting something than it is to understand the same about the lines of assembler code we used to carry out counting.

[2] This is not to ignore the development of the field of software engineering and the many source code management programs and other developments in simplifying and rationalizing the development of computer code. It is merely to observe that programming as practiced frequently falls short of software engineering theory.

[3] For a list of HTML special character tags, see Harris, Stuart and Gayle Kidder, *Official HTML Publishing for Netscape*, Ventana Communications Group, Inc., 1996, pp. 511–512.

CHAPTER 5

[1] (Vintage Books: New York, 1996)

[2] See Negroponte's discussion of bandwidth as it relates to radio waves and cable. To get more bandwidth in a cable network, you can add more cable. The case with the radio spectrum, however, is different. It is a finite resource to which we cannot add.

[3] http://playground.sun.com/pub/ipng/html/INET-IPng-Paper.html 1/20/98

[4] Its description of what it's doing hardly clarifies for me what is meant by relevancy:

Yahoo!! first finds all the keyword matches and then sorts the results according to relevancy within each specific area. Yahoo!! ranks results in the following manner: Multiple Keyword Matches: Documents matching more of the keywords will have a higher rank than those matching less. Document Section Weighting: Documents matching words found in the Title are ranked higher than those found in its Body or URL. Generality of Category: Categories matching higher up in the Yahoo! tree hierarchy (i.e., more general categories) are ranked higher than those deeper in the hierarchy (i.e., more narrowly focused categories).

Yahoo!! Help page: http://search.Yahoo!.com/search/help#works 2/17/98.

[5] A Roman cycle was complete when everything alive at the beginning of a cycle had died. Rome itself was to outlast the cycles "dum Capitolium/ scandet cum tacita virgine pontifex." Horace, *Odes* III xxx.

[6] *Cat's Cradle*, pp. 12–13.

[7] Readers should refer to the "README.TXT" file for the file editor. It may be examined by double clicking on it in the PKZIP listing of contents. The FTP utility is installed by running the "Install.exe" program after extracting the file's contents.

CHAPTER 6

[1] Harris, Stuart and Gayle Kidder, *Official HTML Publishing for Netscape*, Ventana Communications Group, Inc., 1996, pp. 511–512, give an extensive list of HTML special symbols.

[2] Some HTML files have the extension "htm" rather than "html" because they were prepared using the DOS file system which allowed only three letters for a file extension. Windows 95 and MAC machines use the four-character "html" file extension.

[3] There are also a number of HTML editors like *Page Mill* and *Front Page* that have proved popular choices for creation of hypertext documents.

[4] The OCR output used for the text and first HTML versions of the article retain the hyphenation of the article as it appeared in the *New York Times*. These hyphenations have been edited out of subsequent HTML encodings.

[5] This text would have to be added. The first occurrence of the text "Where to Browse for Art on the Internet" is used as the title.

[6] http://www.nytimes.com 1/20/98.

[7] The URL for the article is "http://search.nytimes.com/web/docsroot/library/cyber/week/0121artb.html" 1/20/98.

[8] Recent developments, of a proprietary kind, do allow Web authors some control over type face selection.

[9] http://www.christdesert.org/noframes/script/script.html 1/20/98.

[10] Computers also display text in character mode in which each character is assigned a grid and the screen usually holds 1920 characters (twenty-four lines of eighty characters each).

[11] The easy way to do this is first to load the html file into the PFE32 editor and then to display it on Netscape. One may then change the values for different parameters, save the file with these changes, and then use Netscape's "Reload" button to see the effects of the change. One can switch back and forth between the two programs by clicking on their task bar icons.

[12] http://www.biola.edu/cgi-bin/colorpro/ 1/20/98.

[13] Photographic images can be scanned down to the level of the grains on the film and in ranges of the spectrum not visible to the eye. See the Electronic Beowulf Project images of the Beowulf manuscript http://www.uky.edu/~kiernan/welcome.html. for an example of how modern scanning technology can help restore ancient manuscripts.

[14] http://pages.prodigy.net/bombadil 1/20/98.

[15] http://www.medios.fi/heikki/backgrounds_index.html 1/20/98.

[16] http://pages.prodigy.com/reck/colnmes.htm 1/20/98.

[17] http://www.w3-tech.com/crash/CrashCourse.html 1/20/98.

[18] http://the-inter.net/www/future21/html.html 1/20/98.

[19] See the discussion of helper applications on page XXX.

[20] http://www.realaudio.com/ 1/20/98.

[21] http://www.eat.com/learn-italian/index.html 1/20/98.

[22] http://tucows.rucc.net.au/mult95.html 1/20/98. This site contains links to a number of sites containing virus scanners, HTML editors, and other software and information useful to Web programming in general.

[23] http://qtvr.quicktime.apple.com/ 1/20/98.

[24] There are many varieties of UNIX. I refer to UNIX 5 release 4.

[25] The "CHMOD" command is used in UNIX to control access permissions.

Index